The Campaign Manager

SIXTH EDITION

The Campaign Manager

Running and Winning Local Elections

CATHERINE SHAW

Routledge
Taylor & Francis Group

LONDON AND NEW YORK

First published 2018
by Routledge
2 Park Square, Milton Park, Abingdon, Oxon OX14 4RN

and by Routledge
711 Third Avenue, New York, NY 10017

Routledge is an imprint of the Taylor & Francis Group, an informa business

British Library Cataloguing-in-Publication Data
A catalogue record for this book is available from the British Library

Library of Congress Cataloging-in-Publication Data
A catalog record for this book has been requested

ISBN: 978-1-1385-8927-8 (hbk)
ISBN: 978-0-8133-5079-0 (pbk)
ISBN: 978-0-8133-50890-6 (ebk)

Typeset in Garamond Pro by
Servis Filmsetting Ltd, Stockport, Cheshire

To
Senator Dr. Alan Bates
(March 17, 1945–August 5, 2016)
Thank you for letting me chase rabbits down holes

And a special thanks to Dr. Michael Holstein, PhD

Contents

Preface

> Politics—good politics—is public service. There is no life or
> occupation in which a man can find a greater opportunity to serve his
> community or his country.
>
> —HARRY TRUMAN

RUNNING FOR LOCAL OFFICE CAN BE ONE OF THE MOST DEMANDING YET
exhilarating experiences of your life. Your house will be a wreck, your children ignored, and your partner, whether involved in the campaign or not,
stressed. Yet seeking office or pushing through an issue-based campaign gives
you an opportunity to be a leader, to effect change in your community and
to repay something to the city, county, state, or country you love. The campaign experience also offers you an opportunity to grow personally. You will
be challenged and stretched as never before. When it's all over, win or lose,
you will be a different person, with a different outlook on our political process and a new respect for those who run and serve.

When I first ran for mayor of Ashland, Oregon, in 1988, I had little
prior government or management experience. Many felt I should start at
the council level and work my way up before taking on the position of CEO
of a multimillion-dollar municipality. However, having so little experience
allowed me to view things with a fresh eye. During my three terms and
twelve years at that post, the council, the city staff, the community, and
I implemented dozens of programs, including open space, water conservation, community composting and recycling, voter-approved air-quality
standards, wetland and floodplain preservation, wastewater treatment plant
upgrades, forest management, and restoration and expansion of the library, fire station, and city offices. We also worked closely with our public
school system to find ways to ease its budget shortfalls in the wake of state

education cutbacks. We divested our hospital, helped save a ski resort, and acquired an ambulance service. We installed a dark-fiber ring in our city, providing direct-connect, high-speed Internet access and cable TV services before anyone had heard of high-speed Internet. By having community and government work in partnership, we were able to create and act on opportunities normally available only to large metropolitan areas. Indeed, much of what was accomplished could have happened only because I had previously managed campaigns and knew how to pass legislation in the community at the ballot box.

After each campaign season, I call both winning and losing candidates to interview them about the process. It is astonishing just how little candidates know about their path to victory or defeat. If you know how to run a campaign, especially one based on a broad grassroots organization, that equals power in office. When I was first elected, I had no support from within government; what I did have were hundreds of volunteers who helped me get there and wanted fundamental change once I was elected. Just knowing I could muster signatures and reverse the council's efforts to hobble the powers of my office simply because I held the gavel, or their efforts to force legislation through that neither I nor the community wanted, gave me power to stop them without ever having to pull a petition. As I say throughout this manual, government has a lot of tools in its box. If those tools can be augmented by a community leader who knows how to run and win campaigns, that is the stuff of fundamental change.

There are more than a half-million elective offices in the United States. If you have an inclination to serve and a desire to be a leader in your community, do it. Being in a position where you can have a positive impact on your community and bring about change is more rewarding and fun than you can imagine. Ultimately, the only real credentials you need are integrity, a caring heart, and a strong work ethic.

Since 1985 I have worked on or managed many campaigns in my region. Through years of experimentation and collaboration with other seasoned campaigners, I found organizational techniques that work in political campaigns. This book is the culmination of campaign trial and error and will give you the tools you need to organize the efforts of others on your behalf. Whether you are a novice or a seasoned campaigner, you will find information here to make your efforts more organized and effective.

Good luck, and enjoy the process.

Acknowledgments

A BOOK THAT SPANS TWENTY YEARS BASED ON THIRTY YEARS OF CAM-
paigning creates a long list of people who assisted in its success. Most are
unnamed in this manual but are nevertheless referenced throughout; below I
give context to a few who have helped over the years.

Dr. Michael Holstein, a retired English professor, who edited my first editions, first saw the brilliance of a precinct analysis—or, as he called it, the
open sesame. Through editing, he taught me how to write.

Dr. Alan Bates, peppered throughout the last five editions, had complete
confidence in my ability and gave me freedom to experiment with campaign
systems and theories for better outcomes.

Amy Blossom, former Ashland Branch head librarian, is the name and inspiration behind the job description for the clerical team. If you want a clerical team that comes with a ready set of volunteers, get a librarian. It was also
Amy, along with Barbara Ryberg, who birthed the idea of how to move the
county forward in building renovations that I describe in "The Issue-Based
Campaign" chapter.

Brian Freeman of Crystal Castle Graphics has worked on campaigns with
me since 1986. He is the inspiration of the graphic designer job description:
affordable, fast, creative, and never complains about my wanting something
yesterday. It is impossible to imagine campaigning without him.

Dr. Rita Sullivan has headed up letters to the editor for me for decades; she
found and prodded people to get their letters in.

Blaire Finney miraculously corralled volunteer lists spanning twenty-five
years from dozens of my campaigns; she is the role model for the job description of a data/list manager.

Ron Adams, Rhonda Bohall, and Hal Cloe, formed the job description for treasurer: Attentive to detail and pleasant at all times, they are true professionals.

Sharon Javna and Betty McClendon are the inspirations for the house party–coordinator job.

Karen Starchvick is the name behind the perfect field operative. She's a workhorse.

Chuck Keil, who does my mapping, and Mica Cardillo of Soupala are the techies behind the new get-out-the-vote (GOTV) system outlined in that chapter. They understood the theory and brought it to life.

Ada Fung, my editor at Westview Press, had an organizational vision that improved every aspect of the book.

The thousands of volunteers, who inspired, worked, and contributed time and money, made it rewarding and fun, win or lose.

Oh, and the "very good friend" mentioned under "Theme Dinners" in fundraising? That's Sharon Schaefer.

And finally a thank-you to my family. My husband, Rick, put in countless hours creating outstanding television spots for local candidates and Facebook videos for Bates; no detail was too small. My children have been behind me since the beginning of running, serving, and writing about campaigns. Daniel Golden cowrote five important chapters in this edition, including "Precinct Analysis," "Targeting Voters," and "Getting Out the Vote (GOTV)," and Sarah Golden, who authored the "Digital and Social Media" chapter, jumped in to help Bates in the 2016 midterm by recording interviews, creating the footage my husband edited for Facebook videos. She also helped me in 2017 in my successful bid for the Library Board. Thanks, girlfriend.

Before You Begin

By Catherine Shaw and Daniel Golden

> Play for more than you can afford to lose and you will learn the game.
> —WINSTON CHURCHILL

IN THIS CHAPTER

- How to Use This Book
- A Message for the Candidate
- The Framework
- Know the Law

How to Use This Book

THIS HANDBOOK WAS WRITTEN TO ACCOMMODATE POLITICAL NOVICES and veterans, technical newbies and experts, career political operatives and academics. Each chapter is designed to stand alone—if you're late to the game and lawn signs must go up, flip to the lawn sign chapter and come back for the rest of the story another day. With that said, you should begin with Chapter 2, "Precinct Analysis." Your efforts will be wasteful at best, and counterproductive at worst, without a precinct analysis as the basis for your campaign road map.

Your labors will be most effective when you implement each component of your campaign with an understanding of its relative significance, so I recommend that you read this entire book cover to cover before you get to work. Nevertheless, I realize that some readers will choose to read as they work. This book can accommodate that approach, too, but you should be

1

aware that the earliest campaign activities begin four months before Election Day. Should you choose to read the chapters in this book out of order, I recommend that you review Chapter 8, "Targeting Voters," and Chapter 12, "Getting Out the Vote (GOTV)," as soon as your precinct analysis is complete—otherwise, you might miss the opportunity to identify your base in time for the election.

A Message for the Candidate

This book was written for the campaign manager (CM), and it's almost never a good idea for the candidate to manage his or her own campaign. However, I always recommend that the candidate read it as well. As your campaign revs up, you will constantly find yourself meeting deadlines and going to events with not quite enough preparation time. You will be far more successful coordinating your efforts if you share a common literacy of the same playbook. With that said, if you are managing the campaign for a client who has not read this book, be sure he or she at least reads this section.

Why Are You Running for Office?

The most commonly stated reason first-time candidates give for running is probably some version of "I want to give back to the community that has done so much for me." But never forget: If you choose to run, it can't be about you. The measure of a public servant is his or her success in managing the issues that affect the electorate. Begin with the end in mind—list the reasons you want to serve and let them guide your message. What's broken that you'd like to fix? What's at risk that you'd like to save? If you're running for a school-board seat, your reasons might be opportunity for our children, continuous improvement of the education system, and economic growth. A candidate hoping to serve on a library board might talk about resource management, efficient budgeting, hours of operation, and materials. A seat at the county commission? Your issues could be traffic, air quality, land use, or public safety. There are many good reasons to serve, but none of them are personal.

Many enter public service as a spokesperson for a hot-button issue, but single-issue candidates don't usually make good elected officials. Governance is a complex business; it demands that office holders be attentive to the many facets of the public corporation. Single-issue candidates often struggle with the diversity of duties in office, sitting disengaged until the governing body hits a topic relevant to their issue. It's frustrating for the office holder, their colleagues, and their constituents. However, there's nothing wrong with a pet passion. If your favorite issue is an example for a larger pattern of government dysfunction, you have yourself a platform.

I was first compelled to run for office in 1988, after a sewage leak had contaminated my pond. When the public works director and his assistant came to my home to examine the merits of my complaint, he looked down the steep incline to the pond, some five hundred feet from where we stood, and said, "It's only decomposing plant matter. The city doesn't even have a sewer line down there."

I suggested we walk to the pond so he could see and smell it for himself. He said, "If I were to spend time on every complaint I get from every housewife in town, I'd get nothing done." His assistant cringed.

With no admission of guilt or help from the city, we had the pond water tested, which was indeed contaminated with human waste—and it was from a broken sewer line near the pond. We sent the lab results and bill to the city, and although they reimbursed us, I decided to run for mayor that year, winning my first of three terms. You might say my pet issue was municipal wastewater management, but in my view the sewage leak and subsequent response were symptomatic of a larger problem that needed fixing.

Manage Your Expectations

An effective campaign will consume time and energy. You'll recruit volunteers, raise money (a lot of it), run phone banks, create media presentations, organize canvassers, engage social media, and work tirelessly to get your base to the polls. Don't take the plunge without a sober reflection on your outlook. A good precinct analysis will tell you, among other things, just how pragmatic your candidacy is. Cut your losses if your race is unwinnable. Pay no mind to the voices urging you to make a go of it, in the face of insurmountable odds, to bleed the opposition party of resources. In my experience, fielding a candidate in an unwinnable seat pulls more time and resources to help the unwinnable race than the opposition will spend in either regard.

If you intend to throw your hat in the ring to demonstrate your credibility for some later, more winnable, race, be sure to run a classy campaign. Attack pieces have become ubiquitous in national politics, but the techniques in this book were primarily designed for local elections. The people who run for the school board, city council, mayor, county commissioner, and state legislature are generally well known and respected in their communities. Candidates who run unwinnable races to improve their visibility in the community should never go negative. Even if your outlook is good, though, the rewards for attacking your opponent's reputation in a local race scarcely ever outweigh the risks.

Be Vigilant of Your Campaign's Tone

In *The Odyssey*, Homer describes an island inhabited by the Sirens. Their intoxicating song was known to lure passing sailors to the rocky coast and shipwreck. When Odysseus—the epic's protagonist—nears the island on his journey, he instructs his crew to fill their ears with wax and to tie him tightly to the mast. He was curious to hear the Sirens' song, but if he did, he knew he wouldn't have the sound judgment to pass safely by the island.

Modern economists might call Odysseus a *sophisticated consumer*—someone who constrains their future decisions with the foresight to prepare for their own irrationality. For example, somebody starting a diet might discard all his junk food, not trusting himself to keep clean when the cravings begin.

If you're going to run for office, choose your messaging strategy like a sophisticated consumer. First-time candidates can't appreciate the stress of a heated campaign until they're experiencing it. You'll be deprived of sleep and recreation, you'll feel emotionally and physically exhausted, and when some consultant urgently insists that you must air this ad or mail that literature, you might not have the sound judgment to push back. It will feel liberating to acquiesce the responsibility of decision making to the experts, whose confidence will easily overpower your fatigue. As the saying goes: Fatigue makes cowards of us all.

You must always remember that your name is the brand. In a few grueling months, it'll all be over, and, win or lose, your community will remember how you ran your campaign. I've seen countless candidates enter their races as well-respected leaders in their communities, only to find their reputations in abject disgrace by Election Day. Your opponent will no doubt be well respected in the community as well, and when it comes to local elections, voters won't forget a vicious smear campaign.

As I mentioned above, I never advise that my clients go negative—apart from the risk to their reputations, the evidence that attack ads even work is pretty thin (it may be that negative campaigns depress the opposition's voter turnout, but this book will cover far more efficient strategies to achieve the same ends).

Should you choose to run a negative campaign, never break this rule: Keep it simple and topical. If your attack is confusing, or if you expose a skeleton that had been in your opponent's closet for decades, the voters will assume you're fishing for something—*anything*—to keep the spotlight off you. They will assume you are an empty, Machiavellian candidate, and if you should lose (and you very likely will), that's the way your community will remember you.

Similarly, don't sign off on a flattering character portrait if a salient counterexample might come back to haunt you. Don't present yourself as the law-and-order candidate if you have a criminal record. Don't present yourself as the family candidate if you were ever late making child-support payments. The electorate can be remarkably forgiving of your mistakes, but in my experience, they do not forgive hypocrisy.

In general, the safest messaging strategy is also the most effective one: Stick to the issues, not character. But whatever you decide, make up your mind now, before the rubber hits the road. Don't allow yourself to be swayed in the thick of the campaign.

The Framework

This book provides a field-tested framework for phone banks, campaign literature, fundraising, lawn signs, canvassing, social media, broadcast media, get out the vote (GOTV), branding, and volunteer management. Once you've completed your precinct analysis and settled on a basket of strategies, you should visually organize your campaign plan with a Gantt chart (Microsoft Project is a helpful tool), flowchart, or calendar. Written campaign plans are probably the most common organizational tool, but I recommend something that displays your timeline at a glance. Although your organizational documents will be one of your earliest tasks, the chapter on planning is placed at the end of this manual so campaign teams know what to include based on the various chapters leading up to it.

Chapter 2, "Precinct Analysis," will show you how to efficiently ID voters on a map based on historical voting patterns. It will give you a realistic picture of your chances on Election Day and assist you in focusing resources for the greatest possible return. A precinct analysis will help you geographically parse your supporters from your detractors. Have it ready well before the campaign kickoff.

Chapter 3, "The Campaign Team and Volunteer Organization," covers the small, select group who will develop and execute campaign strategies: the campaign committee and the greater force behind activity implementation, volunteers.

Chapter 4, "Campaign Messaging," details development of a theme and message. Within this chapter, you will also find information on polling, slogans, logo design (also included in the chapter on lawn signs), a voters' pamphlet, and tips on drafting an effective walking piece.

Chapter 5, "Fundraising," outlines the many ways a campaign can raise money through events, direct mail, and candidate and volunteer solicitation calls. This is where you will find sample budgets and a template to help you create your own. There are also expenditure budget sheets.

Chapter 6, "Digital and Social Media," touches on all aspects of social media communication and how best to deploy them in your campaign. Its focus is primarily relevant to down-ballot races, but it also covers systems and strategies that have been successful in well-funded up-ballot campaigns.

Chapter 7, "Traditional Media," provides examples of how to get the most out of your media dollars while effectively communicating with voters. Candidates and issue-based campaigns build credibility from their presence in broadcast and print media. Given the expense and the power of this campaign line item, you'll want to be sure you're getting the best possible return for every dollar you spend on media.

Chapter 8, "Targeting Voters," builds on the precinct analysis to inform a campaign how best to find, mobilize, and target likely voters. It covers all aspects of canvassing, including mapping turfs and organizing and deploying the volunteer workforce. This is where you will find the various forms of direct mail and systems for executing campaign-generated mail plans.

Chapter 9, "Lawn Signs," is an extension of, and related to, "Targeting Voters." This chapter covers design, finding locations, establishing structure for volunteer systems for placement, and maintaining and removing both lawn and field signs. Also included are examples of signs that work.

Chapter 10, "The Candidate Campaign," outlines how best to package the candidate's image. It includes negative campaigning, attacks, debates, and dealing with the press in detail.

Chapter 11, "The Issue-Based Campaign," covers both local and state initiatives and referenda, strategies to pass facility campaigns for community-held resources such as libraries and schools, operating and maintenance money measures, and "monsters in the night": the double majority and the supermajority.

Chapter 12, "Getting Out the Vote (GOTV)," covers the voter activation effort that is critical to a winning campaign, dealing with the hybrid campaign—that is, the election with both absentee mail voting and poll voting—and tried-and-true methods for elections conducted partly or entirely through vote by mail (VBM).

Chapter 13, "The Campaign Plan," orders everything you have to do to run an effective campaign. Your campaign plan should be one of the earliest things you do, but learning to draft one should come last: You'll need a basic literacy of all your campaign activities before you organize them into a plan. Also included in this chapter is a campaign calendar, a graphical alternative to a written campaign plan, which works equally well for organizing campaign efforts.

Chapter 14, "After the Ball," is simply about winning and losing grace-fully, putting your campaign to bed, Election Night, and retiring a campaign debt (should you have one).

Appendix B, "Campaigning on a Shoestring," is designed for running a short three-month campaign on less than $3,000 for either nonpartisan races, parti-san primaries, noncontroversial issue-based campaigns, or those conducted in homogeneous populations where one party dominates in registration.

Know the Law

Before you get to work, visit your county clerk, election office, or city re-corder to become familiar with state and local election laws. For example, in my city, you are not allowed to place lawn signs more than six weeks before an election. You are also not allowed to place them on the strip between the sidewalk and the street. Although home owners plant, mow, water, and care for this area, it is in fact part of the public right-of-way. Placing a lawn sign here could be interpreted in one of two ways: Either you feel you're above the law, or you don't know the law. Neither interpretation bodes well for a candidate hoping to work in government.

Similarly, it is against federal law to place campaign literature in and around mailboxes. Even though you bought and installed your mailbox, the federal government dictates how it can be used. The same goes for the little boxes on the side of your home. Also, publicly owned buildings should not be used for campaign purposes at all—they are maintained, lit, and owned by the taxpayers. Throughout this book, you will find alerts to potential legal missteps noted by "Know the law."

County or city elections will also draw attention to filing dates that you and your treasurer must know. Missing a campaign-expenditure filing dead-line will get you publicity, but not the kind you want. Also, missing the vot-ers' pamphlet deadline can unnecessarily hobble your efforts. Deadlines such as these should be noted in the campaign plan or calendar.

Other than the legal materials from the county clerk, the city recorder, or the secretary of state, everything you need to run a successful campaign is included in this handbook.

THE TEN COMMANDMENTS
OF CAMPAIGNING

Honor thy base

Stay on message

Money is thy savior

Never tell a lie

Aim at the souls that can be saved

Never waste donors' money

Do not commit adultery

Start early

Be prepared in all things

Know who you are

THE CARDINAL SINS OF CAMPAIGNING

Being caught in a provable lie

Committing a crime

Having a relationship with a member of your staff

Committing adultery

Declaring bankruptcy

Precinct Analysis: The Sinners, the Saints, and the Savables

By Catherine Shaw and Daniel Golden

> Spend the time to make the foundation right or you will pay in time and money all the way to the roof.
>
> —TONY NUNES, BUILDER AND FORMER FIREFIGHTER

IN THIS CHAPTER:

- Context of Place
- Nonaffiliated Voters ("Independents")
- The Sinners, the Saints, and the Savables
- Do the Math
- Votes Owed
- Predicting Voter Turnout

Context of Place

MUCH HAS BEEN MADE OF THE GROWING URBAN-RURAL DIVIDE IN America,[1] but political self-segregation dates back at least as far as the very founding of our nation. As David McCullough writes in his book *1776*, British troops suffered great adversity during the siege of Boston, a city sympathetic to the Revolution; they were anxious to move on to New York, where they would enjoy a warmer welcome. Even then, Americans segregated themselves by political ideology.

A precinct analysis identifies voting trends geographically, allowing a campaign to efficiently allocate resources where they count the most. Targeting strategies are conventionally developed from demographic data, but when it comes to effectively targeting voters, geographic data is your first best weapon: Voting behavior is most predictable and usable when organized by neighborhood. Polling data may reveal disproportionate support among some particular gender or ethnic group or age range, but it is a blunt instrument until you map out your supporters and detractors geographically. What we do today, and have done since getting on ships to cross the Atlantic for financial opportunity and religious freedom, is pack up and move next door to people who share core values and think and vote like we do.[2] As Bruce Oppenheimer of Vanderbilt University says, "Democrats tend to live next to Democrats. Republicans tend to live next to Republicans."[3]

Your precinct analysis will provide a road map to target and activate specific voters with canvassing, lawn sign placement, direct mail, and advertising. It's always cost-effective and an indispensable first step for down-ballot campaigns—that is, anything appearing on the ballot below federal and statewide races and issues. We analyze voting trends by precinct because they are generally the most granular geographical unit for which election data is readily available—it might be more powerful to conduct a block-by-block or street-by-street analysis, but county election offices just happen to aggregate voting data by precinct. Just as a presidential campaign will focus its resources within battleground states, local campaigns must focus their resources within battleground precincts.

Get your precinct analysis out of the way as early as possible, as you'll be tight on time once the campaign begins. You only need historical voting data, so you can get started months or years in advance. More important, you won't know whether your campaign efforts are helpful, wasteful, or even counterproductive until you know the literal political landscape of your district.

Social Context

Knowing the social context of cities within a county is just as important as knowing the social context of neighborhoods within a city. This fine-grained knowledge allows the down-ballot campaign to profile voters within a context of historical voting and registration trends.

When I first began tracking voter registration in 1984, my county's partisan makeup was fairly even, with a 2 percent countywide Republican registration advantage. Over the course of thirty-plus years, this advantage moved from 2 percent to 11 percent and back to 2 percent in 2008. In 1986 the registration difference between Democrats and Republicans in my city was

16 percent; now it's 60 percent. Some communities completely flipped in registration, moving from a twenty-point Democratic advantage to a twenty-point Republican advantage. During the period between 2002 and 2006, thirty Republicans moved into one booming town in my region for each Democrat moving in. During the following decade, two hundred Republicans moved into this same town for every nine Democrats who moved *out*.

Similar geopolitical self-segregation is ubiquitous across my state. The new Republicans are landed poor, Roosevelt Democrats, blue-collar workers, undereducated, truck owners, the religious Right, survivalist militia, and people deeply suspicious of government. They resent public education, the educated, and print media. Meanwhile, Democrats are gaining ground with the educated, the moderately wealthy, small-business owners, secular voters, youth, minorities, and unmarried women. This trend is evident across the nation.[4]

Nearly every city in my region has become politically polarized. When areas become extreme in registration, attitudes and voting will also be extreme: A Republican running for office in a heavily Democratic area will be left of (more liberal than) Democrats living in heavily Republican areas. A Democrat running in a heavily Democratic area will struggle to prove his liberal bona fides, just as a Republican in a heavily registered Republican city may struggle to prove her conservative bona fides.

Demographic Data

Many campaign strategists rely on polling data to locate friendly demographics. For our purposes, demographic traits will include gender, ethnicity, education, economic standing, and age. Correlations between political opinions and demographic categories can be helpful, especially with respect to broadcast media—for example, if polls show that your candidate is popular among older voters, you might buy ad spots during the local news when viewing demographics favor older voters. Polling data will be more thoroughly covered in Chapter 8, "Targeting Voters," but you should never rely on a poll at the expense of geographical voting patterns, especially in counties with many small cities, a mix of urban and rural voters, and multiple school districts. A strategy that targets demographic groups as though they voted in a bloc will be inefficient and imprecise, but demographic information can help a strategist target voters with surgical precision when applied within targeted precincts.

Should you have the resources to run a poll or purchase information about voters' lifestyle and consumer habits, break your voting area into zones of similar voting behavior and ask the polling firm to identify support by demographics *and* by region; it will make your targeting activities more effective when you conduct your precinct analysis.

While precinct boundaries are adjusted constantly by county clerks, you should select your zones to remain relatively static across campaigns. Once you have completed your precinct analysis, you'll want to build each zone from adjacent precincts that behave similarly. You might also pick up some hints from US Census data. Zones might include small cities and surrounding precincts, while other zones might divide neighborhoods in large cities.

I break my county into seven zones: One is a city of 20,000 plus surrounding precincts; another is two small adjacent cities and their surrounding precincts. I broke the largest city into two zones, and everything else is grouped into geographic areas. Some of my zones are larger than others, some by population and some by geography.

In another part of the state, I used state house districts for the zones. In another I combined the small cities of the western part of a rural house district as one zone, treated the unincorporated areas of farmland as another, and worked my way across in similar fashion, going west to east and combining like with like, according to geography, cities, and voting patterns.

If your county has organized the precincts in ascending order by geography, you're in luck and you will need to do very little to break your data into and out of zones. This means you can create charts along the way. I like to make charts as soon as I come across interesting data, so that I can study some nuance. However, if the county has a more hodgepodge approach to numbering precincts (often the case, because populations swell and precincts are divided and renumbered), it's best to keep your data together, that is, listed as it comes from the county, until everything is pressed; this will leave all your charts for last. Either way, once precincts are scrambled to make zones for charting purposes, you may need to put them back in the county order for some unforeseen reason. To allow for this, I create a numbered column that is independent of my precinct numbers for quick reorganization.

Microtargeting

Microtargeting is a marketing activity that utilizes demographic, social, and commercial data to predict voting tendencies. In the same manner that retailers with member or discount cards are collecting information each time the card is swiped at the checkout counter, nearly every purchase, Internet search, and social media contact you make creates an information pathway. Marketing professionals know that microtargeting data can be used to predict consumption behavior, and, similarly, you can use it to predict voting behavior.

Practitioners of microtargeting often suggest that a targeting strategy built on "geography, party registration and electoral turnout alone leaves some of your best voters stranded and untouched."[5] That may be true, but a targeting strategy built on precinct analysis alone will always be more effective (and affordable) than a targeting strategy built on demographic data alone. Even if you have the resources to aggressively microtarget voters, you should never do so at the expense of a precinct analysis. A historical study on geographical voting patterns will locate the gold veins; demographic trends will help you locate the gold dust. The two strategies work well together.

Nonaffiliated Voters ("Independents")

So-called independents are registered voters who are not affiliated with a political party. In the District of Columbia and the twenty-seven states where voters register by party, the ranks of independents have surged in the past few decades and now occupy a third of the voter rolls. In the twenty-three states whose voters do not register by party, polls report similar numbers.[6] Political pundits and polling firms have elevated the status of independents, or nonaffiliated voters (NAVs), by assuming they are the undecided voters who tip the balance of an election. Additionally, NAVs are usually presented as though they were their own demographic category, sharing common values and voting priorities. I am aware of no evidence that supports this assumption.

In my decades of experience managing and advising campaigns, I have consistently found that NAVs are just as partisan as Democrats and Republicans, and the best research corroborates my experience nationwide, including polling conducted by the *Washington Post* and ABC in July 2002 and other polling by the *Washington Post*, Harvard University, and the Kaiser Family Foundation in 2007. In the latter study, independents were assigned to one of five categories, with the "disguised partisans" and the "disengaged" composing 48 percent of the polled independents. The "dislocated" (the socially liberal/fiscally conservative) were 16 percent of these voters, with the "disillusioned" (angry voters) and "deliberators" (true swing voters) evenly divided among the remaining 36 percent. These findings are consistent with Bruce E. Keith's findings in *The Myth of the Independent*, first published a quarter century ago, and the trend has only strengthened since then.

NAVs do seem to share one common feature: They turn out less than registered Democrats and Republicans, typically by about twenty points. But with a third of registered voters lacking any party affiliation, the lowest hanging fruit for any campaign is finding your supporters among lazy NAVs and getting them to the polls.

In fact, finding your support, whatever their party-affiliation status, is the main event in a precinct analysis. You can't necessarily parse your supporters from your detractors even among registered Democrats and Republicans. A few years back, I was stuffing envelopes with a volunteer who lived in an area with a Republican registration advantage of eighteen points. I told him that two years before I had worked a campaign in his area and, during the get-out-the-vote (GOTV) effort, discovered that many registered Democrats believed they were actually registered Republicans. "I have a confession to make," he told me. "I'm a registered Republican—always have been—but I've never voted for a Republican in my life."

You will encounter Democrats who always vote Republican (Democrats in name only, or "DINOs") as well as Republicans who always vote Democratic (Republicans in name only, or "RINOs"). Your success in shoring up the support of your base depends first and foremost on your success in locating DINOs, RINOs, and support among NAVs.

The Sinners, the Saints, and the Savables

The overwhelming majority of voters, whether they are registered Republican, Democrat, or neither, will never cross the aisle—when they vote, it's always for candidates of the same political party. So rather than generalizing political preferences by registration status, we'll use historical election data to identify categories of voters: *sinners* (those who will never vote for you), *saints* (those who will never vote against you), and *savables* (undecided, lazy, or persuadable voters).

- *The Sinners*. All of your efforts to engage sinners will only increase the likelihood that they vote, and it will be against you. Once your precinct analysis identifies a neighborhood of sinners, you must avoid canvassing them, calling them, sending them mail, or targeting them with broadcast media. If they do not stay home altogether on Election Day, the best you can hope for is an *undervote*—that is, casting a ballot but not voting in your race, perhaps out of apathy. The best way to keep a sinner apathetic is to keep your campaign invisible to him or her. That includes lawn signs in their neighborhoods.
- *The Saints*. Similarly, saints never cross the aisle, and they also undervote or fail to vote at all. Once you have identified saints, your goal is to activate them (motivate them to fill in your bubble and turn in their ballot). The undervote is now a partisan candidate's biggest challenge. In tight elections, the candidate with the fewest undervotes wins.
- *The Savables*. Also known as *swing* or *undecided* voters,[7] savables do not necessarily vote along party lines. They are typically motivated by hot-button issues, but generally are uninterested in politics. It is tempting to idealize American politics as a Jeffersonian institution, where voters

approach each election with a clean slate, ultimately supporting the candidates who offer the most cogent case to serve. In reality, savables are the exception to the rule. If you've ever shared a Thanksgiving table with extended family, you're probably aware that political persuasion is nearly impossible, even among people who love one another. And you won't have the benefit of annual extended dinners to change your constituents' minds. Your precinct analysis will help you locate savables, and if you find them, it may be worth your while to target them with persuasive campaign materials and canvassing. In my experience, however, it is exceptionally rare to find an election with a significant swing—and I have *never* encountered a campaign for which persuasion was a cost-effective use of resources. Once you have completed your precinct analysis, you will probably find that your winning strategy comes down to activating saints and hiding from sinners.

Election offices, political parties, and political action committees (PACs) often track voters by turnout. Voting frequency will typically be listed next to the registered voter's name as 4/4, 3/4, 2/4, 1/4—that is, people voting in four out of four of the last elections, three out of four, and so on. I refer to them as fours, threes, twos, and ones, respectively; those who voted in one out of the last five elections are zeroes. For the GOTV, they are graded like school: A through F. Fours will take very little prodding to get to the polls. The others can be a little trickier to pin down: Some turn out only for presidential elections, some only in general elections, and others in their own individual pattern. However, with a little push, threes and twos can be activated to get to the polls. Your goal is to surgically activate voters in high-priority precincts who will support your candidate or issue-based campaign. A high-priority precinct is one that has high support but low turnout. It is rarely cost-effective to target "ones" (D voters), and it is never cost-effective to target "zeroes" (F voters). Table 2.1 summarizes general strategies for each voter type discussed so far.

Do the Math

The data you'll need will typically be available at state election offices or your county clerk's office for a nominal fee. I used to get data exclusively from county elections, but recently I contacted Oregon Secretary of State Election Division for an extensive amount of data spanning multiple counties and elections dating back to 2006. If I were to go through each of the counties for this information, it would have cost me $10,000, but the secretary of state's office provided it all for under $400. Similarly, I needed twelve years

Voter	Description	Strategy for *Saints*	Strategy for *Sinners*	Strategy for *Savables*
Fours ("A" voters)	Voters turning out 4/4 of the past elections	Activate with modest campaign effort, e.g., one canvass. An undervote among your saints must be avoided, so give them a reason to care.	You probably can't inactivate these voters by keeping a low profile. Ignore these voters to save campaign resources and hope they undervote your candidate or cause.	Target with persuasive messaging materials. You may need to expend resources to ID these voters, and determine which issues are important to them.
Threes ("B" voters)	Voters turning out 3/4 of the past elections	Activate with substantial campaign effort—a mailer, a canvass and follow up within the GOTV plan. In most cases, this will be the focus of your campaign.	Remain invisible—try not to let these voters know your campaign even exists. If intermixed with saints, expend resources to ID who is who among the nonaffiliated voters.	
Twos ("C" voters)	Voters turning out 2/4 of the past elections			
Ones "D" voters	Voters turning out 1/4 of the past elections	Usually ignore, unless your campaign is exceptionally well financed and you are working with a major registration disadvantage		Ignore to save resources
Zeroes "F" failing voters	Voters turning out once in five of the past elections	Ignore to save resources—the effect of zeroes on any election outcome will always be negligible		

TABLE 2.1 Strategies for the Sinners, Saints, and Savables

of data for Pierce County, Washington, which includes Tacoma. All of the necessary data were available online for free through the state elections division. In order to begin your precinct analysis, you will need election data on six variables across each precinct in your electoral district, for at least two of the past similar elections for your current seat of interest. For example, if you are managing a campaign for a state senate candidate and the previous two elections for that seat were in 2016 and 2012, collect data sets of each of the following variables for both years:

1. *Total registration:* How many voters are registered in each precinct? Notated as A.
2. *Total ballots cast:* How many voters turned in a ballot? Notated as B.
3. *Republican votes cast:* How many votes did the Republican candidate get in your race of interest? For example, if you are managing a state senate race, how many votes did the Republican who ran for the same seat win in previous elections? Notated as VR.
4. *Democratic votes cast:* How many votes did the Democratic candidate get in your race of interest? Notated as VD.
5. *Republican gubernatorial votes:* How many votes did the Republican candidate for governor get? Notated as R.
6. *Democratic gubernatorial votes:* How many votes did the Democratic candidate for governor get? Notated as D.

You may find it more convenient to replace R and D with data on Republican and Democratic registration totals. For example, in Oregon, half of the state senators are elected during the midterms, so they don't ever appear on the same ballot as gubernatorial candidates. So if you were going to define R and D using gubernatorial votes for a midterm senate race in Oregon, you would need data for at least four elections—the past two elections for the senate seat of interest *and* the past two gubernatorial elections. You may find it more convenient to use registration totals for D and R in the same years for which you collect election data, and in fact it will usually be more accurate: Voting behavior is fundamentally different during midterm elections than a presidential cycle.

Registration totals may also be more reliable if your region has experienced rapid demographic changes since the penultimate gubernatorial race. For example, suppose you have collected election data for 2016 and 2012, and in 2013 a manufacturing plant closed in your region. Since then, people have been rapidly relocating out of your district. If you're unsure about the demographic stability in your region, one terrific—and free—resource is the US Census. If the demographics of your district are rapidly changing, it might be safer to use up-to-date registration totals for R and D. On the other hand, if you live in a district with a lot of RINOs, DINOs, or NAVs, gubernatorial votes may be more accurate because actions speak louder than words. If you live in one of the twenty-three states that does not track voter registration by district, you may have no choice but to define R and D according to gubernatorial votes. However, you can also approximate registration percentages using a primary election where only party registrants can vote to nominate someone within the party. For the most part, any of these definitions will yield a robust analysis. The beauty of a gubernatorial race outcome is that voters tend to stick to party when voting for a governor. Whereas voters swing wildly when it comes to congressional races, they tend to revert back to partisan voting within a gubernatorial race. Using the percent that voted for the Republican gubernatorial candidate and the Democratic gubernatorial candidate, precinct by precinct, will give you an excellent indicator of how many votes should go to down-ballot Republicans and Democrats.

Enter each of the six above-mentioned variables—A, B, VR, VD, R, and D—into a spreadsheet. The least cumbersome organization will usually assign rows to precincts (that is, the leftmost column will list each of the precincts in your district) and columns to variables (the first row, that is, the column header, will list the six data types you collected above and the calculated variables below). For graphical simplicity, the first example (presented in figures 2.1 and 2.2) illustrates a transposition of this row-column convention. Choose whichever orientation you feel most comfortable with, so long as you keep consistent.

It's time to begin making the calculations for your precinct analysis. For each precinct in your district, calculate the *undervote* (notated as U) using equation 1, where U represents the undervote, B represents total ballots cast, V_R are votes received by the Republican, and V_D are the votes received by the Democrat:

[Equation 1] $$U = B - V_R - V_D$$

We calculate the quantity of voters who turned in a ballot but failed to vote in your race of interest by subtracting the votes cast for the Republican and Democratic candidates from the total number of ballots cast. Generally, the voter will skip a ballot item for one of three reasons: *don't know, don't like,* or *don't care*. Voters who have not been paying attention to a particular race will "leave it up to those who do know," even while they vote in races elsewhere on the ballot. This most commonly happens in down-ballot races and judge seats where candidates often run unopposed, but it can also occur in statewide races with low profiles. Equation 1 treats votes for third-party candidates like undervoters, which is the most useful simplification for our analysis.

Next you'll calculate the total number of *lazy voters* (notated as L). Lazy voter is defined in equation 2 as the number of registered voters who failed to turn in a ballot at all (recall that A = all registered voters and B = total ballots cast):

[Equation 2] $$L = A - B$$

Third, calculate the total number of activatable voters (notated as G)—that is, registered voters who either undervoted your race or failed to vote at all—using equation 3:

[Equation 3] $G = A - B + U = B - V_R - V_D$

We use the variable G because activatable voters will become the primary focus of your GOTV effort. They may be undervoters or registered voters who didn't turn in a ballot or go to the polls, but one way or another, they didn't fill in the bubble in your current race of interest.

The next two calculations in your precinct analysis will be *Republican margin* (notated as MR) and *Democratic margin* (notated as MD). Equations 4 and 5 define the margin as the gap in votes between the Democratic and Republican candidates running for your current seat of interest:

[Equation 4] $M_R = V_R - V_D$

[Equation 5] $M_D = V_D - V_R$

In reality, you'll only need to calculate one of the margins, since $MR = -MD$. For simplicity, use the margin of the party of your candidate. For example, suppose you're managing a campaign for a Democrat. If the Democrat who last ran for the same seat lost, the margin should be negative. If the Democrat who last ran for the same seat won, the margin should be positive.

Equations 6 and 7 define the *percent votes owed* to the Republican and Democratic candidates in a race (notated PR and PD, respectively). Equations 8 and 9 define *votes owed* to the Republican and Democratic candidates in a race (notated OR and OD, respectively):

[Equation 6] $P_R = \dfrac{R}{D+R} = 1 - P_D$

[Equation 7] $P_D = \dfrac{D}{D+R} = 1 - P_R$

[Equation 8] $O_R = B \times P_R = \dfrac{B \times R}{D+R} = B \times (1 - P_D)$

[Equation 9] $O_D = B \times P_D = \dfrac{B \times D}{D+R} = B \times (1 - P_R)$

Percent votes owed is a unitless fraction quantity: $0 = PR = 1$ and $0 = PD = 1$. Number of votes owed, like every other variable we have discussed, is expressed in units of votes. Number of votes owed and percent votes owed can be calculated over any arbitrary region—it would be equally accurate to tabulate R, D, and B over cities, zones, or your entire district, so long as each quantity is tabulated over the same region. We typically calculate equations 6–9 by precinct, however, because it improves the precision of your targeting efforts. As was the case with the margins MR and MD, it will not be necessary to calculate the percent votes owed for both candidates—don't bother with equation 7 if your candidate is running as a Republican, and don't bother with equation 6 if your candidate is running as a Democrat.

Repeat each of your seven calculations for each of the elections for which you have collected data and for each precinct. At a minimum, your spread-sheet should have six hard-coded data variables and seven calculated variables per precinct for at least two elections—that's twenty-six numbers per precinct if you're analyzing two elections.

Finally, compare your election data with three more calculations, defined in equations 10–13:

[Equation 10] $\Delta G = G_{T2} - G_{T1}$

[Equation 11] $\Delta M_R = M_{R_{T2}} - M_{R_{T1}}$

[Equation 12] $\Delta M_D = M_{D_{T2}} - M_{D_{T1}}$

[Equation 13] $S = \left|\frac{\Delta M}{2}\right| - |\Delta G|$

The triangle character in equations 10–13 is the Greek letter *delta*; it is the mathematical symbol for change. So ΔG is pronounced *delta G*, and it quantifies the total change in activatable voters between elections—recall that G is the sum of people who undervoted or didn't vote. The subscripts denote *time 2* and *time 1*, respectively. For example, if you calculated a G value in some precinct to be 200 in 2012 (*T1*) and 300 in 2016 (*T2*), the *delta* of activatable voters is calculated by $\Delta G = G_{T=2016} - G_{T=2012} = 300 - 200 = 100$. Similarly, you will calculate the change in margin—either ΔMR or ΔMD—by comparing the difference in margins between elections. Again, it is not necessary to calculate both margins: Either the Republican margin or the Democratic margin suffices.

S is the *swing*—for our purposes, the number of voters who might actually have switched between their support for the Republican and Democratic candidates. The bars in equation 13 denote the absolute value—mathematically, the distance between a number and zero. The absolute value of a positive number is itself, and the absolute value of a negative number is its opposite—for example, the absolute value of 10 and the absolute value of −10 are both 10. In Excel the absolute-value formula is denoted "=ABS(X)"; for example, "=ABS(10)" and "=ABS(−10)" will both return an output of "10." The subscript is omitted from the ΔM in equation 11 because one margin is always the opposite of the other—that is, $|\Delta MR| = |\Delta MD|$—so use whichever margin you have calculated.

The swing calculation will help quantify the extent to which voters are persuadable. Suppose you have a precinct where the Democratic margin has grown from 600 votes to 1,200 votes. Have the voters switched their support from the Republican to the Democratic candidate? Not necessarily—you should assume that voters actually crossed the aisle in a precinct only when $|\Delta M| > |\Delta G|$. If your ΔG is 400 over the same period, assume 400 opposition voters either undervoted or failed to vote at all. If your $\Delta G = −400$, assume 400 supporters either undervoted or failed to vote at all. That leaves only 200 votes that can wisely be attributed to the swing. But don't forget: A swing of 200 means only *100* voters actually changed their vote—when a swinger crosses the aisle from Republican to Democrat, the Republican loses one vote *and* the Democrat gains one vote, increasing the Democratic margin by two. This is why equation 13 divides the change in margin by half. So in this example, where $\Delta MD = 1,200$, $|\Delta G| = 400$, and $S = 100$.

As a rule of thumb, a high S value is a necessary *but not sufficient* criterion to engage voters in an idealized Jeffersonian capacity, with the intent of actually changing minds. A very low (large and negative) swing means that changes in voting activity, usually the undervote, had a much larger bearing on the margin than voters changing their mind. Wherever you find a district with a low S, you must identify who is undervoting: saints or sinners. If the answer is sinners, the very last thing you want to do is try to persuade them: Remember, the best you can hope for with sinners is that they don't vote in your election, and a low S tells you that a lot of them won't, if you can only remain invisible. If, on the other hand, you encounter a very low S due to changes in saint activity, you will want to target the precinct, but probably not with conventional "persuasive" messaging—these are not people you need to convince to cross the aisle; you only need to get them to vote.

Figures 2.1 and 2.2 exemplify a precinct analysis for a hypothetical partisan race for dogcatcher. Your spreadsheet should look like these figures, or a transposition of them if you decided to put precincts in the first column and the variables in the header row. If you're managing a campaign for a nonpartisan seat or for a ballot measure or if you're in a primary, still follow along—methods for adapting this analysis will be covered later.

Year	Pricinct	1	2	3	4	5	6
T1: 2012	Registration (A)	1,968	4,956	3,942	3,593	3,096	4,190
	Total Ballots (B)	1,128	3,740	3,117	2,240	2,600	3,549
	R Votes (V_R)	163	1,534	1,248	1,732	1,843	672
	D Votes (V_D)	837	1,604	1,390	487	373	2,307
	Gub. R Votes (R)	178	1,536	1,366	1,881	2,045	740
	Gub. D Votes (D)	884	1,885	1,541	526	393	2,474
	Undervote (U)	=C4-C5-C6	=D4-D5-D6	=E4-E5-E6	=F4-F5-F6	=G4-G5-G6	=H4-H5-H6
	Lazy Voters (L)	=C3-C4	=D3-D4	=E3-E4	=F3-F4	=G3-G4	=H3-H4
	Activatable (G)	=C9+C10	=D9+D10	=E9+E10	=F9+F10	=G9+G10	=H9+H10
	Margin (M_D)	=C6-C5	=D6-D5	=E6-E5	=F6-F5	=G6-G5	=H6-H5
	% Votes Owed (O_D)	=C8/(C8+C7)	=D8/(D8+D7)	=E8/(E8+E7)	=F8/(F8+F7)	=G8/(G8+G7)	=H8/(H8+H7)
	R Votes Owed (O_R)	=(1-C13)*C4	=(1-D13)*D4	=(1-E13)*E4	=(1-F13)*F4	=(1-G13)*G4	=(1-H13)*H4
	D Votes Owed (O_D)	=C4*C13	=D4*D13	=E4*E13	=F4*F13	=G4*G13	=H4*H13
T2: 2016	Registration (A)	1,991	4,949	3,989	3,645	3,125	4,264
	Total Ballots (B)	1,154	3,639	3,122	2,299	2,619	3,549
	R Votes (V_R)	171	879	1,273	1,370	1,880	772
	D Votes (V_D)	855	2,251	1,402	490	376	2,316
	Gub. R Votes (R)	187	891	1,396	1,816	2,070	845
	Gub. D Votes (D)	898	2,545	1,567	530	399	2,494
	Undervote (U)	=C17-C18-C19	=D17-D18-D19	=E17-E18-E19	=F17-F18-F19	=G17-G18-G19	=H17-H18-H19
	Lazy Voters (L)	=C16-C17	=D16-D17	=E16-E17	=F16-F17	=G16-G17	=H16-H17
	Activatable (G)	=C22+C23	=D22+D23	=E22+E23	=F22+F23	=G22+G23	=H22+H23
	Margin (M_D)	=C19-C18	=D19-D18	=E19-E18	=F19-F18	=G19-G18	=H19-H18
	% Votes Owed (O_D)	=C21/(C21+C20)	=D21/(D21+D20)	=E21/(E21+E20)	=F21/(F21+F20)	=G21/(G21+G20)	=H21/(H21+H20)
	R Votes Owed (O_R)	=(1-C26)*C17	=(1-D26)*D17	=(1-E26)*E17	=(1-F26)*F17	=(1-G26)*G17	=(1-H26)*H17
	D Votes Owed (O_D)	=C17*C26	=D17*D26	=E17*E26	=F17*F26	=G17*G26	=H17*H26
	Delta G (ΔG)	=C24-C11	=D24-D11	=E24-E11	=F24-F11	=G24-G11	=H24-H11
	Delta M_D (ΔM_D)	=C25-C12	=D25-D12	=E25-E12	=F25-F12	=G25-G12	=H25-H12
	Swing (S)	=ABS(C30)/2-ABS(C29)	=ABS(D30)/2-ABS(D29)	=ABS(E30)/2-ABS(E29)	=ABS(F30)/2-ABS(F29)	=ABS(G30)/2-ABS(G29)	=ABS(H30)/2-ABS(H29)

FIGURE 2.1

The campaign manager was hired by a Democratic candidate running in 2020, so the light cells are populated with hard-coded data on the 2012 and 2016 races. Formulas as described in equations 1–13 are displayed as they would be entered in Excel. All variables except percent votes owed are expressed in units of votes.

Votes Owed

Before we interpret the findings of our precinct analysis, some explanation is needed on two critical variables: *votes owed* and *percent votes owed*, which we calculated in equations 6–9 and are located on rows 13–15 and 26–28 in figures 2.1 and 2.2, respectively. A votes-owed calculation is possible with election data from a single election. In fact, if you have chosen to define R and D using registration totals rather than gubernatorial votes, you don't need any election data at all.

When you encounter a precinct with high undervoting or low turnout (high G), you'll need to decide if you should activate them—when they *do*

Year	Pricinct	1	2	3	4	5	6
T1: 2012	Registration (A)	1,968	4,956	3,942	3,593	3,096	4,190
	Total Ballots (B)	1,128	3,740	3,117	2,240	2,600	3,549
	R Votes (V_R)	163	1,534	1,248	1,732	1,843	672
	D Votes (V_D)	837	1,604	1,390	487	373	2,307
	Gub. R Votes (R)	178	1,536	1,366	1,881	2,045	740
	Gub. D Votes (D)	884	1,885	1,541	526	393	2,474
	Undervote (U)	128	602	479	21	384	570
	Lazy Voters (L)	840	1,216	825	1,353	496	641
	Activatable (G)	968	1,818	1,304	1,374	880	1,211
	Margin (M_D)	674	70	142	-1,245	-1,470	1,635
	% Votes Owed (O_D)	0.832	0.551	0.530	0.219	0.161	0.770
	R Votes Owed (O_R)	189	1,679	1,465	1,750	2,181	817
	D Votes Owed (O_D)	939	2,061	1,652	490	419	2,732
T2: 2016	Registration (A)	1,991	4,949	3,989	3,645	3,125	4,264
	Total Ballots (B)	1,154	3,639	3,122	2,299	2,619	3,549
	R Votes (V_R)	171	879	1,273	1,370	1,880	772
	D Votes (V_D)	855	2,251	1,402	490	376	2,316
	Gub. R Votes (R)	187	891	1,396	1,816	2,070	845
	Gub. D Votes (D)	898	2,545	1,567	530	399	2,494
	Undervote (U)	128	509	447	439	363	461
	Lazy Voters (L)	837	1,310	867	1,346	506	715
	Activatable (G)	965	1,819	1,314	1,785	869	1,176
	Margin (M_D)	684	1,372	129	-880	-1,504	1,544
	% Votes Owed (O_D)	0.828	0.741	0.529	0.226	0.162	0.747
	R Votes Owed (O_R)	199	944	1,471	1,780	2,196	898
	D Votes Owed (O_D)	955	2,695	1,651	519	423	2,651
	Delta G (ΔG)	-3	1	10	411	-11	-35
	Delta M_D (ΔM_D)	10	1,302	-13	365	-34	-91
	Swing (S)	2	650	-4	-229	6	11

FIGURE 2.2

The campaign manager was hired by a Democratic candidate running in 2020, so the light cells are populated with hard-coded data on the 2012 and 2016 races. Calculated values are displayed as the Excel output in dark cells. All variables except percent votes owed are expressed in units of votes.

vote, will they support your candidate or the opposition? Votes owed are the number of votes a candidate would receive in the hypothetical case where none of the voters leave the bubble blank—that is, 0 percent undervote. If you are dealing with a highly polarized precinct (very high or very low saints-to-sinners ratio), or if you don't have the resources to exhaustively ID voters, votes owed will be your most useful estimate.

The implicit assumption is that nonpartisan registered voters are most likely to mirror the voting behavior of their neighbors—in a neighborhood with 50 Republicans, 50 Democrats, and 50 NAVs, the votes-owed forecast would predict that 25 NAVs will favor the Republican candidate and 25 NAVs will favor the Democratic candidate because the neighborhood is

A	B	C	D	E	F	G	H	I	J	K	L	M	N
Precinct	Reg	TO	Dem Reg	% Dem Reg	Rep Reg	% Rep Reg	Other Reg	% Other Reg	D+R Reg	D reg/D+R = % owed Ds	R reg/D+R = % owed Rs	K x C = votes owed D	L x C = votes owed R
Pct 2	3613	3325	2383	0.66	407	0.11	823	0.23	2790	0.85	0.15	2826	499
Pct 27	4366	3637	1139	0.26	2156	0.49	1071	0.25	3295	0.35	0.65	1273	2364

TABLE 2.2 Breakdown of Votes Owed in Two Precincts

Collapsing other registrants (third-party and nonaffiliated voters) into Democrat (*D*) and Republican (*R*) yields a predictable percent votes owed to candidates according to party affiliation. Multiplied by the turnout, the votes-owed integer is revealed.

home to an equal number of Democrats and Republicans. In a neighborhood with 80 Republicans, 20 Democrats, and 50 NAVs, the votes-owed forecast would predict that 40 NAVs will favor the Republican candidate and 10 will favor the Democratic candidate. The neighborhood is home to four times more Republicans than Democrats, so the best estimate is that the NAVs will support Republicans over Democrats four to one. In other words, NAVs *track* the behavior of their partisan neighbors.

To demonstrate, two precincts are presented in Table 2.2. In this example, 3,613 voters are registered in Precinct 2: 2,383 Democrats (66 percent), 407 Republicans (11 percent), and 823 nonaffiliated or third-party voters (23 percent). Applying equations 8 and 9, the votes owed to Democratic candidates will be the product of voter turnout and Democratic registration, divided by the sum of Democratic registration and Republican registration. Similarly, the votes owed to Republican candidates will be the product of voter turnout and Republican registration, divided by the sum of Democratic registration plus Republican registration. The resulting forecast is that 85 percent of voters in Precinct 2 will cast their vote for the Democrat and 15 percent will cast their vote for the Republican (the actual results show 86 percent voted for Barack Obama and 12 percent for John McCain).

There were 4,366 voters registered in Precinct 27—1,139 Democrats (26 percent), 2,156 Republicans (49 percent), and 1,071 NAVs or third-party registrants (24 percent). Following equations 10 and 11, percent votes owed to the Democratic candidate is $PD = 1{,}139 / (1{,}139 + 2{,}156) = 35$ percent, and the percent votes owed to the Republican candidate is $PR = 2{,}156 / (1{,}139 + 2{,}156) = 65$ percent (the actual results show that 34 percent voted for Obama, 1,240, and 62 percent voted for McCain, 2,264). In eight out of ten precincts, the percent of the votes-owed forecast is accurate within 2 percent. The precincts that deviate from votes-owed percentages are where the swing voters live—that is, precincts where a Democrat or Republican consistently gets fewer or more votes than owed.

Expanding the Test

I have never encountered an election, in my thirty years of experience, for which polling data outperformed the accuracy of a votes-owed forecast. But I wanted to test the reliability of the votes-owed forecast outside my neck of the woods, so I examined election outcomes for two counties in Oregon between 2002 and 2006: Lane County and Jackson County.

Republicans enjoyed an eleven-point registration advantage in Jackson County, and Democrats held an eighteen-point registration advantage in Lane County. For each county I applied equations 8 and 9 to determine the votes owed to Democrats and Republicans. I also looked back at returns between 1986 and 2000 in Jackson County, where data were more easily accessed than in Lane County. The outcome was the same in both counties across all time frames studied: Votes owed were accurate predictors of election outcomes in four out of five precincts.

Outliers

In the one out of five precincts for which the votes-owed forecast failed, could it be that our implicit assumption—that NAVs and third-party registrants behave like their neighbors—was wrong? We conducted a massive three-month study to identify voters in precincts where candidates were not getting the votes they were owed: Where precincts gave more support to the Republican than the votes-owed forecast, all Democrats and nonaffiliated voters were called. Where precincts gave more support to the Democrat than the votes-owed forecast, all Republicans and nonaffiliated voters were called. In all, 23,356 voters were called, and 5,206 participated in the survey. It included only three questions—two "decoys" followed by an ID:

1. In general, do you think the state is headed in the right or wrong direction?
2. In general, do you think the county is headed in the right or wrong direction?
3. In general, do you vote Republican or Democrat?

The resounding finding was that NAVs and third-party voters tracked their partisan neighbors even in precincts where the votes-owed forecast failed. In those precincts, however, the percentage of partisans and nonaffiliated voters who confessed to splitting the ticket—that is, voting for candidates in both parties on the same ballot—was higher. Of all surveyed voters in the selected precincts—whether their precinct leaned left or right and whether they were nonaffiliated, Republican, or Democrat—16 percent to 18 percent offered that they split their ticket. Independents mirrored the ticket-splitting behavior of partisan registrants in precincts where Republicans moved left and others where Democrats moved right. In other words, the swing vote among nonaffiliated registrants mirrored the swing of their partisan neighbors. The important takeaway is not that some NAVs tend not to track their partisan neighbors—we could find no evidence of that. Rather, *knowing where the votes-owed forecast fails will help you identify precincts where voters are willing to cross the aisle* and therefore sharpen your focus in campaign activities.

Whenever I find neighborhoods with a history of election outcomes more favorable to my client than the votes-owed forecasts, I use them to profile other voters outside that area. What do their homes look like? Do they have porches? What are people watching on television when a canvasser knocks on the door? Do they have children? Pets? Do they keep up their homes and property? Are they rural? Urban? These observations will be invaluable when it comes time for your GOTV effort.

Look to the Undervote First

The three factors that might cause a discrepancy between the votes-owed forecast and an election outcome are undervoting, variations in turnout, and voters willing to cross the aisle—in that order. Voters splitting the ticket is the rarest and least usable factor; undervoting is the most common and most informative to an effective campaign strategy. Wherever the votes-owed forecast fails, determine whether it favored you or the opposition, and then determine how much undervoting harmed each party in each precinct. Close races are almost always won by activating undervoters in precincts with a favorable percent-votes-owed value, while flying under the radar to undervoters in precincts with an unfavorable percent-votes-owed value.

In one recent example, a Democratic state representative was running against a Republican businessman for a state senate seat. In one precinct with 3,400 registered voters, the Democratic and Republican candidates were owed 80 percent and 20 percent of the votes, respectively. However, after the ballots were cast, the Democrat received only 79 percent of the ballots cast and the Republican only 17 percent. The remaining 4 percent all came down to undervote. If everyone who turned in their ballots had voted in every single race, the Democrat would most likely have won an additional 1 percent of the vote, and the Republican would have won an additional 3 percent. Determining the votes owed to candidates allows you to determine to whom the undervote should be ascribed. In this example, 34 of the undervotes are attributed to the Democrat and 102 to the Republican.

In another example, I was once hired to analyze a state house seat representing a district with a ten-point Democratic registration advantage, but always elected a Republican—not just a known Republican or an incumbent, but any Republican. Once I charted the previous cycles and attributed the undervote, it was clear that the Democrats were undervoting their candidate. This is an easy fix: The campaign worked the base with canvassers and targeted mail and brought the seat over to the Democratic column. If the undervote is coming primarily from your party, your efforts must focus on waking up and energizing your voters so they care enough to fill in the bubble on their voter card. Voters are not usually activated with vacuous mailers that simply describe the merits of a candidate. A consistent and large undervote for your party's candidates may dictate a more aggressive campaign of comparison pieces, which draw a bright line between two candidates, delivered with a knock at the door.

When some precincts consistently give more votes than are owed to your candidate's party while others consistently give more votes to the opposing party, you know where to concentrate money, voter identification, and campaign efforts as well as which areas to avoid.

Polarized Populations, Skewed Registration, and Nonaffiliated Voters

NAVs continue to mirror their partisan neighbors' voting patterns even as registration percentages shift. Voter registration shifts often occur as economies change, churches arrive, or development reshapes an area. Indeed, voters relocate to a neighborhood near their place of worship or move to find work, better schools, or less congestion. In one Oregon city, the Republican-registration advantage increased by 38 percent between 1986 and 2006. In another city thirty miles away, the Democratic registration advantage increased by 44 percent in the same period.

Subsequent precinct analysis of the two counties in the above study showed that NAVs in both continued to track party affiliation as registration shifted. It's good news if you know how to exploit it: As voters segregate themselves among like-minded neighbors, targeting becomes easier and more cost-effective. If NAVs mirror the voting behavior of their neighbors, the campaign manager is free to target them as she would their partisan neighbors.

Implications for a Campaign

Election vendors are people or organizations selling mail, television, radio, and other communications services to campaigns. They will typically bundle their services with a targeting strategy, which presents a conflict of interest: Vendors are never incentivized to surgically avoid activation of the sinners because their billings scale with the size of their target audience. Furthermore, because vendors tend to live and work in large metropolitan areas, they're generally unable or unwilling to adjust their messaging to suit the subtleties of your region's culture. A campaign that approaches a specific demographic within rural and urban areas with the same strategies—or treats NAVs as though they were some monolithic demographic—is a campaign that squanders its resources to shoot itself in the foot.

Polling firms will normally contact likely voters to test "messages" and various issues that may resonate with voters. Typically, they will aggregate the success of a test message across categories of voters—for example, a polling firm may report that 80 percent of Republicans, 30 percent of Democrats, and 40 percent of NAVs responded positively to a hypothetical message about public safety. The categorical grouping of NAVs, however, will make it difficult or impossible to target them effectively because you cannot assume that NAV voting behavior in one area is reflective of NAV voting behavior in another.

Interpreting the Results of Your Analysis

Let's return to the example analysis presented in figures 2.1 and 2.2, the hypothetical partisan race for dogcatcher. We will discuss the calculated values within each precinct and see how they might inform a campaign manager's targeting strategy.

Precinct 1. The first item of interest is the percent votes owed, located in rows 13 and 26 of figures 2.1 and 2.2. This is a highly favorable area for our Democratic dogcatcher, holding a steady 83 percent of votes owed. The campaign manager decides she needs a good turnout from Precinct 1, but the voters are notoriously inactive: The Democrat received only 855 votes in 2016, despite being owed 955 votes (the results in the 2012 race weren't much better, 837–939). What's more, voter turnout was low in both elections, just below 58 percent. Keeping in mind that people tend to vote like their neighbors, the campaign manager reasons that the activatable voters are also very likely to prefer the Democrat. She settles on a strategy in Precinct 1 of high GOTV effort—lawn signs, canvassing, coordinated block captains, and a couple of informative mailers—without any voter ID effort.

Precinct 2. The campaign manager notices a big ΔMD in this precinct—1,302 votes (the Democratic candidate won 72 percent of the vote in 2016, = D19

/ [D19 + D18], up from 31 percent in 2012, = D6 / [D5 + D6]). Should the dramatic shift be attributed solely to changes in voting activity—that is, changes in the undervote or turnout—or could it be that some voters have changed their party preference? The campaign manager checks cell D27, the swing vote. In this case, 650 voters, about 20 percent, probably voted for the Republican candidate in 2012 and then the Democratic candidate in 2016. Since Precinct 2 is home to voters willing to cross the aisle, the campaign manager decides it might be a good target for persuasive campaign pieces, so she contracts a polling firm to test messaging strategies within the neighborhood.

It bears repeating here that evidence of persuadable voters is uncommon[8]—especially in a general election. It's far more likely that any changes you find in the victory margin, ΔM, will be caused by changes in the undervote. Furthermore, even if you find a precinct populated by swing voters, it's unlikely that any messaging directed by your campaign will succeed in changing minds. I last encountered a substantial swing in a state senate race—the Democratic incumbent won in 2006 by 27 points against a weak Republican and then barely squeaked by in 2010 against a strong Republican, despite a negligible change in voting activity (a very small ΔG). However, 2010 was a good year for Republicans everywhere. The national hostility for Democrats was too much to take on with mailers and lawn signs. Yes, some voters were willing to cross the aisle, but postelection analysis revealed the outcome to be more about depressed Democratic turnout and Democratic undervoting. It's unlikely a persuasive campaign strategy would have been a cost-effective road to victory. Indeed, for the 2010 close senate race, the Democrat's narrow win came entirely from last-minute efforts to activate lazy voters in areas of overwhelming saints through canvassing.

Finally, before you embark on a costly campaign of persuasion, you should take a deeper dive into past elections. Compare the swing vote over at least three or four elections, if you can get the data. If the swing turned out to be an anomaly, perhaps it had more to do with one of the candidates. Was one of them unusually controversial? Was there a scandal? These are the kinds of considerations that give a local campaign manager a big advantage.

Precinct 3. Here we find a heterogeneous mix of voters, with votes owed to the Democrat at around 53 percent. The campaign manager chooses to expend resources on voter ID in Precinct 3. An effective ID effort is costly—every last vote can feel like a struggle, and in districts with tens of thousands of voters, you may wonder if ferreting out saints one by one is worth the hassle. Fortunately, heterogeneous neighborhoods are relatively rare; you'll mostly encounter partisan strongholds, empowering you to activate entire precincts in broad strokes. That's why the campaign manager chose not to squander resources in a voter ID effort for Precinct 1. If you're running a tight race, however, your voter ID efforts in mixed neighborhoods like Precinct 3 could make the difference between a win and a loss. In Precinct 2 of the state senate example discussed earlier, postelection analysis showed that the Democrat nearly lost in 2010, where the Democratic-registration advantage was only three points, because of a 1 percent swing to his opponent plus a 1 percent undervote all attributable to the Democrat through the votes-owed analysis. When the same two candidates faced each other again in 2014, the votes cast by Democrats and Republicans did not change, but what did change was expanding the Democratic base by identifying NAVs in precincts with more even party registration. Indeed, the eight-point win the Democrat enjoyed in 2014 came from additional identified NAVs voting coupled with an increased undervote for the Republican of 500 votes.

Precinct 4. Precinct 4 is a Republican neighborhood—votes owed to the Democrat are around 23 percent. But the change in margin ΔM is pretty big, with the Democrat gaining on the Republican by 365 votes in 2016—about a nine-point improvement. Perhaps Precinct 4 voters are crossing the aisle and the campaign manager should court them with persuasive messaging? Certainly not. The swing vote of –229 is very low (large and negative), indicating that changes in voter activity far exceed the win margin ($|\Delta M| > |\Delta G|$). In this case, the difference came down to a greater undervote among sinners in 2016: The Republican got 410 fewer votes than he was owed (and the Democrat, in fact, got a few *more* votes than owed). The best our campaign manager can do in Precinct 4 is remain totally invisible—ideally, these 410 voters won't even know a dogcatcher race is happening at all, and they'll undervote again. She can't persuade them, and if she tries, she will very likely activate them.

Precinct 5. Another Republican stronghold: The Democrat is owed only 16 percent of the vote. It would be unwise of the campaign manager to waste resources on Precinct 5, but it probably wouldn't backfire so much as it would in Precinct 4—activatable voters fell just shy of 28 percent in 2016, and ΔG is pretty small. It's a neighborhood of active sinners, and nothing is likely to change their behavior.

Precinct 6. In our final precinct, Democrats are owed about three-quarters of the vote. It's definitely friendly turf, and our campaign manager wants to make sure to maximize turnout and minimize undervote. But Precinct 6 has especially active voters, with better than 72 percent voting in the 2016 dogcatcher race (= [H19 + H18] / H16). The campaign manager decides to pursue a GOTV strategy, but not as aggressively as she does in Precinct 1—perhaps a single mailer or canvass, just to lock in the base.

Be Creative with the Data You Have

The votes-owed calculation is your first weapon to parse precincts by voting patterns. But as the idiom goes, you should always cut your cloth according to your cloth. If you can't find the data you need to calculate votes owed—or if by some chance better data are available—you may want to find another way of targeting precincts. If you're lucky enough to find data on candidates comparable to your client and the opposition, the following example will illustrate a remarkably easy alternative.

In 2002 a local physician in my region, a Democrat, ran for county commissioner. On the same ballot, a moderate Republican from Medford—the largest city in the county—was running in a judicial race. Although the judicial race was nonpartisan, he was running against a Democrat, and voters knew which was which. Two years later, I was working for a Democratic state senate candidate, also a physician, who was running against another moderate Republican from Medford. Although they were running in three separate races, the four candidates made two remarkably similar pairs, running in mostly overlapping districts in two consecutive races.

I wanted to use the results of the 2002 races to locate precincts where voters might be willing to split the ticket, so I conducted an analysis on a hypothetical race in which the Democratic candidate for county commissioner runs against the Republican judicial candidate. The senate district was a smaller subset of the entire county, so I limited my analysis to the thirty overlapping precincts. Of course, the candidates running in my hypothetical race were vying for different offices, which meant some voters could choose to support both of them. The resulting *overvote*—that is, the number of votes *exceeding* the number of ballots—totaled 2,307. But 2,253 of these overvotes were concentrated in just eight precincts; the remaining twenty-two precincts had a combined overvote of only 54 votes. In other words, the majority of the swing lived in just eight precincts. Of those eight, however, four were precincts of solid saints—that is, voters who never leave their Democratic candidate. The other four precincts were the same ones that popped off the charts in the precinct analysis as left-leaning. All this meant our entire campaign needed to focus only on four precincts, which is exactly what we did: The candidate and volunteers repeatedly canvassed targeted neighborhoods with targeted literature. We flipped a twenty-eight-year Republican hold on the senate seat while being outspent nearly two to one and with a Republican-registration advantage of six points.

Nonpartisan Races

If your race is in the primary, or if you are managing an issue-based campaign or a campaign for a nonpartisan seat, you will need to translate the partisan variables into a nonpartisan language. Ideally, you will be able to apply historically similar elections or ballot measures.

If you are testing the waters for an issue campaign, again the idea is to look for similarities, especially if your campaign is about raising money. Issue-based campaigns dealing with revenue generally come in two varieties: brick-and-mortar or capital improvements (CI) and operation and maintenance (O&M). Within these two categories are police, fire, schools, cities, counties, libraries, parks, water systems, special districts, and so on. Issue campaigns that have to do with restricting the power of government, such as term limits, the right to die, abortion, and mandatory sentencing, are covered in Chapter 11, "The Issue-Based Campaign." As with candidates, keep in mind that it is best to use identical election cycles, such as a nonpresidential primary, or midterm general, or special election, and so forth, for analyzing issue-based campaigns.

To calculate the percent votes owed for a nonpartisan primary, you must use party turnout, not registration, because there can be dramatic variations of party performance in a primary, depending on what is on each side of the ballot. In this case, rather than dividing party registrants by the combined Democratic and Republican registration totals, you will divide party turnout by the Democratic turnout plus the Republican turnout. For example, if the Democratic turnout is 100 votes and the Republican turnout is 75, to calculate votes owed you would first add 100 and 75, to get 175 votes cast. In this example, the Democrats would be owed 100 out of 175, or 57 percent of the votes cast, and Republicans would be owed 75 out of 175, or 43 percent of the votes cast.

In general, when it comes to increasing taxes, Democrats are more inclined to vote yes than Republicans, but this can break down on many fronts. For example, Republican women of a certain age tend to support library efforts, and Republicans and Democrats alike will often vote for fire districts. Your best bet for conducting a precinct analysis for an issue-based campaign is to follow the above course: There will be patterns of precincts or zones where saints and sinners are apparent. Where numbers are questionable for passage, the campaign must focus on identifying voters in medium- to marginal-support precincts.

Nonpartisan races often come down to organization—especially if one or both of the candidates is relatively unknown. Typically, the campaign with the most lawn signs and the one that shows the most volunteer activity will win. If the candidates are known for right- or left-leaning attributes, then follow the precinct analysis as laid out for partisan races outlined above.

Predicting Voter Turnout

The percent votes owed, PR or PD, will quickly tell you the character of a precinct, but it can't tell you how to allocate your resources efficiently. For example, you may find a neighborhood with a very favorable percent votes owed for your candidate but too sparsely populated to tip the scales of the election one way or another. The quantity of votes owed, OR and OD, actually expresses how much is on the table. But your O can only be as reliable as your B, total voter turnout, and you can't necessarily count on previous elections to predict the turnout in your current race.

Rather than using the most recent election, or an average of a few, use the B reported by your county clerk for a similar past election in the same season. For example, is your election in a presidential or nonpresidential primary or general election? Is it a special or an off-year election?

Next, compare what was on the earlier ballot with what will be on yours. If the gubernatorial race was more hotly contested, your turnout will be higher. If the ballot measures were less controversial, your turnout may be lower. If you are uncomfortable with predicting increases or decreases in voter participation based on ballot issues, you will be close if you simply multiply the percentage of voter turnout of the last identical election by the current number of registered voters. Even if turnout changes substantially in one direction or the other, the parties typically track similarly in turnout, within a couple of points within any election. In other words, in a given precinct, all things being equal, you will not see a substantial increase in turnout for one party without seeing a similar spike in the other party. Once you've predicted voter turnout, a sometimes helpful number is *votes needed to win, VNW*, which is simply half the turnout plus one.

The exception to this rule is a primary. Some primaries do not allow NAVs to participate, and some primaries have candidates on one side of the aisle running unopposed while candidates on the other side have heated races. In the 2008 presidential primary in Oregon, where McCain had a lock on the Republican nomination but Obama and Clinton were still slugging it out,

Democrats outperformed Republicans by ten points in the primary in my county. Clearly, turnout differences will be particularly pronounced when a presidential primary is on the ballot for one party while the presumptive nominee for the other party is the incumbent. Redouble your efforts during the primary if you expect your party to turn out in especially high numbers, even if your candidate is running unopposed in that primary. It is a golden opportunity to lock in your base with a smaller risk of activating the opposition.

Base Party Vote and Maximum Swing

Throughout this chapter, I have underscored the imprudence of campaigns built on persuasion: Swing voters scarcely ever determine the outcome of a down-ballot race, and I have never encountered a campaign that wisely allocated resources to changing minds. That's why the formulation you applied for swing in your precinct analysis (equation 13) describes a *minimum-possible swing:* A campaign manager should assume that voters are crossing the aisle only when changes in the margin, $|\Delta M|$, are too large to explain from changes in the undervote and changes in voter turnout, $|\Delta G|$.

If your analysis of recent elections tells you that victory is impossible even with favorable turnout (that is, high turnout in saint precincts and low turnout in sinner precincts) and favorable undervoting (that is, low undervote in saint precincts and high undervote in sinner precincts), I would ordinarily not suggest that you hang your hopes on a high swing. But suppose you are managing a campaign for a moderate Republican in a district generally safe for Democrats and then your opponent is suddenly caught up in some scandal. You might reasonably wonder in this case if some of the staunch sinners in your district could entertain a vote for your candidate. In this case, you may wish to determine the *maximum-possible swing*, noted SM, to intelligently expand your target precincts.

You should be aware before you begin that the maximum-swing calculation is more involved than our previous analysis. You'll find this method cumbersome and lengthy unless your proficiency with Excel or another spreadsheet technology is fluent. Additionally, the data requirements are a lot more onerous. But if you need to know if extraordinary circumstances have made it possible to flip a previously unwinnable district, the following steps will explain how to do it.

1. First, you must calculate the *base party vote* (notated *BPV*) for each party, or the number of saints and sinners who will *always* remain faithful to their party no matter how terrible their candidate is. You'll need

to dig up historical party registration data and election data, disaggregated for each of the precincts in your district, for as many years back as you can locate. Record in your spreadsheet the number of votes won by each of the Republican and Democratic candidates running in partisan races within each precinct and within each of the races for which you were able to find data. Every partisan race will do—it doesn't matter if it was for the same seat that your candidate was running for, but each election you analyze should span all of your precincts.

In Oregon, and now perhaps Washington and Colorado, all vote by mail has allowed county clerks to increase the size of a precinct to where they are almost zones. In other areas, where populations increase, clerks break up precincts, and sometimes in areas of waning populations precincts are combined. To overcome fluctuations in precincts, you may find it helpful to literally print out old and new precinct maps and overlay them on each other to figure out what is where to capture voting shifts over time. The other option is to simply break things into zones of like-voting areas—small cities, rural, urban, regions, and so on. That way, if precincts change within a zone, it shouldn't impact your efforts.

2. Within each precinct, calculate the *fraction of votes received* (notated *FR* and *FD* for the Republican candidates and Democratic candidates, respectively) for each precinct and each year.

[Equation 14] $$F_R = \frac{V_R}{V_R + V_D} = 1 - F_D$$

[Equation 15] $$F_D = \frac{V_D}{V_R + V_D} = 1 - F_R$$

We first defined *VR* and *VD* as the vote totals in historical elections for your current seat of interest. In equations 14 and 15, however, you must use the vote totals for each individual race you analyze. For example, *FR* will be different for the gubernatorial race and the state senate race within each precinct in 2012 because the Republican candidates will not have won exactly the same number of votes. *FD* will be different for the gubernatorial race in 2012 and 2016 because the Democratic candidate will not have won exactly the same number of votes, and so on.

3. As you can imagine, processing all this data will populate quite a busy spreadsheet. Suppose you are examining three general elections, each ballot contained an average of five partisan races in your district, and

you have fifty precincts in your district. Then you will have calculated *FR* and *FD* 750 separate times *each*, because $3 \times 5 \times 50 = 750$.

Fortunately, you need to know only the *minimum* value for each fraction of votes across all years and elections within each precinct. So looking across three general elections with five races per year, you'll find the smallest value of *FR* per precinct among the fifteen values you've calculated and the smallest value for *FD* per precinct among the fifteen values you've calculated (use Excel's "=MIN()" function to cut down on redundant work). In other words, you have found the very worst that each party has ever performed over your entire history of data within each precinct. You'll be left with an *FR,MIN* and *FD,MIN* for each precinct—that's one hundred calculated variables if you have fifty precincts in your district.

Before you clear out your unused data, however, you must record which *years* each *FR,MIN* and *FD,MIN* were drawn from. For example, if you found that the minimum Republican fraction of votes in Precinct 12 occurred in 2014, record that *FR,MIN* was calculated in 2014 in Precinct 12. You do not need to record the particular race for which each minimum vote fraction was determined, only the year it was determined.

4. You should now have a *FR,MIN*, *FD,MIN*, year of *FR,MIN*, and year of *FD,MIN* for each of the precincts in your district. Next, enter the total Republican and Democratic Party registrations within each precinct for each of the years you have. For example, suppose you found the minimum Republican fraction of votes in Precinct 7 occurred in the 2012 race, and the minimum Democratic fraction of votes in Precinct 7 occurred in the 2014 race. Then you will need to record the number of registered Republicans in 2012, the number of registered Democrats in 2012, the number of registered Republicans in 2014, and the number of registered Democrats in 2014—and do the same for each and every precinct, for whichever dates their *FR,MIN* and *FD,MIN* were recorded.

5. You should now have six variables ready per precinct—*FR,MIN*, *FD,MIN*, the Republican registration in each precinct during its year that each minimum occurred (notated as *ROLD*), and the Democratic registration in each precinct during its year that each minimum occurred (notated as *DOLD*). The last bit of data you'll need is the *current* registration totals in each precinct, notated *RNEW* and *DNEW* for the Republican and Democratic registration totals, respectively. Then use equations 16–19 to calculate the Republican registration fraction for each year recorded (notated as *RFOLD*), the Democratic registra-

tion fraction for each year recorded (notated as *DFOLD*), the current Republican registration fraction (notated *RFNEW*), and the current Democratic registration fraction (notated *DFNEW*):

[Equation 16] $RF_{OLD} = \dfrac{R_{OLD}}{D_{OLD} + R_{OLD}} = 1 - DF_{OLD}$

[Equation 17] $DF_{OLD} = \dfrac{D_{OLD}}{D_{OLD} + R_{OLD}} = 1 - RF_{OLD}$

[Equation 18] $RF_{NEW} = \dfrac{R_{NEW}}{D_{NEW} + R_{NEW}} = 1 - DF_{NEW}$

[Equation 19] $DF_{NEW} = \dfrac{D_{NEW}}{D_{NEW} + R_{NEW}} = 1 - RF_{NEW}$

Don't forget that *ROLD* and *DOLD* will not necessarily be the registration totals for the same years in each precinct—they will each be the registration totals in the precinct for the year in which the *FMIN* values were found—but they will *always* be for the same year within each equation.

6. Now we're ready to calculate the base party vote for each precinct, notated as *BPVR* and *BPVD* for the Republican base party vote and the Democratic base party vote, respectively:

[Equation 20] $BPV_R = F_{R,MIN} \times \dfrac{RF_{NEW}}{RF_{OLD}}$

[Equation 21] $BPV_D = F_{D,MIN} \times \dfrac{FD_{NEW}}{FD_{OLD}}$

Note that the base party vote is *not* expressed here in units of votes, but a fraction between zero and one. Equations 20 and 21 estimate the number of voters totally loyal to each party by taking the worst each party has performed in any partisan race as far back as you could find data and then adjusting it for changes in party registration in each precinct.

7. Finally, we will calculate the maximum swing, *SM*, using equation 22 (recall that *A* is the number of registered voters, precinct by precinct):

[Equation 22] $S_M = A \times (1 - BPV_R - BPV_D)$

If you made it this far, you now have the ceiling of voters in each precinct that don't necessarily always vote for one party in each precinct. If you cannot get 51 percent of the vote from the sum of all swing voters (SM) added up across all precincts, plus the sum of all your base party voters ($A \times BPVR$ or $A \times BPVD$) added across all precincts, your race is truly not winnable—it doesn't matter how strong your candidate is or how scandalous the opposition. As noted before, there may be other reasons for a candidate to run, like getting his or her name to prepare for a run at a more winnable seat down the road. Still, given the work and intrusion a campaign creates on family, friends, and the candidate, your decision might be to simply wait and run for another office when your chances are better.

Don't Confuse Motion with Progress

Not to belabor the point, but I must reemphasize the importance of working smart. Candidates across the nation have called me since the first edition of this book hit the shelves. Almost invariably, as I'm explaining the importance of a good precinct analysis, they interrupt to tell me some version of "I'm just going to go out and start canvassing." I understand the impulse to skip over the spreadsheets and charts. It's particularly common for first-time candidates to lose themselves in a romantic vision of Jeffersonian democracy, talking to their constituents about their passion for the issues. It is your job, as the campaign manager, to temper your client's excitement until you're ready to channel it effectively. Virtually every tight race is won on the undervote, and there is no surer way to activate a sinner than to send a candidate they don't like to their doorstep. Canvassing—and most campaign activities, for that matter—hardly ever persuades anyone: It *activates* voters, to the greatest possible effect. Acting before your precinct analysis is ready would be as reckless as a doctor administering medicine without checking the label or an army general ordering an air strike without knowing whose troops are where. A precinct analysis is the first step to a winning effort.

The Campaign Team and Volunteer Organization

By Catherine Shaw and Daniel Golden

> Behind all political success is attention to detail.
> —LARRY O'BRIEN, ADVISER TO JOHN F. KENNEDY

IN THIS CHAPTER:

- The Campaign Committee
- The Campaign Manager
- The Campaign Chair or Co-Chairs
- Volunteer Organization
- Canvassing
- Phone Banks
- Clerical Team
- Time Allotments for Volunteer Tasks

The Campaign Committee

THE CAMPAIGN COMMITTEE IS THE PRIMARY SOURCE OF EXPERTISE FOR the campaign. This small, select group will maneuver and steer a campaign while drawing on the resources of the community. The committee should consist of individuals who have different personal strengths and areas of ability.

The candidate, the manager, and each of the members must feel safe in speaking candidly without fear of recrimination. Treat them like insiders and keep them informed of any campaign development. You would never want a committee member to first learn about a problem with the campaign in the newspaper or through the rumor mill. Meet with, call, or email your committee members regularly. Be clear about their tasks, expectations, and time commitments; avoid job creep as manager; support their individual efforts in the campaign; and encourage them and listen carefully to determine when they might need additional help.

Once the campaign starts, meet with the committee each week for one hour and always be organized. Typically, after giving my report, I go around the table for individual updates. Committee members need to communicate with each other, and this is when that happens.

Campaign Duties

The following are the duties that must be covered by someone on your central committee:

1. *List management.* Names associated with volunteering, lawn sign locations, contributions, identified supporters, or anyone who has favorable contact with the campaign go to this person. Keeping lists organized, duplicates removed, addresses and phone numbers verified, and categories of individual involvement (lawn sign host, canvasser, coffee host, and so on) is one of the most important jobs in a campaign. Redundant list management, apart from being inefficient, will inevitably lead to repetitive contact of supporters. A well-organized list or data committee member can quickly email any sublist from within the master.

2. *House parties.* This individual is responsible for finding hosts or communicating with those willing to host an event for the candidate (or the speaker in an issue-based campaign). The campaign should have a basket that travels with the house-party coordinator that includes campaign literature, sign-up sheets (see figure 3.1), buttons, and remittance envelopes. The contents of the basket are laid out on an entry table of the home, and, once empty, the basket serves as a collection plate for contributions from the attendees. The house-party coordinator arranges for an individual to make "the ask" for money—typically a prominent community member or local officeholder—and also finds someone to do introductions before the candidate speaks and thank-yous after the ask.

3. *Social media.* This person is responsible for creating, maintaining, and promoting all social media accounts, including Instagram, Twitter, and Facebook (the video team will send videos, as noted below).

4. *Mapping.* This individual provides the maps for canvass packets, lawn sign installation and removal, and the get-out-the-vote (GOTV) webpage that neighborhood captains access (this will be covered in the GOTV chapter).

5. *Letters to the editor (LTEs).* This individual is responsible for finding people to put their names on letters the campaign drafts or to encourage supporters to draft their own: two paragraphs, one thought, five sentences. A good LTE is succinct and easy to understand.

6. *Field operative (field op).* This person is responsible for finding volunteers and turning them out to canvass, put up and take down lawn signs, and populate phone banks. If you have to pay one person other than the campaign manager (CM), this is the one; a good field op is key.

7. *Clerical.* This person gets the direct-mail and money appeals out but might also work on things like lawn sign assembly. Clerical also writes thank-you notes for an issue-based campaign. Typically, this individual has a group of friends or coworkers who can be repeatedly called upon for help or may draw from a list generated from those who checked off "clerical" on a remit. "Clerical" staffs clerical work sessions, not the field op.

8. *Scheduler.* This person is responsible for scheduling the candidate. All requests for attendance at house parties, forums, fundraisers, and such must go through the scheduler.

The following are jobs of individuals who do not necessarily need to be at the weekly committee table but are needed nonetheless:

1. *GOTV webpage.* This will be covered extensively in the chapter on GOTV.

2. *Graphic designer.* Use a pro and one who doesn't complain about stuff you needed yesterday but are only getting to him or her today.

3. *Webpage designer and ongoing maintenance.* This is different from the GOTV webpage mentioned above. On this site you will put all of your published LTEs and explain what's what in a few words—no white papers; post photos and upcoming events.

4. *Video team.* They film and create videos for the campaign Facebook page. These videos should be around a minute long but no longer than 1:20. Your social media coordinator (noted above) is responsible for promoting the videos.

5. *Treasurer.* All money goes to this person (it is his or her address on the remittance envelope). Get one who is attentive to detail. Only

the treasurer, candidate, and campaign manager have access to the bank account. The treasurer, along with the campaign manager and the candidate, is responsible for obtaining and completing the registration forms required for participation in an election. The necessary forms can be obtained from the city recorder's office for city races, from the county elections office for county races, and from the election division under the secretary of state for elections to state offices.

6. *Editor.* Strong written communication is fundamentally important to the success of your campaign materials, and it is surprisingly rare. If your candidate is not a good writer, find someone on your team who is.

7. *Driver.* If you have a candidate who is overcommitted at work or in volunteer activities, is an incumbent, or always runs late, consider getting him or her a driver from the volunteer pool. It is the driver's responsibility to keep the candidate punctual.

Contributions and Expenditures

Your treasurer should be a stickler for detail. Expect the opposition to carefully scrutinize your contributions and expenditures (C&Es) filings. If a mistake is found, it is bound to make the local papers. That sort of damage is completely preventable.

After the C&E forms have been filed, local newspapers may do a story on who spent how much on what. If you are running a modest campaign and your opposition is funded by outside money, make sure that this information makes it to the media. Many states keep track of campaign contributions and expenditures online for review. Running a visibly hardworking campaign with modest funds gives people the sense that your candidate is fiscally responsible.

It's difficult to oppose an extremely well-funded opposition, but it can also work in your favor. In a small community election that involves no TV ads, there is just so much ad space to buy in the newspaper and just so much direct mail to be sent before it becomes clear that the election is being bought. In one campaign I ran, we were outspent five to one by the opposition. When the newspapers ran the usual C&E article, many in the community were stunned by the amount of money coming in from outside interests. Since we had a good idea of how much the opposition was spending, we were ready when the press called for our reaction. We had supporters write and send letters to the editor for those who missed the newspaper articles when they first appeared.

The Campaign Manager

The campaign manager is the single most important position in a campaign. The most effective campaign teams are those with volunteer team members supervised by a strong, capable, and likable manager. Where the volunteer positions entail a modest commitment of time, the CM will sacrifice sleep, social activities, health, and sanity during the most hectic stretches of a race. The CM must be well compensated.

Personality of the campaign manager is at the core of his or her success. This individual must be even-tempered, easy and fun to work with, organized, thoughtful, observant, humble, and impervious to drama.

The duties of the CM vary greatly, depending on the number of individuals working in the inner circle. The CM will typically attend coffees, debates, and events with the candidate and might set up sign-in sheets while lending emotional support. The CM must have good communication skills, and he or she must be prepared to give candid feedback to the candidate. You will find this is easier said than done, when the candidate is an incumbent of an esteemed office. The candidate must trust the CM and be ready to utilize his or her feedback without being defensive.

If you are running a countywide partisan election campaign, having a manager is critical. You need someone to oversee it all and to be a source of support for the candidate. Although I believe it is a mistake to run for office without a campaign manager, if your race is for office in a small city, you can probably get away with it. Whether you're serving as your own campaign manager, have hired one, or your best friend volunteered to do the job, you still need capable people to head up various campaign tasks, as noted above.

A potential campaign manager can be right in front of you: a friend, a community organizer that you've known forever, or a college student. Your CM should be smart, organized, hardworking, articulate, and personable; able to speak to large groups of people and ask for things in simple, understandable ways; know computers; and have presentable clothes.

Teachers make great campaign managers for those with only a fall election, as it forces the campaign to get everything ready during the summer so that your fall campaign will go much easier. The drawback of using a teacher is that he or she may be overwhelmed with school responsibilities during the final days of the general race.

Other potential sources for campaign managers are development directors for local charities, private schools, or nonprofit organizations. These people might consider short-term work for a candidate, and they will have a proven track record. Other leads: people who have worked on other political campaigns, for a United Way campaign or for a heart-and-lung fund drive, and those who have organized local parades, 4-H fair shows, concerts, or county fairs. Also check with colleges nearby for political science graduates looking for field experience. Each summer the Oregon Bus Project (OBP) runs a ten-week course (Policorps) to train future campaign managers and field operatives. Although Policorps is held in Portland, Oregon, the students are from all over the nation. For information on the graduates and the OBP, go to busproject.org.

When running for state legislative office, be prepared to pay the campaign manager handsomely. A good manager speaks truth to power, brings many skills to the table, and can mean big money to your campaign. Individuals, organizations, political action committees, and lobbyists want to contribute to a winning campaign, and your manager is a big indicator. A strong, experienced, well-organized manager will bring an air of confidence to a candidate and campaign team. A candidate should listen to the campaign manager and follow his or her advice.

The Campaign Chair or Co-Chairs

When working on an issue-based campaign, you'll want to select a campaign chair or co-chairs to play a role analogous to a candidate. The chair or co-chairs are the faces of the campaign, and their standing in the community will be directly linked to the campaign's success. Campaign chairs should be uncontroversial leaders with strong social networks, and they may serve either as figureheads or in an actual coordinating capacity. They give interviews to the media, are part of the campaign committee, and work the endorsement circles of the community—the Rotary Club, the Chamber of Commerce, business leaders, and more. The chair(s) should perceptually have nothing to gain personally by passage of the issue. For example, a school superintendent would be an inappropriate campaign chair if you are fighting to pass a school levy.

The campaign's success will rely on the chairs' networks to raise money and activate volunteers and should balance each other, in gender and in interests.

If you cannot find a suitable person to serve as a chair, be sure that a few of your teammates are ready to respond to the press and willing to debate the opposition.

Volunteer Organization

Every campaign consists of basic campaign activities for which you will need to find volunteers, such as:

- Canvassing
- Phone banks
- House parties
- Clerical tasks
- Preparing, installing, and maintaining lawn signs

Finding Volunteers and Creating a Sign-Up Sheet

Those involved in grassroots campaigning must find people willing to help. Finding volunteers can initially seem daunting, but remember, the only people you can be certain will not help you are those you do not ask. First, go to friends and family, and then regularly hold coffees for additional support. Looking for volunteers among those most loyal to causes you advocate is the best way to find and recruit volunteers.

Create a form for sign-ups at coffees, debates, and other gatherings once the campaign is under way to secure volunteer and community support by name (see figure 3.1).

VOLUNTEER SIGN-UP SHEET

I would like to volunteer for the following (please check all that apply):

Name (please print)	Home Phone	Canvass Neighborhoods	Phone Banks	Clerical	Lawn Sign Location Address	Donation	Letter-to-the-Editor	Endor. ad?	Email

FIGURE 3.1 Example of a Volunteer Sign-Up Sheet

Basic Rules for the Volunteer Workforce

Directing volunteers is almost the same for each campaign task. Although the tasks vary considerably, only a small modification is necessary to organize your volunteer force for each specialized campaign activity.

Regardless of the activity, there are seven important things to remember about using volunteers:

1. Don't waste the volunteers' time. Have everything laid out and ready to go the moment they walk in the door. Begin and end on time.
2. Eliminate no-shows: Call (or email) them ahead of time, and let them know what they need to bring, such as clipboards, good walking shoes, a truck, or a hammer.
3. Be clear about their tasks, expectations, and time commitments. Give clear written instructions and deadlines. This is especially important for those on phone banks.
4. Pick the right people for the job. Don't ask out-of-shape volunteers to canvass steep hills; don't assign counterculture volunteers to canvass in conservative neighborhoods; people hard of hearing make great lawn sign installers but should not be on the phones or at the door.
5. Keep volunteers informed and support them. When you call, let them know how the campaign is going. Be sensitive to their schedules.
6. Treat your volunteers as you would highly paid employees. It is a serious mistake to undervalue volunteer time because they're working for free; the respect they get from the team *is* their payment. If anything, it's more important to treat them well.
7. Be organized. Disorganized campaigns lead to irritated and frustrated workers who may not return if things seem poorly run more than once. Some of the very best volunteers will not come back after even one bad encounter, and word will spread quickly in your community that you run a shoddy operation.

Build a Database

No matter where you find your volunteers, a campaign must have a system to organize, direct, and assign responsibilities. I assign this task to one committee person.

Using a spreadsheet program, list all of your contacts from your initial cold calls, family, friends, work, remittance envelopes, and sign-up sheets generated by yours or other campaigns. First, create a master list of activities from which you can break out specific duties that volunteers have indicated they will perform. Here are examples of column labels that could run along the top of your master list: last name, first name, spouse/partner name, house number, street, city, zip code, and phone numbers (cell, home, and work). Volunteer work and service categories (which can be filled in with yes or no) include canvass, clerical, lawn sign, lawn sign installation, LTEs, and endorsement ads. Finally, a column labeled "$" indicates whether a volunteer has also contributed funds, and a column labeled "notes" may contain brief comments.

Although you usually include a column for donations ($), remember, this sheet is for *volunteer* activities. The $ column simply tracks which of your volunteers have also contributed money. The treasurer will track amounts and dates contributions are received. This information is communicated with the data/list committee member who from time to time will print up lists and amounts contributed for the candidate's thank-you notes. Since states have specific filing requirements for campaign donors, it is important to keep track of donor information apart from your volunteer spreadsheet. Check with the elections office or secretary of state to determine the required information on each of your contributors. For example, in Oregon a campaign must list the person who signed the check as the contributor, the contributor's occupation, the address of the contributor, and the name and address of the contributor's workplace.

The "notes" section of your spreadsheet is where you note such information as "Won't canvass hills"; "Don't call early a.m."; "Don't call after 8:00 p.m."; "No phones"; and "Has three staple guns." Also use this section to make a note when someone has been rude ("Do not contact again"), so that other campaign volunteers needn't be subjected to verbal abuse. After hundreds of phone calls, it is impossible to remember such details if a record is not kept somewhere. As the saying goes: The palest ink is better than the most retentive memory.

Organize Volunteer Activities

Once your spreadsheet is populated, create different pages from your master according to activity: phones, canvassing, clerical, lawn sign installation, events, and so on. Always keep a coded master sheet.

No matter the activity, when contacting a volunteer, be sure to have a number of dates lined up for it so that each volunteer is called only once for scheduling. When calling for an ongoing activity such as canvassing, have four or five dates and times, so if one date doesn't work, another may. If a volunteer can do none of the times offered, it is important to determine why and to note this on the spreadsheet. If it is a temporary scheduling conflict, note when the conflict will be resolved. However, if it sounds as though the volunteer will *never* do the activity, offer another campaign job. If it is clear that he or she will never volunteer, that person's name should be removed from the volunteer list. For now, however, the name remains on your working list with a line through it so that you will remember that you called. If you do not do this, you will forget and call again. Whenever you determine that a volunteer wants to change his or her status, be sure to not end the phone call until there is an understanding as to why. If you're working directly from a list on a computer rather than a printout, you can distinguish those who have been called and who will never volunteer by highlighting the cell or changing the color of the font. Get that information back to the data/list member for a master-file update.

A couple of days before the activity, call back (or you may email, depending on time constraints) every volunteer who agreed to work and place a check (✓) in the "CB?" (called back?) column. If the volunteer has forgotten, the call serves as a reminder. If the person inadvertently made other plans, this is your opportunity to reschedule. Potential no-shows, discovered in a callback reminder, are incredibly easy to reschedule. If callbacks are conducted through email, ask for a reply.

Matching Volunteers to Skills

If potential workers indicate an unwillingness to do a particular activity, don't make the mistake of begging and pleading to get help in that task.

I once placed a woman on the phones who told me she didn't like to phone. I found it hard to believe that in this day and age, anyone would have trouble talking on the phone—plus I was desperate. What a mistake. She was painfully uncomfortable calling people she didn't know and projected a poor image of the campaign. I couldn't take her off once I saw my error because that would have called further attention to the problem, making her more uncomfortable. I left her on the phone for about a half hour and then told her that I had finished my work and asked if she would mind if we shared her phone. She gratefully gave it up. Similarly, if a volunteer reports that he doesn't like to knock on strangers' doors, believe him. It is better for the campaign to have people doing what they enjoy.

Some who say they do not like to work phones actually just don't like making cold calls—that is, they do not like to call people who may be opposed to the candidate or measure. Quite often, these same people may be willing to make calls to activate identified supporters, such as in a get-out-the-vote effort. Similarly, some who say they do not like to canvass actually dislike knocking on doors and talking to the residents. However, these same people may be willing to do a literature drop, a door hanger, lawn sign installation, or other tasks where knocking and talking are not involved. If a canvasser returns without notes for lawn signs, has no impressions of voter attitudes, and only partially covered the assigned area, perhaps canvassing is not the best job for that individual. This should be noted in the volunteer data system, and then move that person over to something like lawn sign placement and maintenance.

Supervise volunteers so that workers who have difficulty with one task are not called a second time to help in the same job. For instance, if a volunteer is struggling at a phone bank because age has made hearing more difficult, simply note it in the spreadsheet you use to keep track of volunteers. In this way, campaign workers will not mistakenly call the person again for that task. Similarly, if an individual is great on the phones, keep him or her away from other campaign activities to avoid campaign burnout. Use volunteers where they excel. For example, I've found older men who are hard of hearing make great drivers for lawn sign installation teams.

If it can be avoided, do not place volunteers in jobs where they will have a bad time or where they may reflect poorly on the campaign. Attention to these kinds of details helps volunteers be more successful and keeps them returning to help.

Canvassing

Canvassing remains the most effective and affordable tool in a campaigner's bag of tricks.

Canvassing is not as much about changing minds as improving voter turnout of support, reducing an undervote, and finding support among non-affiliated voters in areas of equally mixed registration. This is all done in preparation for the get-out-the-vote effort. You cannot win if your base voters (saints) stay home, and knowing who among NAVs are actually "lazy saints" increases your chances to activate them in the GOTV. It can also inform other campaign activities. For example, if canvassing reveals the base does not know about the candidate or issue, then mail, media, and digital targeting can be adjusted.

Although there are few, if any, campaign activities that have a greater return on investment than canvassing, it is important to keep in mind that canvassing is not for everyone. Also, some places are too risky for the traditional canvass. Be careful and know the areas you are going into. Never send someone to canvass alone or go alone yourself, and never enter a house, if for no other reason than that your partner will not be able to find you.

Canvassing Map Packets

Map packets for canvassing and for your GOTV effort are related. In order to prepare for your GOTV, voters must be identified, which is done while canvassing and phoning. As outlined in Chapter 2, your voting area will be broken into geographic zones of saints, sinners, and savables. When it comes to saints—that is, areas of 70–80 percent support or more—your canvassing efforts are about activation and prevention of an undervote within your base as well as the nonaffiliated voters who mirror their partisan neighbors in voting behavior. In areas of mixed voter registration and support (55–45 to 45–55), canvassing will be about both locking your party base vote and also *identifying* support among the nonaffiliated *lazy* voters. In areas of sinners— that is, where less than 30 percent will support your efforts—you will canvass only if your campaign has the bandwidth and then only to identify support of those *within* your party. Although this is covered in depth in the GOTV chapter, know that voter identification occurs in the four months leading up to the GOTV.

Creating Canvassing Maps

Creating canvassing maps, or cutting turf, has gotten a lot easier in some ways and more challenging in others. Both the Republicans and the Democrats have systems that allow anyone with practically any ability to map turfs, but they are of inferior quality. We use BatchGeo, which is free, but upgrade to BatchGeo Pro because it is four times faster, has more color options for coding your mapped voters, and can handle larger files. It runs ninety-nine dollars per month.

A canvass map begins with a list. When working from the county voter database, things must be broken down into manageable units. When I conduct precinct analyses for large counties, I use legislative house districts, but that is still forty thousand voters or more, too many to map in a single turf. However, once in a state house district, areas can be broken down into high-priority precincts, and voters can be rated within those precincts by voting activity and party and mapped by neighborhood based on priorities according to where the votes-owed disparities and undervotes pop off the page.

Many election departments keep track of the number of elections in which a voter has participated over a course of years, and parties have voter activation systems that typically include voting history spanning multiple election cycles; this is helpful in grading voter participation. More about this later.

The county voter database typically comes in Excel, which makes loading it into BatchGeo easy. The challenge becomes breaking the county system into smaller neighborhood units for BatchGeo to map. Obviously, the county database can be sorted by precinct and streets, but when precincts contain thousands of voters and streets are long, you must find another way to break it up. I've tried doing it using an online map and a voter list, but it takes a crazy amount of time. Now we use a hybrid system of sorts to create a list using the party voter system and then export that to Excel and then into BatchGeo. It sounds like a lot of work, but it's worth it—the maps are that much better. If you have someone on your team who is capable of working in both Excel and mapping programs, turn this detail over to him or her. I know there are a lot of other mapping programs out there, so look around. One that gets great reviews is Fulcrum because it will also collect and organize data. Another option is to use the extended USPS zip code.

If you have no one who can figure it out, I will refer you to my mapping guru: Chuck Keil. If you have questions, contact him, not me: chuckkeil@ me.com. Also know that if you're dealing with huge lists, your Excel mapper should know a bit about pivot tables, which are helpful in organizing large amounts of data.

Once your lists are loaded into BatchGeo, Google Maps will place bubbles over the homes of those on your list, and immediately below the map it will list the voters on the map. These can be printed or loaded into a handheld device. Canvassers will also need walking pieces and a system to make notes, indicating support, undecided, or no support. Generally, we use numbers: 1, supports; 2, undecided; and 3, nonsupporter. Whatever you decide, just keep it consistent and simple. All of this information gets to your GOTV coordinator because the campaign must know who should be included in the GOTV activation effort. As an aside, the Democratic or Republican turf-cutting systems can also be printed or loaded onto a handheld device.

When dividing precincts for canvassing teams, it is best to use one team to cover both sides of a normal city street. Doing so may require that portions of two or more precincts be included on the same map, but remember: Efficiency is more important than precinct lines; if a precinct jumps a major thoroughfare, do not expect your canvassers to hop across four-lane highways while canvassing.

For each of your teams, make two identical map packets; they can decide who will do what within the turf. Also, attach duplicate packets together; if they get separated, you're bound to have two different teams pick up the same packet and canvass the same area twice, so pay attention to this detail. Finally, number your packets so that you can quickly see if any are missing.

You may either place walking pieces with each of the maps or simply have the canvasser grab some from a pile. Either way, volunteers should take additional walking pieces to avoid running out before they have finished their areas, and if they have too many, it brings them home to drop off the remainders, which is a good thing. It helps to cross-hatch walking pieces into stacks of twenty-five.

It's a nice touch to have your canvassers write on the front of the walking piece "Sorry we missed you" for people not at home, so have pens on hand in a color that stands out, like red or green.

For cheap clipboards, call a local lumber store, and have them cut four-by-eight-foot, eighth-inch Masonite into clipboard-size pieces. You will need metal clips to hold papers secure; the whole setup runs about a dollar per clipboard. Two great things about this setup, besides the price, is that a map of a city that's getting canvassed can be taped to the Masonite so canvassers have a contextual reference for the canvass, and, after the campaign, the oversize metal clips go into a bag and the Masonite stores neatly in a box because nothing protrudes.

Organizing the Canvassers

Have your volunteers arrive fifteen minutes early if they have not canvassed for you before; ask them to read the literature they'll be walking. The campaign should prepare and distribute an instruction sheet that includes a script (to help guide on the first knocks), the purpose of the canvass (such as more lawn sign locations), plus a phone number of whoever remains at the launch site, in case there are any issues.

Very few people ask questions of the canvasser. However, if one arises, the canvasser must be able to direct that individual back to the campaign by way of phone, email, or website. Placing this information on the walking piece is helpful.

Every person who works for you will have a reason for volunteering. Urge your volunteers to think what that reason is before they head out to canvass, and make this directive part of your pre-canvassing spiel. Include things like: "What would motivate you to get out and canvass on a beautiful Saturday when you would probably rather be home with your family?" This is a nice way to let volunteers know you understand what they are giving up to work for you and that you appreciate it. It is also a ready answer for anyone at the door who may ask why he or she should support a candidate: "Well, I can tell you why I'm helping . . ."

Scheduling the Canvassers

More than anywhere else in the campaign, accommodate volunteers' schedules for canvassing. Set up multiple slots for people on a given weekend.

However, if none of those times work, send volunteers out whenever they can go. Nine times out of ten, there will be someone else who can or must fit into the same time slot, thereby providing a partner. If no other volunteer is available at that time, urge the candidate to join in at that time. Volunteers love to canvass with the candidate.

It is important to accommodate your canvassers in other ways, too—for example, if a canvasser prefers to walk her neighborhood or canvass flatlands over steep grades. Figure 3.2 summarizes some good rules of thumb for your canvassers to follow. A big part of a successful canvassing effort is placing the right volunteer in the right precinct: In general, you want peers canvassing peers or neighbors canvassing neighbors. Whomever you assign, remember that when they knock at the door, they represent the campaign.

Bad weather is a blessing for canvassing simply because more people are home. However, in extreme weather conditions, the canvass should be postponed. Driving rain leaves both the canvasser and the home owner questioning the campaign's judgment. A general rule of thumb is if the weather system has a name (other than drought), find another day to canvass.

Canvassing Directions

1. Split the street with a partner (opposite sides of the street; or wraparound method).
2. Walk fast; talk slow.
3. Respect property and lawns.
4. Look for clues, and look at the list for information.
5. Smile; be friendly.
6. "I'm a volunteer." Say it and wear it.
7. Say their name, say their name.
8. Sincerity counts—deliver the message sincerely.
9. Say the candidate's name.
10. Ask, listen, and write things down.
11. Get a commitment: email addresses, lawn sign location, bumper sticker, endorsement ad.
12. "Pitch and lit"—after listening.
13. Get IDs.
14. Take good notes.
15. Move on—don't drag it out.
16. Use good literature placement—no mailboxes.
17. Be aware of stranger danger—be careful; never go inside a house.

FIGURE 3.2 Canvassing Directions

These guidelines will help your volunteers have a successful canvass. (Jefferson Smith, Oregon Bus Project)

A very effective technique for getting more people to canvass is to ask sign-ups to bring a friend. This makes it more enjoyable for those who do, increases your volunteer numbers, and helps reduce the possibility of no-shows. Since canvassing is conducted in pairs, it is an ideal activity for friends or couples.

Canvassers often ask if they can bring their children to help. If the kids are old enough, it should be fine. I started canvassing for my mom when I was in middle school. I believe in children having a hand in campaigns, not least so that they can celebrate the win with their parents. I especially like to have kids along with canvassers when I'm working for a library or school-funding measure. Clearly, they have a stake in the outcome, and it doesn't hurt for the voters to have a stakeholder at their door. Very young children, however, can be a distraction and can really slow down a canvasser. If you are the candidate, you should not tow your kids along—unless, of course, you're a man with a baby (see figure 10.1 on p. 224). (Hey, I don't make the rules.)

Remember, don't put any campaign literature in or on mailboxes, and be sure your campaign material does not become litter. When residents are not home, volunteers should wedge the walking piece into doorjambs, screen doors, and trim boards so that it cannot escape into the wind. If it appears that the residents are out of town and campaign literature and newspapers are already littering the doorstep, skip that home and make a note on the canvassing sheet.

From time to time, candidates should get out and canvass along with the volunteers. Because it is more effective for the candidate to knock on the door, cover as much ground as possible. Start early in the campaign to canvass as many homes as possible. Many voters have told me and candidates I work with that they will vote for any candidate who knocks on their door. It's shocking, really. The only drawback of a candidate's knocking is that he or she often gets hung up talking with voters, so be sure a partner goes along to help cover the area and prod candidates out of doorways.

Occasionally, other campaigns, party headquarters, or a special-interest group will contact your campaign and offer to include your literature in a neighborhood canvass. This is a tempting prospect for any campaign lumbering under a big canvassing schedule. However, the downside is that your walking piece is dropped at the door in a pile along with others and loses the purpose and impact of canvassing a piece to a home; I've even seen bunches of candidate literature bundled with a rubber band at doors. Although this may make it convenient for the canvasser, it also makes it convenient for the home owner to drop the lot in the trash.

Get to Know Your Voters by Where and How They Live

When you canvass, you are moving about in neighborhoods that have supported candidates or causes like yours in previous elections. You can learn a lot by studying the neighborhoods that have popped out as your top- and medium-priority areas. Are the homes historic or modern ranch? Are they well cared for? Is the neighborhood made up largely of working-class or retired people? Minorities, single parents, college students, mill workers? Look for clues as to why these voters may have trouble getting out to vote. Are they simply overwhelmed with life, children, work, school, poverty? As Jim Gimpel, a professor of political science at the University of Maryland, has remarked, neighborhoods tell us about the voters who live there. They "reveal housing preferences, spending habits, racial and ethnic composition, lifestyles, levels of geographic mobility, voting habits and other traits relevant to predicting political participation and attitudes."[1] This is part of the voter identification process outlined in the chapter on GOTV.

Phone Banks

Other than calling people within my volunteer file for specific tasks, I no longer rely on phone banks, even for GOTV. With that said, there will be many campaigns who want to continue to use this method to secure a head count for a fundraiser, to get lawn sign locations, to raise money, and to get the campaign more volunteers. If you plan to do a get-out-the-vote effort on Election Day, you will have to identify voters (voter ID) who intend to vote for your candidate or cause in the months leading up to the election. This can be done while canvassing or by phone. Although conducting a GOTV by canvassing *activates* the greatest number of voters, few campaigns have the volunteer resources to do so and rely on phone banks to do the heavy lifting to identify support.

If it is your intention to conduct a GOTV through phone banks rather than using the neighborhood-captain approach outlined in Chapter 12, the following process will organize your efforts for that and all other phone bank activities.

However, one word of caution on a GOTV phone bank: When word gets out that you're running an organized, well-staffed GOTV, every campaign under the sun will request that you add other candidates or issues to the script. Don't do it: Voters' minds are not changed by dropping a name the week before Election Day. Never allow your phone bankers to slog through a long list of candidates, although they can and should encourage all friendly voters to fill out their entire ballot.

The Setup

Make a spreadsheet listing all volunteers for the phone bank (see figure 3.3). The first column contains their names, and the next has their phone numbers. Then have a smaller column with "CB?" (for "called back?") as the column header; later, a check mark is placed in this column on the printout after a volunteer has been called back and confirmed that he or she will be there for the next day's phone bank. Next are seven columns with dates, one for each night of phone banking. Each phone bank location will have its own spreadsheet, listing only the volunteers who will be calling from that location.

Below the dates, list the starting times of the phone banks. For example, the first bank may run from 6:00 to 7:30 p.m. and the second from 7:30 to 9:00 p.m. Or with so many having unlimited minutes on their cell phones, running one big bank from 6:30 or 7:00 to 8:30 is a far better option. So assuming the campaign needs twenty phone bankers for each night of the GOTV and the phone bank location has only five lines, ask fifteen of your volunteers to bring their cell phones and run one ninety-minute shift.

The names on the spreadsheet are kept in alphabetical order. If your lists are short, this detail is less important, but in a phone bank with two shifts of 10 people for seven nights (as might be the case for GOTV), the campaign will have 140 volunteers working in one location alone. As volunteers let the campaign know whether they can do the early or late shift, the time slot is circled in red so the lead (supervisor) can easily see it. Each night of calling must have a lead responsible for the phone bank. That lead should do the following:

1. Arrive a few minutes early and open the phone banks.
2. Have paper cups for water and red pens for marking precinct lists.
3. Bring enough phone bank instructions so that each caller in each shift will have a set.

NAME	NAME (LAST)	Place lead names here for each night PHONE #	CB?	LEAD NAME Wed. 11/1		Thur. 11/2		Fri. 11/3		Sat. 11/4		Sun. 11/5		Mon. 11/6	
				6:00	7:30	6:00	7:30	6:00	7:30	6:00	7:30	6:00	7:30	6:00	7:30
				6:00	7:30	6:00	7:30	6:00	7:30	6:00	7:30	6:00	7:30	6:00	7:30
				6:00	7:30	6:00	7:30	6:00	7:30	6:00	7:30	6:00	7:30	6:00	7:30

FIGURE 3.3 Example of a Phone Bank Spreadsheet

4. Bring targeted precinct lists with inactive voters or lazy voters—this is provided by the campaign. As an aside, inactive voters are those whose ballots have not yet been received by the county. This information is available daily in states with all vote-by-mail elections. However, in hybrid elections (those with both poll voting and absentee voting), your lists may be just those who have not requested an absentee ballot who live in high-priority precincts.

5. Have the master copy of all volunteers participating at that location, and it's a good idea to have a satchel with cups, pens, and the master calling list inside. For GOTV, secure the precinct calling lists before the phone banks start, and either deliver the lists to the leads or have the leads pick them up, at which time the satchel is passed off as well. In outlying phone banks, these lists are emailed early enough for printing.

6. Welcome the volunteers and give instructions (provided by the campaign).

7. Have callers begin, and then circulate among the callers and answer questions.

8. Fill water cups and distribute one to each volunteer, refilling if necessary. You do not want your phone bank callers wandering around looking for water rather than calling voters.

9. Once questions subside, call *all* volunteers for the next evening's phone banks, using the master lists for the phone bank, and check off the callback column for each confirmation. Afterward, look over the callback column; any last-minute cancellations must be communicated to the campaign as soon as possible so the spot can be filled.

10. The next shift arrives fifteen minutes early for training. Begin anew, providing instructions to the next team.

11. At exactly 7:30, the next crew pulls the first shift off the phones and takes over at their desk, continuing to call down the sheets, picking up where the first shift left off.

12. Again, circulate, answer questions, pick up old water cups and distribute new ones, and be available for as long as necessary.

13. Once questions subside, the lead gets on the phone and calls the next night's volunteer callers. Once that task is complete, he or she then becomes part of the phone bank, calling through to voters until the bank closes.

14. Clean up all remnants of the work crews: cups, pens, lists, and so on. The pens and the master call list are returned to the satchel, along with any unused cups.

15. Lock up and get the satchel to the next lead or back to campaign headquarters.

"Hello, this is (your name). Tonight I am volunteering to help the Ada Kay campaign. As you may know, Ada is running for reelection to the House, and I was hoping you would consider having one of her lawn signs in front of your home."

If no, thank the caller and ask if Ada can count on his or her support in the upcoming election.

If yes, verify address and ask if there are any special instructions for where and how the homeowner would like the sign placed. Then say:

"Someone will be coming by to place the sign about six weeks before the election. We will also have some maintenance crews checking signs from time to time. However, if you would occasionally check the sign and set it up if it falls over, that would be very helpful. When the sign is placed, there will be a note left on your door so you can contact the campaign should it disappear or be vandalized. Thanks for helping us out."

FIGURE 3.4 Example of Phone Instructions and Script for Lawn Sign Locations

Two important things to remember when enlisting phone bank volunteers: Assure them that they will receive training before actually working on the phones, and do not expect your phone bank people to look up phone numbers; calling lists must include phone numbers, names, spouses' names, nicknames (include pronunciations), and, if possible, notes regarding age, hearing ability, and language spoken.

Phone Bank Training

The following is an example of what you might prepare for your volunteers who are phoning for the campaign:

Thank you for your help. Tonight we are calling people who live on arterial streets in hopes of beefing up our lawn sign list. While the lists you're calling have the same party registration as our candidate, they have not been previously identified as supporters. Just so you know, that may make some of the calls a little harder. Please make a note on your list next to the name of the voter whether he or she will take a lawn sign and, if not, whether that person will be supporting our candidate.

Figures 3.4 and 3.5 are examples of materials given to phone bankers.

Before You Pick Up the Phone—

1. *Be proud of what you are doing.* You are working for a cause you believe in. You are on the front line of a campaign.

2. *Think about what has motivated you to give up your time to work for the candidate (or ballot measure).* People will ask how a candidate stands on a particular issue. While you cannot speak directly to that, you can share why *you* are working for this individual (or cause).

3. *Identify yourself only as a volunteer working for the campaign.* In general, you want the candidate's name to make it into the consciousness of the voter, not yours, unless, of course, you know the person.

4. *No matter what else happens, get something from the individual before you get off the phone.* "You can't canvass, ever? How about a lawn sign?" "You have a bad lawn-sign location? Do you have a friend who might want one?" "Can we use your name on the endorsement ad?" "Would you make a contribution?" Whatever. You want them in on the campaign with that single call, or to know how they will be voting. (This is helpful information for the campaign.)

5. And thank you for taking the time to help in this important cause.

FIGURE 3.5 Example of Phone Bank Instructions

What you ask for will vary according to the phone bank. You could be soliciting lawn sign locations, donations, volunteer workers, a head count for an event, or voter ID (that is, finding out whether a voter supports your campaign). Think about your mission, and prepare a short introduction for the caller.

Phone Bank Locations

The ubiquity of cell phones has all but eliminated the nightmare of finding friendly commercial offices with enough lines to accommodate phone banks. Still, you need a comfortable and professional location where people are calling in close proximity to each other and where supervision is easily conducted.

The best locations have plenty of rooms and desks, such as offices for lawyers, real estate offices, or physician offices; you can also use party headquarters, but caller ID will reduce the number of pickups on the receiving end. Wherever you end up, the location should have some landlines for volunteers without access to a cell phone or whose calling plan limits their minutes. The remaining ten to fifteen volunteers at the phone banks use personal cell phones.

What makes this approach so ideal is that voters are more apt to pick up a phone call if their caller ID indicates a real person, a friend or neighbor, is on the other end of the call rather than "party headquarters." This hybrid phone bank approach allows the phone banks to be as large as necessary to get through the required calls for the task in front of you.

One note of caution: Remind the cell phone users to bring chargers.

Sample Phone Bank Scripts

Scripts should be drafted prior to each campaign activity. While it is preferable to have callers ad-lib, they generally need a prepared script for the first few calls until the volunteer is comfortable with the task. When calling for money, the calls will be a bit longer and more involved, so I usually start by asking the person who answers if they have a moment to talk. However, with volunteer recruitment, the calls are so short that you can just cut to the chase. The following paragraphs suggest some sample scripts for typical campaign phone sessions.

- *Lawn sign location.* "Hello, I'm a volunteer working for the Kate Newhall campaign for state senate. Tonight we're looking for locations for lawn signs. Will you be supporting Kate in the general election? Great. Could we place a lawn sign? Let me verify your address. Someone will be coming by about six weeks before the election to place it. We also have a crew who will be maintaining these signs; however, if it needs some attention, maybe you could help with it. Great. Thanks."
- *Special activity.* "Hello, I'm a volunteer working for the Pam Marsh campaign for the house. Did you receive the invitation for the campaign dinner this Saturday? The restaurant needs a pretty accurate head count, so we're trying to get an idea of the number of supporters who will be attending the dinner for Pam. Will you be joining us?"
- *Canvassing (Variation A).* "Hello, I'm a volunteer helping in the Peter Buckley campaign. We are hoping to canvass the city this Saturday with a last-minute door hanger and need about eighty-five volunteers. There will be no door-knocking, just great exercise. Can you help?"
- *Canvassing (Variation B).* "Hello, I'm a volunteer working for the John Doe for Mayor campaign. Our notes indicate that you might be willing to canvass. Is that correct? Great. I have a number of dates for some upcoming canvasses. Do you have your calendar handy?"
- *GOTV for absentee and mail-in ballots.* "Hello, I'm a volunteer from the Jane Doe campaign. We're down here working on phone banks tonight

to turn out as many of Jane's supporters as possible. As of a couple of days ago, your ballot had not yet been received at county elections. Is it possible you still have it at home?"

- *Voter ID.* "Hello, I'm a volunteer working for the Amy Amrhein campaign. As you may know, Amy is a candidate for the school board. Do you know if you'll be supporting her this November?"

With any of these scripts, if I call and discover that someone is undecided or leaning, I ask whether the person would like more information from the candidate or campaign committee. Finally, whatever a potential supporter might say, ask volunteers to make a note so that the campaign can follow up if need be. If you get a negative response, get off the phone as quickly as possible, and make a note for the campaign.

Clerical Team

The clerical team is an extremely important part of your campaign. Normally, you think of people sitting around, addressing, stamping, and stuffing envelopes. While these tasks might make up the bulk of your clerical team's work, you should think of this group in broader terms.

Always reduce your campaign activities into the smallest sensible subtasks. For example, on the day that lawn signs go up, you *cannot* expect your lawn sign team to arrive early in the morning, assemble lawn signs onto H-wickets, organize lists, and then head out for two hours of installation. Instead, use a clerical team to come in days ahead of time to assemble signs, and then another clerical team can organize the map packets and lawn sign lists for either printed lists or handheld devices.

Your clerical team is crucial in keeping your campaign tight and organized. Use them creatively wherever they can help with your workload or with organizing an upcoming activity. Here are some examples of how the clerical team can be used:

- Stuff, stamp, and address a mailing in all forms: fundraising direct mail and general direct mail on issues
- Lawn sign assembly
- Assemble maps and lists for a canvass
- Write and send thank-you notes for money or volunteers' time
- Prepare items for a fundraiser, such as a yard sale or an auction
- Set up for a campaign gathering—decorate, print name tags, and so on

To set up a campaign activity requiring clerical workers, contact people who have indicated they will help with clerical work on sign-up sheets or noted on a returned remit envelope. If you need additional volunteers, try the League of Women Voters, your friends and neighbors, library volunteers, and senior groups that support you. Given how much fun a clerical work party can be, it is usually pretty easy to turn out a crowd.

A clerical work party is a social time in campaigns; it's a time to chat with friends while helping with a cause everyone supports. It's a time to share war stories about canvassing, to talk news, to gossip, or to do whatever else while having coffee and cookies over a simple task. These meetings are enjoyable and highly productive for the small effort involved.

It is important for people to be comfortable while working and sitting for two or more hours, so be sure to have enough table space for each volunteer. Do not do clerical work in an already cluttered house. Because no one's back is getting younger—and many of the clerical volunteers are older—I take the time to put together a comfortable work area. Avoid having people work on their laps in soft, overstuffed couches and chairs; they will not be as productive. It would be like cleaning house or doing yard work in flip-flops—you can do it, just not as efficiently.

Have some snacks around but not on the table where work is being conducted.

Have everything set up. Do not waste your volunteers' time.

Do one activity at a time. If the task is to get out a mailing or assemble lawn signs, do just that. When the task is done—hopefully ahead of schedule— don't bring out more work. Remember, as with any other task in a campaign, you have made a verbal contract with your workers. Asking your volunteers to work beyond their commitment will create hard feelings. Workers who complete a task early and then go home feel good about their participation and feel that they are helping in a well-organized effort.

Prevent idleness by keeping all the necessary materials at each workstation. Have extras of everything you need—staplers, sponges, stamps, envelopes, rubber bands, electric screwdrivers, drywall screws, washers, or whatever else the task might require.

Time Allotments for Volunteer Tasks

Below are some general guidelines for what volunteers can do in a designated amount of time. From here, you can calculate how many people you'll need to accomplish a task in the time available. For the task to be completed by a certain date, work your way backward from that date, as outlined in Chapter 13, "The Campaign Plan," so that you have enough time to complete the task, given your resources and task goals—number of calls to make, signs to put up, homes to canvass, and so on. (This should all go into your campaign plan.)

Phone Banks

In general, each volunteer can complete twenty to thirty calls per hour, depending on the nature of the calls. In a GOTV effort, people can make fifty calls during a ninety-minute shift. So, for example, if you want to make four thousand calls by Election Day and have only one phone bank location and six phones, you will need people on all six phones, for two ninety-minute shifts, for seven nights. Naturally, if you have callers bring cell phones, the number of calling nights goes down and the number of volunteers per shift goes up.

Canvassing

Some precincts are huge, by either population or geography, and can have anywhere from 300 to 3,000 voters per precinct or 200 to 1,800 homes. Use voter lists to get an accurate number of houses in each precinct.

Two types of canvassing are used for our purposes here: a knock and a simple lit drop without knocking.

- *Knock.* Depending on how hilly, rural, or compact a neighborhood is, if canvassers can cover 10 to 15 houses per hour, that means a precinct with 120 to 200 houses would require six canvassers working two to three hours each to cover the distance. When canvassing in apartment buildings, a canvasser can cover twice that many, and if it is a rural area or hilly maybe half.
- *Lit drop.* A literature drop can be done quite a bit faster than a knock canvass. With a drop, again depending on the street grade and the density of homes, a canvasser can cover twenty-five to thirty homes in an hour, more for duplexes and apartments.

Clerical (Direct Mail)

A five hundred–count mailing requires a fifteen-person clerical team working one hour to stuff, stamp, seal, and address envelopes.

Lawn Signs

One lawn sign team—a driver and an installer—can put up about twelve lawn signs an hour. So, if you have two hundred lawn signs to place, you will need sixteen people (eight teams) working two hours each.

Your campaign committee and volunteer teams are central to a winning campaign effort. A thoroughly organized and properly executed volunteer structure minimizes wasted time and reflects well on the campaign manager and candidate.

Campaign Messaging

Leaders can conceive and articulate goals that lift people out of their petty preoccupations and carry them above the conflicts that tear a society apart.
—JOHN W. GARDNER

IN THIS CHAPTER:

- Campaign Theme and Message
- Message Development for Candidates
- Polling
- Campaign Slogans
- Logo
- Walking-Piece Development
- Voters' Pamphlet

Campaign Theme and Message

ALTHOUGH POLITICAL STRATEGISTS USE THE WORDS THEME AND MESSAGE in different ways and sometimes interchangeably, for our purposes a *theme* covers the overarching issues that capture the spirit of what voters want, such as government free of corruption, whereas a *message* is a single idea used to bring that theme to the voters, such as integrity.

For example, if you're working on a campaign to fund cocurricular activities that were eliminated from your school district because of budget cuts, your *theme* will probably include the idea of reinstating these programs. However, your *message* will center on the idea that it is no longer enough for students to have a 4.0 GPA if they want to get into a good college or land a better job—they must also be involved in cocurricular and extracurricular school activities. Briefly, your message is "opportunity."

A theme embraces what the voters want and defines the candidate or issue-based campaign in that context, whereas a message is a believable application of the theme to the voters that cuts through to the emotional level. The voters want great schools, which must have a combination of challenging course work and cocurricular activities. You sell these programs for what they are: opportunities for students. The proposed programs help students get into competitive universities or land great jobs, they are the reason some kids stay in school, and they represent another layer of preparation that enriches the next generation's future. It all comes back to providing opportunities for youths to excel. It isn't about money; it isn't about how little your property taxes will go up. If you're justifying money, you're on their message.

When you're selling a bond measure to maintain money for operation and maintenance (O&M) of a community asset, such as a library, you are not selling what a great deal the voters are getting or how this generation owes it to the next; you're selling more: a community resource that is properly managed and protected from cuts. That's your theme. Your message, however, is about community. It's about a place where old and young can gather, as they have for hundreds of years, to read a book, study, and connect with others.

On the other hand, if you're selling a *capital improvement* project, the campaign actually does sell money; you're selling "a stitch in time saves nine": It is cheaper to repair roads now rather than later, to fix leaky roofs to public holdings, repair wastewater systems to avoid federal fines for spilling wastewater into streams, to upgrade wiring to make classrooms safer. What a campaign should *not* do is mix operation and maintenance arguments with capital improvement (CI) arguments. O&M is about keeping the library open; CI is about protecting the asset. O&M is about more teachers per student; CI is about boilers exploding. O&M is about hope and opportunity; CI is about being responsible. There's a difference.

A campaign message is a tool to keep the candidate and team focused. It is a concept back to which all roads go. Take the message "It's the economy, stupid," used in President Clinton's first run. All the issues that fell under his campaign (environment, education, crime, and health care) came back to the message: We need to protect our environment to ensure better *jobs* in the future, we need to provide our children with better education if we want a *workforce* that can compete on the world market, providing opportunities for everyone to get a college education means *keeping America competitive*, affordable health care allows a family *to get ahead*, high crime is destroying our communities and marginalizing *businesses*, and so on. Everything comes back to the message "the economy," and addressing the theme issues that base voters want will lead to a better economy. This message had added strength in that it suggested the incumbent was unaware that the electorate was concerned about the economy. Good messaging always suggests that the opposition is either unaware or complicit in the problem your campaign and election will strive to solve.

A campaign message is a story you tell over and over, a story you can tell in a few seconds: "It's the economy"; "This is about opportunity"; "It's the small issues"; "It's hope"; "It's about community." A well-crafted message moves the debate away from which candidate can be trusted to whom the voters trust to do the job. A theme and a message articulate the point that the candidate knows *what* job needs to be done and will be the one more likely to do it.

Message Development for Candidates

Get your committee together and brainstorm:

- Your strengths and weaknesses
- Your opponent's strengths and weaknesses
- What's working and what needs attention in your community (at the heart of this bullet point should be why you're seeking the office for which you're running)

Using the issues that need attention, you will frame your message so that it underscores your strengths, your opponent's weaknesses, and hopefully makes a liability out of your opponent's strengths.

For example, let's say some of the items that need attention in your city are poorly maintained streets, a dilapidated or inadequate water supply and system, and a forest backdrop that has become a potential fire hazard of standing dead trees from bug kill.

Your opponent has voted against infrastructure (weakness) but has brought in a lot of jobs (strength). Without ever mentioning your opponent, you will frame your message of "It's about responsibility" this way: "Before we spend tax dollars to lure outside business to our front door—indeed, to compete with our neighborhood stores—let's make sure our house is in order. For too many years, we have neglected our water system; for too many years, we have failed to maintain our roads; for too many years, we have ignored our forest interface. Let's get our priorities straight."

In a debate setting where your opponent touts his efforts to attract more business, you may frame the response this way: "Let's work to retrain and expand the businesses we have rather than offering tax breaks to outside businesses so they relocate." Your loyalty and responsibility lie with helping the businesses already in the community.

Identifying what needs attention, defining a problem, is as strong as or stronger than white papers outlining detailed reforms.

Related to this is framing your candidate. By taking a critical look at your candidate and listing the strengths and weaknesses, your campaign team is better able to shape and communicate the theme of a campaign through the message. For example, a woman who is energetic, feisty, and steadfast translates into pluses and minuses. The opposition may frame her as pushy, shrill, dogmatic, or overbearing, but for your campaign those are just other words for fighter, integrity, and honesty.

The charge of the campaign committee is to frame the negative into a positive: Pushy becomes persistent; dogmatic becomes steadfast and straightforward, which go with honesty and integrity. All this is communicated through the message that flows from what the candidate represents. For instance, if a community is being overrun by developers and the quality of life is compromised by the inherent impacts of growth, couple a message of thoughtful, planned growth with a candidate's strengths of persistence and willingness to fight for the soul of the community. Again, the message is planned, thoughtful growth, and every question answered comes back to this message—all under the umbrella of the theme "quality of life."

Through this process, campaigns identify issues that create relationships with the voters, and *that* translates into money, volunteers, and votes. For example, people in a particular neighborhood are concerned about development, so the campaign underscores the creation of a park near the neighborhood. It is not about stopping growth but rather about mitigating the negative effects of growth. The campaign looks at the impacts growth has on the community and presents approaches that allow growth without compromising quality of life. This in turn will create relationships within the community. For parents and teachers, growth affects class size; for others, it's about traffic, open space, or availability of resources, such as water. If you present yourself as antigrowth, you risk being tagged as a single-issue candidate. Instead, lead people to where two worlds can coexist or even enhance one another rather than prophesying what will happen if these two worlds are allowed to collide. In short, planning for growth is good for business, education, resources, neighborhood integrity, and so on.

If your opponent has not defined himself or herself, you can work this process in reverse and define that person for the voters: "My opponent is pro-growth."

Polling

Polling provides a campaign with a snapshot of public opinion. While a benchmark poll looks at ranking multiple issues among voters before any campaigning or distribution of information has been done, tracking polls provide ongoing feedback on the impact a campaign has in swaying public opinion over the course of the campaign.

Getting Data Without a Poll

If your campaign has no money or, more to the point, does not want to spend thousands on a benchmark poll, you can get much of the information a benchmark would give you, for free. Using recent voting history of issue-based campaigns can provide candidates with an idea of voter opinion—precinct by precinct. For example, in one general election, Oregon had twenty-five ballot measures before the voters. Among other things, the measures covered issues involving school funding, gay and lesbian rights, mandatory sentencing, campaign-finance reform, drug-related property forfeiture, land use, taxes, powers of the state legislature, tobacco settlement funds, baiting traps, background checks for firearm purchases, and linking teacher pay to student performance. Although some of these measures passed (or failed) in every county, that does not mean they passed or failed equally in every precinct within the county.

If you're running a campaign in a state that is not as measure happy as Oregon, potential campaign issues in your voting area can be ferreted out in other ways: letters to the editor, minutes of city council or county commission meetings, editorials, general news stories, blogs following local articles, and county and city elections. Given that issues pop up in candidate elections, reviewing which issues were at the center of those campaigns can be very helpful.

Recently I worked on a county commissioner campaign in which the candidate had been elected to his conservative city council post on a no-growth platform. Knowing that growth was an issue in my city as well and that the two cities represent opposite ends of the political spectrum, we knew we had an issue that would transcend the county's political schism: growth and the effects it has on our region.

Alternatives

Many small communities conduct citizen surveys to track residents' concerns and to assess city employees' job performance. This is part of the public record and is available for the asking. You can get similar information, minus the job performance of the governing body, at the local Chamber of Commerce. The census also has a wealth of information broken down by city, county, region, and state such as ethnic diversity, income, single-parent homes, percentage with higher-education degrees, and more.

Special-interest groups that support your candidate or issue may have recently conducted a poll to track voter support of a particular issue, especially if that issue has been or soon will be placed before the voters. Such polls typically assess support according to voter profile within a region, county, or city.

And don't forget to check the local college, as sometimes political science departments conduct polls.

Benchmark Polls

Conducting a benchmark poll may be the most efficient and accurate way to determine voter concerns before you develop your message. As First Lady Rosalynn Carter remarked, "It is difficult to lead people where they do not want to go." While it is important to have elected officials with strong core values, it's equally important that officials listen to and embrace "where people want to go." Take that information to help present your message in a believable and compelling way, to encourage your voters to see their values as your values: They're the same. Having a clear reading of voter concerns will help your campaign develop and direct a message that will be heard. It can also inform you about when to keep quiet and where to avoid which issues. Generally, a benchmark poll is done before a campaign, and it can be invaluable in developing a campaign strategy, theme, and message.

A good benchmark poll can take as long as thirty minutes per call. It will include questions that lead to information about the following:

- The name recognition of the major candidates
- The favorability of that name recognition
- A voter's knowledge of state and local politics
- The degree of a voter's partisanship
- The issues most important to the voter, by gender, age, and party affiliation
- The education, age, and gender of those who support you and of those who support your opposition
- The income level of those who support you and your opponent
- Whom the voter will support if the election were held tomorrow (or which direction the voter is leaning)

- What form of message works best, both for your candidate and for the opposition
- What attacks will hurt the most, for both you and your opposition

A good benchmark poll can be expensive but will provide specifics that influence to whom you communicate what message.

Push Questions

Good benchmark polls include push questions. Push questions, not to be mistaken with push polling, "are recognized by all the major associations and leading political consultants as a valid and legitimate research tool for the purposes of testing ad messages and examining the collective viewpoints of electorate subgroups."[1]

Push questioning will ask whether a statement is very, somewhat, or not at all convincing and will do so for both the candidate paying for the poll as well as the opposition. The questions will test both positives and negatives on each side of the debate—and will do so equally.

Polling for Dollars

If you're working on a state legislative race, a professionally conducted poll can mean money for your campaign. Lobbyists and PACs are reluctant to give money to campaigns that "think" they will win. However, show that you're close to your opponent in a legitimate poll, and checkbooks will open. To spend thousands on a poll in hopes of attracting PAC money is risky and works against common sense. Still, it happens, and if the numbers are good, it can pay off.

Professionally conducted polling tends to be expensive. To cut costs, you might consider offering to include other candidates in the poll if their campaigns will contribute to the cost or ask a PAC or state party to help financially by paying the polling firm directly.

Polls can also cost a campaign support and money if they indicate yours is a losing effort. If your registration is wildly skewed in favor of the opposition, save your money.

Tracking Polls

Tracking polls are generally brief, with only a handful of questions, and are most helpful when conducted regularly throughout the campaign. A tracking poll may be used to do several things:

- Track candidate or issue support
- Fine-tune a campaign message
- Tell you whether a particular campaign event or ad has left you or your opponent vulnerable
- Determine whether negative campaigning, on either your part or that of your opponent, is helping or hurting (this is generally tracked in a quick-response poll following an ad)
- Indicate what groups are still undecided

Tracking Polls on a Shoestring

Not long ago I hired the Campaign Solutions Group in Los Angeles to conduct tracking polls; they created a random call list using criteria I specified and made the calls. Also, for a few cents more per voter contact, they retained each contact's name and correlating response, data we used to augment our voter ID efforts. The bill for these services came in at $590, with a margin of error between 3 percent and 4 percent for each of the two tracking polls; the polling showed our candidate was in a dead heat, winning the election with 50.2 percent of the vote, compared to his opponent, with 49.7 percent. We mapped the captured IDs using BatchGeo, which gave us a quick glimpse of where our support was strong and weak in areas of equal registration.

After the final vote was counted, the opponent actually had 49.8 percent to our 50.2 percent (we won by 281 votes out of nearly 50,000 cast). This polling approach gave us an exact and accurate percentage of the final vote for a very affordable price.

In another campaign, I used the Solutions Group to poll Spanish-speaking voters for an issue-based campaign. It was remarkably affordable, as I was charged only for actual calls where the voter engaged.

Tracking Polls Without the Poll

If you cannot afford a tracking poll, there are some telltale signs that will give you an idea about the progress of your campaign and that of your opponent. Here are just a few examples:

- *Attendance at debates.* At the beginning of a campaign, while voters are still undecided, attendance at debates is often high. Once voters have decided how they will vote, they tend to stay home. This phenomenon will vary from city to city. If it happens in a city in which you enjoy support, that's great. If voters are still coming out in droves to hear you and your opponent in an area that normally would not support you, that's bad news for your opponent.

- *Your opponent, who had been straddling the fence, suddenly moves to the extreme of his or her base.* Chances are, when a candidate moves toward the base, it's because information has come in that the opponent thinks the race is close and the base is wavering. Remember, just because you're not polling doesn't mean your opposition isn't polling. Trying to lock your base late in a campaign is difficult and can be a sign that a campaign is in trouble.

- *A week before the general election, canvassers report that people still do not know your candidate.* In general, astute canvassers bring back valuable information about your candidate or issue-based campaign. If they report that many people still don't know your candidate, you must find a way to go back and grab your base to avoid an undervote. Not ideal, but it can be done.

Push Polling

Push polling is a form of negative campaigning and comes to the voter through telemarketing, disguised as a legitimate poll. The objective of push polling is to *persuade* voters, *not* to gain information. And since they are only about persuasion, push polls typically do not collect data.

Because many confuse push questions with push polling, it is important to again underscore the difference. As indicated above, benchmark polls ask push questions that reveal the dark side of *both* candidates. Campaigns do this so they know the effectiveness of hitting an opponent or receiving hits from the opposition with little-known, but truthful, information. Campaigns want to know what will work for and against both their campaign and the opposition.

Benchmarks take twenty to thirty minutes, whereas tracking polls are relatively quick, grabbing a snapshot of a moment. Only a very specific voter will invest twenty or thirty minutes in a benchmark; many more will jump in on a tracking poll.

Push polls use the goodwill of tracking polls, which are based on brevity ("If the election were held tomorrow, would you vote for Candidate A or Candidate B?") to persuade unwitting voters. Push polls typically take under five minutes, but unlike their tracking-poll sister, they add a little "something something" at the end to close the deal.

Here is how Rachel, a blogger on the *Huffington Post*, described a push poll regarding the Obama and McCain 2008 presidential campaign in Ohio:

When I said that I was voting for Obama, they asked if I would be more or less likely to vote for Obama if I knew that he voted to let convicted child sex offenders out early, voted to allow convicted child sex offenders to live near schools, is for sex education in Kindergarten, voted for some offensive and incredibly graphic abortion procedure, and so on and so on for 5 minutes. This was a really offensive push-poll. They also brought up the statements of Rev. Wright and Michelle Obama.[2]

That is a push poll: it typically shares with the voter something inflammatory and typically skewed. Because there must be some tangential thread between the question and truth, push polls can tip leaning voters—both ways. Push polling is condemned by everyone yet seemingly is done all the time—or so some think.

In one campaign on which I worked, a Democratic state representative and doctor ran against a local Republican businessman and beloved philanthropist. Both candidates were identical on every single issue, from sales tax to education to choice. However, the Republican enjoyed a 6 percent registration advantage and was so well known and well liked that he could routinely turn out four hundred people for a six o'clock breakfast or three hundred for a Tuesday lunch. Yikes.

Then a friend called, upset. Apparently, her husband had received (ostensibly) from our campaign a call that was obviously "push polling," she said. After assuring her that it was not us, I asked her on what she had based her allegation. She said her husband was asked whether he would be more or less likely to vote for the Republican if he knew he was blind.

The truth is, our opponent, who had suffered from macular degeneration for most of his life, *was* legally blind. However, I do not believe you can poll for prejudice because, when you try, voters lie. Indeed, there are many examples of campaigns in which polling for prejudice resulted in unreliable data. The so-called Bradley effect in the 1982 California gubernatorial race is one such example, and the appeal to people's prejudice through their love of the Confederate flag in Georgia and South Carolina in the 2000 gubernatorial races is another.[3]

Indeed, before our benchmark poll, I argued against a question regarding our opponent's vision impairment. It seemed disingenuous if we allowed a doctor to attack an opponent on a disability; some might even see it as cruel. So, I contended that if we would *never* use it, why ask? Indeed, polling this question could actually inflame the narrow swing vote needed to win. Some on our team argued that "to ask" was not "to use."

Don't be fooled: If you have a handgun in your pocket while committing a robbery, the jury doesn't care if you never intended to use it. Voters are no different. In small communities, friends share information about telephone polls.

Clearly, our opponent was asking this push question on his benchmark poll, and knowing that offered important information to our campaign: They wondered about their candidate's disability. Knowing the opposition was worried or at least curious about voter response to our opponent's macular degeneration was gold. Indeed, service in government is largely about being able to move quickly through unbelievable volumes of material and grasp information for effective communication, in a glance. How to convey and indirectly remind voters of this without being heavy-handed became the goal (see figure 4.1).

Campaign Slogans

The slogan is a simple statement about why voters should vote for you or your issue. It should also imply why *not* to vote for your opponent or what a "no vote" may lead to in an issue-based campaign. Your slogan must not depart from your campaign message, and it should evoke a gut emotion. One effective slogan used in an issue-based campaign in California simply said, "Share the Water." Who can argue with the idea of sharing? It is a friendly thought that is encouraged throughout our lives. It also implies that the water is not being shared.

Slogans can be very effective, but do not invent a slogan just to have one. Using your campaign message, design a slogan that underscores and reinforces the message. Look back on the list of your strengths and the issues important to your community. Once you think you have a slogan, brainstorm on all the ways it could be used against you or hurt your cause. Work through this process until you come up with the right combination. In one open-space campaign, we used the slogan "Parks: Now and Forever." People who opposed the measure saw our slogan and used their own modification: "Parks: *Pay* Now and Forever," a very clever counterslogan. We should have chosen ours more carefully.

A negative slogan—that is, one that indirectly references your opponent—should be avoided. Two actual slogans, one for the state legislature and the other for Congress, "Now Let's Choose Leadership" and "A Leader We Can Be Proud Of," both committed such an error, and both lost. The first comes across as arrogant, especially for an outsider running against a well-liked incumbent; it was even more problematic in that the outsider needed some of those who had previously voted for his opponent to swing over and vote for him. Hard to accomplish when your slogan insults the voters; after all, the voters assumed they had voted for leadership in the past. "A Leader We

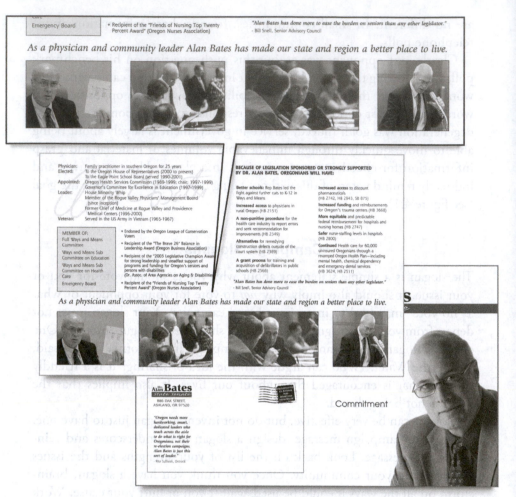

FIGURE 4.1 Example of a Full-Color Brochure That Subtly Addresses Voters' Concerns with the Opponent

Democrat Alan Bates ran for a state senate seat recently vacated by a twenty-eight-year Republican veteran; the seat had a six-point Republican registration advantage. His opponent, a highly respected, fabulously wealthy, and generous philanthropist, was legally blind. Once we discovered that the opposing campaign polled for, and was concerned about, his disability, the challenge became how to subtly remind voters of the importance of sight in dealing with the sheer volume of material coming across a legislator's desk. (Brian Freeman, Crystal Castle Graphics)

Can Be Proud Of" was intended to remind the voters that the incumbent had misbehaved while in office. Effective slogans stem from messages that are about the voters and the community. If they reflect on the candidate, they should reinforce the positive: Experience. Leadership. Commitment.

In 2008 a police officer of a neighboring community but living in Ashland, Oregon, wanted to run for city council. He had run and narrowly lost in 2006 after the Green Party attacked his occupation and Republican registration. (In Ashland there's a pronounced anti–law enforcement sentiment, and better than eight in ten voters cast a Democratic ballot.)

With the previous loss under his belt, he tried again in the 2008 election cycle. To remove party bias, he changed his registration to nonaffiliated. His opponent in the nonpartisan race was both a green Democrat and an incumbent with loyal supporters. However, she also had detractors. She was publicly accused of micromanaging city departments and grinding council action to a crawl. Some believed she was responsible for elevating the dysfunctional city government to national attention when a therapist was hired and received $37,000 in tax dollars to help the council work together more productively.[4] With 86 percent of the voters supporting Barack Obama, we looked for a way to piggyback on those coattails without being obvious. To do so, we used the same font as Obama (Gothic), took an Obama lawn sign to the graphic designer to match the colors exactly, and used the slogan "Change Starts Here." Our candidate won by eighteen points.

For a local restaurant tax to fund wastewater treatment plant upgrades and open-space land acquisition, our opposition used the slogan "Don't Swallow the Meals Tax." This is a clever slogan because it works on different levels: People who swallow something are duped, and then, of course, the tax was on food.

A while back, Oregonians put together an initiative to overturn a previously voter-approved ballot measure allowing physician-assisted suicide. The new initiative was well financed, with billboards and lawn signs everywhere. In the upper right-hand corner of the signs, they had the previous measure's number (16) in a circle with a line through it. Next to that was the slogan "Fatally Flawed," and below the slogan was "Yes on 51." While this was clearly a professional campaign, they mistakenly used a very ambiguous approach. Basically, they meant to state that the previously passed ballot initiative (Measure 16, for physician-assisted suicide) was "fatally flawed" and that a yes vote on *this* measure (51) would overturn that one. However, the way the sign was laid out, it appeared that Measure 51, not 16, was "fatally flawed."

During the campaign, an organizer called me to help defeat the referendum. I suggested that the campaign did not need any help; it needed only

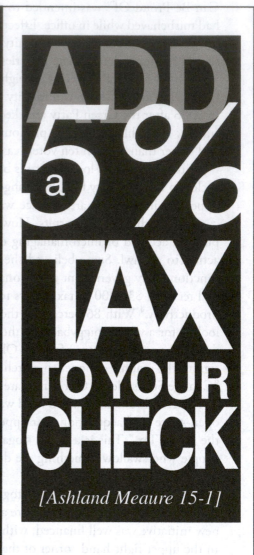

BROCHURE DESIGN BY ERIC BRADFORD WARREN

DON'T SWALLOW THE MEALS TAX

[VOTE NO ON 15-1]

Measure 15-1, Ashland's proposed meals tax, is a regressive tax because:

15-1 IS NOT A TOURIST TAX. THE BURDEN OF THE TAX WILL BE PAID BY YOU, THE ASHLAND CONSUMER.

FOOD IS A BASIC NECESSITY. THIS TAX WILL SEVERELY IMPACT STUDENTS, THE ELDERLY, THE POOR, AND OTHERS ON A FIXED INCOME.

IT IS NOT A LUXURY TAX. BECAUSE OF TODAY'S BUSY SCHEDULES, AN AVERAGE OF 48c OF EVERY FOOD DOLLAR IS SPENT ON PREPARED MEALS OUTSIDE THE HOME.

IT WILL AUTHORIZE INCREASES UP TO 5% WITHOUT FURTHER VOTE FROM THE PUBLIC.

IT IS CONFUSING, DIFFICULT TO MANAGE, AND COSTLY TO IMPLEMENT.

IT IS SHORTSIGHTED. IF THE STATE LEGISLATURE IMPOSES A STATEWIDE SALES TAX IT COULD NEGATE ANY LOCAL SALES TAXES.

IT WILL PUT ASHLAND ON THE MAP AS THE ONLY CITY IN AMERICA TO IMPOSE A MEALS TAX WITHOUT FIRST HAVING AN OVERALL SALES TAX IN PLACE.

ADD a 5% TAX TO YOUR CHECK

[Ashland Meaure 15-1]

Back   **Front**

FIGURE 4.2 "Don't Swallow the Meals Tax" Brochure

Brochure layout: two-panel, front and back, pictured above. Note that the front and top back of the brochure are visually striking, but the lower, dense, reversed type is hard to read. Also note that this brochure went to press with a typo on the front panel. This is not the responsibility of the graphic designer but rather the campaign team. Avoid errors like this by having a number of people proofread the text. (Eric Bradford Warren) to adopt the same slogan that the opposition had used: "Fatally Flawed." Because voters naturally associate a negative slogan with a negative vote, every "Yes on 51" lawn sign, billboard, and commercial would become a "No on 51" pitch. Whether the team members took my advice or came to it themselves, the "No on 51" campaign co-opted the same slogan of the "Yes on 51" campaign, and with very little money the referendum was defeated at the polls—only this time, instead of losing by one point, the referendum lost by twenty. Further, because the "no" campaign co-opted the slogan of the "yes" campaign, those supporting the referendum had to create a new slogan, reprint field and lawn signs, and replace all installed billboards and field signs with the new look. Changing the look of a campaign in the middle of a cycle is a death knell.

As a general rule, you don't want a negative slogan or idea associated with a yes vote ("Fatally Flawed"). It's preferable to have a negative slogan, such as in the meals-tax example given above, associated with a no vote and a positive slogan ("Share the Water") associated with a yes vote on a ballot measure or proposition. In the campaign to overturn the measure allowing physician-assisted suicide, the slogan "Yes on 51" campaign expected too much of the voter.

During my first run for mayor, I used the slogan "Building a Better Community." I chose this slogan because of citywide concerns about growth and development. I wanted a positive slogan that suggested to the voters that more was not necessarily better and that it was "community" that needed to be built, not indiscriminate construction. I also wanted a more inclusive government that involved the citizens in solutions.

People love to throw exclamation points into campaign literature and especially slogans. Avoid this. In one local campaign, a candidate committee and I came to the slogan "It's about integrity." We landed on this because the candidate was hardworking and came across as earnest. It also didn't hurt that her opponent, a local real estate agent, was using his position in the legislature to pass legislation to protect his industry and because of reversals of his votes after which special interests contributed to his campaign coffers. For example, the tobacco industry contributed to his campaign after he changed his mind on a vote to impose a cigarette tax to fund children's health insurance. However, at some point, the period in the slogan turned into an exclamation point: "It's about integrity!" Truly a good slogan ruined.

The following slogans are examples I have pulled from brochures in my files:

"It's about people, not politics"
"Experience * Leadership * Commitment"

"Unbought and unbossed"

"Because nothing counts like results"

"Straightforward, Fair, Effective"

"Tough, committed, fighting for us"

"Experience money can't buy"

"This is about governing . . . and I've done it"

"People over politics"

"The Change Will Do Us Good"

"It's Time for a Change"

"Change We Can Believe In"

"Change starts here"

For more ideas, go to www.presidentsusa.net/campaignslogans.html or http://en.wikipedia.org/wiki/Political_slogan.

Logo

I use the lawn sign image as the logo on my walking piece, Web banner, Facebook page, and TV and newspaper ads. I think it adds continuity to a campaign, conveying a subtle message that it is well organized and connected.

A logo is like a trademark. It can simply be how the candidate's name is written, or, for an issue-based campaign, it can be an image. Figures 4.3, 4.4, and 4.5 present some examples. Obviously, if you have a name like that of Shayne Maxwell, a candidate for the Oregon Legislature, you want to take advantage of it in your logo: "Maxwell for the House." In the Maxwell for the House race, we continually had people say "Good to the last drop" after hearing her name (figure 4.3). It did not hurt that she ran in an area whose residents were predominantly seniors—and undoubtedly still bought their coffee in a Maxwell House can with the slogan "Good to the last drop" across the top. Think about the candidates' name, and come up with creative ways to link it with the office being sought or the campaign, like Audie Bock, who used a play on her name in a reelection campaign for the California State Assembly: "Bock by Popular Demand," or state representative candidate Jeff Barker, who used his dog's image to differentiate himself from his opponent, Keith Parker.

Walking-Piece Development

Up until a few years ago, I used a combination of a brochure and walking piece. A walking piece is basically a mini brochure with no space for a recipient address, stamp, or return address. A brochure typically folds and may

FIGURE 4.3 "Maxwell for the House" Walking Piece

Example of a logo using the candidate's name to piggyback onto a positive corporate slogan. We used this walking piece to get newspaper endorsements to homes in the district; the back had photos, a bio, and individual endorsements. (Crystal Castle Graphics)

have more pictures and more copy—such as endorsement quotes from notable people saying amazing things. However, I now exclusively use a walking piece and size it to fit on half of a sheet of eight-and-a-half-by-eleven-inch paper. Doing so saves money (no folding, and less paper used) and allows the campaign to print on demand from home printers. Although this is an expensive way to print, it can buy a campaign time until it knows what's what. For example, a campaign may not know early in the process if there will be

COMMITTEE FOR THE CARNEGIE

FIGURE 4.4 Example of a Logo for a Campaign to Restore and Expand Ashland's Carnegie Library

The logo builds one idea on top of another. (Design by Crystal Castle Graphics)

FIGURE 4.5 Example of a Logo Using Lettering That Appeals to the American Love of Baseball

(Design by Eric Bradford Warren)

opposition but may still need literature to bring to coffees. Always print on card stock, something in the eighty-pound range; I like 80# Xerox Elite or 80# Vellum Bristol.

In a candidate campaign, the walking piece serves as the principal piece of literature for canvassing, forums, and house parties. It should include photos, a biography, and information that identifies why the candidate would be ideal in public office. If the candidate has previously held office, it will underscore past accomplishments and activities to bring them to the attention of the electorate. Unless the campaign plan calls for developing different pieces for the primary and the general election, the walking piece should be free of partisan politics because it travels with the candidate to all public functions.

In an issue-based campaign, the walking piece may give a sense of time and history reflecting on community goals and ideals. An issue-based walking piece should clearly explain what is before the voters, delineate the potential impacts of yes and no votes, and include testimonials from important community leaders.

Though the campaign committee will help develop the campaign message and theme, you should have only one or two people work with you or the candidate in writing the walking piece. Obviously, you want one who can write. The initial writing takes only a few hours, but it is often followed by many rewrites. These rewrites return to the committee for approval. If the committee does not like what it sees, you need time to make the necessary corrections before delivering the material to the graphic designer and printer.

Copy

The walking piece, like a voters' pamphlet statement, should be no more than 325 words and should include the following:

Occupational background. Include names of companies or jobs held and actual years worked at each—not "27" but rather "1983–2010," that sort of thing. If the candidate has a laundry list, then forgo the years to save on word count.

Prior government experience. This is where the planning commission and such gets listed—not Little League coach or pink lady at the hospital.

Educational background. Include degrees and the universities or schools and years the candidate attended. If he or she did not get a degree, just list the school with no actual dates, and hopefully voters will think a degree was involved.

Military service. If the candidate served in the military, this is important; indicate years and rank. If he or she never served, omit this category.

Community service. This is where the Little League and pink-lady stuff goes; if the candidate received special awards or recognition, bullet-point those here as well.

Proven leadership. Next is a short list of candidate accomplishments that relate to the office sought. For a reelection campaign, list what the candidate and the body on which he or she served accomplished while in office. Bullet-point this stuff, too. People are going to look at the walking piece for ten seconds, so be brief and articulate.

Together we can do more. The next section will offer bullet points regarding issues that your town or community could be doing to make its corner of the world a better place. For example, economic development, dealing with the homeless, upgrading the wastewater treatment plant, placing electric lines underground to prevent future outages, safeguarding the water system by removing dead and dying timber from the watershed, getting sidewalks installed near schools—that sort of thing.

Values we respect. Depending on word count, the final section will consist of two to four short quotes from prominent community leaders. They, not you, will say just how great the candidate is. They, not the committee, will describe the crumbling school or closed library or dilapidated park system that increased taxes will fix in an issue-based campaign. For nonpartisan races, this is where the voter is reassured. For example, if the candidate is a businessperson, the copy will balance that strength with a quote from a credible person who may be considered antibusiness. If the candidate is on the Left, get a quote from someone on the Right. One caution: Do not choose people who are extreme; you want to balance a candidate's weakness with someone just slightly over the line in the other camp. Think about the candidate's strengths versus the opponent's, and enhance your candidate's strengths at your opponent's expense.

Partisan races can easily do that, but if you are well known as a Democrat or Republican, then just get quotes that will activate your base. Use respected people within your base who have a following of their own and are actively engaged in various activities within the voting area; balance geography with quotes of respected people from outside your immediate community.

When I ask people for a quote, I also ask if I can edit it down for space. No one says no to that. If the individual is busy or unsure about sounding articulate or on point, offer to draft a quote for approval. The best quotes come from the heart and often reflect about the candidate in a way that you would never conceive.

Also important to note here is that your endorsements can actually say what you highlighted under "Proven leadership." Indeed, reinforcing what you want emphasized while underscoring humble roots can be powerful: "He was always there for us with great advice, and he set an example by working hard. He's a born leader" (Sally Smith, Borden Foods supervisor).

And now a word from our sponsor. When you complete all the above sections and find you still have space for a few words, the candidate can make a special appeal: "It would be an honor to serve our city. I hope I can count on your vote." Then have the candidate's signature appear on the walking piece under this appeal.

Pictures

Before the campaign literature is laid out, the candidate should search personal files for family photos and visit a professional photographer. If a professional will not volunteer his or her time, this is a good place to spend money; amateurish photos will hurt your campaign. If the first sitting does not produce the right array, ask for a second. Email a head shot to local papers, as you want them to use your photo rather than one generated by their news team. After you're elected, continue this practice.

Pictures break up the text to give the walking piece a substantive feel; include at least one picture of the candidate to increase face recognition. Select other photos to create an image of who this person is. There may be pictures of the candidate at work, with the family, at play (e.g., batting in a softball game or fly-fishing), with seniors, or at a preschool, a public school, a hospital, or a park. Include whatever might both positively connect the candidate with his or her lifestyle and characterize what is important in the community.

Whether the campaign is doing a studio shot or one of the candidate on the stump, be sure to bring extra clothes for different settings. Campaign literature that shows a candidate at a school, at a senior center, in a park, with family, or whatever ostensibly intends to show the individual in his or her everyday life over a period of time; if the candidate is wearing the same clothes in each shot, the result appears contrived and the opportunity to evoke specific emotions is lost.

Avoid photos that picture the candidate standing or sitting coincidentally near a celebrity. Novice campaigners are eager to show they hobnob with the elite and will select pictures that show themselves in the general proximity of a celebrity—elected or otherwise. If you want to use a photo of your candidate with the governor, be sure it is a photo of your candidate with the governor. One walking piece I saw had the candidate looking around a plant that was situated behind the governor, who was being photographed with other people. This is interpreted by the voters for just what it is.

Some candidates when being photographed with a "name" lean toward or tilt their head toward the celebrity ("I'm with him"). This pose suggests weakness on the part of your candidate and may have a subtle but negative influence on the voters.

When selecting photos for issue-based campaigns, look for ones with movement and that elicit emotion. The photos in figure 4.6B were used for funding youth sports programs, water conservation, and state funding for seniors and public schools. The bottom right had the caption "What future do we offer them?"

Urge the photographer to take some pictures of the candidate outside. Change the background, walk toward the camera, sit on a bike, and lean on the handlebars. (This particular pose, with or without the bike in it, makes a great shot.) Arrange for people to meet you and the photographer for a few shots that can be taken outside, in front of businesses, with the backdrop of trees or historic buildings (see figure 4.6A). Capture the candidate in a quiet moment reading over papers, through a window at night burning the midnight oil, conferring with a colleague while leaning over a desk, or engaging with the family from last summer's vacation.

When selecting pictures for either a candidate or issue-based campaign, be sure to look at the whole picture, not just the subject of the picture, especially what lies behind the subject of the photo. A dearth of quality photographs during a campaign puts a strain on everyone. Take care of it early.

Layout

The layout depends on size, how much you want to say, and the quality and quantity of photos. Do not make the mistake of trying to save a hundred bucks by doing this yourself or by using someone just because he or she has a desktop publishing program. Having a professional graphic designer throughout the campaign saves time and eliminates stress.

A good way to get ideas on layout is to go over past political campaign literature. Often you can find the look you want and then emulate that look. Some examples of different types of brochures and walking pieces are presented in these pages, but your best resource will be the politically experienced graphic designer or layout artist.

Photo by Christopher Briscoe

Photo by Cathy Shaw

Photo by Christopher Briscoe

Photo by Marietta Gilmour

FIGURE 4.6A
Examples of Candidate
Photos That Work Well
in Walking Pieces or
Campaign Brochures

FIGURE 4.6B
Examples of Photos
That Work Well in an
Issue-Based Brochure

When selecting photos for
issue-based campaigns, look
for ones with movement and
that elicit emotion. These
photos were used for funding
youth sports programs, water
conservation, and state funding
for seniors and public schools.

The challenge is to arrange your 325 words so as not to overwhelm the recipient. By placing text in boxes, using bullet points, and shading pullouts, the copy becomes easier to see and read.

Avoid long narratives and leave high school accomplishments behind. Same with "born and raised." In my first run for mayor, my opponent had his picture taken in front of the local high school with the caption "When he graduated, he never dreamed he would one day be mayor of Ashland." Candidates love to underscore their longevity in a city, county, state, or region. Voters put very little into presumptive entitlement to an office based on birthright. Similarly, voters care less about experience than you'd imagine. Candidates and committees who want to pack in every inch of history at some point must decide between including everything, with nothing read by the voter, or a partial list, which is read by most. Remember, if George Donner had left either the organ or the wood cook stove behind, his family might have made it over the Sierra Nevada before the snow fell. Finally, brochures designed for mailing can be reconfigured for a walking piece. One will reinforce the other, and the two can be done at the same time by your graphic designer (see figures 4.7 and 4.8).

Voters' Pamphlet

Although much of the voters' pamphlet statement may be dictated by election offices, portions that are not dictated allow for highlighting, italicizing, underlining, and such. Here are ten dos and don'ts to consider when accenting your portion of the voters' pamphlet:

1. Use a professional photo of the candidate and face it toward his or her written submission to the pamphlet. This is where you will use your candidate's best "mug shot." Photos of poor quality get worse when printed in the voters' pamphlet; think DMV.
2. Let others do your bidding through testimonials, and put their names in boldface, not the testimonial. A common mistake is to boldface what someone says about a candidate rather than the endorser's name. When entire lines are boldface in a small area, they will make anything in between the boldface area seemingly disappear into the page. You do not want endorsers' names to disappear. If voters don't know a candidate, they will look for prominent names; make these names easy to find (see figure 4.9).
3. Boldface headings. Voters will often skim a pamphlet, so boldface what you want them to see. The ten-second rule of direct mail applies here

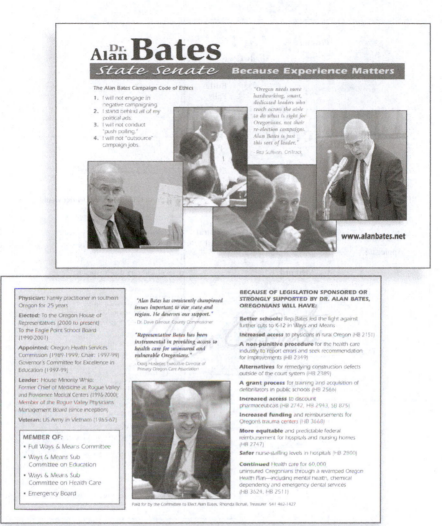

FIGURE 4.7 "Example of a Candidate Walking Piece on Half Sheet of Paper, Both Sides."

This particular walking piece was created from the brochure featured in figure 4.1. Full color. (Crystal Castle Graphics)

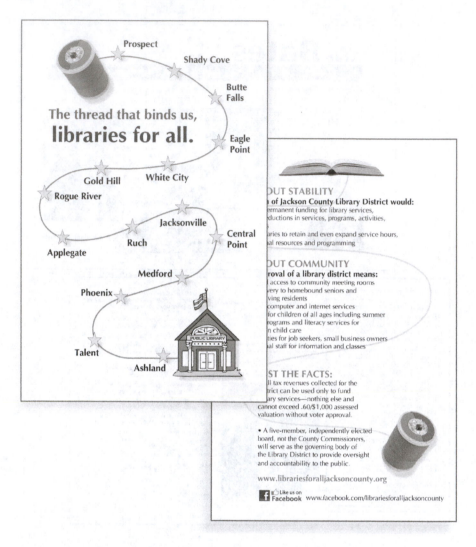

FIGURE 4.8 Example of an Issue-Based Walking Piece Created for a Library District Campaign.

The genesis of the thread connecting the community libraries and the Coats and Clarks thread spool came from a librarian who made bookmarks for each of the libraries located in each of the seven zones; we simply piggybacked onto her idea. (Crystal Castle Graphics) as well. Do not randomly make words boldface in the **middle** of a sentence or a bullet point.

4. Avoid using all caps. An exception may be headings; otherwise, it looks FRANTIC when words are capped in the middle of sentences. Similarly, do not use exclamation points.

5. Do not use narratives. No one cares where you spent your childhood summers or what you were thinking when you moved to your community. Keep the pamphlet crisp with bullet points and breathing space between lines. Break things up.

6. Cite accomplishments. If your candidate has held office and the community is a better place because of legislation he or she designed, highlight those accomplishments. When listing legislation, be sure to place bill numbers next to the claim; this gives it authenticity.

7. Place your website address at the bottom, and place your voters' pamphlet statement on your webpage.

8. Use the available space wisely. Do not bunch everything at the top, leaving white space below. Lay out your submission so it fits comfortably in the available space. Rather than creating distance between lines using the return key on your keyboard, instead go to the "Format" tab in Word and then insert spacing between lines using "Paragraph."

9. Do not use the voters' pamphlet to attack your opponent: Stay on the sunny side.

10. Don't exaggerate; don't lie. Candidates like to beef up their résumés when running for office, and although he or she might get away with that in direct mail or in advertising, knowingly listing false information in a voters' pamphlet is a felony. Nevertheless, there are ways to get the most out of what you have. For example, you attended Harvard as an undergraduate but dropped out before receiving a degree. Later you were accepted into graduate school at Stanford University, solely on the basis of your Graduate Record Examination scores, and there you received a master's degree in communications. Under "Education," you would list "Harvard, undergraduate; Stanford, master's in communication." While voters may assume you received an undergraduate degree at Harvard, you never actually did. If you completed only a couple of years of undergraduate work at a college or university before heading out into the real world, you would simply list the institution without referring to any degree or year of graduation. If you list more than one without a degree notation after any of them, voters will know you attended but never graduated.

Jackson County Library District Director, Position 2

Cathy Shaw

Occupation: Campaign consultant, since 1998; Author: (The Campaign Manager. Running and Winning Local Elections: six editions), since 1996.

Occupational Background: Legislative Assistant, Alan Bates, 2001-2004; Mayor of Ashland, 1989-2000; Development Director, Planned Parenthood of Southern Oregon,1994-1999; Stanford Medical Center, 1981-1983, 1985; Ashland Women's Health Center, 1977-1980.

Educational Background: SOSC (SOU) Credential Program, 1980; UC Davis, Bachelor of Science, Early Childhood Education, 1975.

Prior Governmental Experience: Library Budget Committee, 2015-16; Ashland Community Hospital Board,1998-2000; Mayor of Ashland, 1989-2000; Ashland Budget Committee, 1987-2000; Jackson County Human Services Committee, 1980.

Libraries Matter.

"Cathy brings a thorough knowledge of government and love of libraries as an essential element of a democracy. I am so happy to endorse her; she'll do an excellent job." **Marian Telerski**

"It was Cathy Shaw's strategy that got our library buildings renovated and our district funded. Without reservation, we support her candidacy for the library board." **Jim and Gayle Lewis**

"There are many reasons to support Cathy's candidacy for the library board but the most important is her commitment to bring library management back home." **Karen Starchvick**

"Cathy has exactly the experience the Library needs. She understands local government, knows how to work well with other people, and when it comes to understanding what the people of Jackson County want, she literally wrote the book." **Peter Sage**

"I first met Cathy Shaw during the Medford School Bond campaign; she was organized, hardworking, focused, and a team player—the kind of person we need in this transitional time for our libraries." **Mark Wisnovsky**

"Cathy's commitment and efforts on behalf of our libraries has helped to make our communities better. I'm grateful for her willingness to serve on the Library District Board." **Peter Buckley**

"Cathy's ability to advocate and organize others in pursuit of important issues in our county, especially our libraries, makes her a perfect choice for the board." **Bill Thorndike**

"Please join us in supporting a tested community leader who has contributed so much toward the success of our libraries." **David Lane**

FIGURE 4.9 "Sample of a Nonpartisan Voters' Pamphlet Statement Using Only Endorsement Quotes for Copy."

This Voters' Pamphlet includes former mayors of small cities in the district, business leaders, a former member of the Oregon House, and community leaders with a specific voter following.

State Representative, 5th District

Pam Marsh

Democrat, Independent, Working Families

OCCUPATION: Executive Director, Ashland Emergency Food Bank (2012-present); Co-owner, Green Springs Inn and Cabins (1994-present)

OCCUPATIONAL BACKGROUND: Co-manager, Green Springs Inn & Cabins (1994-2004); Coordinator, Santa Clara County Cities Association (1992-1994); Field Representative, California Legislature (1984-1988)

EDUCATIONAL BACKGROUND: Southern Oregon University, BA 2005; UC Berkley, (1973-1975)

GOVERNMENTAL EXPERIENCE: Ashland City Council (2012-present); Ashland Planning Commission (2006-2012); Ashland Charter Review Commission (2004-2006); Palo Alto, California, Planning Commission (1985-1993)

As an Ashland city councilor I've worked to ensure that city government is transparent, fair, and efficient. Now I am running for State Representative because I know how much government matters. Decisions made by state officials affect the way we govern our communities, run our businesses and raise our families.

With strong leadership, Oregon can:
— Pass legislation that meaningfully reduces greenhouse gas emissions
— Support heath care that emphasizes prevention and provides high-quality services for all
— Fund programs for high-risk families to prevent abuse and prepare young children for kindergarten
— Ensure that high school graduates are prepared to enter college, trade school or the skilled job market

Education is key:
"As the owner of a rural resort, I understand the challenges of running a small business. And as Executive Director of the Ashland Emergency Food Bank, I see the social and financial realities facing families in southern Oregon who are struggling to make it through the month.

"We need to build a sustainable, broad-based economy that offers opportunities for individuals to grow and succeed. Adequate funding for K-12 and continuing support for SOU's transition to a self-governing institution are critical to this region's long-term economic development."
Pam Marsh

"I'm grateful that Pam has stepped up to serve in the legislature. She will be an outstanding representative for our district."
Rep. Peter Buckley

"Pam will continue the open-door policy that's been a hallmark of Peter Buckley's tenure. She's accessible, hardworking and understands the importance of the agricultural economy in southern Oregon."
Mark Wisnovksy, Vintner

Pam.MarshforOregon.com

FIGURE 4.10 "Example of a Partisan Voters' Pamphlet Candidate Statement"

This Voters' Pamphlet, for a partisan race in a heavily Democratic legislative House district, includes a combination of testimonials and proposed areas of focus.

Primary Voters' Pamphlet and Nonpartisan Races

Remember, your objective in the primary is to lock your base. Given that the voters' pamphlet goes to every registered voter and is referred to by most, you need to be in it, whether you have an opponent or not. While your text should keep partisan material to a minimum, those whose names are included in testimonials may be closely aligned with your party. Each testimonial should bring voters on board, from both the name and the text. Here, less is more. On one issue-based campaign, there was a vote to change the Ashland City Charter to a weak-mayor form of government. Opposed to this idea, I initially thought about filling every square inch of the voters' pamphlet just with names in opposition, but ultimately decided that six names were stronger than a long list of hundreds, especially since the six were a former congressman, a sitting state senator, a sitting state representative, a current county commissioner, a well-known and well-liked former radio personality who was also a former county commissioner, and, finally, a former mayor of Ashland. The voters' pamphlet was the entirety of the campaign opposing this shift of power. We turned it away by 28 percent.

General Election Voters' Pamphlet

A statement for the general election voters' pamphlet will look a lot like the one for the primary, except for the candidate statement (see figure 4.10) or testimonial section. For the general election, you are looking for names and statements that will give voters in the other party permission to jump ship on the party and split their ticket or undervote. However, you must also speak to those within your party, so look for balance in the big names you use.

The Takeaway

A walking piece should include enough text to inform the voters but not so much that it overwhelms the recipient at first glance. Use photos to evoke emotion and reinforce the text, ones that alone, without text, could tell your story. And never lose sight that the brochure or walking piece reflects on the campaign in more ways than words and photos: Use paper that feels good to the touch and a layout design that is both inviting and compelling.

The walking piece is key to your campaign. You will walk it door-to-door and hand it out at debates, house parties, and fundraising events. The message must resonate with voters who receive the walking piece, which will state in subtle and not-so-subtle ways why people should vote as you want them to vote. It should also imply why they should *not* vote for your opponent.

Fundraising

Never put your own money into the show.
—*THE PRODUCERS*

He who gives early gives twice.
—*CERVANTES*

IN THIS CHAPTER:

- Early Endorsements = Early Money = Early Media Buys
- Campaign Budget
- Direct Mail for Money
- Special Events
- Candidate Calls to Raise Money
- Calling for Money for Ballot Measures
- Raising Money Online
- Fundraising Through Email
- Tips for Successful Fundraising
- Fundraising Ideas That Take Less Than One Month of Preparation
- The World's Smallest Brochure: Direct Mail That Works
- Thank-You Notes

THIS HANDBOOK SUGGESTS A NUMBER OF WAYS TO STRETCH YOUR campaign dollars. Still, no matter how many volunteers or friends with special talents you may have, eventually you will have to spend money to get your message out. Production and media buys require up-front, cash-in-hand transactions. The US Postal Service will not send mail on a promise, and most places that print anything for campaigns require payment when you pick up the product. Although volunteers can cut your debt load and are a valuable resource, they're not enough.

The bottom line is, if you want to get your message and your candidate's face or name into the public view, you must raise and spend a certain threshold of money to be competitive. What that threshold is depends on your race, the voting population, and which campaign activities you intend to implement.

There are always stories of winners being grossly outspent, but history indicates the inverse, especially as you move up the food chain. However, the down-ballot candidate can often level the playing field with shoe leather and common sense. For example, in a recent election, a local city council candidate ran into his opponent while canvassing, and they struck up a conversation, during which his opponent revealed that she hated canvassing hills and was sticking to the flatlands of the city. He immediately got in his car and drove to the hills, where he systematically canvassed for the rest of the cycle. He eventually won all the precincts in the steepest parts of the city, including his opponent's precinct, and prevailed in the election, even though his opponent had a robust lawn sign campaign, attended thirty meet-and-greets thrown by her friends and neighbors, and outspent him two to one.

Both the message and the quality of candidates (or issues) matter when it comes to raising money. However, campaign organization is a major factor in determining whether contributors are willing to "invest" in your campaign throughout the election cycle. Relationships that develop as a result of the candidate, the campaign team, your message, and your organization will bring in early money and early endorsements from individuals, companies, political action committees, and formal organizations. Indeed, a well-run, well-organized, hardworking, professionally executed campaign does not go unnoticed by the electorate. The voters correctly assess the job a candidate will do once in office by the campaign he or she runs to achieve that office. That is true from president of the United States to the county tax assessor. Further, when voters determine that a campaign is disciplined, they equate that with winning and contribute time and money.

Early Endorsements = Early Money = Early Media Buys

Early money is a way to communicate to the public that a cause or candidate has the necessary support to pull off a win. Unfortunately, contributions from individual donors tend to arrive late in a campaign, as things heat up. When supporters see the campaign in the paper and on television or hear it on the radio, they know this takes money. What they may not realize is that media time must be bought weeks in advance. *Early money is critical to*

CAMPAIGN ACTIVITY	COST IN DOLLARS
Brochure	
Layout and design 110.00	
Printing (7,500 full color)..495.00	
Lawn Signs	
Design 100.00	
Printing (250 @ $2.24 each-2 color-two sides) 560.00	
Wickets@ $1.00 ea 250.00	
Voter lists from County for absentee, GOTV, or	
access to voter activation network 50.00	
Direct Mail: 1 piece: postcard (saturated)	
Postage, layout, mail charge...3,000.00	
Photocopying, misc. office supplies..60.00	
Candidate Photo Session...165.00	
Voters' Pamphlet 300.00	
TOTAL...$ 5090.00	

FIGURE 5.1 "Example of a Campaign Budget for a Candidate in a Small-City Race"

a successful media campaign. That's why many candidates take out personal loans to get their campaigns rolling.

The urgency to raise money for media buys changes with each election cycle and is influenced by other races on the ballot that may be competing for media time. For example, down-ballot races in an area with competitive November campaigns may have to buy television by August to secure time for the general election.

Know the law: In some states, you may not legally begin collecting money until you have filed with the county clerk, city recorder, elections office, or secretary of state. However, from the moment you decide to run or work on a ballot measure, you can begin calling and lining up pledges that will come in as soon as you file.

Campaign Budget

Putting together a cursory budget sheet based on the activities you intend to conduct throughout the campaign is relatively straightforward; all it takes is a few phone calls. Figure 5.1 is an actual budget sheet from a local city council race. This race covered a city of 19,000 people and 8,000 homes. There was no TV or radio advertising or paid staff.

If your budget is tight, consider omitting direct mail; that means you could run a campaign of this size for two thousand dollars. However, if you're intent

CAMPAIGN ACTIVITY	COST IN DOLLARS
Direct Mail	
Fundraiser letter: 1,000 pieces, three times	
Design	300.00
Printing and postage, plus remit envelope	3,000.00
Targeted mailer: black-and-white, 25,000 pieces	
Design	300.00
Printing and mailing	5,000.00
Walking piece: 5½ x 8½, color, 30,000 pieces	
Design	300.00
Printing	2,000.00
Precinct Analysis	900.00
Voters' Pamphlet	300.00
Lawn Signs (600)	2,400.00
GOTV	
Voter registration database from county	100.00
GOTV inactive reports (four reports)	400.00
Data consultant; mapping, GOTV $3K/mo	15,000.00
Media Advertising	
Facebook ad & testimonial development	12,000.00
Cable buys	0.00
Network buys	0.00
Radio development: five spots at $250 each	0.00
Newspaper (small local only)	125.00
Facebook and Online Advertising	20,000.00
Other Advertising	
Insert in chamber newsletter	0.00
Car/business signs, 500 pieces	0.00
Campaign Management ($5,000/mo for 5 months)	25,000.00
Office Supplies	200.00
Celebration Party	800.00
TOTAL	**$88,125.00**

FIGURE 5.2 Example of a Countywide Issue-Based Campaign Budget

on sending direct mail, note that printing costs have gotten very competitive, so go online to find the best deal. Be sure you print only once; multiple short-run printing jobs will really drive up your costs. You can also save money by organizing and sending the direct-mail piece through your campaign clerical team. The post office will give you particulars about how to bundle and how many it can handle in one day. Chapter 8, "Targeting Voters," includes a step-by-step process for sending your own direct mail.

Figure 5.2 is the budget from a countywide issue-based campaign. This county covers about 2,000 square miles and has about 180,000 residents (approximately 100,000 registered voters). Note that newspaper, television, and radio advertising has zeroed out, as Facebook advertising allows more reach to a targeted audience. By the end of the campaign, you can be spending some real money on Facebook, so hit it early before competition heats up.

Figures 5.3, and 5.4 are examples of budget components for a state senate race. Figure 5.3 is the expense portion, figure 5.4 the income portion.

Interestingly enough, by 2012 direct mail moved to the back of the bus in part because voters are numb to it but also because of the general expense. Similarly, TV has become so fractured that it, too, is decreasing in effectiveness. By 2016 we dropped all radio, TV, and print media for down-ballot races—even countywide races. Print media has gotten prohibitively expensive, and penetration can be low. For example in my area, the two newspapers have about a 10 percent reach.

Issue-based campaigns do not receive a political ad rate and pay full freight on TV, so TV advertising in an issue-based campaign for anything other than well-financed statewide races is out. Meanwhile, social media and online advertising have stepped up as better tools, especially for the down-ballot campaign.

In 2014 we generated testimonials for Facebook with interviews of individuals prominent in their field. The 1:20 videos cost close to $5,000 each (generally what a TV spot costs to produce), and we produced six of them that were directed to targeted voters by interests. For example, two were farmers, one was a home health care provider, two others testified regarding important bills passed by the member up for election, and another was candidate testimony taken from a forum on climate. All were powerful and heartfelt. We targeted according to audience interests and pumped a lot of money into getting them viewed. When viewership started to decline, one was pulled and replaced by the next one that targeted another audience by interest. By the end of the campaign, as we approached Election Day, we were spending $1,000 a day on Facebook. The budget allocated $10,000 for Facebook ads (figure 5.3), but we ended up closer to $30,000.

Because Facebook misses a lot of the senior population who still watch network television, I farmed out all of our TV production and buys. Sadly, the ads were of poor sound quality—a shotgun mic was used rather than a lapel mic—and unimaginative. But at least they were expensive. Still, farming out the television ad production and buys can save a lot of headaches and allow the manager and team to focus the campaign in more productive ways.

Fact is that much of the lobby will give money only to vendors, not directly to a campaign. I assume it's a way for people to grease each other's palms while saying to donors, "See, we sent this or that mail piece that won the election." If you're working on a campaign where direct mail, television, and

CAMPAIGN ACTIVITY	AMOUNT	CAMPAIGN ACTIVITY	AMOUNT
Walking piece		**Advertising**	
Lay-out & design	200.00	**Radio**	
Photography	500.00	Spanish	2,000.00
Printing: 20,000 pieces	700.00	Production (2 spots)	500.00
		Television	
Direct mail (small issues, very targeted)		Production	
Education	TBD	Buys	56,000.00
Health care	TBD	(Fox, Cable, Network)	
Environment	TBD	**Online**	
Jobs and the economy	TBD	Spotify	1,000.00
Activation	TBD	Pandora	1,000.00
Total not to exceed:	45,000.00	Webpage ads 6	6,000.00
		Facebook advertising	10,000.00
Polling		**Print**	
Bench mark poll: Senate leadership	In-kind	LTEs only	
Tracking Polls	5,000.00	**Voters' pamphlet**	500.00
Research		**Office supplies**	
Candidate	3,250.00	Postage, pens, software,	2,000.00
Oppo	1,250.00	Telephone burners	500.00
		Staples, envelopes, etc.	2,000.00
Lawn signs		Printer cartridges	1,500.00
Design & layout (done)			
Printing	$2,400.00	**Headquarters**	
Wickets (harvested)		Rent,	1,625.00
		Burner phones	300.00
Field signs (printed)			
		Fundraising	
Staff		10 coffees @ $300 ea	3,000.00
Campaign manager	26,000.00	Mailings	2,400.00
Deputy / fundraising	20,000.00	Postage for t-you notes	1,000.00
Field op	17,000.00		
Lists and mapping	15,000.00	**Senate leadership pledge**	35,000.00
Treasurer	1,000.00		
GOTV webpage management	5,000.00	**Total:**	**$330,525.00**
Paid canvassers	TBD		
		Local fundraising	(27,000.00)
Volunteer support		Already expended	(8,000.00)
Food, refreshments	1,000.00	Cash on hand	(127,103.49)
Supplies	1,000.00		
Paper	300.00	**Must raise**	**$168,422.00**

FIGURE 5.3 Example of an Expense Budget for a State Senate Campaign

Note: Wickets (harvested) means they were attained from a previous campaign.

FUNDRAISING ACTIVITY	COST IN DOLLARS	ANTICIPATED INCOME IN DOLLARS (AND AMT. IN BANK)
Donor/volunteer mailing (600 pieces)	600.00	6,000.00
Physician mailing (500 pieces)	500.00	6,000.00
DO mailing (200 pieces)	200.00	4,000.00
State/nation physician mailing (1,000 pieces)	500.00	1,000.00
Pharmacists	150.00	1,000.00
Local education association		3,000.00
Nurses' association		20,000.00
League of environmental voters		TBD
State education association		TBD
Pledges		14,600.00
Money in the bank		90,840.00
Deposit 8/27		3,475.00
Events		
Chiropractors		2,000.00
Portland physician event		3,000.00
Local physician event		1,000.00
Optometrists (20 pieces)		1,000.00
Owed for Medford fundraiser	1,000.00	
Misc. gatherings	1,000.00	2,000.00
Donations from other senate members- _____		10,000.00
TOTAL	3,950.00	168,915.00

FIGURE 5.4 Example of a Fundraising Budget for a Physician's State Senate Campaign

radio are all unnecessary expenses, you run the risk of upsetting a whole lot of people who have car and house payments on their second and third homes in Hawaii who want to send mail and purchase airtime after charging a lot for lousy ads. Take it from me: Don't fight it. Decide where their one-size-fits-all strategies will do the *least* harm (television that no one sees and direct mail that no one reads) and let them have at it. *But* be sure to have the final checkoff on all their work.

Finally, to estimate how much money your campaign will need, consider talking with people who have previously run a similar race. Some will have budgets with predicted and actual money spent. Some state election offices have contributions and expenditures by race on file, and a little time with these records provides an opportunity to reconstruct what was spent, and where.

Figure 5.5 is a template of a budget sheet you can use or modify for your purposes. Many local campaigns are too small and underfunded to have a

Campaign Activity	Amount	Campaign Activity	Amount
Walking piece		Lawn signs	
Layout & design		Layout & design	
Printing		Printing	
Photography		Field signs	
Staff salaries		Printing, shipping	
Campaign manager & other staff		Lumber or metal stakes, etc. for installation	
Treasurer		Office supplies	
Headquarters		Postage, pens, software	
Rent, phones, etc. (list it all)		Telephone, fax	
Website		Staples, envelopes etc.	
Facebook & online advertising		Television	
Direct mail (do this for each piece)		Production	
Layout and design		Buys	
Printing		(Again, use the ad rep of each station to set up a schedule and budget according to exposure you want. Put total here.)	
Postage		Radio	
Lists and labels (or)		Production	
Mail house (they handle labels, postage)		Buys	
Misc. Printing		Fundraising expenses	
Bumper stickers		Staples, envelopes, etc.	
Flyers		Invitations, layout, printing	
Body badges (canvassers & volunteers)		Postage	
Letterhead, envelopes		Decorations	
Print Advertising (I would run a separate budget sheet for print advertising and include the number of ads, the size of ads, and the cost of each with reductions as to the number of runs)		Prizes	
Polling		Volunteer support	
Benchmark polling		Food, refreshments	
Tracking poll		GOTV	
		Voter ID lists	
		Absentee lists	

FIGURE 5.5 Sample Budget Form

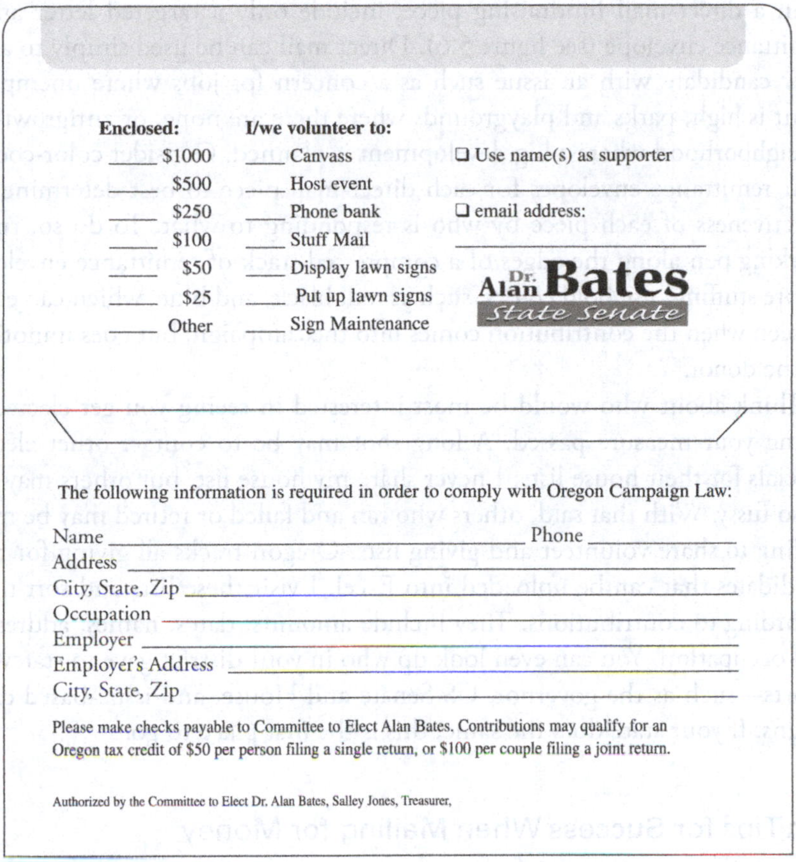

Enclosed:	I/we volunteer to:	
_____ $1000	_____ Canvass	❏ Use name(s) as supporter
_____ $500	_____ Host event	_____
_____ $250	_____ Phone bank	❏ email address:
_____ $100	_____ Stuff Mail	_____
_____ $50	_____ Display lawn signs	
_____ $25	_____ Put up lawn signs	**Dr. Alan Bates**
_____ Other	_____ Sign Maintenance	*State Senate*

The following information is required in order to comply with Oregon Campaign Law:

Name _____ Phone _____

Address _____

City, State, Zip _____

Occupation _____

Employer _____

Employer's Address _____

City, State, Zip _____

Please make checks payable to Committee to Elect Alan Bates. Contributions may qualify for an Oregon tax credit of $50 per person filing a single return, or $100 per couple filing a joint return.

Authorized by the Committee to Elect Dr. Alan Bates, Salley Jones, Treasurer,

FIGURE 5.6 Example of a Remittance Envelope

remote campaign headquarter or even staff. However, I included a staff section just in case you need it. Feel free to photocopy or scan this page and modify it to fit your budget needs.

Direct Mail for Money

While direct mail can help create a relationship between your campaign and the voter, it is also an opportunity to raise money where those relationships are established. Given that efficient direct mail requires a mailing list of an already identifiable group of voters, I prefer to see which lists I can get and then formulate a letter or mail piece that will appeal to those voters. Remember, *your direct mail is only as good as the list to which it is sent.* Carefully match your appeal to the people you are targeting.

In a direct-mail fundraising piece, include only a targeted letter and a remittance envelope (see figure 5.6). Direct mail can be used simply to align your candidate with an issue such as a concern for jobs where unemployment is high, parks and playgrounds where there are none, or antigrowth in a neighborhood where a big development is planned. Consider color-coding your remittance envelopes for each direct-mail piece to best determine the effectiveness of each piece by who is responding to what. To do so, run a marking pen along the edges of a compressed stack of remittance envelopes before stuffing; use bold colors, such as red, black, and blue, which can easily be seen when the contribution comes into the campaign, but goes unnoticed by the donor.

Think about who would be most interested in seeing you get elected or seeing your measure passed. A long shot may be to contact other elected officials for their house lists; I never share my house list, but others may not be so fussy. With that said, others who ran and failed or retired may be more willing to share volunteer and giving lists. Oregon tracks all giving for filed candidates that can be uploaded into Excel. I visit these lists and sort them according to contributions. They include amounts, dates, names, addresses, and occupation. You can even look up who in your district gave to statewide efforts—such as the governor, US Senate and House, and issue-based campaigns. If your state does the same, this is the first place to go.

Ten Tips for Success When Mailing for Money

1. Solicit only targeted lists.
2. Always include a remittance envelope (figure 5.6).
3. Use quality paper stock and printing. Keep graphics and fonts simple and clean.
4. Personalize the letter: "Dear Suzi" works better than "Dear Friend," and always include a PS. The PS should not be a throwaway; this is often the only thing that is read in a fundraising letter, so make it count.
5. Keep the letter short: I use a single piece of heavy-weight paper, laid out in landscape, cut in half, then folded in half. This way each piece of paper will generate two letters of solicitation and looks like a greeting card from the outside. (Note that this size restricts your ability to have the contributor's name and address at the top—only a "Dear Bob and Mary" will fit; that means everything must be kept in order.) The front of the folded half sheet can be simply a picture of the candidate or a list of accomplishments; a report card of sorts (see "The World's Smallest Brochure: Direct Mail That Works" in this chapter).

6. Use a size of envelope that does not scream junk mail; six and a half by four and a half inches (number 6) works best. This size envelope will comfortably hold the folded half sheet of paper and your remittance envelope. You want everything to match, so since the remittance envelope is always white, make both the letter and the envelope white as well. Avoid using business-size envelopes (number 9).

7. Personalize the envelope: Have volunteers hand-address or select a font that gives the appearance of a hand-addressed envelope when printing your list directly onto it. Don't print your picture on the outside of the envelope.

8. For fundraising direct mail, first-class stamps get a far better response rate than bulk, but there are some pretty classy bulk-mail stamps out now. Placing the stamp so it is slightly crooked also helps with the response, as it indicates a human placed it. For non-fundraising direct mail, I use a bulk-mail permit number that gets printed in the upper right-hand corner when everything else gets printed. Have the graphic designer create a sort of canceled-stamp look with the bulk-rate number. Check out the bulk-mail stamp I use in figure 4.1. For saturated pieces (mail that goes to every household in a postal route), covered in Chapter 8, "Targeting Voters," the post office has other criteria.

9. Print the return address on the *flap* of the envelope with only the address: Do not print the candidate's name or place a campaign logo on the envelope, just an address. Printing the return address on the flap gets the recipient one step closer to opening the envelope and potentially giving. Omitting the candidate's name and logo keeps everything clean and unrecognizable as political mail. By the way: I make the return address on the envelope that of my data team member, so lists can be updated if mail is rejected. The remit envelope address is that of the treasurer, so deposits are made promptly; after the deposit, the remit envelope goes to the data team, where pertinent information is gathered and entered.

10. A direct-mail piece followed up with a phone call substantively increases your response rate.

Determine a Baseline Budget for Direct-Mail Solicitation

1. Decide how many mail pieces you intend to send throughout the campaign and schedule those on your campaign plan.
2. Look at some other direct-mail pieces you like, and get a cost estimate for layout and design.

3. Decide which groups you are mailing to, and then determine the number of households that will receive the piece; this helps dictate the budget.
4. Use this number to figure your printing and mailing costs for each piece. With a first-class stamp plus remit and folded eighty-pound paper, they will run around one dollar each. However, with bulk mail and cheap paper, sixty-five to eighty-five cents each is a good ballpark figure.
5. Multiply the per-piece cost by the number of direct-mail pieces you want to send.

Special Events

Special events are campaign-sponsored activities intended to raise money and support for the campaign. Although I have had many successful special events for campaigns, given the campaign time expended for the return and the fact that people who attend are usually supporters who have already given and have every intention of voting for the candidate or cause, you will find that the more efficient fundraising effort goes to dialing for dollars, direct-mail solicitations, and coffees. Nevertheless, it is important to stress that special events are not just about raising money; they increase public visibility and education, energize volunteers, and strengthen bonds.

When approached as an opportunity to advertise the candidate and cement relationships, special events can be worth the necessary resources. But do not underestimate the commitment involved and the strain special events put on the campaign committee, the volunteers, and the candidate. Even if someone other than the campaign committee is sponsoring the event, you need to be ready to help to avoid poor turnout. If it looks as if an event will have marginal attendance, have the field op or clerical team call through the list of invitees. Know that one-third of those who say they will attend tend to no-show. Cancel or postpone events (including coffees) where potential attendance looks poor.

Holding a Special Event

Preparation for events takes place in four stages:

1. Define
2. Plan
3. Promote
4. Conduct

Tips for handling each of these stages are discussed below.

1. Define the purpose and type of event. Be clear about the purpose. Is it to attract donors, raise money, raise support, thank volunteers and supporters, or just get the word out on the measure or the candidate? Consider your budget when deciding what type of event to hold; figure roughly what it will cost the campaign and what income it is likely to generate, and then ask yourself if it is worth it. Don't forget to consider the economic climate in the community. When considering an event, always ask: Does this make sense? Does it fit? Does it feel right?

2. Plan the event. The location must be secured; often availability of the venue will dictate the date of the event. For indoor events, avoid using a huge hall or room unless you are expecting a huge crowd. When selecting locations, I look for places where rooms can be closed off in case of poor attendance. No matter how many people come, the event should appear well attended and successful, leaving attendees with the impression that just the number expected came.

Some events require licenses or permits from local government. The theme of the event, whether it is a candidate luncheon or auction for a school bond, now influences the details of the event.

Create a timeline and budget, to ensure things are done and in the proper order. If you assign one person to oversee or assist the sponsor, be sure he or she has some experience or the right personality; provide ample volunteer help.

Here is a list of the things that could be included in a budget:

- Site rental
- Food
- Drinks
- Rental (sound system, tables, chairs)
- Printing
- Supplies
- Mailings
- Entertainment
- Professionals
- Parking (if it is difficult, you will need valets; high schoolers work well for this task)
- Advertisements
- Decorations
- Insurance
- Fees

- Use permits
- Liquor licenses
- Cleanup
- Awards, door prizes
- Thank-you mailing

Know the law: Prohibitions against holding political fundraisers in public buildings must be considered. Official government seals are prohibited on campaign materials. Know whether there are other community events that might conflict, such as a graduation ceremony or the annual Chamber of Commerce dinner. And know what may compete on TV, such as major sporting events.

3. Promote the event. Promotion of an event must coincide with the type being held. For example, printed invitations with a telephone follow-up might work well for a formal dinner (always include a remit with an invitation), while a yard sale may just require flyers around town and an ad in the local paper. Whatever the means, people must be assigned to accomplish it. Invitations must be printed; flyers must be designed, printed, and distributed; ads have to be written and delivered. All this takes time and people, and you will need to plan accordingly.

To promote a special event properly, have a target audience in mind and determine where to get lists of the people in your target audience. A narrow focus, such as teachers, doctors, or human-service advocates, may necessitate only acquiring mailing lists from the special-interest groups these people belong to or support. If your audience is broader, as it would be for a neighborhood bake sale, you can make a list from a general source, such as your voter database.

4. Conduct the event. Arrive early: Early access provides an opportunity to set things up and test all systems before people arrive. Once people start to arrive, your focus is on hospitality. How you greet people and work with them will set the tone of the event. Allow adequate time for the candidate to circulate. Do not schedule or allow the candidate to "help" operate the event; his or her only job is to mingle with supporters. If it is a large event with many tables, leave one open seat at each table. This allows the candidate, spouse, campaign manager, or other prominent attendee to comfortably sit and authentically engage for a moment at each table. At the door, have sign-in sheets, remittance envelopes, and name tags. Place a name tag below an attendee's right shoulder, where it can be read discreetly by the candidate as he or she shakes the attendee's hand. Bring lawn signs for attendees to install back home.

Always keep track of those who did so for postelection retrieval. Thank everyone, even the people who sold you things. Assign individuals to help with cleanup: Never leave an individual to clean up alone.

Candidate Calls to Raise Money

Direct contact by the candidate remains the quickest, cheapest, and most effective way to raise money. It is very difficult for people to turn down the candidate on a direct ask. When calling, do not sound apologetic. Remember, as the candidate, you're willing to do a job that few want to do. If people support your core values, ideas, and effort, they must show that support by contributing to your campaign. While the campaign manager can call for moderate amounts of money, the calls to major donors should be conducted by the candidate or surrogate such as a spouse, a sibling, or a parent.

First put together a three-ring binder that has individual sheets of all those who will be called. Each individual should include phone number, address, giving history, party registration, employment, as well as what name the candidate should use when speaking with the donor (is it Katherine, Kathy, Katy, Kate, Kit, or Kay?). Because it is so difficult to get a candidate to actually do this, schedule time each day to make the calls and assign a person to assist with the task. The assigned campaign worker stays with the candidate throughout the call time and makes notes on the call sheet for the candidate, such as previous attempts to call and revealed information from the donor that may be referenced in future phone calls: "How's your mother? She was sick last time we spoke."

Calling for Money for Ballot Measures

When fundraising for ballot measures, it is sometimes easier to raise money for a specific item, such as lawn signs. Let people know what you are trying to buy and how much it will cost, so they can contribute accordingly. For example, I might tell people that I am trying to raise $3,500 for a last-minute ad campaign and ask what they can give toward it. If you are going to use a phone bank for fundraising, use just a few people who are committed and are identified with the measure in the community. Provide each caller with a list of the people you want called; the list should include their giving history along with their phone numbers.

Since people prefer to sign on to something that's going to fly, I tell potential donors that we are *X* dollars away from our goal. Keep track as pledged dollars roll in, and if the campaign hasn't received the check within a week, remind the donor with either a phone call or an email.

In general, a fundraising solicitation is the quickest and easiest way to raise money for ballot items, but it requires a good list and clerical team.

Raising Money Online

Given the online fundraising success of the McCain campaign in 2000, the Dean campaign in 2004, the Obama campaigns in 2008 and 2012, and the Sanders and Clinton campaigns in 2016, as well as online giving during national crises, Web-based fundraising must look like the answer for easy, cheap money. After all, it doesn't involve stamps, printing, folding, stuffing, or a clerical team.

According to Blue State Digital (BSD), retained by Obama "to manage the online fundraising, constituency-building, issue advocacy, and peer-to-peer online networking aspects of his 2008 presidential primary campaign," by October 2008 better than half of Obama's eventual $750 million raised came through the Obama website using the BSD online-tools suite.[1]

However, before you opt out of the inefficient and costly means of raising campaign dollars through direct mail and events, consider this: Although there will always be exceptions, online contributions for down-ballot races are a relatively small part of a campaign's overall income stream.

In 2008 former Speaker of the Oregon House Jeff Merkley (D) challenged incumbent and Republican Gordon Smith for the US Senate. In that race, Merkley raised and spent a little more than $6 million to Smith's $13 million.[2] In a recent interview, Jon Isaacs, Jeff Merkley's campaign manager, explained that Merkley received less than 16 percent from online donations (compared with Dean's 2004 and Obama's 2008 online contribution percentages of 53 percent) and that this amount was only after the campaign received national attention that Smith was vulnerable. For now, down-ballot campaigns should add the Internet to the fundraising toolbox while continuing to employ more traditional fundraising methods such as events, direct mail, and dialing for dollars. The following are ten tips to help your online fundraising efforts. These tips are based on observations by David Erickson of the e Strategy Internet Marketing Blog.[3]

1. Make it easy to contribute by allowing supporters to donate small amounts of money, $20 or less. Lowering the barrier attracts more donors.
2. Create multichannel marketing: Place donate buttons everywhere— within Internet ads, social networking profiles, or in blog posts. This provides as many opportunities as possible for people to contribute.
3. Use spot color to make the donate buttons pop on the website.

4. The website should be able to reload the donation form with information the donor gave previously (name, employment, address, zip code, and phone number). Small contributors often give repeatedly and do so at times impetuously, following an irritating comment by the opposing candidate or in support of something your team has said or done. Make it easy.

5. Include next to the donation form a short video of the candidate underscoring the importance of the donor's support.

6. The design of the donation form is important. Place labels so the donor does not have to look back and forth to fill in data, and include only the information necessary to complete the donation. The submit button should be obvious.

7. This is not the time to gather unrelated information about your contributor. You want the donor doing only one task: giving money. Remove all distractions, and omit from the donation page any links that will take the donor away from it.

8. Give donors opportunities to give incrementally, $20 per month or whatever amount they choose, so multiple donations continue to come in with little or no campaign effort.

9. People are more likely to give to a candidate or a cause that their friends endorse, so build in incentives to encourage supporters to "bundle" their friends for giving. Besides bringing in money, it also expands a campaign's financial network.

10. Your website is integral to the success of fundraising. People will not give to a cheesy website. It must look professional; colors, font, layout—all this matters. Spend some time and money on the design of your site if you hope to attract money with it.

For more ideas, check out "The Political Consultants' Online Fundraising Primer" from the Institute for Politics, Democracy, and the Internet (www.ipdi.org/UploadedFiles/online_fundraising_primer.pdf).

Fundraising Through Email

With the introduction of Facebook, Twitter, and donation buttons on webpages, campaigners have mistakenly moved email to the back of the line. While Facebook is a fabulous tool for mobilizing large numbers of supporters for your cause in a short amount of time, I've found that email has remained a mainstay for raising money quickly and efficiently, but only if done in a very personal way. Recently, I helped a candidate retire a small campaign debt following a losing bid for a local office. Contacting only those who had previously contributed to the campaign and individuals I knew personally, I sent a two-paragraph appeal that was individually addressed to each of the potential contributors to keep it personal. Of those I emailed, 19 percent said no, 16 percent did not respond, and 64 percent contributed. Within the two paragraphs I placed a "date certain" (about two weeks out) when the campaign would be permanently closed; doing this gave individuals a sense of urgency to respond. After receiving the contribution, I emailed the individual to acknowledge that the check arrived and thanked the contributor along with the acknowledgment. As with all successful fundraising, email solicitations work best if they are as follows:

1. Short
2. Personalized
3. Personal (the individual making the request knows the potential contributor)
4. Clear about intent (to retire a debt, raise money for a display ad, fund printing of a last-minute flyer—that sort of thing)
5. Finite—that is, they have a timeline (as in the example above, let a potential donor know when the event, ad, flyer, or whatever you're trying to fund will occur)

Tips for Successful Fundraising

Campaigns are about emotion, not intellect.

- Be visionary, present a vision, address opportunity. People need to feel that investing in a campaign will make life better, both now and in the future. Make your case larger than the office you seek or the program you hope to fund.
- Invite donors to invest in leadership, solutions, and vision. Through a candidate or a campaign, people are making an investment in their community. Generally, people contribute to a campaign or candidate because they believe that they will get something in return. Describe to the potential donor expected change a victorious election will bring. Use issues that are in front of voters.
- Do not look at fundraising as though there is just so much money and no more. Money flows like a river; don't think of it like a pond. There's plenty of money if you can show that the gifts will be used wisely. This applies to both candidate and issue-based campaigns.
- Sell hope. You're offering something that the voter wants: opportunity, vision, solutions, parks, better schools, less traffic, lower crime rates,

cleaner air, or whatever. Look at your campaign as the vehicle for the voters to get what they want. Charles Revson, founder of Revlon, said, "In the factory, we make cosmetics. In the stores, we sell hope."

- There's a difference between an underdog and a losing effort. People want to help an underdog but usually will not help finance a lost cause. Presenting your campaign as an underdog suggests that people are investing in the American Dream.

- Stay on message. Your message should always be at the center of every appeal. Incorporate it into the ask while keeping the targeted donor's profile and interests as the focus.

- Be organized. Because people equate organization with winning, by showing a strong organizational core, you are more likely to get people to give.

- Think community. Community campaigns are the most successful. Such a campaign presents issues that people understand. It presents solutions, involves volunteers, and encourages investment in the future. Do not talk about the mechanics of the campaign. The candidate or campaign should represent opportunity, solutions, answers, and the ability to meet community needs.

- Don't be afraid to ask for money. Asking for money is how you fund a campaign.

- And finally, never think of fundraising as begging. As John D. Rockefeller once said, "Never think you need to apologize for asking someone to give to a worthy object, any more than as though you were giving him an opportunity to participate in a high-grade investment."

Fundraising Ideas That Take Less Than One Month of Preparation

Candidate announcement. When it comes to first-time candidates, who need money yesterday, it seems presumptuous to just send an appeal letter out of nowhere. To get around that, I send an invitation to an announcement party for the candidate (see figure 5.7). The invitation is printed on card stock, landscape, and two-up, like the world's smallest brochure, shown in figure 5.8. The purpose of the invitation is to actually get a remit in the hands of as many probable supporters as possible. In the invitation I urge the recipient to return the remit (with or without money) to give the campaign an indication of support, willingness to host a lawn sign, and so on.

In an introductory event, don't suggest a donation amount or impose a cover charge. First, if the candidate is unknown, people will not attend rather than blindly give money. Second, if the candidate performs well and the

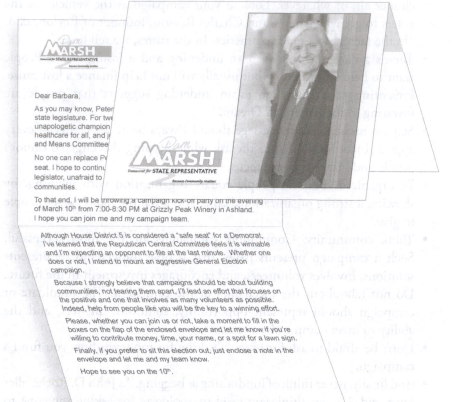

Dear Barbara,

As you may know, Peter [...]
state legislature. For tw[...]
unapologetic champion[...]
healthcare for all, and j[...]
and Means Committee[...]

No one can replace P[...]
seat. I hope to continu[...]
legislator, unafraid to [...]
communities.

To that end, I will be throwing a campaign kick-off party on the evening
of March 10th from 7:00-8:30 PM at Grizzly Peak Winery in Ashland.
I hope you can join me and my campaign team.

Although House District 5 is considered a "safe seat" for a Democrat,
I've learned that the Republican Central Committee feels it is winnable
and I'm expecting an opponent to file at the last minute. Whether one
does or not, I intend to mount an aggressive General Election
campaign.

Because I strongly believe that campaigns should be about building
communities, not tearing them apart, I'll lead an effort that focuses on
the positive and one that involves as many volunteers as possible.
Indeed, help from people like you will be the key to a winning effort.

Please, whether you can join us or not, take a moment to fill in the
boxes on the flap of the enclosed envelope and let me know if you're
willing to contribute money, time, your name, or a spot for a lawn sign.

Finally, if you prefer to sit this election out, just enclose a note in the
envelope and let me and my team know.

Hope to see you on the 10th.

PS. Grizzly Peak Winery is located at 1600 E. Nevada St. Ashland.

FIGURE 5.7　**Invitation to a Candidate Announcement Party**

Front of a direct-mail fundraising letter for first-time candidates; inside is an
invitation letter to a campaign kickoff event.

crowd swells behind the candidacy, people will give more than any contribution the campaign might suggest to get in the door. For example, if the
admission charge is $25 for a meet-the-candidate event at someone's home,
typically many attendees can give more; however, the campaign will get only
the $25 cover. To lend credibility to a political newcomer, bring in a well-
known political figure, such as the governor, and schedule two events back-
to-back in two cities. The first event can run from 6:00 to 7:30 in one city
and the second from 8:00 to 9:30 in another. Arrange ahead of time for one
or two people at each gathering to announce they have just written a check
for $1,000 and would encourage all to give as generously as possible. In one

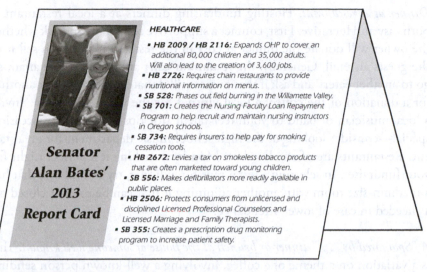

FIGURE 5.8 Front of 'The World's Smallest Brochure'

Front of a direct-mail fundraising letter; inside is a direct-appeal letter.

campaign, more than a decade ago, we raised $10,000 in three and a half hours with this approach; there was no suggested contribution on the invitation, no cover charge to get in, and virtually no one knew the candidate before the events; having the governor introduce the candidate at both events was a big draw.

For down-ballot candidates, this is often the only direct-mail solicitation you will need to send. With a good list, a good turnout, and good responses to the original letter, it can yield enough money to get the candidate to coffees or personal solicitation.

Personal solicitation. The candidate calls for money.

Coffees sponsored by a supporter. These can be easy and quite successful, and they should be ongoing throughout the campaign season. They are a great resource for contributions, finding campaign workers, and obtaining email addresses and lawn sign locations. The drawing card is the combination of the candidate and the hosts of the coffee. As noted, one committee person should oversee house parties, and that individual may also be the one who selects the homes of such gatherings. Good hosts tend to have good lists, but it is also helpful to provide the hosts with a list of all the registered voters living near their home: Encourage hosts to walk invitations to their neighbors for better attendance.

Dinner at a restaurant. Hosting fundraising dinners at a local restaurant is both easy and lucrative. First, contact a supportive restaurant and ask whether the owner will donate the dinner at cost in the restaurant and then sell it to the guests at retail. Generally, the restaurant can't afford the whole affair, so go to another eatery and ask if that owner will donate the dessert, ask another for a donation of the coffee, a local vintner for the wine, and so on. Invite a local musician or band to volunteer talent (for tips) to make the occasion special—consider looking at the high school music department for great talent. Restaurants are often closed on Mondays, making it a perfect night for your fundraiser. In selecting a restaurant for a dinner, try to find one that has a medium-size room with another adjoining it that can be used or closed off as needed in case of lower attendance.

A "Sponsored by . . . " dinner or brunch at the house of someone well known. This is a variation on a theme of a coffee, involving a well-known person sending invitations to well-heeled friends and providing a lavishly catered meal. We have brought in thousands in our small area at this type of dinner.

Theme dinner. These are great fun. First and most important, you need an incredible friend who is willing to open his or her home and prepare the food with other friends. A theme dinner usually will focus on a period in history (such as the turn of the twentieth century), an author or a set of authors, an important leader, and so forth. For example, you might have an evening focusing on Jane Austen. One friend would research her life and prepare some text that may be read throughout (or between) courses of the meal. The meal features the types of foods eaten during that period. A theme dinner can also center on many authors. In this case, your really great friend might prepare favorite dishes of certain authors or dishes featured in books—for example, *Like Water for Chocolate.* We have done this with high school girls and boys acting as the servers (dressed in black and white). We used different people to read appropriate passages from books that pertain to the courses being served.

    As these dinners are a real treat—almost like time travel—and a lot of work, so charge plenty. Make sure you sell enough tickets to make it worth your while before you head out to shop for groceries and spend days cooking. This type of dinner can be sold as an auction item for a specific number of people and a minimum bid; whoever receives the winning bid gets to invite his or her friends to the feast. Another approach would be to auction seats with a limited number of seats on the block. One theme dinner we conducted was an auction item for public television and sold for $5,500.

Small auctions. Approach businesses and friends to get donations and combine donations to make more attractive prizes. Auction a pair of shoes from a local shoe store or a backpack from a mountaineering supply store; find someone willing to give tennis lessons or golf lessons; ask a historian to donate a tour of your town's historic district, a pilot to donate a ride in a private plane, a day of fly-fishing, a rafting trip, and so on. A great auction item that's easy to gather is ninety-nine bottles of wine. Supporters donate single bottles of wine, and wineries and private brewers are asked to donate mixed cases.

Softball tournament. This requires a lot of work and makes very little money, but is great fun and a perfect project for that guy who wants to help but doesn't quite fit in anywhere else. The admission fees go to the campaign.

Yard sale. Speaking of a lot of work, a yard sale is another option. If you're going to plan one, get a huge yard and plenty of donations, old and new. Advertise the great stuff in advance. A successful yard sale will bring in a couple of grand a day and off-load unwanted things in the bargain. However, the setup and cleanup are time-consuming.

Birthday party for the candidate. The price of admission in dollars should be the candidate's age in years. This works best for incumbents.

Raffle. This requires someone to be completely on top of the event, someone who can really track where the tickets are. You need one to three big prizes and some lesser prizes plus a bunch of people to sell tickets. Again, you can combine things to create a big prize, such as dinner for two, plus two theater tickets, after-theater dessert, and a nightcap at a popular spot, or a donated weekend in a cabin at the lake, in the woods, or near a ski resort. Do you know anyone with a condo in Hawaii? If a supporter has a lot of frequent-flyer miles, he or she could donate the required miles to get your winner to the final destination.

"An afternoon with . . . " Have a local celebrity or author put together entertainment or a reading. How about asking the governor to pop in as he or she is moving through town? Have some great donated pastries and assorted hot beverages on hand.

The World's Smallest Brochure: Direct Mail That Works

Most direct mailings have a rate of return of 3 percent to 6 percent without callbacks. Generally speaking, a campaign does not want to send a direct-mail piece that costs more money than it brings in, so the challenge lies in designing a piece that has a higher rate of return and is inexpensive to produce.

People have become very sophisticated at detecting junk mail. To increase the rate of return, the piece must first get opened; second, it must be read (at least in part); and finally, it must be compelling enough to motivate the reader to give. Anything in a business-size envelope (a number 9) with an address label, a bulk-mail stamp, or a meter mark is suspect and apt to be thrown away unopened. So the first task is choosing an envelope size that will increase the odds the recipient will open it.

I've found the size that gets the best rate of return looks like an invitation or a greeting card from a friend; that is, six and a half by four and a half inches (a number 6). This size is large enough to hold a remittance envelope (without folding) and will comfortably hold a half sheet of paper folded in half. Given that a shorter letter is more likely to be read, do not make the mistake of folding an eight-and-a-half-by-eleven-inch sheet in four.

Once the envelope is open, it is important that the piece offer information, be pleasing to the eye, and have a weight and feel that says the recipient is important, without looking lavish or expensive. The challenge, then, is how to make it all fit in a small format.

To accomplish such a package, my graphic designer and I created the world's smallest brochure: a half sheet of eight-and-a-half-by-eleven-inch eighty-pound vellum Bristol, folded in half with a photo of the candidate and a list of his accomplishments and ratings on the front (figure 5.8). The inside had another photo of the candidate and a letter with a PS on the state's tax-refund policy on political contributions; each piece was personally signed by the candidate in either blue or green ink (never use black). The back had an endorsement from the governor. Given the space constraints, we skipped the usual business-letter practice of including the donor's address in the upper left-hand corner. Some letters had a "Dear Friends" salutation, and on others we used no other identifier than the recipient's first name to make it a personalized letter; this created more work, but was worth it. To keep everything looking sharp, the letter, envelope, and remittance envelope were all printed on white. To encourage the recipient to turn the envelope over (one step closer to opening it), I omitted campaign identifiers like the name, slogan, or logo and printed the return address on the envelope flap rather than on the front in the upper left-hand corner.

To test a "Dear Friends" salutation versus a personalized one, I divided the mailing into two parts. The first was sent to five hundred people who had canvassed, had a lawn sign, or volunteered time to the campaign in some way; some had contributed already. This group had a letter that began "Dear

Friends," which allowed me to have the whole thing printed, cut, and folded at a local print shop (be sure to have the paper scored for easier folding). Using a clerical team of sixteen seniors, we hand-addressed, stuffed, sealed, and stamped the envelopes (using bulk, not first-class, postage) in one hour and fifteen minutes. The mailing cost was $425 (85 cents apiece)—for printing, postage, paper stock, layout, and remittance envelopes.

Because the candidate was a physician, I sent the second mailing to one hundred local physicians he knew, either personally or peripherally, using a letter designed to address their interests. This mailing was identical to the "Dear Friends" mailing except for four things: the text of the letter, the personalized salutation, a first-class stamp rather than a bulk stamp, and a computer-generated "handwriting" font on the envelope. A volunteer printed and stamped the envelopes. One side of the letter was printed at a local print shop, and I used my printer to merge-sort the personalized salutation and letter on the other side; I cut and stuffed the letters as they came out of the printer. Changing the postage from bulk to first-class increased the price by 14 cents per piece, but saved an enormous amount of time going to the post office and dealing with the bulk-mail process. The cost of the second piece was $1 each, for a total of $100.

For the five hundred "Dear Friends" letters, the rate of return was 19 percent, with an average donation of $61. This $400 mailing brought in $5,795. The mailing with the personalized salutation and first-class postage stamp had a 53 percent rate of return, with an average donation of almost $97. This $100 mailing brought in $5,125. The two mailings combined realized a twenty-to-one profit. We did not make follow-up phone calls for either mailing.

Given the expense of this mailing, send it only to your best list of supporters, volunteers, and lawn sign hosts. However, I have also sent this format to less targeted lists, and it has always paid for itself.

Also, because there is no room to get in an address or full name of the recipient on this size letter, we've changed a couple of things to make life easier for the clerical team. First, we number the envelopes and the corresponding letter that goes in the envelope. Hiding the number for the envelope is easy: place the number where the stamp will be placed; it gets printed on at the same time the address is printed. For the letter it's a little trickier. I make the number very small and just place it at the bottom of the note or bury it at the end of the candidate's letter heading. Let me stress that with no room for a recipient's return address and full name on the letter, it is incredibly easy to mix up letters and envelopes. Numbering the envelope to correspond with the letter solves that challenge.

Thank-You Notes

With the introduction of computers and desktop publishing, a printed thank-you note does not carry the same weight as a handwritten note from the candidate, his or her spouse, or the campaign manager. Most people know that computers not only can generate a personalized thank-you note but can also print a signature. While a campaign should send a thank-you note or receipt for a contributor's tax records, if you are working with a candidate who is willing to scratch a few lines in his or her own handwriting, it really goes a long way. Besides thank-you notes for contributions, it is important to send notes to volunteers who have gone above and beyond the call of duty and to anyone who hosts a coffee or facilitates a campaign event. For example, I send personal thank-you notes to my neighborhood captains in the GOTV; I use the cartoon graphic located in the GOTV chapter to make small cards on which I jot a personalized, albeit brief, thank-you.

Because thank-you notes are fairly expensive to send, I look at them as an opportunity to strengthen a relationship between the donor and the candidate. To do this, I put together a printed personalized thank-you note for the candidate to sign but will look for some small thing the candidate can add to the note after it is printed. I also go through the lists of contributors with the candidate to identify those he or she knows personally; this doesn't take long and can be done over the phone; keep those notes apart from the rest. If the contributor has been involved with the campaign in some small or large way, attach a Post-it to the thank-you note as a reminder for the candidate. For example, if the campaign receives a contribution from someone who also baked all the cookies for a coffee earlier in the campaign, I tell the candidate to acknowledge that effort one more time in the contribution thank-you note: "Still thinking about those great treats you brought to the coffee last month. Hope all is well, and thanks again."

When responding to contributors from a targeted mailing, such as doctors, teachers, dentists, lawyers, or some other special-interest group, I will include in the body of the thank-you letter updated campaign information so the contributor feels more a part of the inner circle. Only a small portion of a thank-you note is about the gift. The real power of it is to curry the donor for the next "give." In local elections, personal communication with donors is about investing them in the campaign.

In all preprinted thank-you notes, be sure to have the candidate sign in off-color ink that isn't associated with generated signatures; green is best.

For thank-you notes that do not need a contribution receipt, have special stationery that can be printed on demand. On the front may be a picture of the candidate on the campaign trail or a collage of the candidate in different settings. I usually ask my graphic designer to put together the layout and then email it to me so that I can print out the cards as needed. However, if your design uses just one photo, it is pretty easy to drop it in yourself (see figure 5.7).

To generate this stationery, lay it out in landscape format so that each sheet of paper will make two note cards; again, use paper that is slightly heavier, such as eighty-pound vellum Bristol or eighty-pound Xerox Elite. Include matching preprinted, stamped envelopes so that the candidate need only jot a note before the notes are stuffed, sealed, and mailed.

PS. If your campaign is short on money, you can also send thank-you notes by email.

Digital and Social Media

By Sarah Golden

Marketing is no longer about the stuff that you make, but about the stories you tell.

—SETH GODIN, AUTHOR, ENTREPRENEUR, AND MARKETER

IN THIS CHAPTER:

- Digital Strategy
- The Website: Where People Come to You
- Social Media: Where Conversations Happen
    - Facebook
    - Twitter
    - Online Video
- Outreach: Where You Go to People
    - Email
    - Digital Advertising
    - Other Digital Tools

THE DIGITAL WORLD HAS FUNDAMENTALLY RESHAPED EVERYTHING. From how we communicate to how we choose a restaurant and how we get news, we live in a completely changed world.

Campaigns are no exception. In some ways, it's silly to have a chapter about digital campaigning within a campaign book. Digital techniques and tools are now woven through every aspect of campaigns, offering the ability to manage information and people, communicate, create content, fundraise, and get out the vote (GOTV).

But even though the tools have changed, the rules of campaigning haven't: You strive to run an efficient and effective organization, communicate your key messages to potential voters, get people to the polls, and win.

The tips in this chapter are based on the trends from recent elections, and, given the speed at which technological innovation is disrupting things, much of this is likely to change significantly. Because of the quickly changing landscape, we've aimed to keep this chapter focused on larger trends and best practices, as new programs and software will certainly arise and others will die between when this book is published and when you read it.

Because of this, we recommend you take time to research recommendations in this chapter to better understand where the technology is and what it is able to do. Magazines like *Campaigns and Elections* offer good insight into digital trends. We also recommend www.epolitics.com, which does a good job of keeping its finger on the pulse of digital campaign trends.

First, we will take a look at digital strategy, outlining how to think about a healthy digital diet. Your digital strategy should be broken into three broad categories: a place to welcome people who come to you (your website), a venue for two-way communications (social media), and a method to actively reach out to people (email and advertising). Then we'll provide a brief overview of the digital tools that are disrupting how we campaign. This section offers a glimpse into software designed to make life easier, which you should consider implementing at the start of your campaign.

Digital Strategy

Your digital strategy should work hand in glove with your umbrella strategy. A well-defined, adaptable campaign strategy can harness the power of new media to effectively reach specific audiences in personal ways. The following steps are designed to help you think about the through line of your digital strategy and how it can fit into the other tactics and strategy of the campaign.

Creating Your Digital Campaign Plan

At the start of your campaign, consider the following steps to understand what gaps digital campaigning can fill. Revisit this throughout the campaign to ensure you're serving your umbrella strategy. Digital media strategist Colin Delany says digital campaigning always does one of three basic tasks: recruiting, mobilizing, and messaging. Any time you're evaluating a tactic, ask whether it helps you achieve one of those three goals.[1] If the answer is yes, ask

FIGURE 6.1 Jon Ossoff, a candidate in Georgia's Sixth District, aims to recruit followers while inspiring through his vision with a clever hashtag—#FlipThe6th.

yourself if that's the most effective way to achieve that goal. All tactics have an opportunity cost, so use your time wisely.

Step 1: Understand your goals. Of course, you are trying to communicate to voters and get your target audience to vote for your candidate. But along the way, there are other smaller milestones and goals. Create a digital campaign plan that outlines your ultimate goal and identifies smaller interim goals. Getting specific about your intentions and who needs to move to get you there will help you figure out how to get to where you're going efficiently. Some questions to ask yourself include the following:

- Who are you trying to reach? Which demographics and market segments are most important to move? What do you want them to do? For example, you may want to activate the Latin vote, accrue more volunteers, or get more millennials to turn in their ballots.

- What are your goals of your social media profiles? Do you want to engage in conversations with voters? Do you just want to create a record of your campaign? Do you see it as a vessel for amplifying your content?
- What metrics would you like to achieve? Do you want to grow your mailing list to a certain number or get a certain number of followers on Twitter? While numerical goals can help provide guideposts, don't forget that this is about getting votes IRL, so remember the big picture.

Creating guideposts help you determine your target audience, develop your content, optimize your advertising campaigns, and utilize your resources well. You could have a good idea of some goals now, and they could evolve as the campaign develops, so revisit them throughout the campaign. Remember to nestle these short- and long-term goals into your larger campaign strategy.

Step 2: Determine your digital media mix. Once you know where you're going, focus on devising the most effective way to achieve that goal. Assess your time, money, and resources, and determine what social media platforms get you where you're going. Don't expect voters to start using a platform to find your content; keep in mind where your voters already spend their time—like Facebook and Google—and optimize your strategy around that.

Step 3: Backmap from your goals. Once you've determined your long- and short-term goals, identify what tactics you and others need to execute to achieve them. This process, called *backmapping*, helps create deadlines and breaks down large goals into doable steps to make sure things stay on track. This is identical to creating a campaign plan: Start where you want to end, and work your way back to the beginning.

For example, if you want your website to launch by a certain day, break down deadlines to make sure all details are taken care of. If you want to reach a specific target segment, think about what endorsers and messages may help you. Then plan out when you need to engage those messengers, how you will test messaging, what content you would like to use (a video testimonial or memes?), and a date to deploy a social media ad campaign.

Put all of these dates into a digital media plan, and refer back to it to make sure you're on track and that your goals are still the most valuable targets as the campaign evolves.

Step 4: Develop your assets, voice, and values. Know your candidate's strengths, and develop a voice and plan that plays to them. Social media is a place to speak your passions and define the difference between you and your opponent through sharing your perspective and beliefs. It is your opportunity to

Bernie Sanders ✓
@BernieSanders

Follow

I got into politics not to figure out how to become President. I got into politics because I give a damn.

Retweets Likes
23,873   42,415

2:42 PM - 11 Dec 2015

465   24K   42K

FIGURE 6.2 Bernie Sanders established himself as a passionate and authentic politician, which added to his popularity.

share directly with voters the candidate's opinions, reactions, and values. Social media communication doesn't need to sound like talking points—it's powerful when it sounds genuine.

People respond well to those who are authentic, compelling, lively, funny, and/or smart—and they can feel when you're faking it. In other words, they want to hear your voice. Often social media posts that perform well and are shared widely are humorous. But if your candidate isn't funny, social media isn't the place to force it. Just ask Hillary Clinton; during the 2016 campaign, her tweets that aimed to be funny were at times cringeworthy and sounded overhandled.

Step 5: Test it and revise it. Pay attention to your analytics and what resonated well with your audience. See if it got you closer to your goal. Use that feedback to examine whether your tactics are the most effective way to reach your goal. Additionally, new goals can emerge while you're on the campaign trail. Revisit your digital media plan often and make sure your strategy and tactics remain the best use of resources.

Tips for Creating Your Digital Strategy

- *Draw boundaries with social media.* Social media can be very time-consuming. It takes regular monitoring and takes time to get your voice and content right. And once you log on, it's easy to get sidetracked by clickbait, pictures, and cat videos. It's actually created by scientists to make you do this. Carve out how you want to use it, and stick to that.

- *Get a social media manager.* The thing about social media is some people really, really like doing it. Find one of those people that you trust and ask him or her to help monitor your accounts and conversation. This is not a substitute to spending time creating content in the candidate's own voice, but this person can help make sure everything stays on track.
- *Track analytics in a single spreadsheet.* Ask your social media manager to set aside a certain time every week to review your analytics across your social media profile; take a look at your following, reach, interactions, engagement, and best-performing post. This summary will allow you to see which accounts and post types are performing best and can help you dictate where to focus your energy.
- *Find software that works for you.* There are programs that can help automate posting, organize content, and make sense of the noise. Research what fits your needs, read reviews, talk to people who have used it, and test out the interface before committing.
- *Keep your finger on the pulse.* Be sure you have Google alerts set up so you know when there are mentions about your candidate, your opponent, and your issues. Knowing what others are saying gives you valuable insights into how you should position and respond. Some vendors can also offer more in-depth monitoring across social media. Consider this if digital media is a big part of your strategy.
- *Integration is key.* Make sure your email, social media, video, and website work together and promote one another. Together, these are more than the sum of their parts. Separate, they're inefficient.

The Website: Where People Come to You

The role of the website in a local campaign is ever evolving. Once the center of the candidate's online presence, the website plays a more narrow role as engagement features have largely migrated to social media. For example, Obama's 2012 campaign offered opportunities to join eighteen different constituency groups. In 2016 no presidential candidate had a feature like this. There were still "issue" pages that explained the candidate's position on certain issues, but individualizing was left for social media.

With social media keeping you connected, a website can focus on what it does best: acting as the campaign's storefront, greeting people who wander in and want more information, and providing opportunities to recruit them to your campaign. It is your rock throughout the campaign where you can capture everything you don't want to dissipate into the ether of the digital world and a home base for your other digital tactics and strategies.

Plug-and-play website templates have made building and hosting your website easier and cheaper than ever before. There are dozens of free or cheap do-it-yourself platforms (I like Squarespace) that allow you to customize with no coding experience, drastically lowering the cost of getting a beautiful site off the ground and allowing you to easily update your content and structure.

Website Design Tips

- *Keep your messaging and branding tight, and make sure the site is up-to-date and functioning properly.* The website is like your campaign's front porch: If it looks like a mess and seems unloved, people will make assumptions about what's inside. Make a good first impression so people stick around long enough to drill down into content.
- *Use content hierarchy.* This is the idea of using formatting to help communicate your key messages. Use font sizes, headers, layout, and emphasis to help quickly communicate the structure of your content. That allows those who are just browsing your website to glean important information, and it works as signposts for those looking for specific content. Content hierarchy makes sure your website has something to offer for everyone—whether they are on your site for fifteen seconds, one minute, or ten.
- *Make it user friendly.* Finding content should be intuitive. Visit other websites and borrow ideas for layout and structure. Before launching your site, share it with five people. Only five are needed to identify 85 percent of a website's problems.[2]

Website Content Considerations

- *Provide pertinent information—but not too much.* Streamline what you want to say, and make sure your key messages pop by using the media that best makes your case, including photos, infographics, stats, videos, and stories. Make your case, say what's important, and get out.
- *Always be recruiting.* If people are visiting your site, they are clearly willing to take some time for politics, so give them ample opportunity to join your campaign. Include newsletter sign-up boxes in the footer of every page and embed tools so people can easily volunteer, donate, share your content on social media, or host a lawn sign.
- *Customize the user experience.* Many template sites make it easy to add a splash page (or landing page, cover page, or microsites) where you can tailor content that relates to the materials that drove voters there (see figure 6.3). For example, if you're running an ad campaign highlighting

FIGURE 6.3 An example of a customized landing page to welcome Obama website visits from Reddit. Note the personalized headline and clever picture placement.

your candidate's position on education, you can make a customized splash page that speaks to that specific ad and funnels people to the action.

Digital Considerations

- *Make sure your website is responsive and mobile-friendly.* Template platforms do this well. Everything is moving to mobile, so check on different devices and browsers to make sure everything is showing up as it should. Make sure buttons are clickable and forms are easy to fill out.

- *Connect your website to your social media accounts, and make sure all your materials include your website's URL.* Have buttons on your website that easily take the user to your Facebook, Twitter, and YouTube pages. This makes it easier for people to find you across platforms and increases your search-engine optimization. And once they get to your website, you have a chance to turn them into a volunteer and donor.

- *Make it personal.* Some technology packages make it so your campaign websites can appear different to different visitors. Just like online retailers show you products you may be interested in, websites can bring you to different pages depending on your past campaign interactions.[3] If you're already on the email list, it could take you to a volunteer form. Or if you're a known donor, you might see a more prominent donate button. Some software programs—like NationBuilder—provide this type of customization.

- *Include dynamic elements in your site.* This gives the appearance that the site is fresh and updated frequently with minimal maintenance. You can insert your Twitter feed or news feed or embed a scrolling ticker of endorsers.

Website Content Checklist

There is no one-size-fits-all for websites, though there are common content staples:

- Background information and a head shot.
- Your platform, broken down by issue. This is where you can include the nuances to your position.
- Your endorsers, along with quotes or videos, when available.
- Ample opportunities for the visitor to get involved with the campaign. Provide splash pages, footers, and widgets to encourage people to sign up for your newsletter, become a volunteer, and donate.
- Campaign collaterals, such as your television ads, radio spots, direct-mail pieces, brochures, or voters' pamphlets.
- A media kit. This should include photos, videos, and a press contact person for easy access for the media. You may also include a Q&A with basic information about your campaign or a quote sheet.
- A blog. Your candidate does not need to keep a blog, but if he or she feels compelled to communicate in long form, the website is the place to do it. This blog can also host statements and press releases. The most effective blogs are no more than four hundred words.

Website Monitoring

There are some simple analytic programs you can harness to see how people are using your website and what's important to them. Template sites like Squarespace offer limited free analytics. It is also free to set up a Google Analytics. Both of these can tell you things like the following:

- What pages are most visited, and how long users spend on each page, giving you valuable information regarding what your voters want to know about
- Which outreach efforts are driving traffic to your site
- Where people drop off your site
- The path users take through your site and how many pages they viewed before leaving
- How many new versus returning visitors come to your site

Alone, these analytics are just numbers—but you can extrapolate feedback that can inform your campaign. Your website traffic gives you valuable information about which content is creating buzz, what issues people are looking at, and what recruitment techniques are most effective. Some constituent relationship management software (CRMs) integrate with website analytics to give you more insights. (More on CRMs later.)

Social Media: Where Two-Way Conversations Happen

Social media wasn't fringe in the 2012 election, but by 2016 the election lived and breathed on the Internet. Social media is now central to how we understand politics and candidates, confirm our worldview, and express support. It's no longer just a tool within an election toolbox; it's a weapon.

According to the Pew Research Center, a majority of Americans now say they get news via social media, and half of the public turned to these sites to learn about the 2016 presidential election.[4] And it's hard to beat the reach; in 2017, 69 percent of the public used some type of social media, a trend that has been on the rise and will likely continue.[5]

The Role of Social Media in Local Elections

Social media offers huge advantages compared to the campaigning of yesteryear. It gives you more flexibility to be creative and innovative, especially as creative tools have become cheaper and more user friendly. Today there are many free or cheap programs that let you easily create graphic designs, edit video, create infographics, post blogs, and develop engaging content—meaning you can free up a chunk of your budget.

- *Connecting with your community.* Political websites have largely moved away from hosting comments and interactions on their websites; instead, they're doubling down on compelling social media to interact with potential voters. And this seems to work for voters—after all, they're already on social media. The number of registered voters who follow candidates for office on social networking sites has steadily increased.[6] Voters are following politicians' social media profiles to bypass traditional journalism to hear directly from the candidates, feel more connected to politicians, and get breaking news from the source.
- *Reaching more people for less.* In the past, large, targeted outreach efforts required a ton of money, which skewed effective communication toward interests with deep pockets. Now digital platforms, together with targeted digital marketing, allow you to reach voters and have a

dialogue with voters at a much lower cost. Bernie Sanders, for example, was able to reach out directly to voters who previously felt ignored by the political establishment.

- *Receiving instant feedback.* The speed of social media allows you to test messaging and instantly find out what works and what doesn't. If you're toying around with a couple of different messages, you can send out tweets and see which performs best. That feedback can help you decide which subject line you'll use in your next email blast or which punch line to use at your next debate.

- *Engaging micro influencers.* Social media opens up a world of supporters advocating on your behalf—something more powerful, genuine, and personal than more traditional campaign advertising. A 2016 study from Nielsen shows that 80–85 percent of people trust recommendations from people they know—higher than any other form of promotion.[7] Social media makes it easy for voters' friends, neighbors, pastors, and tennis partners to become micro influencers and support your campaign, which could mean more than radio spots, brochures, mailers, emails, or online ads (which, by the way, nearly half of consumers block).[8]

- *Turning active fans into volunteers.* A Pew poll showed that Facebook users who log on multiple times a day are 2.5 times more likely to attend a political rally or meeting, 57 percent more likely to try to persuade someone how to vote, and 43 percent more likely to have said they would vote.[9] That means your fans are a good place to start when looking for volunteers.

- *Rapid response.* Social media offers a venue to instantly reach out to the whole world, giving your campaign the ability to answer attacks and address issues quickly. Use this as a place for rapid response to push back against attacks and unfavorable coverage and let people know where you stand on the most pressing issues of the day. Effective response tools include social media content, ads, videos, and mass emails to supporters asking for their help in setting the record straight.

- *Poising you for serving in office.* Setting yourself up right during the election can help you be better at your future job, as you've already established a line of communication with constituents.

Tip: Keep It Short and Tell the Rest with Visuals

Social media is a noisy place. At the time of this writing, people post 293,000 status updates and upload 136,000 photos on Facebook and 300 hours of video to YouTube every minute. Every second, 6,000 tweets are published. There's a lot of competition for eyeballs, which makes it increasingly difficult to communicate complex issues or in-depth thought and, for better or worse, means you have to catch the user's attention quickly. A picture is worth more than a thousand words because you could never get social media users to read a thousand words. So think about how you can communicate your content with visuals, and use the post for context. With the power of communicating with visuals, it makes sense that the photo-sharing platform Instagram was a staple of the 2016 presidential election.

- *Vision trumps all other senses.* We are incredible at remembering pictures. According to John Medina, author of *Brain Rules*, if we hear a piece of information, three days later you'll remember 10 percent of it. Add a picture and you'll remember 65 percent.[10]
- *People look more than they read.* Eye-tracking studies show Internet readers pay close attention to information-carrying images.[11] In fact, when the images are relevant, readers spend more time looking at the images than they do reading text on the page. It also shows that users ignore purely decorative images—so avoid posting fluff.
- *Video will dominate the Internet.* Cisco projects that global Internet traffic from videos will make up 80 percent of all Internet traffic by 2019.[12]
- *Visuals encourage engagement.* Tweets with images receive 150 percent more retweets than tweets without images.[13] Facebook posts with images see 2.3 times more engagement than those without images,[14] and organic engagement is highest on posts with videos (13.9 percent) and photos (13.7 percent).[15]

Think about how you can communicate your messages and calls to action with visuals. There are endless ways to do this; find a way that resonates with your voice and style. Here are a few examples that we have had success with in the past:

- **Make videos.** Marketing research shows four times as many consumers would prefer to watch a video about a product than to read about it,[16] so a video helps communicate to more people. See more in the "Online Video" section below.
- **Create an infographic communicating your candidate's platform and strengths.** Using a simple visual language can help voters understand what the candidate's top issues are and why they're important. Infographics are "liked" and shared on social media three times more than any other type of content,[17] and they're a great way to pack in a lot of information.

FIGURE 6.4 Obama's digital skills gave new prominence to social media. This tweet, posted during the 2012 election, expertly used a powerful visual to respond to Clint Eastwood's appearance at the Republican National Convention, where the actor spoke to an invisible Obama/ empty chair.

- **Take pictures from the campaign trail.** Tweet a picture of the pancake breakfast you attended with a key takeaway. Post a picture of your volunteers stuffing envelopes. Tweet a picture of you putting up a lawn sign. The visual world and multimedia give you the ability to paint a sensory and emotional experience that frames your campaign. Don't take this power lightly.
- **Create memes—images with simple text—to convey key points.** These images are easy to spot in news feeds and are incredibly flexible. They could be cute, funny, or sincere or could convey a key statistic.
- **Use GIFs.** GIFs—graphics interchange format—are like a tiny digital flip books. They can capture things from popular culture, your videos, graphics, animations—just about anything. They're a popular element to add to social media posts and emails to communicate additional information, add levity, and add movement.

Tip: Do Less Better

Don't spread yourself too thin. Focus your efforts where people already are. We saw this trend on the national level between the 2012 and 2016 elections. In 2012 Obama had a presence on nine separate social media platforms: Facebook, Twitter, YouTube, Instagram, Pinterest, Tumblr, Google+, Flicker, and Spotify. In 2016 Sanders, Clinton, and Trump were all on substantially fewer platforms. All three had the same staples (Facebook, Twitter, YouTube, and Instagram), Clinton was on Pinterest (which has a high number of female users), and Sanders was on Tumblr (which has a high number of young users).[18] That's it.

On the local level, where you have a smaller pool of people to contact and a smaller budget to play with, this becomes even more important.

Tip: Sometimes Social Media Takes on a Life of Its Own

Social media loves a good riffing session. One misstep can trigger a meme that can spread like wildfire. For example, Romney's "binder full of women" comment, the ObamaGirl, or Trump's #ManyPeopleAreSaying hashtag. These are unlikely on the local level, and there's little you can do to protect yourself. If it happens, remember to keep it in perspective; being defensive could give it more attention than it otherwise would have.

	2008		2012		2016		
	Obama	**McCain**	**Obama**	**Romney**	**Sanders**	**Clinton**	**Trump**
Facebook	x	x	x	x	x	x	x
Twitter			x	x	x	x	x
YouTube	x	x	x	x	x	x	x
Instagram			x		x	x	x
Pinterest			x			x	
Tumblr			x			x	
Google+			x	x			
Flickr	x	x	x	x			
Spotify			x				
Myspace	x	x					

FIGURE 6.5 Candidates Are Using Only Staple Social Media Platforms

Source: Pew Research Center, "Presidential Candidates' Changing Relationship with the Web," July 18, 2016, http://www.journalism.org/2016/07/18/presidential-candidates-changing-relationship-with-the-web/.

Social Media Best Practices

- *Keep up the dialogue.* Respond to messages and comments. Interact with your users and others in your communities. People love getting attention on social media—psychologists have discovered it releases dopamine, so people literally get a high from their social media love. Making the conversation two-way is also an asset. The interactivity of social media offers an unprecedented means for two-way communication, allowing you to listen to your supporters and engage on issues that matter to them. If you listen, you can learn a lot about how to inspire and connect with your support base.
- *Be authentic.* Keep your posts compelling, lively, smart, and conversational. Try to avoid posting official statements or press releases. Write from the first person and personalize your message.
- *Brand carefully and confidently.* Take a step back and think about how all your content works together in concert. What are you communicating about your candidate? How does your social media presence read as a whole? Think about what you post and how you post, and make sure you align with your other branding sessions.
- *Keep it catchy.* You cannot underestimate people's attention span. The cacophony of content constantly rolling into people's feeds means the competition is stiff. Value your audience's time like a gift and respect it.
- *Social media is mobile.* The majority of social media traffic comes from smartphones, so think about how you design your content with the expectation that it will be viewed on a mobile device.
- *Develop a visual identity.* Develop a visual identity guide and stick to it (see figure 6.6). This should include colors, fonts, logos, and other elements that you should use throughout your material. It should also tie back to your other collaterals and lawn signs to create strong cohesion throughout the campaign.

Facebook

Facebook is still king of social networking by a substantial margin. Nearly eight in ten online Americans (79 percent) use Facebook, more than double the share that uses Twitter (24 percent), Pinterest (31 percent), Instagram (32 percent), or LinkedIn (29 percent). What's more, Facebook users rose 7 percent from 2015 compared to 2016, indicating that the platform's dominance isn't likely to wane anytime soon. And Facebook audiences are active; 76 percent of Americans who use Facebook now report that they visit the site on a daily basis.[19]

FIGURE 6.6 Bernie Sanders did a good job of establishing a visual identity. This tweet captures his brand while leveraging a magical moment on the campaign trail: the time a bird landed on his podium during a rally.

Getting Started

Recognizing the role it plays in politics, Facebook launched Facebook Elections, which is designed to set up a page for a candidate. It will help you get a short, custom URL—ideally one that is consistent across social media platforms—and select a profile and cover photo to represent you on Facebook. Pick one that visually ties to the identity of the rest of your campaign. Facebook also shares best practices for setting up your page and posting. Best practices are constantly changing, so check in to see what Facebook and other blogs recommend.

Yelling in a Noisy Room

Facebook has become so ubiquitous that every cause, musician, business, and adorable dog has its own group page, which has led to a surge in the number of pages out there. In 2016 the number of group pages passed 50 million,[20] with each page posting on average 1.48 times a day. The explosion of content has led to the decline in organic reach—there's just too much competition—with one study indicating organic reach has dipped to 2 percent of followers in some cases.[21] And as is the way with noisy spaces, some accounts are compensating by posting more often, meaning the organic reach will likely continue to decrease.

There is an algorithm that determines what shows up in whose feed. It is constantly changing and it's based on thousands of user-specific details, meaning nothing is ironclad, but we know several important factors:

- How much interest the user has expressed in your past posts. Does he or she often interact with your posts?
- How well the post is performing with other users. If you get likes right out of the gate, it's more likely to show up in others' feeds.
- How well your past posts have performed. With social media, past performance *can* be indicative of future results.
- The type of post the user prefers. If that person often interacts with videos, a video is more likely to appear in his or her feed.
- When the post is posted. Posting updates while your audience is online, or is about to be online, helps raise the visibility of the post.

These factors highlight how important engagement is to the algorithm; three of the five above factors have to do with others' engagement. You can help get more engagement by boosting a post—an advertising campaign that promotes just a single post—which can lead to more of your content appearing in their, and other people's, feeds.

Building a Following

With the explosion of Facebook group pages, people can be picky about what they "like." Getting those likes can also be worth the effort, as those people's friends can see that they've expressed support for your election. Think of these as endorsements from community members—and all they need to do is click. And, of course, give your voters a reason to like your page by providing them compelling and useful content.

Ask your current friends and contacts to like your candidate's page—and ask them to do the same with their friends. In the beginning, consider throwing some advertising dollars behind a "like" campaign to build a following. Once you have a base, it's easier to get others on board through the bandwagon effect.

It's important to promote the page wherever you can—have a link on your website, on your Twitter account, and any other materials you make, such as emails, direct mail, campaign literature, and advertisements.

Once you've created your page, it can "like" other pages, too. Create a list of companies and organizations in the community and follow them. This way you can keep your finger on the pulse of what others are talking about and interact from your campaign's page, which can make you more visual and appear plugged in to your community.

Posting Best Practices

- *Post regularly, but not excessively.* You want to stay connected, but you don't want to be annoying. Posting five to ten times a week is a good rule of thumb.
- *Be pithy.* Short posts perform better and give you a better chance to be noticed. Lead with your main point to avoid getting lost between an article about Kylie Jenner and a cat video. The best-performing Facebook posts are only forty characters long.

FIGURE 6.7 Hillary Clinton shares a classic campaign moment with her online following. This picture helps reinforce one of Hillary's main assets—her strength with families and children.

- *Be visual.* As mentioned, visuals outperform text alone, so think about how you can combine posts with visuals or video that help make your point.
- *Make hypersharable content.* Shared content is the best type of promotion you can have, so make something you want people to share.
- *Amplify your content.* Use Facebook to post your op-ed or a letter to the editor. Share a picture of your lawn signs.
- *Go behind the scenes.* Share candid photos and videos that highlight your personality, what you're up to, and what you care about. This helps build credibility by letting people see how the sausage is made.
- *Share what matters to you.* You can engage on issues people are talking about and add your perspective.
- *Interact with other public figures.* Commenting on others' posts puts your name in front of more people.
- *Create a record of your campaign.* Even if someone isn't following you, they may be interested to know more as Election Day rolls around. If you've kept your Facebook page up-to-date, users can scroll through and quickly get an idea of where you've spent your time and energy.

Analytics and Management Software

The Facebook platform offers built-in analytics, called Insights, that will automatically appear in your page's Admin Panel and transform data into feedback for your digital campaigning. Here you can figure out what content encourages the most engagement, the demographics of your followers, and the best time to tweet.

Other platforms are designed to help your page perform better. For example, ActionSprout allows you to select Facebook pages to monitor and then lets you know what is trending and popular from those pages. You can follow other local politicians' accounts to gain inspiration for content, organizations in your community to find out what they're doing, and local news outlets to see what content is engaging the community the most. Additionally, it can tell you who your superfans are by indicating who interacts with your content and how often, who could turn into future volunteers.

Twitter

Twitter has become a favorite platform of politics. We elected a president who has harnessed the power of Twitter and used the new medium to flip everything on its head in a fantastic media landscape upheaval not seen since John F. Kennedy and Richard Nixon made television a crucial part of elections.

Hillary Clinton ✓
@HillaryClinton

[Follow]

I'm running for president. Everyday Americans need a champion, and I want to be that champion. –H hillaryclinton.com

12:27 PM - 12 Apr 2015

Hillary Clinton 2016
The official website for Hillary Clinton's 2016 presidential campaign
hillaryclinton.com

↩   ⟲ 96,138   ♥ 104,473   ⓘ

FIGURE 6.8 Hillary Clinton announced her candidacy on Twitter, a choice that reflects how mainstream the platform is.

And even before the election, it was clear Twitter had hit the mainstream; between the 2012 and 2016 elections, the White House launched an official Twitter handle for the commander in chief (@POTUS), and both Hillary Clinton and Ted Cruz announced their candidacies on Twitter.[22]

But for all the prominence Twitter has gained, it is difficult to figure out how to use it. It is a cacophonous mess. The first presidential debate in 2016 inspired a record-breaking 10 million tweets. That is, until the second debate broke that record with 17 million tweets. That is too much content for anyone to be able to handle. Hashtags can help, a word or acronym used to add context to a tweet that helps others organize and view content, but the quantity of tweets means what you put out there will be buried quickly. There are so many tweets, news outlets have begun posting online articles that curate top tweets about specific events to help us make sense of the noise.

Why Bother?

If you're just starting out, it's hard to get noticed. So what's the point of maintaining a Twitter account during your election?

- *Creating a record of your campaign.* While this is something you do on Facebook too, you can get away with more Twitter posts, so you can share the little things you don't want to enshrine on your Facebook wall.
- *Communicating with voters directly.* People are able to reach out to you directly on Twitter—an incredibly egalitarian communication platform. If you're interested in getting a pulse on your district, you can see what people are talking about through geolocated searches.
- *Connecting with journalists.* One of the most active demographics on Twitter is journalists. On Twitter, you can alert your favorite and target reporters about campaign news and updates they should know about. The journalist will become more aware of your efforts and may be more likely to write about you in the future.
- *Finding influencers.* A small number of people are making the most of the noise on Twitter. These people could provide valuable endorsements for your activities. You can find people by hand, or some CRM software can help identify who in your network is most influential.

Getting Started and Building a Following

The proliferation of tweets upped the volume in an already busy Twittersphere, and it can be difficult to rise above the noise and be noticed. Here are a few tactics to help you get started:

- *Fill out your profile completely.* This will help people find you, and it is a good place to share information about yourself. How this is done and best practices change, so if you have any questions search for a step-by-step guide; there are many out there.
- *Ask your friends, family, and supporters to follow you.* Provide many opportunities to follow by including your Twitter handle on your website, in every email blast, and on campaign materials.
- *Identify voters and community leaders and personally engage them.* This can also give you an idea of what your voters are talking about in real time. Platforms like Hootsuite allow you to create channels to monitor this easily.
- *Use software to track your following and find new followers.* Using one will give you feedback about what content is pulling people in and pushing them away and allow you to engage with new and recently lost followers to see if you can get them back. I like Audience.
- *Give them a reason to follow you.* Post interesting and thoughtful content.
- *Run an advertising campaign to get a base number of followers.* Followers are a bit more expensive on Twitter than Facebook, but developing a base can encourage others to follow through the bandwagon effect.

@johnfritchey
John Fritchey

I've been kissing hands and shaking babies all morning; not sure why people are reacting strangely. Oh. Damn. Never mind.

2 Feb 10 via Twittelator

FIGURE 6.9 An example of a candidate who has done a good job of establishing himself as a jokester.

Posting Pointers

- *Post often.* Tweets are so ephemeral, feel free to post often. Remember to keep the value high; don't post silly things just to fill the space. There are no hard-and-fast rules, but one to ten times a day is safe.
- *Post important content multiple times.* If there's a great article or endorsement you want to highlight, post it three to five times. You can schedule this to go out on different days throughout the week.
- *Find software to help you make sense of the Twitter noise.* Some programs—like Hootsuite or Tweetdeck—allow you to schedule tweets to ensure you have a pipeline of key content teed up for the day or week. Additionally, it allows you to create content channels so you can monitor conversations, hashtags, or select users. A word of warning—these programs allow you to add multiple Twitter accounts to a single interface, but encourage staffers to keep their accounts separate. It is far too easy to accidentally post a tweet to the wrong account, which could cause an unnecessary PR headache. Rogue tweets are more common than you would think, and while they're often deleted within minutes, they can cause embarrassment.
- *Follow journalists and influencers and talk to them.* Respond to their tweets to help alert them to your account.
- *Be careful about tone.* Snark sometimes doesn't come through in 140 characters. If you're running for office and not known as a jokester, it's probably best to tag a snarky tweet (j/k, #snark.) Though it may be a little lame, at least it won't have to be explained later.
- *Avoid sounding like a texting teenager.* Don't use numbers as words (it's *for* not *4*, *to* not *2*, *skater* not *sk8r*). One hundred and forty characters isn't a lot of space, but think of that as a challenge to be pithy. Stay elegant.
- *Pay attention to analytics to see what works, and do more of that.* Take a look at what performed well and emulate it in future posts.

What to Tweet About?

- *Tweet updates from the campaign trail.* Tweet about a rewarding interaction you had with a voter. Tweet about your debate tonight. Tweet all those pictures you're taking along the way. This creates a record of your activities and helps paint a picture of how hardworking you are as a candidate—and what type of politician you may be.
- *Tweet about campaign successes.* You can tweet about a new endorsement or meeting a fundraising goal.
- *Tweet about your materials.* Do you have your new website up? Tweet about it. Are your lawn signs printed? Tweet a picture.
- *Tweet about your platform and issues you care about.* Twitter is one of the most direct ways you can express yourself. Through it you can help remind people why you care and help others get on board with your vision.
- *Tweet news articles.* If you or your opponent appears in the news, you can tweet it out along with a snippet of your commentary. Additionally, if a news article appears that speaks to a key plank of your platform, use it as an opportunity to tweet and show others what you believe in.
- *Retweet at your own risk.* Many profiles state "RT is not an endorsement," but be prepared for people to associate whatever you retweet with your campaign.

Online Video

Cheap camcorders, smartphones, and free online video hosting sites have made video easier to access than ever.

House your campaign videos in a single location, like a YouTube account. (No need to focus on subscribers or likes; you can focus that energy on your Facebook and Twitter accounts.) Fill out the profile completely; sometimes users search for information directly on YouTube, so make sure all clips are properly titled and tagged. This also increases your search-engine optimization.

Videos should be short and to the point. Unless you are skilled in cinematography, don't expect viewers to watch more than thirty seconds. Avoid unedited content or poor video or audio quality, unless it captures a rare or special moment.

A friendly reminder: Because videos are so accessible, it's more important than ever to stay on message. We saw the danger of saying things in an off-hand manner in 2008 when a tape captured Obama saying Midwest voters "cling to guns or religion," in 2012 when a hidden camera captured Romney disregarding 47 percent of the country and reinforcing the stereotype that he was an out-of-touch rich guy, and in 2016 with a leaked video that caught Donald Trump on a hot mic bragging about sexually assaulting women.

What's Video Good For?

- *Talk about your platform.* One local candidate talked extemporaneously on twenty-three subjects he felt were important in the county and posted these separately by subject matter. Besides imparting his depth of knowledge of county business, the clips were incredibly informative for the average person. His site received 65,000 hits—a huge amount for the small market in which it was posted. Use clips such as these on the site on the "Issues" page.
- *Use your opponent's words against him or her.* You could upload anything your opponent may have said that could be damaging to him or her. If the opponent is an incumbent and the official government meetings are taped, go through and pull out damaging moments and place them on your site. These should be kept brief (under three minutes).
- *Tell a story about an issue that matters.* A candidate for Berkeley City Council recorded a video of himself telling the story of talking to a woman with Alzheimer's at a local coffee shop. The story was touching, poignant, and memorable—and allowed the candidate to segue into talking about his vision for city assistance for the elderly. The video performed incredibly well, surging past other posts on the account.
- *Show videos from the campaign trail.* Posting videos from rallies, events, or interactions can help make potential voters feel connected to the campaign.
- *Get video testimonials.* Have influencers from the community talk about why they support the candidate. We once had key leaders from different sectors talk about why our candidate knew the issues he championed, which helped drive home his key platform. We edited them into short, super-shareable videos to post on Facebook, Twitter, and YouTube (which you can embed on your site).
- *Make an ask.* Your donation page could feature your candidate asking for support or regular donors communicating why they have contributed to the campaign.

Videos and Social Media

Both Facebook and Twitter have begun hosting their own videos—and pri-oritizing content posted directly to those platforms in their algorithms. That means that, in addition to posting on YouTube, if you want to share the video on social media, you should upload it directly to the platform. The difference in analytics pays off for the extra time spent.

Tip: Be sure to add captions. Eighty-five percent of videos on Facebook are watched without sound as people are scrolling down the feed.[23] So either include captions or tell a story that doesn't need words.

Other Social Media Platforms

There are a surfeit of social media platforms out there, and you've likely heard about interesting and creative uses of many of them. When considering using them, remember the rule of thumb: Ask if it helps you reach your goals and then if it's the most efficient way to do that.

Instagram

After Facebook and Twitter, the social media platform that makes the most sense for local elections is Instagram, a photo- and video-sharing platform. It's has a huge number of users—28 percent of US adults[24]—and lends itself well to capturing moments of the campaign.

LinkedIn

LinkedIn, a social media platform for professionals, is excellent for business-to-business interactions but is less helpful for local political campaigns. If you have a LinkedIn profile already, make sure it's clean and up-to-date and has relevant skills listed. Reach out to some friends and ask them to endorse you for those skills, too. If you have job experience that really shows off your qualifications for office, you could also consider asking an old colleague to write you a reference. You could also search your contacts to identify potential donors or endorsers. If LinkedIn isn't your thing, during an election isn't the time to learn.

The Others

Different social media platforms attract different demographics, so in some cases it may make sense to tap into that. For example, women tend to spend more time on Pinterest, and college-age people are much more likely to use Snapchat. But remember to ask yourself if that is the most efficient way to accomplish your goal.

Outreach: Where You Go to People

Email

Old-fashioned email is still crucial to raise money, motivate volunteers, and keep supporters engaged. Emails have a much higher response rate than social media—sometimes by a factor of ten—as supporters can view it at their leisure (versus social media posts, which a person may miss if they're not online when you post).[25] They're also good at reaching those people who aren't on social media.

Software can help your campaign use emails effectively. There are programs dedicated to email like MailChimp, Constant Contacts, or a constituent resource management system, which allow you to do the following:

- *Easily customize your emails with a plug-and-play template builder and layout options.* This makes it easy to create actions, like signing a petition, sharing information on social media, or donating, and can help turn email-list subscribers into volunteers and boots on the ground.
- *Keep your email mobile-friendly.* Everything is going mobile; emails are no exception. If your email is not mobile-friendly, it may be ignored. Software can help.
- *Analyze your campaigns with built-in reporting features.* This will allow you to monitor who opened, clicked, and engaged with your emails. You're also able to see things such as if people have unsubscribed.
- *Provide an easy way for people to subscribe.* People can subscribe to your lists with sign-up forms you can embed on your website and link to on social media profiles.
- *Segment your audience for hypertargeting and A/B testing for messages and subject lines.* Programs linked to CRMs will also allow you to segment factors such as who has donated or where people are located.
- *Share information gathered from email blasts and connect it to the rest of your database.* This saves time and removes the annoying need to swap out data and information.

In 2016 data companies got into the email game, linking big data associated with a person's email address to create a more complete picture, including things like a person's interests and his or her likelihood of voting or donating.[26] If this functionality becomes more widely available, you may be able to segment your lists based on what type of messaging would resonate best, allowing hypertailored email campaigns.

Email Tips

- *Don't spam.* Only email people who have opted in to your list.
- *Email with a purpose.* Be thoughtful when emailing en masse. Every busy person's in-box is already overflowing with impersonal emails, so make your emails minimal and be sure you have something to say. Templates can help create clear call-to-actions, be it to donate money or volunteer for a canvassing shift.
- *Use clickable subject lines.* The power of your subject line makes all the difference in opening rates. Strive for lines that are compelling and authentic and correspond to the content within. Obama's 2012 and Clinton's 2016 campaigns extensively tested subject lines and found that short, catchy lines such as "Join me for dinner?" and "Hey!" performed best. A/B testing can help you hone in on what works best for your audience.
- *Collect email leads.* Give people plenty of opportunities to opt into your email list (like on your website). These leads are the most likely to help you meet volunteer and fundraising goals, so don't give up this effort.
- *Integrate with social media.* Be sure to include links to your social media profiles on email blasts.
- *Personalize landing pages.* You can create a landing page on your website that corresponds directly to your asks. Squarespace's splash pages make this easy to do.
- *Make sure emails and social media aren't competing with one another.* One way to think about the difference: Social media is a place to engage with supporters consistently over time; emails spur action at critical moments.[27]

Digital Advertising

Digital advertising is now a staple of a promotional diet. In 2012 digital advertising made up 1.8 percent of ad dollars. Four years later, in 2016, that number jumped to almost 10 percent and is expected to grow as more people cut the cable cord and turn to online sources for news and entertainment.[28]

Digital ads have the ability to be much more targeted and personal than traditional advertising, and the commitment is far less. Most digital advertising services charge you by the number of impressions made, meaning you can make much smaller buys than on TV, in print, or on radio. Additionally, you are able to microtarget, which allows you to hone in on your target locations and demographics.

Digital advertising is a quickly changing field. As it's the primary revenue source for most social media platforms and search engines, it's an area where companies are constantly updating their interfaces and offerings to remain cutting edge. Facebook, for example, introduced a new ad product tailored specifically to political campaigns that allowed candidates to advertise specifically to the most politically active and influential Facebook users.[29]

Additionally, software is emerging to help campaigns get even more precise. Some software offers household IP targeting, which helps hone in on specific households to get crazy granular with targeting. Services like Mobile Conquesting allow you to reach voters on their smartphones (you can even target by political party affiliation), and you can reach very specific groups of people with targeted display and video ads across all devices and geographically targeted to the specific area the campaign wants to reach. The mercurial nature of digital ads make it especially important to research before committing dollars, so take a look at what's available when you're ready to launch your campaign to see what makes sense.

Creating an Advertising Strategy

- *Consider your goals and your interim goals.* Remember your digital media plan? Revisit your goals and figure out whom you want to do what to achieve them.
- *Understand your audience.* Carefully craft personas to target the exact people you want to move. Think about their behaviors, interests, and consumption patterns.
- *Create an advertising budget.* Determine how much money you have to spend on your push and how you'd like to divide it between the different platforms. Two to five times the amount it costs to create the content is a reasonable rule of thumb when designing a promotional budget—though that may need to adjust to accommodate content created on the cheap or for free.
- *Figure out what advertising mix will help you reach your goals.* Social media allows you to create different types of ad campaigns that drive the user to different actions. Decide which tactic will get you to where you want to be.
- *Create awesome content.* Your ad is just as good as your content, so be thoughtful about what you advertise. Keep your target demographic in mind and create messaging and content that connects with them.
- *Social media allows us to get specific with who sees our content.* Marry your advertising campaigns with your precinct analysis to target geographically, and use social media's targeting tools to drill down on

> *Tip:* You can focus group cheaply on Twitter and Facebook. Set up ad campaigns promoting different messaging and topics using multivarients. People's responses will tell you which language and topics are resonating with microsegments. Facebooks reaction buttons and comment board can provide invaluable feedback on what demographics care about and what language works.

multi variants to get specific about who you're reaching. Thanks to information Facebook has gathered on its users, you can get specific; you're now able to promote an ad to single moms with a dog from a neighborhood you need to engage. In one campaign, we created a series of videos with community leaders highlighting our candidate's strengths. We were then able to promote to the demographics and neighborhoods we had identified as high priority in the days leading up to the election. This helped activate the vote with those we needed the most.

- *Launch the campaign and monitor regularly.* Digital campaigns give you real-time feedback and can be easy to change. Listen to what your analytics are teaching you, and try it again from the top.

Things to Keep in Mind

- *Get help.* If you aren't familiar with creating ads on social media, it can be time-consuming and frustrating, and you may not make the impact you want. There are plenty of firms out there that will help you create and execute your strategy, which could save you more than crappy ads will cost.
- *Go where the people are.* In the 2016 election, the majority of advertising dollars went to Facebook and Alphabet (Google's parent company), which makes sense with the number of people using that software. Pandora, the streaming radio service, is well positioned for political ads, and video-streaming services like Hulu or YouTube could be a great home for your video ads.
- *Take analytics with a grain of salt.* Between ad-blocking software, the cacophony of content on people's feeds, and the fact that an estimated 37 percent of digital ad impressions come from bots, not humans,[30] it's hard to know how much of an impact your ads are really making. Pay

attention and take cues from analytics, but remember you're aiming to connect with real-life people, so don't lose yourself in the numbers.

The Future of Advertising

Social media allows for you to advertise with a high level of precision—you can target folks in specific zip codes with specific likes and specific beliefs. And as you've no doubt noticed, Big Data is getting more sophisticated by the day. With marketers working toward honing revenue models online, we know that every purchase we make, every search we type, every movement we make, and every reaction we give are filed away to create remarkably reliable deductions about who we are.

A new data-driven subbranch of psychology, called psychometrics, is emerging to develop models that assess human beings based on personality traits and what will motivate us. With that information, content can be curated that isn't just based on our values—it can be based on our driving forces. It's not hard to envision a future where this type of software could be deployed affordably—and effectively—at the local level. We could tailor messages to activate our lazy voter by tapping into their psychological motivations.

Digital Tools

Thanks to technology, just about everything in this book is changing. Throughout this book you have gotten tried-and-true tactics, and for just about all of them there is now a digital counterpoint.

Between the time this is written and when you run for office, there will likely be a whole new suite of software options available, so do some research to figure out what's right for you. If you're curious about what types of things could assist you, here's a taste of some functionality software offers.

Note that many platforms bundle several of the following features. Choosing software can be expensive—it costs money to use and takes time to learn—so make sure you're getting the functions you would use and aren't paying for bells and whistles you don't need.

Software Can Help Manage Your Network

Political constituent relationship management software helps organize, track, and analyze communication and contacts across a campaign. CRM software is an efficient, centralized way to build and manage your campaign's network.

CRMs can help keep a Rolodex of volunteers, organizers, donors, vendors, lawn sign recipients, voters, and anyone in between across all levels of your campaign. They will allow you to keep track of basically anyone you cross paths with and can maintain their contact information, keep a record of interactions, and allow you to recall them by different categories and tags.

It's sort of like a dynamic, multidimensional spreadsheet that allows you to sort and recall information easily. Using a dedicated CRM will eliminate the problem of maintaining multiple separate data spreadsheets, many of which are not designed to interact with each other.

So if you're wondering, "Who donated more than five hundred dollars but hasn't given any money for the last three months?" your CRM can help. And if it's integrated with email distribution functions, it would also let you craft a pitch to that specific segment and email only them.

Some CRMs—like NationBuilder—allow you to match a supporter's email address and social media profiles to help identify those more influential on Facebook and Twitter. This can help you identify which supporters can act as your social media influencers, too.

CRMs come with different features, support options, price points, and functionalities. Do research to figure out which one has the functionalities your campaign needs. Once you've identified one, be sure you take it for a test drive. These databases can be central to your campaign, and you want to be sure you choose one that is intuitive and user friendly. Read reviews and talk to people who have used it. Features to look for include integration with social media and email in-boxes, ability to send email blasts, and integration with your website. In the 2016 cycle, popular campaign CRMs included Salesforce, Pipedrive, Hubspot, and NationBuilder. Once you've chosen a CRM, implement a protocol immediately to ensure information is entered in a consistent way. CRMs can get messy quickly, especially with multiple users, and the more organized it is, the more functional it is.

Software Can Streamline Your Canvassing and Grassroots Operations

Apps are emerging to help manage canvassing and outreach. Software can help plan out canvassing routes, analyze effective techniques, and track volunteers' location and productivity. On the canvasser side, mobile apps can provide addresses, talking points, phone numbers when people aren't home (so the canvasser can leave a message on the spot), and an ability to instantly add information from the field to the database. If you're interested in using canvassing software, look for one that integrates with your CRM to make sure you're capturing data in one central location. Research what works for your campaign. One popular platform in 2016 was ECanvasser.

Software Can Manage Your Call Banks

Calling software can help automate the calling outreach process. There are programs that can help create call lists, provide auto dial-out features, and allow you to send out campaign updates through SMS (short message service or texting). Others also send automated GOTV voice messages, which I recommend against, because everyone hates automated calls. [31]

It makes sense to use software that integrates with your CRM so you know the history of those you are calling—whether you are fundraising, getting out the vote, or polling—and can easily capture the information from your latest outreach. Platforms also offer options to stay in touch with supporters via text messages, which could be helpful for getting out the vote. Research what software works for you. Two popular platforms in 2016 were CallHub and TeleForum.

A word of warning: Some of this software may make it *too* easy to connect with people. Be considerate; people don't want to feel harassed. Too many impersonal touches may turn people off from the campaign. We saw this in outreach during the 2016 campaign in Reno, Nevada. As a swing state close to the California border, people flooded over to help in election efforts. The result was a lot of angry Nevadans who wanted some peace and quiet and were instead called and canvassed to the point of madness.

Software Can Help You Step Up Your Fundraising Game

Online fundraising is now key to elections. In 2012 the two presidential campaigns together pulled in more than $1 billion online. Fundraising software can help you manage, track, and analyze donor and fundraising efforts. Functionalities include the following:

- Providing the ability to accept donations in the field on a tablet or mobile phone via mobile credit card readers
- Targeting precisely, so you can fundraise to a particular segment
- Enabling supporters to raise more money for your campaign by tapping into their network of family and friends on social media
- Providing code to easily embed user-friendly plug-ins where people can contribute
- Gamifying fundraising, allowing supporters to set their own fundraising goals and providing built-in social sharing
- Compiling financial reports instantly

- integrating with your CRM to track donations and provide analytics so you know what's working

Additionally, new platforms tap into more widespread support. More groups are now working to be more strategic about elections from a macro view and are orchestrating support for local, state, and national races. Platforms have popped up so people can identify candidates near and far that they would like to support, such as Swing Left and Crowdpac. If your candidate is combating in an important district, it may be worth investigating what national networks could lend support.

Software Can Give You Feedback About the ROI of Campaign Activities

Analytics and data can give you powerful insights about what is working in a campaign, and more options will surely emerge and become more user-friendly. One example is Civis Analytics, a company backed by Eric Schmidt of Google fame, which is an incarnation of an analytics tool built for the Obama 2012 campaign known as "Optimizer." That idea evolved into a data science platform in the cloud that introduced the targeting methods of corporate marketers into political campaigns and strives to make sense of data and uses that to make predictions and recommend next steps.

Other software can improve the data you do have. Accurate Append, for example, boasts of billions of data points on US voters and consumers. It aims to help clean up email and phone lists by verifying which email addresses and phone numbers are valid and filling in gaps where it can.

The Upshot

- Digital platforms can be time-consuming. Make sure you have a strategy and always ask yourself if what you're doing is the most efficient medium to achieve your goals.
- Tools and tactics are always changing, so do your homework before investing time in programs and tactics.
- Draw a contrast between you and your opponent to energize the base, especially with lazy support.
- Tell your main messages with stories and visuals. The digital world is becoming increasingly more visual, mobile, and pithy. Play to that.
- Remember, if your base doesn't care and doesn't vote, you can't win. Communicate with authenticity and make the cause important.

Traditional Media:
Print, Radio, and TV

> What we are voting on is far more important than buying cereal. The
> last thing we should be doing is advertising that dumbs us down.
>
> —CINDY WILSON, FREELANCE PUBLIC RELATIONS AND MARKETING SPECIALIST

IN THIS CHAPTER:

- Print Media: Paid and Unpaid
- Fielding Questions from the Press: Top Tips
- Radio
- Television
- Ad Production
- Placing Your Buys on Television: Research, Research, Research

SIMILAR TO ANY BUSINESS, CAMPAIGNS NEED TO EFFECTIVELY TARGET media dollars for the best contact-to-cost ratio. Both benchmark polls and a precinct analysis will inform a campaign where and who should be targeted, but if a benchmark poll is financially out of reach for your campaign, a precinct analysis will give you a geographic road map as to which neighborhoods, precincts, and communities will support—or not support—your candidate or issue-based campaign. As with other campaign activities, your message must be at the foundation of your media campaign.

Print Media: Paid and Unpaid

Americans have become as divided over their opinions of the credibility of news sources as people have become isolated by partisan leanings in their neighborhoods and cities. Just as Democrats and Republicans have isolated themselves geographically, they have also done so with news and general programming. Further, the programs people listen to and watch break down by age as well. For example, nearly six in ten young voters get their news online, while older Americans receive news from more traditional venues—such as newspapers and network television news.[1]

Newspaper readership, which has been in steady decline for more than a decade, now hovers around 20 percent (see figure 7.1).[2] If you know the demographic breakdown of your supporters (gender, age, race, income, education) and who gets information from where, a campaign can more effectively target the right audience in the correct medium with the appropriate message.

The relationship between newspaper credibility and partisanship should also be taken into consideration when targeting voters. People tend to watch news that reinforces preconceived attitudes of politics, world events, and domestic issues. Needless to say, this relationship plays out when it comes to newspaper endorsements for candidates and issue-based campaigns; not receiving one hurts a candidate or cause more than receiving one helps. Newspaper endorsements do, however, continue to influence voters in primaries and citywide races of communities with overwhelming Democratic registration.

Similarly, where a campaign advertises underscores an assumption about a candidate or cause in relationship to the viewer. Given that campaigns are often won or lost by the undervote, campaigns must communicate, excite, and draw a clear line that differentiates the candidates with the base voters.

Still, no matter what presence your daily newspaper holds where you live, issue-based campaigns and candidates on either side of the aisle should never squander opportunities with local papers. Thoroughly prepare for interviews, editorial boards, and any campaign events that will be covered by the media.

Unpaid Print Media (Earned Media)

Local papers in my area no longer attend candidate announcements, but if they do where you're running, know that the announcement of your candidacy or your issue-based campaign is the first piece in your earned media tool kit. Here are some tips to make the announcement more successful:

1. Announcements should be timed to have the biggest impact and the best news coverage. Have your campaign team gather as many supporters as possible for your announcement, and make it in a public place that is both well known and well liked by your community.

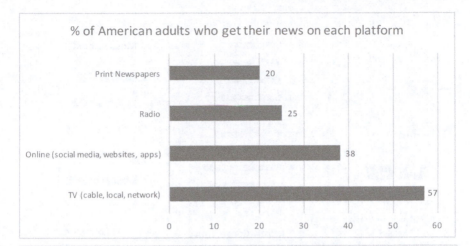

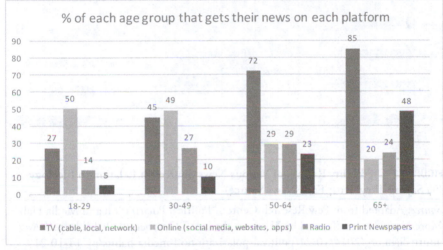

FIGURE 7.1 Knowing Where Voters Get Information Allows a Campaign to Target an Audience with Its Message Appropriately

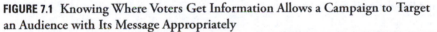

Source: Adapted from Pew Research Center, "The Modern News Consumer," July 7, 2016, http://www.journalism.org/2016/07/07/the-modern-news-consumer/.

2. Know the law: Avoid announcing on publicly owned property, such as a school or a civic building, and do not involve people who are on taxpayer-funded payrolls (such as school or government officials) during the workday, even during the lunch hour. While an announcement may be legal on publicly owned property, collecting money for a political cause may not be, and it is typical for people attending an announcement to hand the candidate a check.

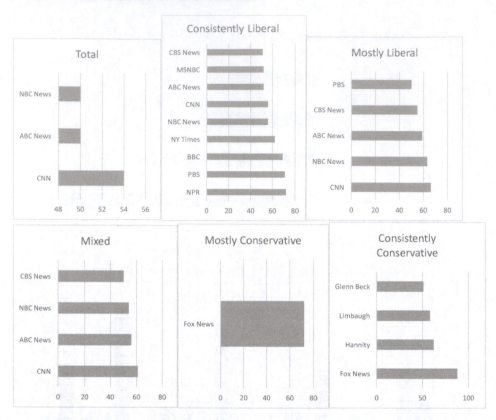

FIGURE 7.2 Credibility Ratings of Various News Sources in Relation to Ideology (% Saying They Trust Each News Source)

Source: Adapted from Pew Research Center, "Political Polarization and Media Habits: More News Sources Trusted by Those on the Left," October 20, 2014, http://www.journalism.org/2014/10/21/political-polarization62-media-habits/pj_14-10-21_mediapolarization-12/.

3. Schedule the announcement at the convenience of television crews rather than newspapers. Getting your face in front of the camera is important, and the print media can be covered with a press packet. Keep in mind that local television news crews typically work late at night and are not available until late morning.

4. Know the schedules of the press. An announcement should be held at a time and place that is convenient for the press, even if it is not convenient for your supporters. Call the local papers, and ask what time would work best for them, given their deadlines. If your announcement is too late for the newspaper reporters to attend, have printed news releases emailed to those who will miss it. Be sure to include a photo.

5. Make press packets available electronically.
6. Know what's going on in your community for the best coverage. Avoid major holidays, three-day weekends, Fridays (fewer people read Saturday's paper or watch Friday's evening news), and take advantage of community events where your candidate can be noticed, such as Fourth of July parades, in an inexpensive and effective way.
7. Have everything ready ahead of time. I recently witnessed a candidate announcement that was well attended with a retired congressman and dozens of community leaders who stood and waited while the candidate and his wife put up a banner with masking tape. It fell just as they finished, and the crowd waited as the process began anew.
8. Keep announcements short, know what you will say, and rehearse it over and over so you sound natural and well spoken. If you're nervous and think you'll need help, jot down some bullet points.
9. Line up supporters to write letters to the editor immediately after your announcement. Letters should be short and simply say how glad that individual is to hear you decided to join the race. Letters should also mention one or two things that are central to your message.

Letters to the Editor

Letters to the editor show a voter cares enough about a candidate or ballot measure to take the time to write a letter and get it to the paper. E-letters are limited in length, which is good, because short letters are more likely to be read and are often the lead letters, giving them prominence, plus newspapers tend to run them more quickly than more traditional letters to the editor.

Once published, letters are in the public domain, so the campaign can pull nuggets from them to use in endorsement ads, on a webpage, and in a brochure. Referenced quotes in advertising have more credibility.

Assign a committee member to oversee letters to the editor. This coordinator should be willing to write sample letters, provide general instructions and tips to potential letter writers, and be prepared to remind supporters about getting letters to the papers. It is one of the most difficult jobs of a campaign, so choose this person carefully, and do not assign any other campaign tasks to him or her.

Early letters stand out and tend to have a greater impact than later in the season, when competition heats up. Brevity is key; a good rule is for a letter to cover one subject and to be no longer than one or two short paragraphs. As important as a letter may be, the heading placed above it is more important. Shorter letters mean more boldfaced titles, which will be read, even by those just scanning the page.

Many papers have cutoff dates for letters to the editor. Get this information for each local paper, and place the date on the campaign plan, calendar, or flowchart. Most people procrastinate, so keep supporters apprised of the deadline as it approaches.

Other Free Media Coverage

Some newspapers have a public interest section that serves as a community chalkboard. If your candidate is speaking at the Rotary Club or the League of Women Voters, or if one of your committee members is giving a presentation on your ballot measure, be sure it gets into the community activity section of the paper. Figure 7.3 is an actual example from a local paper.

COMMUNITY

Dogs need vaccines and licenses
The Jackson County Animal Care and Control Center reminds the public of its on-going license checking program. All dogs over six mouths of age are required to have rabies vaccination and a dog license. Citations will be issued for violators.

In responding to the public's request, the center will be informing the public of the areas that will receive concentrated checking in the near future. The White City area will be the next on the list.

However, people are reminded that officers work all areas of the county. License checking may be done in any area at any time.

The goal of the license checking program is to achieve voluntary compliance, so people are urged to be sure their dogs are vaccinated and licensed.

House candidate to speak
Bev Clarno, Republican candidate for House District 55 will be the featured speaker **Wednesday** at the luncheon meeting of Jackson County Republican Women at J.J. North's in Medford. The luncheon will begin at 11:30 a.m., reservations are requied. For more information call 000-0000.

County fair entry books available
The Exhibitors Entry Book for the Jackson County Fair, July 19-24 and the Harvest Fair and Wine Fest, October 8-9, is now available from local Grange Co-Ops, the Jackson County Library and at the Fair office at the fairgrounds. Anyone interested in entering the fair competitions, both 4-H and Future Farmers of America (FFA), or Open Class must obtain an entry book.

Oregon poet will read in Ashland
Oregon poet and artist Sandy Diamond will be reading from her new book, "Miss Coffin and Mrs. Blood; Poems of Art and Madness," at Bloomsbury Books 7:30 p.m. on Monday.

CORRECTIONS

Christensen runs for city recorder
Barbara Christensen has obtained a petition to run for city recorder in November. Her name was misspelled in Thursday's paper, due to a reporter's error.

FIGURE 7.3 Example of the "Community" Section from a Local Paper

On this day, two candidates got some free ink.

Paid Print Media (Earned Media)

With declining readership, newspapers have increased rates for display advertising to the point that they can be out of reach for the down-ballot campaign. Considering the dwindling numbers that read newspapers, the lack of credibility they have with Republicans, and that newspapers miss most voters under the age of thirty, campaigns should consider whether this is a preferable way to spend limited campaign dollars. Still, should you choose to do so, there are three advertising formats that work well in newspapers: emotional, informational, and testimonial (endorsement). None of these ads are mutually exclusive.

- *Emotional ads* use pictures or other images and copy that will elicit emotion in the voters. Children at school, a couple talking privately, a child drinking clean water from a hose, congested streets, historic buildings, kids engaged in school activities, seniors, and before and after pictures—such as a forested hillside next to a clear-cut or a meadow juxtaposed to development on the same land.
- *Informational ads* are generally used with issue-based campaigns and are designed to let the voters know some bit of important information, such as the impact a losing tax measure may have on their lives or their pocketbook if it wins. For candidate races, comparison ads are an effective information format.
- Finally, *testimonials* or *endorsement ads* use a third person to speak on behalf of a candidate or cause. While those listed or quoted may be movers and shakers in a community, testimonials and endorsement ads can also feature the average person. The testimonial approach is especially effective in a candidate race: It's more effective for someone else to say you're great than for you to say it.

Advertising Formats for Newspapers

Political campaigns tend to look like clutter, a sort of strip mall of democracy. Whenever possible, organize your efforts and give a sense of continuity and neatness to your campaign. Use your logo in all campaign literature, or bring some thread from one medium to another to create continuity. Use your lawn sign as an identifier in print ads, television spots, direct mail, and social media ads and on badges for canvassers. It's your trademark, and it should be used just as a major corporation would use its trademark.

Although there are many formats for newspaper ads, here are a few examples that have helped move campaigns forward in the print media.

CATHY GOLDEN ON INDEPENDENT MANAGEMENT AUDITS

"Ashland city government is long overdue for a management audit by an outside professional firm. It just makes good economic sense.

Management audits consistently pay for themselves in money saved, improved service, and higher staff morale. And they let taxpayers know exactly what they're getting for their money."

Cathy
GOLDEN
FOR MAYOR

Building a Better Community

FIGURE 7.4 Example of Candidate Ad Made to Look Like a Newspaper Article

(Crystal Castle Graphics)

Create newspaper ads that mimic a news story in layout. Place the candidate's picture as a fairly prominent part of the ad. Select and place a headline with copy alongside the candidate picture. Ad copy should be no more than three paragraphs long, should cover only one subject, and should include the campaign logo and slogan. Figure 7.4 is an example.

This format can be rotated with five or six different headings and copy, and the picture of the candidate should vary to alert the reader that the content is different. This format works well as a *two-by-four*—two columns wide by four inches high. Smaller ads like this are more affordable and get placement on top of other ads, directly under newspaper copy. I have seen local races effectively place ads, daily, on each page of the paper.

A two-by-four lends itself well to informational and endorsement ads. Informational ads for issue-based campaigns should also adopt a uniform look that is recognizable to the public. Figure 7.5 is an example of an ad used in an issue-based campaign for school funding. The font, layout, and design intentionally lead the voter to connect the ad with schools. Similarly, the endorsement ad shown in figure 7.6 uses the same two-by-four format and visually links itself to other ads advocating for the same school tax measure.

Testimonial or endorsement ads are among the most effective you can use anywhere in a campaign, but they lend themselves especially well to newspaper advertising. Unfortunately, too many campaigns attempt to cram too much into this format. Remember, newspapers are inherently cluttered, so

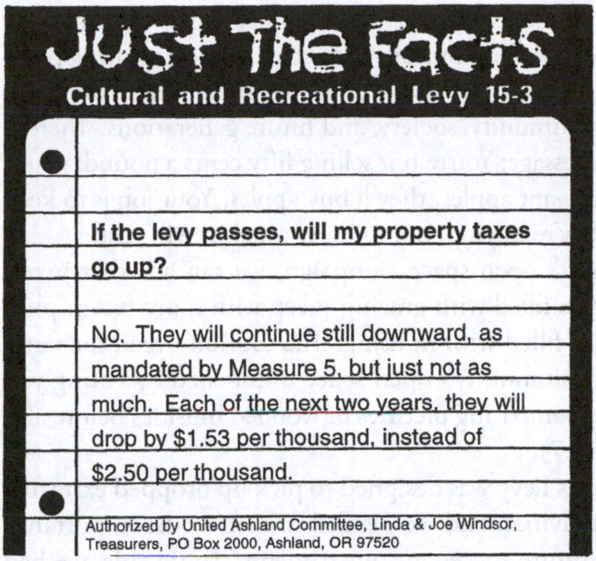

Just The Facts
Cultural and Recreational Levy 15-3

If the levy passes, will my property taxes go up?

No. They will continue still downward, as mandated by Measure 5, but just not as much. Each of the next two years, they will drop by $1.53 per thousand, instead of $2.50 per thousand.

Authorized by United Ashland Committee, Linda & Joe Windsor, Treasurers, PO Box 2000, Ashland, OR 97520

FIGURE 7.5 Example of an Information Ad

This ad uses graphical cues that we typically associate with schools to help the reader identify the ad with the tax measure. (Crystal Castle Graphics)

Thoughts on
Cultural and Recreational Levy 15-3

"If the citizens of Ashland desire to maintain the academic and cultural assets of their community, then it is imperative to find some method of funding for the schools. The community is fortunate that the city of Ashland is in a position to generate some funding for this purpose." -- **Sam Hall,** former Ashland Schools Superintendent

Vote Yes on 15-3

Authorized by United Ashland Committee, Linda & Joe Windsor, Treasurers, PO Box 2000, Ashland, OR 97520

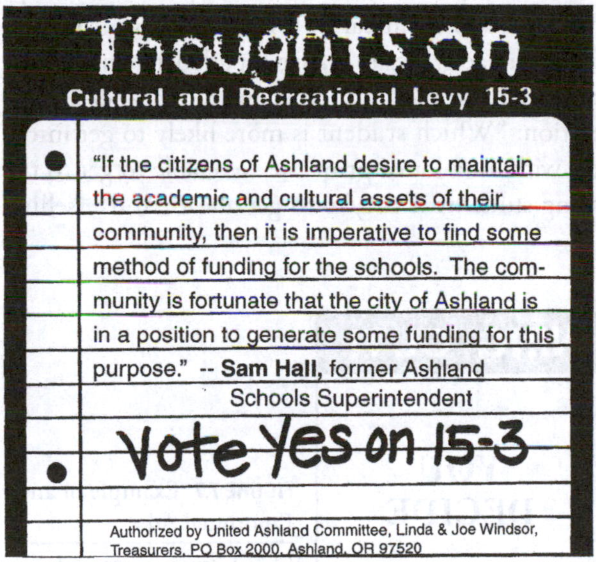

FIGURE 7.6 Example of a Two-by-Four Newspaper Endorsement Ad for an Issue-Based Campaign

By design, this ad links itself to schools and other ads for the same tax measure. (Crystal Castle Graphics)

help your ads breathe. Keep the pictures simple and memorable. Pictures in small-format ads are difficult to see and work best with a close-up of only one person: the candidate (not the individual giving the quote). Resist the temptation to show the candidate shaking hands with the person lending the quote. Keep all ads clean and minimal.

As the campaign progresses and the candidate gains endorsements, some of these candidate ads can be recycled to emphasize a point.

Issue-based campaigns generally do best with ads that tug at emotion. Expanding a library, adding curriculum options for a school, and acquiring parkland are not about how affordable the projects are but rather about what the projects will do for your community, society, and future generations. There is no price for that. Stay on message: You're not selling fifty cents a pound; you're selling apples, and if voters want apples, they'll buy apples. Your job is to keep people focused on what they're buying, not on how much it will cost.

For example, in Ashland's open-space campaign, we ran ads that juxtaposed pictures of open fields filled with grazing sheep with more recent photos showing the same fields filled with housing. The caption urged the voter to help leave some of the community's open space untouched by voting yes. Similarly, we ran other ads comparing pictures of wooded hillsides before and after development (figure 7.7).

Ashland's Youth Activities Levy was designed to pick up dropped extracurricular and cocurricular activities, and we needed to convey the importance of these programs to the future success of our students. To do this, we had one ad that juxtaposed two transcripts of the same student. One transcript had an excellent GPA; the other was identical in GPA, but also included a list of all the student's cocurricular activities in leadership, debate, and sports. The caption read: "Which student would you rather hire?" Another ad was identical except for the caption: "Which student is more likely to get into a great college?" In these ads, without a lot of print, we were able to get to the heart of the challenges facing students if they're to get ahead. You're selling

TIME IS RUNNING OUT!

YOU
DECIDE

OR

The revenues generated
by Measure 15-1 will
help preserve the land
that gives Ashland its
unique character.

Paid for & authorized by the *Good for Ashland!*
Committee, Hal Cloer, Treasurer, PO Box 0, Ashland, OR

IT'S GOOD FOR ASHLAND! VOTE YES ON 15-1

FIGURE 7.7 Example of an Emotional Ad

(TAO Productions and Crystal Castle Graphics)

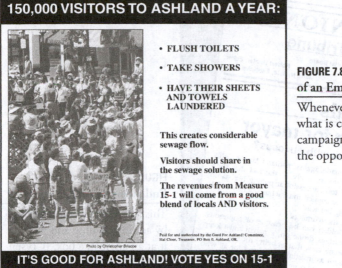

150,000 VISITORS TO ASHLAND A YEAR:

- **FLUSH TOILETS**

- **TAKE SHOWERS**

- **HAVE THEIR SHEETS AND TOWELS LAUNDERED**

This creates considerable sewage flow.

Visitors should share in the sewage solution.

The revenues from Measure 15-1 will come from a good blend of locals AND visitors.

Paid for and authorized by the Good For Ashland! Committee, Hal Cloer, Treasurer, PO Box 0, Ashland, OR.

Photo by Christopher Briscoe

IT'S GOOD FOR ASHLAND! VOTE YES ON 15-1

FIGURE 7.8 Another Example of an Emotional Ad

Whenever possible, use what is coming at your campaign and redirect it to the opposition.

opportunity, not twenty-five cents per thousand; if you're discussing the impacts the measure will have on the home owner's property tax, you're on the opposition's message.

When local restaurants opposed a food and beverage tax for funding parkland acquisition and upgrades to the wastewater treatment plant, they argued that the tax was on the tourists who visit our city each year to enjoy the Shakespeare Festival. We agreed. They then said it was a tax on locals. We agreed again. To say this dramatically, we ran an ad with a picture of the city's central plaza on the Fourth of July, when more than 30,000 people drop in for the day. The caption pointed out that 150,000 visitors each year use our parks, have their bedding laundered, and flush toilets (figure 7.8). We took what was coming at us and redirected it back at the opposition, implying that visitors, like residents, should help pay for the systems they use.

Endorsements and Endorsement Ads

Endorsements from support groups, editorial boards, and business and community leaders can mean both money and votes for your campaign. As you get endorsements, place them on your webpage and Facebook page, and incorporate them into your brochure, direct mail, and newspaper, television, and radio ads.

Endorsement ads or testimonials can take many forms. You can list the names of hundreds of people who support you, hopefully showing a broad

FIGURE 7.9 Example of an Endorsement Ad

This ad was made more striking by adding shading and placing it at an angle in a box. (Crystal Castle Graphics)

cross-section of your community; you can pull quotations and names from letters to the editor; or you can have a page of logos from businesses that endorse you, with a caption identifying you. Figure 7.9 is an example of an actual ad that included the endorsement of a newspaper's editorial board.

Endorsement ads listing hundreds of names have gotten a lot easier. All campaigns should collect names of supporters, usually from remit envelopes or on sign-up sheets, to list on the campaign webpage. I like the names to scroll and move with the webpage visitor from page to page. These names can easily be gathered and listed in mass for a regional newspaper ad. However, another way is to isolate each of the local community tabloids and list supporters from just those communities in corresponding tabloids. For example, in my county there are a dozen or so cities, half of which have local newspapers that are usually printed monthly. For the small publications in targeted communities, I place an endorsement ad with selected supporters from just those communities. I like to present the copy with the candidate message by way of endorsement quotes at the top of the ad, and then I list twenty or thirty prominent people from just that city, directly below the endorsement quotes.

Always maintain a field in your campaign database for an endorsement-ad sort. Use the computer to sort names alphabetically to help you find duplicates. However, when it comes time to run the endorsement ad, randomly list the names so people read through them all, searching for familiar names. Also, random order allows you to put your big names in prominent locations, like at the top of columns or just above a prominent quote.

In my first mayoral campaign, we ran the endorsement ad on eighty-pound bright-yellow paper, printed three-up, with a die-cut (a hole at the top) so it could hang from doorknobs. On the front at the top was the logo and the phrase "Join us in voting for Cathy Golden for Mayor." Below was a list of hundreds of names, which continued on the back to cover both sides of the door hanger. At the crack of dawn, the Saturday before the election, about sixty volunteers covered the city in two hours. No matter where voters traveled in the city that day, these yellow endorsement door hangers could be seen hanging from doorknobs.

After the food and beverage tax passed, funding parkland and wastewater treatment plant upgrades, restaurant owners began placing a postcard on every table in every restaurant in town. On one side, it asked patrons to let the city know what they thought about the meals tax, and on the other side of the card was my name and address at city hall. Obviously, the idea was to have patrons tell me that they hated the tax. Naturally, some postcards said just that; however, many came in with glowing remarks about Ashland and how happy the visitors were to contribute in some small way to the beauty of our community. I saved these cards. Eventually, opponents of the tax pulled a petition and referred it back out to the voters through the initiative process. Once the referral qualified for the ballot and it was clear that we would have to run another campaign, I took the postcards supporting the tax and printed them verbatim in an endorsement ad (figure 7.10). Because I had not asked permission to use the names of the people who sent me postcards, I used initials. Again, take what is coming at you and redirect it to the opposition.

Use both endorsements and published letters to the editor in online advertising. For a campaign website, assign a campaign committee member to troll the newspaper for letters and then select a memorable sentence from each. This sentence is what goes on the site with a "more" link that will open the full letter for those who want to read it. Prominent endorsements are

168

We *LIKE* the Meals Tax

We've been coming to Ashland since 1970. OSF is the impetus, but we've come to love the charm of your city/area. We make three trips a year into your economy. Since the ambience of the area attracts us, we don't object to contributing to ambience things like park areas, and mundane things like sewers. We're not paying the total cost with our 5% meal tax, just a contribution (maybe $25 a year). It's a small price to pay for the joy we get in return. How would the critics finance these things? And if you don't have them, folks like us wouldn't come. Don't be foolish, there's no free lunch – and we had a picnic in the park last night. 5% was only $1.50.
– R.S.
Eugene, OR

I applaud the wisdom of your voters in implementing this tax. I hope it continues.
– B.C.
Edmonds, WA

As frequent summer vacation visitors to Ashland, my wife and I are pleased to make a small contribution to the well being of your beautiful city through the tax. We feel it to be a good idea, not unreasonable.
– J.R.M.
Portland, OR

Paying 5% on our meals is a small price to pay to help keep Ashland the lovely city it is.
– T.W. **Talent, OR**

As a frequent visitor to Ashland, I welcome the opportunity to help pay for parks, open space and water treatment. The 5% tax seems appropriate to me.
– K.R.D. **Corvallis, OR**

I think you would be CRAZY NOT to collect this tax. These services benefit tourists, like us, therefore we should pay for them. This tax should focus more on visitors who put demands on your open space and utilities. Restaurant oriented taxation does that.
– J.H.J.
Winters, CA

I think the restaurants are foolish to oppose this tax. I support it and think we should have one in Eugene.
– G.S.
Eugene, OR

Good for you! Deal with your real problems ... I'm glad to chip in my share.
– M.P.
San Luis Obispo, CA

Although I work at a local coffee shop and am surrounded by opposition to the meals tax, I still support it. Please stick with your aims and goals no matter what pressure the restaurant owners put on you. 'Good Job!'.
– **Ashland, OR**

We have been annual visitors to Ashland for the past 16 years, and we do not feel burdened to support this sales tax for Ashland's parks and sewers (both of which we USE).
– R.K.
Los Altos, CA

Save our funding for park acquisition
VOTE NO ON 15-1 and YES ON 15-2
Paid & authorized by the Good for Ashland Committee, Jean Crawford, Treasurer

FIGURE 7.10 Another Example of an Endorsement Ad

Again, whenever possible, redirect back to the opposition what they send your way. (TAO Productions and Crystal Castle Graphics) scattered throughout the pages of the campaign website, and of course all endorsements scroll on the page. As noted above, the scrolling names follow the visitor from page to page.

One caution on endorsement ads for those running for a judge or district attorney: Listing a disproportionate number of attorneys and those making a living in law enforcement can backfire. Voters need to know a judge or DA will be impartial once elected, and when too many who potentially will work with or come before the individual seeking office, voters become wary. One way around this issue is to simply omit identifiers that might typically be used to precede or follow a name such as "atty.," "JD," "Capt.," or "Lt."

The avenues with which campaigns communicate with the voters are fairly standard. However, in politics, when the period during which you must attract the voters' attention and move them to support you—and vote for you—is so short, irritating ads can hurt more than help. You want ads that create a buzz in a memorable way to break out of the clutter. A creative and memorable political campaign costs no more than one that is indistinct in every way.

Years ago, I was involved in a campaign for a circuit judge. In the campaign war room was a local newspaper columnist who had been riding me and city hall for years. From time to time, I had responded to his missives with guest editorials that were as hard-hitting as those he had aimed at me. Our ongoing feud was well known in the community. One evening we happened to sit directly across the table from each other during a campaign committee meeting. Everyone in the room knew the backstory, and the tension was palpable. While we were discussing possible newspaper advertising, I suggested that the columnist and I be photographed back to back, arms crossed, looking directly at the camera. The caption would read, "They can only agree on one thing: Phil Arnold should be elected circuit court judge." We ran the ad. People in our community loved it and commented on it repeatedly.

Campaigns are the most fluid segment of the advertising market, and nowhere is it more important for your campaign to adapt to changing circumstances and new information than in advertising.

Placing Your Newspaper Buys

For newspaper advertising, talk to the person who sells display ads for your local papers. Although newspapers often include ad layout as part of the package, it is best to have your ad designed by a professional outside the newspaper. It is also worth paying extra to choose where in the paper the ad will be placed. Requesting placement typically adds 15 percent to the cost of the ad, but as the saying goes: in for a penny, in for a pound. Salespeople will tell you that it's not necessary to request placement and that they will do all they can to get you what you want for no extra money. This works about half the time. I have found that the personal bias, at least with small papers, gets your ad placed where they want it, not where you want it. If you can afford it, pay for placement.

The best spot for ad placement is opposite the editorial page, which some papers no longer allow for political ads. Pages 2 and 3 are also good choices. Stick to the outside of the page, not the fold. Much farther back in the paper, and your ad is at risk of disappearing. Don't forget the television listings section. In many papers, this section is tabloid size, and a full-page ad there costs a third as much as a full-page ad in the regular paper. Plus, people, especially seniors, keep the TV section around all week.

If you have the money and the space is available, a full-page or half-page ad on the back of the newspaper can work wonders. One local woman running for state representative bought the top half of the back page. Most of it was a color reproduction of a watercolor by a local artist of the hills surrounding our city. It was the best newspaper ad I'd ever seen. She won by a handful of votes.

One way to mitigate the high cost of media advertising yet still reach newspaper readers is to pay your daily to place an insert in its paper for your campaign. Given that newspaper readers are more likely to vote and are better educated, older, and more inclined to support schools, parks, and civic endeavors, this may be the happy compromise for getting the word out for a candidate or an issue-based campaign to a targeted audience at a reasonable cost.

Fielding Questions from the Press: Top Tips

1. *Project the image of a credible community leader.* What kind of clues are you giving that speak louder than your words? Avoid nervous behavior: Don't click your pen repeatedly, jingle change in your pocket, or twist your hair. Avoid verbal ticks, such as "like," "um," "if you will," "quite frankly," "you know," and "to be honest." Toeing the ground—looking down and moving your foot in a half moon with your toe—abdicates power to the other person. So does crossing your feet while standing (you're making yourself smaller). Stand with your feet no farther apart than shoulder width. Use your hands as a way to emphasize what you're saying. Speak in a clear, firm voice, and look directly at the reporter. Keep your hands away from your face; this is a hard thing to remember when you're sitting behind a desk.

2. *Be sure you know your subject well.* Reporters do much better if you're to the point and they don't have to do a lot of work to figure out what you're saying. Frankly, you don't want them to; reading a reporter's summation of a long candidate ramble typically ends with the candidate groaning and saying: That's not what I meant.

3. *Think about your audience.* Although you may have the reporter in front of you at that moment, it is the voter who will be reading what you say the next day. Talk to your base first, and then consider potential swing voters. Always draw a strong line on core values to help rally the base behind you.

4. *Try to keep a positive spin on everything.* Reporters like to print controversy, but if that will hurt your cause, do not go there. Remember, you do not have to answer the question being asked; you just have to sound as if you're answering it.

5. *Unless it's your intention, don't answer a question that hasn't been asked.* Candidates often will hear one question when another is asked or want to offer up more information than is necessary. Shorter is better. Keep on your message, and do not let a reporter pull you off.

6. *Take a moment.* When the press calls, take a moment to think about what you will say, call someone for help if you need it, jot down some notes, and then return the call.

7. *In general, return all calls promptly.* As a rule, the earlier you're interviewed, the higher up you will appear in an article.

8. *Avoid going "off the record."* Watch your post-interview banter as well.

9. *Never speak when angry.* Calm down, and then do the interview. It's always preferable to wish you said something than to wish you hadn't. As Ambrose Bierce said, "Speak when you are angry and you will make the best speech you will ever regret."

10. *Select where the interview takes place.* Think about the backdrop and whether its visual effect can further your message.

Radio

Generally speaking, candidates seeking an office in a small town might be well advised to discard radio and television, focusing on mixes of the other media. On the other hand, candidates running for a countywide seat, state senate, state representative, mayor of the county's largest city, or further up the food chain should consider television and radio.

Morning and evening drive time is still the most coveted of all time slots on radio and has arguably the largest reach. However, equally important is that many workplaces also pipe in radio stations all day for workers and patrons. Needless to say, radio stations know and track their audience for advertising purposes, so reaching certain segments of the population through radio is pretty easy. And by the way, average commute times for cities can be found in the US Census.

"Radio ads are narrowcast, targeted toward particular audiences with distinguishing characteristics." Listeners choose a station that appeals to their sensibilities: Christian rock, oldies, classical, country/western, hip-hop, NPR news and information, Latino, or contemporary music formats. Because radio listeners' loyalty is predicated on a specific format, listeners do not surf, and campaigns can actually target one audience on one station with a specific message and target a completely different audience on another station with a completely different message.[3]

Because radio paints a picture with words and sounds, it should be treated differently than television. Nevertheless, a few years back, one of my clients ran a sixty-second radio spot from two thirty-second television ads we produced. Because the ads were rich with Foley work (background sound) and had scripts that could stand alone without the TV images, it completely worked. As a side benefit, the ads playing in two media reinforced each other with no additional production costs.

Radio spots are generally sixty seconds long, which allows the campaign plenty of time to tell a story, and due to their length "radio ads really do impart more information." Further, research indicates that the more voters are "exposed to campaign ads on the radio, the more importance they attach to the information they receive from such ads."[4] In one local primary, a candidate running for circuit court judge ran a very effective radio campaign. He had inadvertently missed the deadline for the voters' pamphlet in the primary and was facing a well-heeled opponent who was everywhere, including on television. The voters' pamphlet is one of the most respected and effective tools a campaign has in Oregon, and not appearing in it is a death knell. To overcome his opponent's money and organization, the candidate saturated radio stations with a great ad reminding voters that he was the one who *wasn't* in the voters' pamphlet and blamed it on his campaign manager, himself, whom he said he then fired. It was clever and memorable enough to help him survive the primary and eventually win in a runoff in the general election.

But let's be clear: Radio is for some campaigns more than others, so know who you're targeting and do it with the right message. For example, "Republicans report higher levels of exposure [to radio] than similarly situated Democrats," and "men are significantly more likely to find radio ads important than are women, and more religiously active citizens rely significantly more on radio ads for campaign information than do otherwise similarly situated secular citizens." Also, Caucasians report "less influence from both radio and television ads than do non-Caucasians."[5] Indeed, campaigns should not overlook the power of radio in communicating with Hispanic populations, especially in more rural areas where Spanish-language radio and television stations are limited. According to Laura Sonderup in "Hispanic Marketing: A Critical Market Segment":

- Radio is a proven, effective medium in targeting Hispanics.
- The most unique aspect of Spanish-language radio stations is the amount of time spent listening.
- The Hispanic population often listens to the radio all day.
- The entire family may listen to one station and tune in, on average, twenty-six to thirty hours per week. This ranks more than 13 percent above the general population.[6]

Once you know the audience you want to reach, contact radio stations and ask for a schedule to achieve your goals. Multiple stations are often located under one roof, and salespeople know who listens to what.

Television

Before deciding to advertise on television, your campaign must first determine whether the medium is within your financial reach and whether it is worth it. If you're running for office in a small city or down-ballot in a countywide race, such as tax assessor, there are much better ways to spend your money than buying television time, such as video ads on your website or within social media. And if you're involved in an issue-based campaign, a couple of things may help make this decision both easier and harder: First, television is a great way to brand a community service (like pools), but issue-based campaigns do not enjoy the same political rate break as candidates.

Is It Worth It?

Television once had a vast reach, especially in rural areas, which often had access to only a few local stations and limited cable penetration. But with streaming services like Netflix and Hulu, DVRs, cable TV, and digital set-top boxes, television's best and most reliable reach now is to older voters who watch upward of thirty-five hours per week. Middle-aged voters are best reached by mail and millennials through the Internet and canvassing. But if a campaign has the resources, television can legitimize a candidate or campaign issue more quickly and effectively than any other medium—especially with older voters who actually vote.

Although the costs for television ads near major media markets can be prohibitively expensive, that is not necessarily true in more rural areas. For example, in my market, production for a thirty-second TV spot runs from $500 to $5,000 and anywhere from $8 per spot on cable to $3,300 for a thirty-second ad on a top-ranked network program. Spending $3,300 for a thirty-second spot is completely unnecessary for the down-ballot race, as any campaign can get equal reach with increased frequency on cable or on network television during the day or close to prime time.

Cable Television: A Better Buy

In larger media markets, cable remains affordable, and in small markets, it can be downright cheap, depending on the station, show, and placement. For example, in small markets, a campaign can buy a thirty-second spot on cable for about $10. While $10 sounds cheap—and it is—remember, you're typically buying six spots per day on six to seven cable channels for three weeks. It adds up.

Cable advertising is often available only on rotators. That means you buy six spots, and the station will rotate your thirty-second ad through a time slot, like twenty-four hours or (for a little more) from 6:00 p.m. to 12:00 a.m. I've never found this to be a problem and research my buys with that in mind. People watch at all times of the day and night; the trick is to line up your buys on a daytime rotator with shows that people watch during the day and an evening rotator for cable networks and programs that tend to get watched more at night.

Much of cable has become narrowcasting, with networks that cater to specific viewer interests, such as the History Channel, the Weather Channel, HGTV, and cable news like Fox and MSNBC. Beyond cable networks, the level that television viewing has been analyzed both in and out of the trade is worth researching to target a specific demographic your campaign wants to reach.

After the 2016 presidential election, the *New York Times* ran a fascinating piece underscoring just how close culture and politics are when it comes to TV viewing. It is not only about the urban-rural divide but also about suburbs, geographic regions, race, and party. They tracked viewers according to Facebook "likes" by zip code.[7]

To research viewer demographics juxtaposed to your targeted audience, check out Pew Research, the Television Bureau of Advertising (www.tvb.org), the entertainment section of *Business Insider*, and Nielsen Online (nielsen-online.com) for Web audiences by site, size, demographic profile, and behavior. Once a campaign knows its audience, a small amount of time in research can help target both Internet advertising and television audiences and save money.

Fat-Free TV

Although production for television should be left in the hands of a professional, the more you know about the process, the more input you'll have in the finished product. There are a number of ways to stretch your campaign dollars if you decide to use television advertising.

Whether you're cutting the ad yourself in a software program or have hired a media consultant, it's important to do as much front-end work as possible. Research the strengths and weaknesses of your candidate so that strengths may be accentuated in ads that establish a candidate and weaknesses so that the team is better prepared to quickly respond to attacks.

Your campaign should also research the strengths and weaknesses of the opposition. Even if you do not intend to run negative ads, by researching the opposition's flaws, you can juxtapose your candidate's strengths with your opponent's weaknesses even though they're never directly mentioned; they simply become implied: "Jane Doe will not miss important votes" implies that her opponent has.

Gather as much background information about your candidate: images in the form of newspaper articles, childhood and current family photos (especially ones that help underscore what you want to project), career history, and a list of names and phone numbers of close family and friends the media consultant can contact. This small effort not only makes for better ads but also helps your consultant do his or her job efficiently. Also, collect newspaper clippings of the opposing candidate for possible use in advertising.

As an aside, the local community-access station is often hungry for programming and may be willing to produce shows for a candidate at little or no charge. Such productions can provide some outstanding material for your producer to use in an ad or a portion of an ad.

Finally, don't forget to check what is available within your community. In one election, we did not have enough material for a particular ad a candidate wanted, so an appeal was put out in the community for any video on the candidate. One local resident had footage of all the candidates in a Fourth of July parade. Although the quality was marginal, converting it to black and white and slowing the motion gave it a timeless quality; it added a great deal to the ad.

Ad Production

Before you hire someone to produce your ads, check to see what level of expertise already exists within your campaign team. Digital cameras can capture video of amazing quality, and the average consumer is becoming incredibly adept at editing and producing short works. Volunteer producers can also be found at local cable-access stations, where fledgling producers may be willing to work for the experience and exposure. One note of caution: Contact the local TV stations beforehand so you can meet required formats.

Finding Outside Talent

Finding a good production team can be as easy as noting which locally produced ads you like—whether they're political spots or for commercial businesses. I am continually amazed at the poor quality of local ads in my area: picture quality, graphics, and sound. But from time to time, one will stand out and include rich visuals and Foley (sound) work. Typically, the advertising department knows who produced what, so give them a call for details.

Make Ideas Your Own

Spend time reviewing other political spots online for ideas and script inspiration. There is no reason an agency cannot model your ad after another campaign somewhere else in the country. Stanford University's Political Communication Lab has archived thousands of political ads: http://pcl.stanford .edu/campaigns.

Keep It Simple

- Be sure the final product does not include unnecessary or distracting motion like clever swirls and bizarre dissolves.
- Avoid a voice-over that is trying to cram in as many words as humanly possible; a thirty-second television spot should have no more than eighty words.
- It is always preferable to have the script written by the campaign.
- If it is written by the producer, the campaign committee should review and approve the script.
- Any on-screen type should reinforce what's being said rather than introduce new thoughts.
- A film-like softness can be created with lighting.

- Movement adds a great deal—whether it is the candidate walking door-to-door (hopefully toward the camera) or panning across a still photo.
- Enough still photos with a great script and a professional voice-over can make a fabulous ad at affordable rates.
- Reserve talking-head ads for a candidate who is responding to an attack or for featuring local stars or incumbents with clout who are willing to publicly endorse a candidate or cause.

B-Roll

B-roll is supplemental footage that can be inserted into an ad to enrich the story being told. There are plenty of occasions for the media team to attend events that include both candidates, providing a venue to capture footage of each. Seizing opportunities of this nature allows your campaign to study both candidates and pick up material for additional ads or for use to intercut with the main shot in an interview format. Anytime a candidate attends a debate, send someone to catch it on a smartphone or digital camera, and if a local station or public access channel has a debate or candidate forum, ask for a copy or the link to online access; after all, they do have professionals lighting the stage and working the cameras. Over the years, we have cut a number of 30-second spots from recorded candidate forums but now use this sort of footage just for 1:20 spots to promote a candidate's position on his or her Facebook page (and we promote it heavily). Look to your community for possible B-roll opportunities or see what's available online of ordinary people doing ordinary things to cut into and enhance your ad—just Google "B-roll."

Streamline Production: Ten Tips to Save Money and Improve Your Television Spots

1. As a candidate, if you're delivering a speaking part, know your part and be fully prepared.
2. Bring a change of clothes. Typically, a production company will get all of the shots for multiple ads in one day and will attempt to create or re-create events and settings that are quite different. So the candidate may be featured (supposedly) at a day care center, a business, a senior center, and so on. If the candidate is wearing the same clothes in each of the settings, viewers will notice, and the ads will lose the very thing they hope to frame. If you are going from farm to senate chambers, dress appropriately for each setting.

3. If the ad involves testimonials, provide the scripts ahead of time and impress upon those involved that they need to know their parts. It is more effort than you can imagine getting an average person to sound plausible in advertising; there's a reason advertisers use actors for testimonials.

4. Find locations that convey message and image. Think about these ahead of time—for example, a backdrop of traffic congestion for a candidate underscoring indiscriminate development, air pollution, quality of life, and that sort of thing.

5. Use of candidate, community photos, and newspaper headlines with a professional voice-over reading a great script will create a credible and very affordable ad with a professional look. Check out online pros who can email you the voice-over (VO).

6. Get enough baseline footage so that more ads can be cut without sending the crew out again.

7. Try using just music and no VO. Because TV is so noisy, if a thirty-second ad appears with only music, everyone looks.

8. For a relatively small cost, your campaign can purchase stock images to convey a message or create an emotion. This is especially important when your ad covers delicate issues such as domestic violence. Shutterstock is one source, but there are others; Google "stock images."

9. Send a professional photographer or talented amateur to early campaign events, for both your candidate and the opposition. You'd be amazed at how handy this footage can be.

10. Buying television and radio is not a complicated prospect in a small media market, especially if you're willing to do some research and have a clear idea with whom you want to communicate. This small effort will save a campaign 15 percent on the buys—a price break that is normally given to the production company making the buys. Do not fall victim to agencies that make your television spot for free, knowing they will make their money, and then some, on the buys. Once an ad is made "free of charge," a campaign feels disinclined to ask for changes and obligated to use it, especially in a small market where agencies are headed up by friends or acquaintances.

In one campaign cycle, I received a call from a candidate who was working with a local advertising agency. The candidate had gone heavily into debt in the nonpartisan primary race, outspending the opponents nearly three to one, and he wanted to know how to get to a win for the general election. After looking over all his materials, which were rather rudimentary, I looked at his TV spot. It was awful. I told him he had to ask the agency to make a new one. He said, "But it was done at no charge to my campaign." I pointed out how much money the agency made placing the buys at his expense; still, he could not bring himself to ask for a better ad. He lost the general, even though he outspent his opponent again. A bad ad—free or otherwise—is just that: a bad ad.

Great Ads Don't Just Happen

In television and radio campaign advertising, there are generally three types of ads: establishing, comparison, and response/attack. Whatever the format of your ad, certain overriding principles apply to all.

Know your objective. What does the campaign hope to accomplish with the ad?

A good ad begins with a good script. The fewer spoken words, the better; aim for fewer than eighty. Although you're buying thirty seconds of ad time, it is actually twenty-nine and a half. Too often, campaigns compensate for long scripts by having the narrator read faster. As Pascal said in 1656, "I have only made this letter rather long because I have not had time to make it short." Take the time.

The first ad should establish the candidate. Establishment ads tell a story about who he or she is; your ad must stay focused on just that aspect of the candidate. It should tug at emotion, providing a voyeuristic glimpse into the candidate's personal life, past and present. It's a time capsule of what this potential community leader will bring to the table in terms of experience and core values. Is she a fighter? Has he volunteered for country or community? Has the candidate had unique challenges in life that have shaped who he or she is? This is a good place for the old photos you had the candidate dig up.

Show clear comparisons between the candidates. This can be implied or direct.

Use language that reflects that of your voters. Don't talk over people's heads, and don't talk down to them. Talk about issues the way real people would talk about them.

Make the ads believable. Whether you are attacking your opponent or promoting your objectives, be accurate about accusations and specific and realistic about promises and programs you want to bring to the voters once you are elected.

Look at other political ads—a lot of them. Political ads are available on many university websites as well as candidate sites. As mentioned above, there are thousands of political ads dating back to 1994 at the Political Communication Lab at Stanford University with more posted each election cycle.

Let others do your bidding. Using family or prominent, respected community leaders can be an effective tool for an outsider to establish authenticity and credibility of a candidate. Using on-the-street people can show that an incumbent is still connected to everyday people.

Use black and white. What color does for direct mail, black and white does for TV. It's an effective tool to get noticed and to create mood, intimacy, and a sense of history for the candidate or issue-based campaign.

Ads should be easily distinguishable from one another. In a recent election cycle, a local ad firm cut four ads, each with the candidate sitting in a large leather chair talking directly to the camera. Other than the script, they were identical. Given that the opposition was making age an issue, the candidate could have met that criticism without actually acknowledging it by showing images of him fly-fishing knee-deep in a river. Instead, what he got were four ads that looked identical to the average viewer.

Use motion. When a candidate speaks directly to the camera, have him or her moving forward, either to a stationary camera or to one that moves with the speaker.

Use still photography and create motion by zooming in or panning pictures. By mixing childhood photos with more current images, you can tell a story about the candidate in a controlled, evocative way. Still photos work well for issue-based campaigns.

Carefully select the music. Do not think you can simply use images or music because you downloaded it off some secondary site on the Internet. Copyright infringement is a serious business, where campaigns may be fined up to $150,000 in statutory damages for willfully infringing on copyrighted material—and that includes instances where there is no actual proof of damages.[8] Don't risk getting your campaign on the front pages of the local paper for the wrong reasons: There is an abundance of copyright-free music available for purchase. The Music Bakery has a great selection, but many online services are available. Most sites do not expect payment for a piece until you download it for use. Heads-up: Selecting music takes a lot longer than you can imagine.

A few years back, we made a spot for a candidate who wanted different music than we were proposing for his ad, so we sent him to Stanford Media's website to view other political ads and find something he liked better, which he did. We were then able to very closely match what he liked. You want to be involved in your production; you should always feel you can tweak an ad so it is more to your liking.

Answer attacks. Sometimes, answering attacks can simply be a pivot and deflect motion. In a 2014 state senate race, our candidate was being hit from multiple angles with incessant negative campaigning that covered our candidate's divorce from decades ago as well as his voting record of the past decade. Since our opponent's hit pieces were revealed to the voters through direct mail, television, and radio, we responded to the general morass using a thirty-second spot that we produced for TV and our candidate's Facebook page, which the campaign promoted heavily. We cut the copy into parts of sentences and had different community leaders from different occupations give a few words of the copy and then cut it all together in one coherent script.

The ad opened with the candidate in front of a hundred-year-old red barn:

"How you run your campaign reflects how you will serve."

This line was followed by a cacophony of negative ads produced by the opposition overlaid with newspaper headlines claiming the opposition campaign had sunk to the level of Willie Horton–type ads. This then cut to the testimonials of community leaders:

"They say if you don't have a record to run on" (local business leader)

"then you paint your opponent as someone to run from." (former county commissioner and physician)

"Alan Bates's opponent is using attack ads" (cattle rancher from a corner of the district)

"to distort his record," (former mayor from a small town in the district)

"discredit him, and scare you." (former teacher)

"Don't be fooled by negative ads." (small business owner and city councilor)

"I'm Alan Bates, and I'm proud of my campaign." (then back to the candidate in front of the barn)

Each of the people delivering lines had different backdrops reinforcing their occupations; all had tag lines. It was sixty-two words.

Remember, television is about emotion, not information. In 2016 Gerald Daugherty, a Republican county commission candidate for Travis County in Texas, ran an ad that was dubbed the Best Political Ad of the Year. "Please Re-Elect Gerald . . . Please!" was viewed nearly 4 million times across the nation and is worth a look if you haven't seen it: https://www.youtube.com/watch ?v=wzjRwNUQDRU.

The audio is primarily of the candidate rambling on about this or that issue while doing things around the house, at the table with family and friends, and grilling steaks on the barbecue; it is entirely possible that everything he references is actual. The underlying theme is his wife begging voters to reelect him, ostensibly to focus his governing obsessions in government rather than while folding laundry or whatever. When you look at the ad, there is little doubt it played a role in the candidate's three-and-a-half-point win, especially given that Hillary Clinton won the county by nearly eighteen points. After the election, the campaign updated the outcome online, which you can also find at the above website.

Placing Your Buys on Television: Research, Research, Research

The advantage of television, like radio, is that the market has been thoroughly researched, offering the campaign ample detail about where to best target specific voters. There are many sources you can use to research who views what, such as Cabletelevision Advertising Bureau, Rocky Mountain Media Watch, Simmons National Consumer Study, Nielsen, and Doublebase Mediamark Research. Industry-tracking firms know who is watching what according to age, education, voting history, income, geography, and gender.

What is helpful for the campaign is that by using industry resources, you can develop and run ads that speak to an audience that is more likely to vote and one with highly specific demographics. Knowing who watches what helps a campaign avoid overtargeting a particular demographic group as well as reach the kind of voters who, with a little information, will support your efforts. Indeed, if your campaign can produce great TV ads for around five hundred dollars, why not run a different ad on different cable stations at the same time? After all, the airtime is the same, so the campaign is only out the production costs.

The Buys

Political candidates must be offered the lowest unit rate. However, be aware that if you come in at this rate, your time is "preemptable" by other buyers. This means you can be bumped by someone who is willing to pay the full price. Usually, you will be moved to a "comparable," that is, a spot with similar demographics. A second tier, at a slightly higher rate, is "preempt-able with notice." At this rate, the ad rep must let you know you're about to be bumped so that you can pay more to secure the spot. Finally, the most expensive rate is nonpreemptable. You pay for this rate, and you're gold: No one moves you.

If you're working on an issue-based campaign, there may not be any price break for TV ads. If that is the case, add at least 20 to 50 percent to your television budget buys. With that said, on one campaign for a school bond measure, I called a sales rep at one of our three local stations and suggested that "local" issue-based campaigns were different from statewide initiatives, which came fortified with millions in special-interest money. Convinced, the station gave us the candidate rate, so I called the other stations and told them what their competition was doing for the community and got similar breaks across the board.

Because most campaigns run their media with greater frequency as the election approaches, open time slots for media buys become scarce. If you do not secure your media buys early, there could be nothing available as the election deadline draws near.

That does not mean you have to deliver finished products the day you buy ad time. All the production work can be done later. But it does mean that in August or September, if you're going to buy thirty seconds on *60 Minutes* for November, you must have the cash in hand.

Make your buys early, and make them at nonpreemptable rates. This is done for two reasons: First, you lock in the time so no one can bump you, and, second, you also lock in the rate. As an election approaches and demand increases, so do rates. One local sales representative told me that during the 2008 season, a statewide issue-based campaign called from Portland with $64,000 to spend in three days. She said that by then, our region was com-manding Portland metro rates. Buy early if you know you're going to do television, and if you end up changing your mind, you can always sell the time back to the station.

With that said, if you're working in a campaign cycle with little competition, such as a special election or a midterm primary, a campaign may be safe buying television at preemptable rates.

Buy Smart

There are a few ways to reach your targeted audience and hit that critical mass if dollars are short. Television costs are based on the size of the audience: The bigger the audience, the higher the cost. For example, a thirty-second ad in the *Breaking Bad* finale cost $400,000. However, by purchasing less expensive time slots, when the audience is smaller (smaller rated), a campaign may air ads more frequently for less money and still meet the desired reach and frequency.

If you know you will be advertising on television but really don't have the funds to keep a critical presence for more than a week, buy your television time starting closer to the election and work your way back. As money becomes available, you can buy ads for more and more days preceding your buy. Also, by purchasing the time closest to the election first, you don't run the risk that this highly coveted time will be unavailable later. Smaller-rated "avails" (available time) are usually the last to go, so there may even be some opportunity for in-fill close to Election Day, but don't count on it. As a side note, the timing of ad placement changes dramatically when elections are run entirely or almost entirely with vote by mail (VBM). With all VBM, ad timing for television, like everything else, moves up, and campaigns must peak the week before, during, and after ballots are mailed, or three weeks before the actual Election Day.

Rules and Regulations

The following are general rules and regulations as they apply to political advertising. Nevertheless, be sure to get media packets from your local stations and familiarize yourself with individual station requirements.

- You must be a qualified candidate for public office or an authorized campaign organization to promote a person's candidacy for office. Political action committees and noncandidate campaigns (issue campaigns) do not fall under the political advertising guidelines.
- Reasonable access for political "use" will be provided to all legally qualified federal candidates during the forty-five-day period before a primary or primary runoff election and the sixty-day period before a general or special election.
- While candidates may request specific programming, the station reserves the right to make reasonable good-faith judgments about the amount of time and program availability to provide to particular candidates.
- All ads must comply with the visual sponsorship identification requirements of the Communications Act. In other words, they must all have a disclaimer. The disclaimer ("Paid for by . . . ") must last at least four seconds and be at least 4 percent of screen height. Who or what follows the disclaimer depends on who paid for the ad and whether the candidate authorized it.

- Any spot for a political candidate or on behalf of an announced candidate must include video or audio use of the candidate's image or voice or both. In many areas, political ads may not be placed just before, during, or just after news programs.

As populations become more segregated by political ideology, it follows that Democrats believe and are swayed by some media just as Republicans believe and are swayed by other media, but what is more interesting is the cultural bifurcation of TV viewing along political and geographic lines. Knowing with whom you want to communicate by age, gender, and affiliation will inform your media buys.

Targeting Voters

By Catherine Shaw and Daniel Golden

If you would persuade, you must appeal to interest, rather than intellect.

—BEN FRANKLIN

IN THIS CHAPTER:

- Finding the Likely Voter
- Voter Gaps
- Finding Priority Precincts
- Direct Mail
- Urban Versus Rural

IF YOUR CAMPAIGN IS BLESSED WITH AN ABUNDANCE OF CAPABLE volunteers, your targeting strategy need not go further than your precinct analysis. Chapter 12 will walk you through a proven get-out-the-vote (GOTV) system that efficiently deploys your volunteers to activate your supporters with surgical precision across your entire district. If you must budget your volunteer hours, however, you may have to cull your targeting approach. This chapter provides a framework to sharpen the focus of your precinct analysis with demographic or geographic data, as well as methods to prioritize precincts in your targeting efforts.

Finding the Likely Voter

Your ideal target is the friendly, lazy voter—someone likely to prefer your issue or candidate, but needing a little motivation to actually vote. It would be wasteful to target highly active voters—they'll cast a ballot no matter what you do, and as covered in Chapter 2, it would be a blunder to bet the farm on changing any of their minds. Predictors of *voter participation* (the likelihood that a voter will cast a ballot without undervoting) provide a less precise but cost-effective shortcut that may help your campaign narrow its focus onto lazier groups. The five most reliable indicators, in order, are as follows:

1. Voting history
2. Education
3. Income
4. Absentee voting
5. Age

Voting History: The Most Reliable Predictor of Participation

The record of a voter's participation "exceeds the effects of age and education" in its power to predict future participation,[1] and those who participate in a primary are 42 percent more likely than nonprimary voters to participate in the general.[2] Your county clerk, elections office, or city recorder will usually provide four years of voting history for everyone registered within their jurisdiction—whether you vote is a matter of public record; *how* you vote is not.

If you have trouble locating voter files from a governmental office, or if you'd like to find extended voting histories, you might also ask your political party, a voter contact service, or local PAC (political action committee). Campaign vendors specializing in direct mail will also have access to voting histories.

We sometimes refer to voters by their voting score or the number of ballots they cast in the past four similar elections—so "four," "three," "two," "one," or "zero." Each voting score is conventionally interchangeable with a letter grade—"fours" are "As," "threes" are "Bs," "twos" are "Cs," "ones" are "Ds," and "zeroes" are "Fs." You should assume that fours always vote, no matter what you do. Threes and often twos can be motivated to vote (*activated*) with a little prodding from your campaign. It would be wasteful, however, to expend your resources hoping to activate ones, unless your race falls in the same year as a presidential general election.

Education

Education is a consistently reliable demographic predictor of voter participation, and education data are readily available on the US Census website.

Income

Wealth also correlates positively with voter turnout, and income data are also readily available at the US Census website. Be aware, however, that education and income are confounded predictors—high-performing voters are more likely to be wealthy *and* educated, but educated voters are also more likely to be wealthy. Only 41 percent of voters with an annual income below $15,000 voted in the 2008 presidential election, compared with 78 percent of those with an annual income above $150,000.[3] Voter performance is nondecreasing across every income bracket: the more you make, the more you vote.[4]

Absentee Voting, Early Voting, and Voting by Mail

Absentee voters account for a significant fraction of the electorate. Before permanent absentee registration was available in Oregon, about a quarter of the electorate voted absentee—after voters could permanently register absentee, that number rose to 41 percent, and they cast nearly two-thirds of the votes: 73 percent of absentee voters returned their ballot.[5]

The density of absentee voters varies among regions, but participation is consistently high. For example, the Field Institute reports that in 2008, 29 percent of California's absentee ballots were cast by voters in the San Francisco Bay Area, compared to Los Angeles' 13 percent. By the 2012 general election, 43 percent of the state's voters were permanently registered absentee, casting 51 percent of the vote. Their turnout was 82 percent, while only 60 percent of their nonabsentee counterparts' voters cast a ballot.[6]

Political parties typically register absentees at different rates. Again, in California's 2008 general election, 46 percent of poll voters were Democrats, compared with 30 percent Republicans, whereas Democrats held only a 4 percent margin over the GOP for mail-in ballots.

If your targeting strategy includes absentee voters, consider the Field Institute's research on demographic trends among absentee registrants, showing they are more likely to be as follows:

- Elderly, although this margin has narrowed over past elections
- White non-Hispanic (70 percent, versus 23 percent Latino)
- Female (54 percent, versus 46 percent male)
- More conservative (32 percent, versus 24 percent liberal)

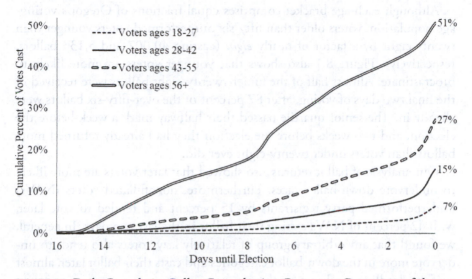

FIGURE 8.1 Daily Cumulative Ballot Count by Age Group, as a Percentage of the Final Ballot Total

These data describe ballot returns for the 2006 general election in Jackson County, Oregon. However, it is reasonable to expect similar age-participation trends across the United States.

Age

Younger Americans consistently underperform their elders on Election Day. Slightly more than half of eligible voters under thirty are registered, compared to 75 percent of Americans over the age of sixty-four. And among those registered to vote, seniors outperform millennials by twenty points in presidential elections and nearly forty points in midterm elections.[7] Americans between the ages of eighteen and twenty-four outnumber Americans between the ages of sixty-five to seventy-four by 7 million, but they cast 1 million fewer ballots in 2004 and 6 million fewer in 2006 and 2010.

In Oregon final activity reports list every voter who participated in the election and include the date ballots were received. (Oregon switched to all vote by mail [VBM] in 1998, effectively registering every voter absentee. The county clerk mails ballots out two or three weeks before Election Day and reports when each voter returns them.) Our research of a 2006 general election final activity report for Jackson County shows that older voters are more likely to vote *and* more likely to vote early. Figure 8.1 illustrates cumulative ballot returns by age group in the sixteen days leading up to Election Day.

Although each age bracket comprises equal fractions of Oregon's voting-age population, voters older than fifty-six outperformed voters younger than twenty-eight by a factor of nearly *eight* (casting 40,007 and 5,133 ballots, respectively). Figure 8.1 also shows that younger voters are more likely to procrastinate: Almost half of the under-twenty-eight ballots were received in the final two days of voting, after 87 percent of the over-fifty-six ballots were already in. The senior quartile passed their halfway mark a week before the election, and two weeks before the election they had already returned more ballots than voters under twenty-eight ever did.

Our analysis of ballot returns also showed that later voters are more likely to undervote down-ballot races. Furthermore, nonaffiliated voters (NAVs) underperformed party registrants by 15 percent and tended to vote later, with 42 percent of NAVs casting their ballot in the last two days. In general, we found that any arbitrary group of relatively lazy voters also tends to undervote more in the down-ballot categories and casts their ballot later, almost as if the deadline sneaks up on them.

One implication of these findings is that older voters make up their minds early. Campaign managers in states with extended early voting or VBM or significant absentee registration should target these voters first and GOTV last. Young voters and NAVs in high-priority precincts require special attention from your campaign to ensure they vote all the way down the ballot—once voting starts, these groups should be at the top of your GOTV list.

Voter Gaps
Youth Voters and the Growing Age Gap

It has become common knowledge that younger Americans are more liberal than their elders. Scott Keeter, Juliana Horowitz, and Alec Tyson of the Pew Research Center write that "young voters are more diverse racially and ethnically than older voters and more secular in their religious orientation. These characteristics, as well as the climate in which they have come of age politically, incline them not only toward Democratic Party affiliation but also toward greater support of activist government, greater opposition to the war in Iraq, less social conservatism, and a greater willingness to describe themselves as liberal politically." The researchers conclude that "this pattern . . . suggests that a significant generational shift in political allegiance is occurring."[8]

Such a shift may prove to be consequential in presidential races, but younger voters are slow to show their numbers down the ticket. In my home county, the 2008 Obama campaign aggressively registered new voters and reregistered NAVs to the Democratic Party before the primary. Within a few months, the Republican registration advantage shrank from eleven points down to two. Unfortunately for the Democrats, the spoils of their precipitous growth were reserved for the top of the ticket: Obama received 8,000 (8 percent) more votes in the general election than any of the down-ballot Democratic candidates—7,000 more than the Democratic candidate for US Senate, a well-esteemed state senator with an unpopular opponent. Like I said, young voters simply undervote more. Vote totals for down-ballot Republican candidates, on the other hand, fell only 100 shy of John McCain's. The same pattern persisted through the 2012 and 2016 generals, with Democrats undervoting their down-ballot candidates by eight and thirteen points, respectively.

Joe Green, the president and cofounder of NationBuilder, argues that undervoting is just a fact of life in down-ballot races: "For local campaigns, most citizens have no idea who's running for office and are therefore open to persuasion—a significant fact since local elections can be swung by just a few votes. And since persuasion at the local level happens by direct voter contact, field organization is the key to victory. The campaign that does it better, wins."[9] That's especially true of relatively new and lazy voters: If you're managing a down-ballot campaign, your top priority must be identification and activation of friendly NAVs and new registers. And given the ineffectiveness of direct mail, phone calls, and TV advertisements with these voters, and the comparative success in engaging them by canvassing and using social media, down-ballot campaigns would do well to shift strategies.[10]

Activating Young Voters

A great deal of researchers and institutions have examined the problem of political disengagement among young Americans, and some have published data-driven solutions. The overwhelming consensus—independently reported by the Michigan Democratic Party's Youth Coordinated Campaign, Green & Gerber, George Washington University's *Young Voter Mobilization Tactics Booklet*, and Tufts University's CIRCLE[11]—is that young Americans are most easily activated by personal contact. Actually, the same is true for every demographic: Door-to-door canvassing consistently beats TV ads, radio ads, lawn signs, and print media. These alternative messaging channels, however, are uniquely ineffective when it comes to young Americans. It seems that even the content of your message is irrelevant—negative or positive, partisan or nonpartisan, young Americans care more about the messenger than the message. Phones can also be a significant motivator, but a single call is just as effective as several[12]—should you contact young voters by phone, you'll do better to call each of them once close to Election Day rather than some of them repeatedly.

Ironically, most campaigns focus their energies at senior voters because they turn out in higher numbers. But when you accept that voter persuasion is, at best, the highest-hanging fruit you can pick, it becomes apparent that high-performing demographics should be at the bottom of your messaging priorities. Besides, you help to break a vicious cycle when you activate the youth vote: Young people vote less out of cynicism—they disengage from their civic duties because they doubt that government works in their interest. So candidates are elected that disproportionately prioritize the interests of older demographics, which perpetuates the cynicism of younger voters.

Newly activated youngsters tend to activate the elders they know in a "trickle-up" effect.[13] This is especially the case within immigrant communities, where the youngest generation is more likely to speak English fluently. And the habit is sticky: When a voter gets to the polls once, he or she is more likely to return. Getting young people to vote early nurtures a new generation of voters.

Ethnic and Gender Gaps

The Pew Research Center, Public Opinion Strategies, Women's Voices, Women Vote, and the *National Journal* have conducted extensive research on demographic voting trends. Some of their salient findings include the following:

- Women vote more than men.
- White people vote more than people of color.
- White men usually vote for Republicans.
- White, undereducated whites usually vote for Republicans.
- Married women usually vote for Republicans.
- Unmarried women usually vote for Democrats.
- About one-third of Hispanics are registered to vote, and one-third of that total actually votes.

Remember, wherever research identifies a low-performing demographic, your opportunity is to find and activate supporters within it—you stand to gain a lot less by focusing your resources on demographics that are likely to vote anyway.

Finding Priority Precincts

We have discussed research findings to help you locate your lazy supporters within demographic groups, but your precinct analysis is still the sharpest tool in the box—remember, like-minded Americans tend to live in clusters, so lazy voters usually support the same candidates and issues that their neighbors do. We will identify friendly precincts with PR or PD (percent votes owed), notated here simply as P, since you will use only the value relevant to your candidate or issue.

Voter turnout (notated as T) will measure precinct-level voter participation; it is the quotient of *all votes cast in your race of interest* (notated as C) divided by *total registration* (notated as A).

Recall that your precinct analysis was built primarily or entirely from historical election data, so if you're running a campaign to elect a candidate, the *votes cast in your race of interest* is calculated by $C = VR + VD$, the sum of votes cast to the Republican and Democratic candidates who last ran for the same office.

Calculate the voter turnout of every precinct in your district by $T = (VR + VD) / A$. If you are managing an issue campaign, the *votes cast in your race of interest* will be the sum of "yes" votes and "no" votes ($C = VY + VN$) in your district's most recent similar-issue race. Don't worry if the electorate is considering your issue for the first time; just use the turnout for a race in the same category—for example, if your race is a ballot measure for a municipal bond to finance after-school programs, calculate C using any recent school-funding measure held in a similar election cycle. Calculate the voter turnout of every precinct in your district by $T = (VY + VN) / A$.

This formulation of T does not differentiate between voters who failed to cast a ballot and undervoters—either are eligible for activation. However, if your precinct analysis indicates that a low undervote among likely supporters provides a clear path to victory, you may prioritize supportive areas with a high undervote over supportive areas with low turnout—after all, convincing a voter to finish their ballot is an easier sell than convincing a nonvoter to begin one. In this case you can calculate T with ballots cast in the denominator instead of total registration, $T = C / B$.

Having determined P and T values for each of the precincts in your district, begin by ranking them according to support:

- High support (H/S) may include precincts with $P = 64\%$.
- Medium support (M/S) may include precincts with $52\% = P < 64\%$.
- Low support (L/S) may include precincts with $36\% = P < 52\%$.

Then rank each precinct according to voter turnout:

- High turnout (H/T) may include precincts with $T = 70\%$.
- Medium turnout (M/T) may include precincts with $61\% = T < 70\%$.
- Low turnout (L/T) may include precincts with $T < 61\%$.

Prioritize your precincts in this order:

1. High priority: H/S + L/T; H/S + M/T; M/S + L/T
2. Medium priority: M/S + M/T; H/S + H/T; M/S + H/T
3. Low priority: L/S + L/T; L/S + M/T; L/S + H/T

The parameters dividing each priority levels (64 percent, 52 percent, and 36 percent support levels and 70 percent and 61 percent turnout levels) are chosen more by art than science. If you live in a district with especially polarized precincts, higher parameters may be more suitable for you. If you live in a district with relatively mixed precincts, you might prefer lower parameters. Your turnout parameters will depend on the election cycle. For example, you may find $T = 30$ percent during a midterm primary, whereas $T = 70$ percent in a presidential general election. The ideal turnout parameters will evenly distribute your supporters between the three priority levels—you may have to play around with your data to find the numbers that work for you and that maintain a relatively even number of precincts in each of the categories.

Direct Mail

An election vendor from another part of my state pitched me on a mail plan a few years ago. My candidate was a vocal supporter of schools, and the Oregon Education Association (OEA) had endorsed him. The vendor wanted to target demographics where schools polled well with an aggressive pro-education message. Our poll had broken the district into zones; however, the vendor bluntly lumped together cities with unique voting patterns.

For instance, two demographically similar cities—predominantly white, well educated, and middle class—were grouped into a zone where schools polled favorably. However, an analysis of historical election data and the zone polling data indicated only one of the cities supported school measures. The residents of the other were dissatisfied with the management of their school district, and they responded unfavorably to OEA, higher education, back-to-work vocational programs, and Head Start. Notwithstanding, the vendor was determined to send *twenty-one* mailers to every Democrat and Republican woman and most of the NAVs, including education-themed mail pieces, in these two distinctly different cities—a total of 800,000 pieces of mail. My client was braving a six-point registration disadvantage; I knew his only path to victory was a high opposition undervote, and that would be possible only if our campaign could fly under the radar in some areas on specific messaging. I struggle to imagine a more expensive way to stir the hornet's nest.

The vendor also wanted to target a city where my client enjoyed a fifty-point registration advantage with all twenty-one mailers. "I think two mailers and a brochure will be adequate," I explained to him in a conference call, "just to remind the base to turn out and support their guy. Anything more would look wasteful."

"You send only two pieces," he bellowed back, "you'll lose. You'll *lose!*" They never say, "Send twenty-one, you'll win. You'll win."

His unprofessional demeanor might have been unusual, but his mail plan exemplified a universal dilemma. Mail vendors bill their clients by volume; they have every incentive to overstate the scope of your target and depth of their medium. Vendors won't appreciate how political self-segregation has fractured your district into politically homogenous silos. They can't understand how a deluge of junk mail might frustrate your supporters or activate your detractors. As Upton Sinclair said, "It is difficult to get a man to understand something when his salary depends upon his not understanding it."

One might argue that direct mail doesn't have to preclude precision or moderation. A campaign manager with the fortitude to weather the sales pitch could certainly contract a vendor to surgically target high-priority precincts with only a couple mailers. But I have never encountered a peer-reviewed article, data set, or compelling anecdote to suggest that direct mail can activate voters; some researches argue it never does.[14] Speaking candidly, I'm not even sure the premise is coherent. If you have a physical address, you probably don't even notice the mechanical ceremony immediately following your trip to the mailbox, in which you reflexively discard everything screaming for your attention. And voters with PO boxes are known to read almost exactly zero campaign mailers, as they consistently toss unsolicited letters before they even leave the post office. Whichever medium your campaign chooses, the fundamental objective remains *finding and activating lazy supporters*, at the lowest possible cost and greatest possible precision. Direct mail does none of this.

Nevertheless, if your race is for a legislative seat, direct mail will be sent on your candidate's behalf. The push from lobbyists and legislative leadership is simply too great to overcome. Both have money to spend, and they'll prefer to give it directly to the vendors, whom they trust as political strategists. If your candidate loses, they will assume it could have been a win with more mail. Win and they'll assume it was *because* of the mail. Instead of pushing back, try to develop a cordial relationship with the remotely located movers and shakers in your party; it's the only way to minimize the damage their mailers will do to your campaign.

What You Need to Know About Direct Mail

Direct mail typically falls into three categories: advocacy, comparison, and attack. Advocacy mailers sing the praises of one candidate, comparison highlights distinctions between candidates, and attack goes after a candidate on a personal or public level.

Advocacy ads are the weakest in terms of voter activation and work best for incumbents. Advocacy mailers don't really work for challengers, unless the challenger has a long list of community involvement or accomplishments to show from a different elected office. Voters regard comparison pieces as the most honest and trustworthy.[15]

The most credible studies on the influence of attack advertising on performance and persuasion found the following:

1. Strong attack pieces can demobilize the electorate.
2. Pure attack pieces reduce turnout and harm the *sponsoring* candidate's share.
3. Attack is weakly and negatively related to turnout (advocacy is weakly and positively related to turnout).[16]

Whereas canvassing is about activating voters who, according to past precinct voting patterns, are inclined to vote for your candidate, direct mail is about activating voters around specific issues that transcend voting tendencies.

Direct mail should cultivate a relationship between your campaign and the voters around issues that resonate with your base. When it comes to reducing the undervote, comparison pieces that contrast your candidate from the opposition on issues work better than attack or advocacy pieces.

Direct mail's advantage over traditional media—TV, newspaper, and radio spots—is its precision. A mailer can target any voter in your database with a piece on the exact issue that will resonate the most, if the campaign does its research. You must know the issues that influence your base and your opponent's stand on them. Your database must be organized and detailed, with voter-specific details like registration, voting grade, age, gender, neighborhood, marital status, general economic category, educational level, and whether there are children at home. Other helpful information, if you can find it, includes hunting and fishing licensure, membership in advocacy groups (such as the Sierra Club and the National Rifle Association), veteran status, and union status and profession (especially for teachers, police officers, firefighters, and health care workers). Just about any voter-specific information—demographic, professional, and area of interest—can sharpen the precision of a mailer's message.

Effectiveness of Direct Mail

Direct mail basically has two forms. As noted in Chapter 5, the first is a fundraising letter mailed in an envelope, designed to move the voter by the way an issue is presented in the copy or by the effect of the person who sent the letter (or both).

The other type of direct mail generally comes as a glossy, full-color, flat or folded, oversize piece of paper that is issue and voter specific. This type of direct mail is not about raising money but is similar to fundraising direct mail in that it goes, theoretically, to targeted voters, specifically voters who care about specific issues. Because the "swing is gone,"[17] direct mail has become about keeping your base with you, motivating your base to actually color in your bubble, and maybe encouraging the other team to undervote their candidate.

For direct mail to be effective, the bright line of division between you and your opponent regarding some issue that base voters care about must be repeated throughout the campaign season in all of your communication and media and must relate back to your message.

Direct Mail to Hit Your Opponent: It Takes Research, Opportunity, and Timing

Pointing out how your opponent has voted while serving in office does not constitute negative campaigning, and juxtaposing actual votes with campaign claims in direct mail keeps an opponent's inconstancies in front of the voters.

A voting record is not only a verifiable set of facts, but one that goes to the very essence of why we have elections. Have at least one volunteer dedicated to researching your opponent's voting record. If you're running for a state assembly or legislative race, the party will do this for you. Voting history of a candidate is helpful for both direct mail and candidate debates.

Direct mail should be both clever and simple. Democrat Jeff Barker, a candidate for the Oregon House, faced Republican Keith Parker in the general election and found that the voters were having trouble differentiating the two because of their similar surnames. To help voters, Barker incorporated into the mail pieces a barking dog that strongly resembled his family dog, who was in campaign photos. Barker won by 44 votes out of 15,720 votes cast.

Being clever can also backfire. A few years ago, a special election was held in Oregon to backfill falling revenues in the state budget. Opponents of the tax measure said that government, like everyone else, needed to tighten its belt. In response, proponents of the tax measure sent a direct-mail piece featuring the gut of an overweight man with a belt cinched about as tight as possible (figure 8.2). The message was to underscore the difficulty schools

Vote YES on Measure 28

Because WE can't do this anymore.

FIGURE 8.2 Example of Direct Mail That Can Reinforce the Opponent's Argument

Be sure the image you present to the voters is the image you want to communicate.

were having with budget cutbacks as Oregon faced monumental budget deficits that biennium. However, in the context of the criticism leveled against the measure, one look at the photo brought to mind the *opposition's* message: Cut the fat.

Reference Your Comparison Pieces

When doing a comparison piece, be sure to footnote each of the assertions made about your opponent and your candidate. Include where, the date, and a bill number—that sort of thing.

Direct Mail on a Budget

If you are campaigning in a relatively small area, combining direct mail with canvassing can save a campaign a lot of money and is far more effective than mailing a piece to the voter. Some years back, I ran a campaign in which we canvassed direct mail attached to the walking pieces. In that campaign, we were trying to get approval for an open-space program designating where future parks and walking paths would be in our city. Each neighborhood of the city was slated for a park in the plan. So we drafted a specialized campaign piece pointing out what kind of park each specific neighborhood would get and asked four to six supporters from that same neighborhood to allow their names to be printed on the specialized piece. Neighborhood volunteers hand-carried it into the appropriate neighborhood as part of our canvassing effort. With this approach, the campaign piece became both a personal letter and an endorsement.

Walking direct mail to the door is also a good way to time your mailing. For example, in the campaign for the open-space program, the voters approved the open-space program but turned down the funding proposal. The city council immediately sent another (almost identical) proposal out to the voters, and it went down as well. At this point, the entire voter-approved park component would be threatened without a funding package. In a narrow vote, the city council presented the public with a proposal for a prepared-food and beverage tax to fund both parkland acquisition and Department of Environmental Quality–mandated upgrades to the wastewater treatment plant.

However, no city in Oregon had a tax on prepared food and beverages, and the industry did not want a domino effect starting in southern Oregon. As a result, our opposition included all but one eating establishment in Ashland, the Oregon food and beverage industry lobby, local businesses, and real estate agents who did not want land taken out of the inventory for parks. Again, our campaign had little or no money for lawn signs or advertising, and because of the controversy, people told us they were reluctant to write letters to the editor.

The weekend before Election Day, we hand-delivered a direct-mail piece to every home in the city. In the piece, we pointed out nothing more than who was financing the opposition. This tactic worked for two reasons. First, it clearly showed that our side was rich with volunteers, as close to one hundred people walked the streets for that canvass. Second, we canvassed the city on the same day the opposition coincidentally featured a half-page ad in the local paper underscoring who opposed the funding and who paid for the ad, reinforcing what our flyer said. Given that our measure passed by 150 votes out of 5,000 votes cast, clearly the flyer juxtaposed with the opposition's display ad helped tip the scales. This program—both the parks component and the funding mechanism—won state recognition in the Cities Awards for Excellence Program.

Mail Preparation

A lot of money can be saved by having a group of dedicated volunteers willing to repeatedly prepare and send your direct mail.

Mailings to individuals. Be sure to have the bulk-mail stamp printed on your piece to save time and effort. Make sure you have a bulk permit number; it runs about a hundred dollars, and it will quickly pay for itself. Your political party or a friendly campaign might also allow you to use theirs. Personally, as noted in Chapter 5, "Fundraising," I prefer first-class stamps, especially for money requests; it avoids the whole bulk-mail process and improves response and return from the recipient. The return address should always be part of the printing to save time.

Once you have decided on a plan and the direct-mail piece has been written and printed and is back at your home or headquarters in boxes, here's what you do:

1. Organize a clerical work team to assemble your direct-mail piece; have everything lined up and ready to go when people arrive.
2. If the mailing is not a flat or postcard, it must be stuffed and addressed, or sealed in some way—like with a sticker. Hand-addressing increases the number of people who will open the piece and look inside. However, printing envelopes with a font that appears as though it were handwritten is almost as good and saves a lot of time. Do not use labels, or recipients will throw them away unopened.
3. Visit the post office or go online to get all the particulars for bundling and preparing your bulk mailing.

Saturation mail. Given that voters are relocating to live near those who share similar political and social attitudes, campaigns can actually save money on direct mail by saturating a city (or postal route). A saturation piece goes to every mailbox regardless of whether a registered voter lives at the address or intends to vote; while this may drive up the cost of printing, it can be worth the savings in postage. Also, because a saturated piece is delivered to every mailbox in a given postal route, there's no need for bulk-mail permits or for printing addresses on the pieces. For candidates, this method works well in nonpartisan races and for partisan primaries in small cities of homogeneous populations that are overwhelmingly registered with one party. It is also effective for just about any issue-based campaign where there's broad support with a need to remind and activate voters regarding an upcoming issue on the ballot.

Every Day Direct Mail: EDDM

Every Day Direct Mail (EDDM) is an alternative to your mail house printing, organizing, and sending your mail piece and charging you for that service.

You will find step-by-step directions for political mailings on the US Post Office's website and instructions on using EDDM at www.usps.com/business /political-mail.htm.

According to the postal service, "USPS® Every Door Direct Mail® (EDDM®) is an affordable targeted advertising technique that lets you map your marketing mail audience by age, income, or household size. You can use the EDDM mapping tool to choose the ZIP Code™ and carrier route that will target your best possible customers—current and future. The EDDM mapping tool is easy to use and discounts are available even for small businesses."[18] The USPS website just keeps getting better; they want this to be easy for people to use.

You will still create your piece and have the graphic designer and printer follow the instructions from the post office regarding acceptable format, but by counting, sorting, and delivering it to the post office, campaign money can be saved. All the forms for the bundles are available online, so your team can arrive at the post office prepared. And since every piece is addressed to "Local Resident" or some generic phrase, without individual addresses, postage costs are cut. As an aside, the return address should always be part of the printing so as to save volunteer time in preparing the mailing.

After checking the postal website, you can also personally contact your regional Postal Service election-mail coordinator whose job it is to answer questions and give additional advice as you need it. The website will give you a list of the closest mail coordinator. They may not be in your town, but they are great on the phone.

The site gives you the regulations related to the mailing, size of piece allowed, format for the addressee, and the indicia to have printed on your piece (this is the equivalent of the stamp). Follow their guidelines when printing this. There is a limit of EDDM pieces you can bring in on any one day (usually 5,000), so you must batch your mailings accordingly—this is where your clerical team helps. Be sure to keep count of the number of pieces; you'll need that information for postage, and don't forget to bring the campaign checkbook. If the team counts one stack, weighs it, and then matches that weight on future stacks, it will save time.

From the postal website, go to "Launch EDDM," put in your zip code or city, and it will give you an option of choosing city, rural/highway, or PO boxes. Depending on your area, you will determine who you are targeting. You can choose residential only or a combination of residential and business. Then, if it matters to your campaign, you can break it down by age of household or by income level per postal district.

Often at the end of a campaign, when the committee suddenly decides to create and send another direct-mail piece, the grassroots campaign cannot pull together the people to get the piece out on time. If so, consider a mail house. The mail house can download which party you want, eliminate household duplicates, and print the name and address directly on the piece.

Be aware, however, that mail houses are often flooded by last-minute requests from political candidates, which can affect timing.

As noted above, direct mail is different from targeting neighborhoods for canvassing in that you are directing your pitch for voter interest rather than for voting patterns. Also keep in mind that by using direct mail, you can address subjects that, if put in a more public forum, might activate a lot of heated letters to the editor. Well-targeted direct mail should reach potential friends of the campaign and let them know where you (and or your opponent) stand.

Targeting voters for persuasion and activation is central to winning a down-ballot campaign. By taking advantage of the wealth of available data that examine voter habits, a road map emerges, revealing how and when to reach voters effectively.

Urban Versus Rural

As you have undoubtedly discovered from your precinct analysis, voters have very different attitudes within an incorporated city as opposed to rural areas outside the cities. Small cities provide great targeting opportunities for the campaign.

1. There exists far more area-specific information available through the US Census for small cities than for their rural neighbors in the same county.
2. Many small cities are a single postal route, so a saturated mailing to a city is more affordable than mail sent to rural voters.
3. Small cities are easier to canvass and easier to get volunteers to canvass.
4. Small cities often have many citywide elections covering issue-based and candidate elections that provide additional information to your targeting model.

Targeting voters based on demographics in combination with a precinct analysis allows a campaign to get the most benefit for resources expended. It is important for the down-ballot candidate and issue-based campaigns to be aware of the many approaches to targeting voters as well as what works best with your targeted constituency.

Lawn Signs

The seeds of political success are sown far in advance of any election day. . . . It is the sum total of the little things that happen which leads to eventual victory at the polls.

—J. HOWARD MCGRATH, FORMER DEMOCRATIC NATIONAL COMMITTEE CHAIRMAN

IN THIS CHAPTER:

- To Be or Not to Be
- Logo and General Information
- Lawn Sign Installation
- Field Signs
- Maintenance and Removal
- Untargeted Activities: Bumper Stickers and Buttons

To Be or Not to Be

LAWN SIGNS ARE A VOTER TARGETING TOOL; THEY SHOULD NOT BE placed everywhere but rather where the campaign wants to activate support. Consider the following before deciding to use them:

- Lawn signs work best in nonpartisan races, partisan primaries, and issue-based in areas of homogeneous and supportive populations.
- Outside of nonpartisan races, lawn signs are *not* about voter persuasion; they're about activation.
- Placed in enemy territory, lawn signs do more harm than good.
- The number of lawn signs placed randomly for a candidate or issue does not necessarily coincide with a win.
- The number of lawn signs placed in areas of greatest support may increase turnout and minimize undervotes, helping to push a candidate or issue over the top in close races.

- Lawn signs are a great way to increase name or issue recognition where a candidate or an issue already enjoys support or a registration advantage.
- Lawn signs are a high-maintenance relationship.
- Know the law: Many cities, towns, and counties have restrictions on when, where, and for how long political signs may be placed.

Lawn sign placement and maintenance is a great campaign activity for those who want to volunteer in a campaign but are not interested in working directly with the public. Although it's a huge time and money commitment, with enough volunteers a well-run lawn sign campaign is an excellent way for a voter to feel involved in a campaign while elevating candidate name recognition or increasing awareness of a ballot issue. Lawn signs also demonstrate support for a candidate or an issue within a community. However, that is really all they do.

The campaign should endeavor to secure as many locations for the lawn sign installation day. If enough signs go up—especially at individual residences—their sudden appearance gets noticed. After the initial installation, lawn signs should be placed as voters request them or permission is secured during canvassing. Send all canvassers out with a few lawn signs for immediate placement as voters authorize them throughout that activity. The slow growth of signs after the initial boom signals to voters a growing support. Slowly building your locations from the initial push has many benefits:

1. Voters are becoming sensitive toward and suspicious of political machines, so when a campaign suddenly appears everywhere—especially with field signs—the signs call attention to themselves rather than the candidate.
2. A slow build has the look of a grassroots effort.
3. Signs placed once with little movement or infill become part of the landscape and lose impact, almost becoming invisible as a campaign moves closer to the election.
4. Unknown candidates have difficulty getting locations before they're well known. The steep climb from obscurity to public figure dictates a hybrid lawn sign placement approach: Get as many locations as possible to start and then infill like crazy throughout the election cycle.

When the day arrives to place your first round of lawn and field signs, it is important, as in all campaign-related activities, to have everything ready and organized for the teams. Also note that it is especially important that people work in pairs in this activity: one to drive and the other to navigate and install.

Logo and General Information

Lawn signs are basically a campaign's logo and, like trademarks, must easily identify your cause or candidate. You need to develop a "look" that distinguishes your campaign from all others on the landscape. Visit local vendors who print lawn signs to get some ideas; they often save one of each sign they have ever printed. This way you can shop for ideas for style and color combinations without any out-of-pocket expenses. When you're designing your sign, keep in mind that using two colors costs a lot more than one but is well worth it (figures 9.1 and 9.2). To save money, a two-color (or even three-color) look is achieved using a solid color printed over the white stock while leaving the lettering with no color (see figures 9.3 and 9.4). This produces white lettering on what looks like colored stock. Using halftones (a mix of the

FIGURE 9.1 Example of a Lawn Sign Using Logo and Theme: Campaign for the Carnegie

In an issue-based campaign—especially for capital improvements—it is advantageous to connect a positive image with the ballot item. This logo was in red, black, and white and was so well liked that voters who had never had a lawn sign before called and requested one for their yard. (Crystal Castle Graphics)

FIGURE 9.2 "Maxwell for the House" Lawn Sign

This sign was done in two colors, puce (lettering) and turquoise (the bar); playing on a corporate slogan and using unusual colors helps a candidate stand out.

FIGURE 9.3 Example of a Low Budget Yard Sign

Using one color (deep blue) with halftones in the silhouetted trees behind the lettering and reverse type on the name, this sign appears to have three colors rather than one. Although the design measured ten by twenty-four inches originally, the final size was twelve by twenty-four inches, with the website eventually added to the bottom. (Crystal Castle Graphics)

white sign and the solid color showing through) in the design or part of the lettering creates a "third" color. The result is very classy and quite affordable.

There are basically two types of lawn signs: a plastic sleeve that is placed over a croquet-type wicket and corrugated. Corrugated comes in two forms: one with the interior tubes running horizontally and the other with vertical interior tubes. If your intention is to use wooden stakes, be sure the signs are printed with the tubing running horizontally; otherwise, they will bend and flop in the wind. Corrugated signs printed with the interior tubing running perpendicular require H-wickets, which slide up the tubing, to hold the sign in place.

Whether using the plastic sleeve or corrugated lawn signs you will need something to hold them upright, such as the croquet-style wicket, H-wicket, or four-foot lawn sign stakes. All of them add around a dollar per sign to the overall cost of your lawn sign.

You can count on your lawn signs plus stakes or wickets costing four to five dollars each, depending on the size of the sign you print, the quantity, and number of colors. Budget accordingly.

Obviously, the size of your lawn sign can affect the cost of printing as well as the cost of stock. A typical sign is eighteen by twenty-four inches, although I've seen some very effective signs that were nine by twenty-four inches (figures 9.3 and 9.4). This longer, narrower size works well if your candidate has a long name that fits comfortably in that space. Smaller signs do the same work of a larger sign but are more stable against the elements and give the appearance of a modestly funded campaign. Oversize signs are more trouble than they're worth.

FIGURE 9.4 Another Example of a Low Budget Yard Sign

This low-budget sign used a deep blue-green background with halftones of light green and reverse type on the name for a three-color look. It measured nine by twenty-four inches—half the size of a normal lawn sign and half the price. (Crystal Castle Graphics)

Know the law: Some cities have restrictions on sign size.

Another style of lawn sign uses a U-shaped metal rod, like a large croquet wicket, that holds a printed plastic sleeve. This type of sign costs as much as or more than the conventional lawn sign because the wickets, which are practically indestructible, are quite expensive to buy and even more expensive to ship. Still, the sign stock itself does not need to be attached with hardware to stakes or shoved into H-wickets before being installed, thereby omitting the advance work to prepare the signs for placement. The downside of these signs is that they are not particularly attractive. Also, two notes of caution: first, the wickets come in all sizes, making borrowing someone's U-wickets less certain, and, second, even a small amount of moisture will cause the steel wickets to rust and get all over your hands and vehicle during installation and removal. Since it is the wickets that drive up the cost, we now save the metal hoops. To store wickets, make a two-bar modified sawhorse that the wickets simply straddle. H-wickets, like wooden stakes, should be bundled in groups of twenty-five. Wickets thrown into a pile until the next campaign are a nightmare.

The most pervasive sign is a corrugated sign placed on an H-wicket. The H-wickets are surprisingly flimsy and often need a little help getting into the ground, so be sure your installers have mallets and metal spikes to drive a pilot hole, especially if there's been little or no rain.

Lawn signs should be a work of art. You want the homeowner hosting the sign to be pleased with its look. You know you have a winner when people call and ask for a lawn sign simply because they like how it looks (figure 9.5).

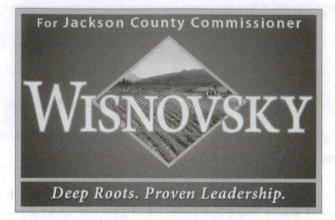

FIGURE 9.5 A Full-Color Lawn Sign Design

We developed this lawn sign design to mimic a wine label; it worked well because our candidate was a vintner and ran for office in a predominantly agricultural area. The sign was full color and wildly expensive but became a huge part of the campaign. Rather than being screened onto the corrugated plastic, it was a laser picture. With lettering in orange, background in blues, and the grape fields in the middle of a full-color picture, it was a gorgeous logo and sign that could be seen forever. (Landeros Design)

Location, Location, Location

Getting good locations to display your signs is the second half of using lawn signs effectively. Often people who have run for office in previous elections will have a record of their lawn sign locations. Try to get such lists, and call those people first. This works best when you share a political ideology with a former candidate. Similarly, cold-calling registered voters using geographic location as the first filter and then party registration as the second is a brutal but effective technique for securing authorization. Indeed, if your objective is to place between 600 and 1,000 lawn signs on the first day, the best approach is to begin the process with phone banks. For this many locations, you would need ten people calling for ten nights for ninety minutes per night. And that's with good lists.

Another option is to canvass for lawn sign locations starting on collector and arterial streets to quickly place lawn signs in high-visibility areas first, where they will offer the greatest returns. Subsequent canvassing can fill in other less-traveled routes.

Just remember, lawn signs are not campaign buttons; they are a valuable campaign resource and should be used appropriately.

Assembling Lawn Signs

Somewhere in the midst of finding locations and cutting turf, lawn signs must be assembled or at least organized. As noted above, be sure to have everything ready for your volunteers. If you're using corrugated signs with horizontal tubing on wooden stakes, you will need electric screwdrivers, screws that are the proper length, washers, and stakes. It's a nice touch to have tables for the workers; I use old doors on saw horses, but if none of that is available, your lawn will do. Also, when using wooden stakes, have the graphic designer move it slightly off center about two inches so nothing is blocked by the stake.

To assemble 600 signs, you will need ten electric screwdrivers (ask volunteers to bring theirs from home), 1,200 screws and washers, 650 stakes (there's always damage), a couple of trucks (to disperse the signs to installation meet-up locations), and about thirty people to do the assembly.

H-wickets for corrugated signs with vertical tubing are quick and easy to assemble only if the H-wicket is spaced exactly into the sign without bowing out or in. Improperly spacing the tongs of the H-wicket will cause the sign to distort. Look for two letters on the sign that are the perfect distance for the H-wickets, and then inform your assembly volunteers as to where they are; it will make the job go faster. For 600 signs with H-wickets, you need ten people for two hours and no hardware or tools.

Cutting Turf

Because down-ballot campaigns are generally smaller and more manageable, lawn sign installation can still be conducted without using spreadsheets or mapping programs, but why? Mapping lawn sign locations using BatchGeo and Google maps is fast and accurate, and, frankly, anyone can do it. It takes a fraction of the time, and the way the little red dots are dropped onto the map directly from the address on the Excel sheet is completely civilized.

You can certainly use a party-system mapping program, but once your locations are in Excel, BatchGeo produces better maps and faster.

If you're working in a small city where streets are familiar, you can easily use the old-school system of marking locations on a real estate map or precinct maps from the county and accompany those with a list or index card that includes the address, name, phone number, and any special installation

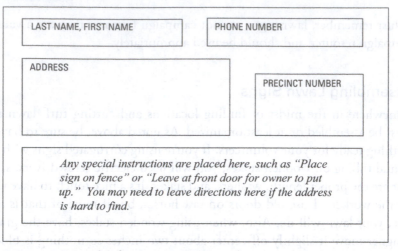

LAST NAME, FIRST NAME	PHONE NUMBER
ADDRESS	PRECINCT NUMBER

Any special instructions are placed here, such as "Place sign on fence" or "Leave at front door for owner to put up." You may need to leave directions here if the address is hard to find.

FIGURE 9.6 Example of a 3x5 Lawn Sign Card

instructions (see figure 9.6). For campaigns covering more than one small city, BatchGeo is the only way to go.

After loading your Excel spreadsheet of addresses for your lawn sign locations into the mapping program, you will have a bird's-eye view of your coverage areas, which now must be broken down into manageable units for the installers (see Figure 9.7). Typically, I find it easiest to work city by city, but in large cities I break it down to east-west and north-south, depending on man-made or natural barriers that could slow down installers. Examples of barriers might be rivers, highways, drainage ditches, parks, or just geographic distance (one city to the next). Whatever your map looks like, you want to minimize the back-and-forth of your volunteers during lawn sign installation. Depending on distance between locations, installers may be able to cover anywhere from ten to thirty signs in a two- to three-hour period. Because rural areas take longer to get from one location to the next, I restrict my signs to urban neighborhoods where locations are thick with signs that will go up quickly. The rural areas are reserved for field signs.

When I print my map, I also print information about the home that is included in my Excel spreadsheet, such as name, address, phone number, and installation instructions (if there are any). The list is the detailed information of the map. Needless to say, this avoids the need for the cards (figure 9.7).

Lawn Sign Installation

Typically, I will prepare and attach a list of the location addresses, a map, and door hangers (figure 9.8) to a clipboard and place that on top of the

FIGURE 9.7 Example of a Lawn Sign Map

Accompanying the map should be a list of names, addresses, phone numbers, and special installation instructions (if there are any) for the install team.

appropriate number of lawn signs for the packet area spread out in my front yard. Installers can then shop for the turf they prefer and begin earlier than I care to wake up. Always be sure to add a couple of extra signs to each pile in case one breaks or a neighbor asks for a sign during a team's installation.

If volunteers arrive singly, pair them up upon arrival, as placement crews work best in pairs. If the volunteers are placing corrugated signs with wooden stakes, they will need only a mallet and maybe a metal pole for making a pilot hole. Similarly, installation teams placing corrugated signs with H-wickets or plastic-sleeve signs with U croquet wickets may also need a hammer and metal spike for pilot holes when the ground is hard.

Assigning crews is then simply a matter of handing them a clipboard with the map and address list along with the appropriate number of signs and stakes (plus extras). Ask as many volunteers as possible to bring tools or borrow enough ahead of time from friends. Be sure everything the campaign borrows is labeled and returned promptly.

I like installers to bring the map and location lists back to me so I know the task was completed or whether any addresses were missed. If you do not want installers to make the trip back to your launch location, they can scan and email it back to the campaign. If that isn't an option, simply number each of the areas and ask installers to sign up prior to installation so you

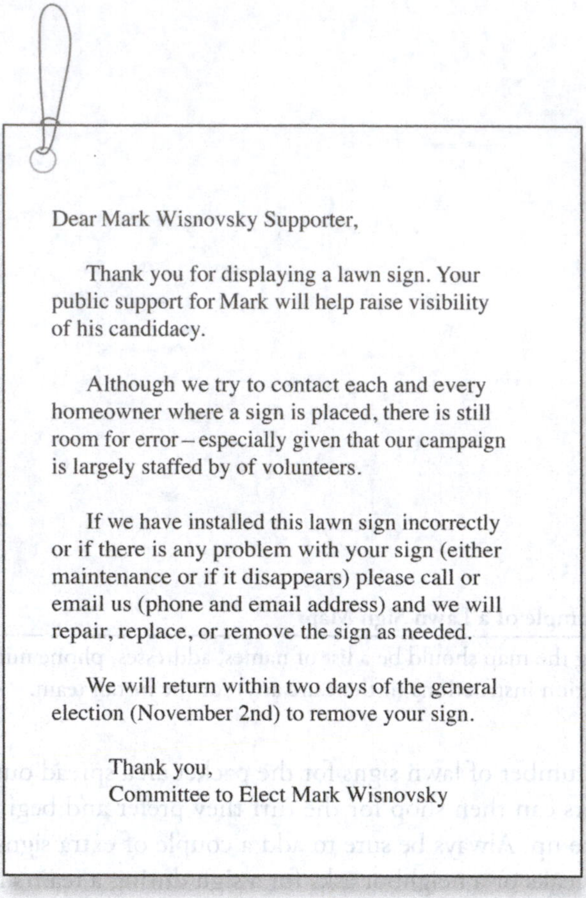

Dear Mark Wisnovsky Supporter,

Thank you for displaying a lawn sign. Your public support for Mark will help raise visibility of his candidacy.

Although we try to contact each and every homeowner where a sign is placed, there is still room for error – especially given that our campaign is largely staffed by of volunteers.

If we have installed this lawn sign incorrectly or if there is any problem with your sign (either maintenance or if it disappears) please call or email us (phone and email address) and we will repair, replace, or remove the sign as needed.

We will return within two days of the general election (November 2nd) to remove your sign.

Thank you,
Committee to Elect Mark Wisnovsky

FIGURE 9.8   Example of an Instruction Door Hanger for Lawn Sign Hosts

Hole-punch an upper corner and include enough rubber bands within the packets for the instruction cards. These are hung by your teams on the doorknob of each address where a sign is placed.

know who did what, and then contact the team by either email or phone to follow up.

As stated earlier, poorly designed, poorly constructed lawn signs can hurt a campaign more than help. If you are going to use lawn signs, they are way too expensive and too labor intensive to cut corners on design and production. If you can't raise the money to do them right, don't do them.

Even so, sometimes you must deviate from this rule for strategic reasons. In one issue-based campaign, because of a lack of funds, we printed only one-third the normal number of lawn signs. Although they were carefully placed to maximize visibility, they soon began to disappear (it was a very controversial money measure). People who wanted signs were calling, and others were calling to request replacements. We knew it was a close race, and our diminishing number of signs looked as though our support was waning.

So, using the same color of ink as our signs, I hand-painted more signs in my barn on the back of old poly-tag lawn signs. In the middle of the night, I placed them throughout the city. I did not want them to be next to each other; rather, I wanted to create the impression that homeowners had taken the initiative to paint their own signs and put them up. I wanted the look to be one of individual rebellious support for our side and angry opposition to the money fighting our effort. We won the election by fewer than 300 votes out of 5,000 cast.

Finally, no matter how careful you and your team are, mistakes happen: Addresses get inverted, people hear yes when no is really spoken, and signs get vandalized or stolen. Further, if you have an incorrect address and do not know it and the homeowner pulls out the sign, your maintenance teams may assume it disappeared for completely different reasons and continue to replace it.

In short, the host of your lawn sign must be able to reach the campaign in case something goes wrong. To make this easy, the campaign should include a door hanger for each of the locations where a lawn sign is installed. These notes are printed four-up on brightly colored paper, usually shocking orange or yellow (you want them to be seen), and then they're cut so that each sheet of paper makes four. If you punch a hole in the corner for a rubber band, the installer can hang it from the door knob (see figure 9.8).

A few years back, I worked on one of the most disorganized campaigns of my career; suspecting trouble, I decided to meet installers just in case the campaign manager didn't show (she didn't). Although I had given the manager door hangers the previous week, for some reason they had been loaded into her car and were nowhere to be found on installation day. By the time the campaign manager arrived with the hangers, all of the installation teams were out, and this is what I learned: The accuracy of mapping programs makes the door hanger less critical than when signs were being installed back in the day. So, if you're out of time and feeling overwhelmed and cannot quite get it together to get a door hanger on the knob, don't worry.

Finally, be sure the signs are installed perpendicular to the street, not horizontal. The point of lawn signs is for people to see them from a distance as they drive by.

Requests

Lawn sign requests throughout the campaign season should be accommodated. However, this means your campaign must be discerning about initial lawn sign placement. Hold some back to replace lost or vandalized signs and to accommodate requests. Avoid placing signs on cul-de-sacs unless the majority of people in that cul-de-sac have expressed support during voter-identification efforts. If your campaign is running short of signs with no intention to print more, avoid overloading some streets while leaving others bare. Let supporters know—from the beginning—that the number of signs is limited and that the campaign needs to place them where they will do the most good.

If you printed a limited number with more requests coming in than can be filled, the campaign may decide to print a second run. Just know this: It is cheaper to print too many at the beginning and throw some away that never get placed than to print a short run. Short runs can run as much as seven to ten dollars per sign. Print enough the first go-round.

Be Aware of Guilt by Association

In nonpartisan races, voters are constantly looking for clues that may reveal the true political ideology of a candidate. If you are placing lawn signs in areas of overwhelming registration for one party, do not place your signs alongside those of the other party. The same goes for field signs just outside of cities or towns that are overwhelmingly registered one way or the other. Signs do not persuade, but they do inform. If voters of one party suspect you are actually aligned with another and have that suspicion confirmed by lawn sign placement, it works against your efforts. Voters look to contextualize a candidate, and lawn signs are the easiest way to do that.

Finally, avoid placing your sign in yards already teeming with political signs. Keep in mind that voters are highly sensitive to visual cues, and so I look for opportunities to couple an unknown candidate with one who is both well known and well liked. Voters know their neighbors and look to those they respect for help in making decisions about candidates and measures. They also spot patterns.

Field Signs

Typically, field signs are printed at the same time as your lawn signs and are simply a giant rendition of the smaller sign. Campaigns will often print a few on both sides and others on only one side to save money. One-sided signs can be placed on the sides of buildings or become half of a *V* where two signs are necessary to get maximum visibility.

Although I believe a top-notch lawn sign campaign will beat out a field sign campaign any day, campaigns with more money than volunteers often drop lawn signs in favor of field signs. And indeed, a well-located field sign can be very effective in raising name recognition for campaigns.

With that said, field sign locations can be tough to find. Many cities have restrictions on the size of a sign, which would limit your field sign locations to outside city limits for a citywide race—hardly worth the money. But in races in large geographic areas, locations can be found by contacting real estate agents who have parcels listed along highways or in cities, ranchers, farmers, and owners of large vacant lots. I've even had luck with farmers "renting" me a spot on an edge of their property that abuts the freeway. Also, some counties now list property and owners online, so if you find a location you like, consider looking for the owner through the county tax assessor's office.

The volunteer crews putting up field signs should have some construction experience so the structure can withstand wind and the weight of the sign. They'll need metal fence posts, a ladder for height and mallet or post driver to pound in the metal fence post, a screwdriver or hole punch, and zip ties to thread through the hole you just punched, to secure the sign to the post. Using existing structures, such as established fence posts, to support one side of your field sign will save time and effort. Given the size of field signs, a pickup truck for installers is a must.

Know the law: Be sure to contact city and county authorities regarding size requirements and any other regulations on field signs.

Another area of potential conflict for field signs is along state highways where a state highway right-of-way may extend as much as fifty feet on either side of the road. Although cities and counties may look the other way when a campaign encroaches on a right-of-way, the state generally does not. To have field signs installed only to have them ripped down by state workers is maddening and wasteful. And when I say ripped down, I mean ripped down. State workers do not take the time to carefully disassemble your field sign for reuse, and good luck trying to locate the sign among various state highway yards. Save the campaign time and money: Call the local office of the state department of transportation, and ask about any locations where you are uncertain of the right-of-way.

Maintenance and Removal

Large or small, campaign signs must be maintained once they are up. Maintenance crews travel with installation supplies—whatever those may be.

Ostensibly, maintenance crews are ready to repair any ailing sign they see in their normal daily travels, but from time to time the crews may need to travel their assigned placement routes for a more systematic check of the signs—such as after Halloween. For this level of maintenance, both lists and maps can be emailed to volunteers.

Besides maintenance, there will be the ongoing duty of filling new lawn sign requests. If there aren't too many requests, you can assign new locations to the appropriate maintenance or installation crews or have volunteers assigned to do this task on an ongoing basis. Believe it or not, having the candidate help with new location installations is great PR. As the campaign progresses, voters increasingly recognize the candidate and will often honk and wave as they drive by. Such a simple thing makes the candidate appear more accessible and "like one of us." In one campaign I worked on, the candidate, a local physician, went out and helped put up field signs on the weekend. He reported that a lot of people honked and waved and that some even stopped to help or say hello. A couple of days later, when the signs that the candidate himself had helped erect fell down, I got a number of calls from people I did not know asking if they could help get the signs back up for "Doc." Ultimately, his initial efforts got him a lot of mileage and then brought additional workers.

In another campaign, there was a street where all the lawn signs disappeared every night. The man who put the signs in that area was also in charge of maintenance and just happened to drive this street to and from work each day. After the signs disappeared and he had replaced them a couple of times, he decided to take them down on his way home from work and put them back up each morning on the way to work. You can't buy that kind of loyalty.

It is best to get requested signs up as soon as possible. However, if there are too many requests, it may be necessary to organize another day for placement. If you do this, be sure to include all of your current locations so that signs can be replaced if damaged or missing.

Most localities have regulations requiring campaign sign removal within a certain number of days postelection. Whatever the regulations, your crews should be lined up and ready to remove all your lawn signs the day after the election. Although field signs can be removed the weekend following the election, if the lawn signs are left up longer than a day, home owners begin to take the signs inside or throw them away, making it difficult or impossible for your crews to retrieve them.

Field or lawn signs printed on poly tag must be dried prior to storing, or the paint will delaminate. If stored properly, both poly-tag and plastic-bag signs seem to last indefinitely, which is money in your pocket for the next election. At a minimum, you will want to retrieve the stakes or wickets for future campaigns. Since you have to get the signs down eventually, you might as well look organized and responsible by retrieving them as quickly as possible.

Pickup trucks greatly increase the speed of lawn sign retrieval, so consider an early mass email to party faithful, on your Facebook page, and to the volunteer list, asking for help from people with pickup trucks. This simple request is the easiest way to bring in new workers who would normally *never* volunteer in a political campaign.

Depending on density of placement, a single team with a pickup can retrieve an area that required two or three teams for placement. Here again, volunteers work in pairs with maps and address lists. When installing signs I try to assign areas close to the homes of my installers, simply because they know the terrain, and the same can be done for retrieval. Keep track of who is picking up what areas and whether they've received a map and list directly from you or by email. Also, have a small group back at the launch site to disassemble the signs.

During one primary campaign, gas prices went up immediately after signs were installed, and I was disinclined to send volunteers back out to pick them up just to have them reinstalled in October. So as an alternative, I mailed a postcard to each house that hosted a sign and asked the host to bring in the sign after the primary. I also indicated on the postcard when it was legal to put them back up before the general and in addition sent another postcard when it was time to place the signs before the general. I included my phone number on the postcard in case a sign went missing. It completely worked. Supporters pulled in their signs and put them all back out before the general election on the designated day. It worked so well I continued the practice even after gas prices went down.

Signs with H-wickets can be stored with the H-wickets still installed—they hang neatly from hooks on a garage or barn wall; however, if the campaign has no intention of using the sign again or you're using wooden stakes or the U-wickets, they should be disassembled for storage and all parts harvested for reuse. This is a great time to get together a volunteer thank-you party to disassemble lawn signs, put them away for the next election, and bundle wickets or stakes in sets of twenty-five with twine or zip ties. Duct tape works well to hold wooden stake bundles but is a nightmare on metal wickets. I find it depressing to look at piles of lawn signs in my yard, so I have a small group back at the launch site to disassemble signs as removal teams bring them in.

Untargeted Activities: Bumper Stickers and Buttons

Bumper stickers are an inexpensive way to familiarize the community with your name or ballot measure. Although bumper stickers are used predominantly in large city, county, state, and federal races, they can also be quite effective in the small down-ballot election simply because they continue to be a novelty there.

This is one application for which I would relax my strong recommendation to place your campaign logo on all your materials. Bumper stickers are small and hard to read, so clarity is what is important. On a bumper sticker, ideally you want your candidate or measure before the voters, nothing more.

A bonus with bumper stickers is that they are occasionally left on cars and bikes if a candidate wins, giving the community the impression that the individual is well liked in office. People who like to display bumper stickers are often willing to kick in a dollar or two to buy them.

Three points of caution on bumper stickers: First, should you decide to print bumper stickers, be sure to print them on removable stock. Second, urge people to drive courteously while displaying your name on their cars. If they are rude on the road, the only thing the other driver will remember is the name on the bumper sticker. Finally, keep in mind that the use of bumper stickers (like campaign buttons) is an untargeted campaign activity.

Buttons are walking testimonials or endorsements. If supporters actually wear them, this tool further serves the goal of getting your name in front of the voting public. My experience is that very few people put candidate buttons on each day, and these items tend to add clutter and expense for the campaign.

However, since all canvassers should have some sort of official identification with the campaign, this is what I recommend: At a stationery store, buy a box of the type of plastic name holders used at conventions and meetings. Ask the graphic design artist who put together the lawn sign logo to make a miniature version of it, sized to fit in the plastic badges. Also ask the designer to lay out as many of these as will fit on a sheet of paper. Reproduce on card stock as needed, keeping the original to make more throughout the campaign. Cut out your miniature "lawn signs," and slide them into the plastic holders. After the campaign, you can reuse the plastic name badges.

When it comes to using lawn and field signs, don't hesitate to be creative and bold. You never know what will work. Bold, however, does not mean elaborate. Simple signs with a simple theme are the easiest to read. Given the work and expense of lawn signs, if you choose to include this activity in your campaign, make it as successful as possible.

The Candidate Campaign

No man ever listened himself out of a job.
—CALVIN COOLIDGE

I don't care if he did it or not, just get him to deny it.
—LYNDON JOHNSON

IN THIS CHAPTER:

- The Lay of the Land
- Packaging the Candidate
- Stay on Message
- Outsider Campaign Versus Incumbent Campaign
- Debates
- Public Speaking
- Write-In, Third-Party, and Nonpartisan Candidates
- Negative Campaigning
- Dos and Don'ts of Attacks
- Recall

IN 2008 PRECINCT ANALYSES BEGAN TO SHOW A MARKED CHANGE IN voter behavior: With the 2008 election and each subsequent midterm and presidential cycle, fewer voters showed a willingness to swing over and vote for a candidate in the opposing party. Indeed, as the swing went down, undervotes increased, indicating that Republicans and Democrats would either vote for their party's nominee or undervote the office.

Specific issues that once moved voters to ticket-switch their ballot now appear to play a smaller role than in election cycles prior to 2008. All this means that partisans must find a way to energize their base, that is, make the base care enough to fill in the bubble on the ballot.

This chapter is about projecting a positive image before the voters and thereby minimizing the potential nitpicking that the public might do. You will also find suggestions on how to redirect negative questions at your opponent, turning the ammunition back on him or her. For a candidate, this is not a time to be defensive. Take criticism as a gift and an opportunity.

The Lay of the Land

Each elective office has specific powers and duties associated with it. For example, my city's charter says the mayor is the chief executive of the municipal corporation and will closely oversee the workings of city government. Laced throughout the document are other stipulated duties associated with the office, such as appointing department heads and duties in relation to the city council. The charter sets up a strong-mayor form of government. In a nearby city, the charter establishes a weak-mayor form of government, giving the appointment powers to the city manager and city council; the mayor runs the council meetings, votes in case of a tie, and cuts ribbons.

Before running for mayor of Ashland, Oregon, I spent a great deal of time familiarizing myself with council business and city documents, but I never read the charter. Then, within my first six months in office, the city council members set about stripping the powers of the office of mayor. Their intention was to do it through a simple resolution, which, unlike an ordinance, does not need a public hearing and cannot be subject to a mayoral veto. As they put it, they didn't want to "take" the powers; they merely wanted to "share" them with me and to "help" me do a better job. I was young, just thirty-five, and felt both attacked and betrayed as some of the council were personal friends. No help came from the administrator, who was probably equally concerned about my ability and wanted the power to appoint department heads to fall under his jurisdiction. No support came from fellow councilors, who initiated the coup and wanted equal say on city appointments.

Department heads, who did not want to work for a woman—especially one as young and inexperienced as I was—aligned with the administrator, even though they technically worked for the mayor. Word came back that many at city hall were saying disparaging things about me, including name-calling—my favorite was "the meddling housewife." I represented a change of the status quo. The problem wasn't necessarily that I would wreak havoc on the city or that the existing system wasn't working all that well. There is just a general suspicion, especially in government, when moves are made from the known to the unknown. The council's overall proposed action would result in moving Ashland from a strong-mayor form of government to a weak-mayor form of government, all without going to a vote of the people, all without changing the charter.

Things heated up quickly. I did not want to go down in history as the mayor who lost the powers of the office. I floundered in meetings as I tried to find footing. I simply could not figure out how to stop the train. Then another southern Oregon mayor told me he thought his city's charter was modeled after Ashland's, and if they were the same, what the city council was doing was illegal. He said, "Read your charter." Simple, obvious, good advice. I did just that.

At the next meeting, armed with information, I held my ground, recited the powers of my office, and threatened to take the council's actions to a vote through the initiative process if the council members persisted. They backed off. Four tumultuous years followed, during which time three department heads and the city attorney went. By the time I left office, twelve years later, there had been a changeover of all department heads, and the administrator and I had moved from a relationship of suspicion to one of trust, understanding, and mutual respect.

Before you run for office, know the powers and duties of that office; attend meetings and familiarize yourself with the lay of the land. Wouldn't you prefer to know before you run whether you're suited for the kind of work that goes with the office? You should also know something about the system: how land-use laws work, how property and other taxes are distributed, the revenue stream, the expenditure stream, and which follows which.

It's also important to know the lay of the land of your community. In one election a candidate appeared in a debate at the Rotary Club. Prior to making a point, he asked if there were any businesspeople in the room. He was not joking.

Packaging the Candidate

Although your political views may be at the center of your message and decision to run, a candidate is selling a lot more than policy. People are looking for an individual who will represent their community, city, school, county, or country in a professional way. Elected officials fulfill the role of continually answering to the public trust. If the community believes in the candidate, then it will believe that its money is in good hands.

To meet voter expectations, the candidate must always look the part. Dirty clothes, missing buttons, unpolished shoes, holes, and strained clothing can all leave a bad first impression.

Be disciplined in all things while campaigning; eating well and losing weight help keep stress levels down and appearance at an optimum. Whatever improvements can be made in your appearance and dress, make them; it is the little things that assist candidates to look and feel the part. A crumpled look may be endearing at home, but not to voters. Inattention to personal appearance translates into inattention to detail and incompetence.

Dress in a consistent style. This gives the community the impression that you are stable and know who you are. Do not do things out of character. We all remember the picture of Michael Dukakis in the military tank. Cowboy hat and boots worked for Ronald Reagan but not for Bill Clinton. It did not work when Bob Dole began dressing in khakis and running shoes in an effort to appeal to younger voters in his bid for the presidency. One candidate in eastern Oregon who wore Pendleton shirts changed to three-piece suits midway through the campaign because his numbers were sagging at the polls. After his makeover, the numbers dropped further. Behave and dress in a way that is consistent with who you are. Sagging numbers don't improve with a new outfit.

Barack Obama wore only gray or dark blue suits in an effort to pare down the number of decisions he has to make in a day.[1] While selecting your clothes may seem inconsequential, it all adds up when it comes to the day-to-day grind of running for, or serving in, office. Finding ways to minimize stress is central to a win and to service.

One final thing to keep in mind is that while you are a candidate, you should resist working on other campaigns, either issue or candidate based. Voters are suspicious of candidates who appear to be manipulating an outcome in too many arenas. Your only task is to get yourself elected; once in office, work on as many campaigns as you please.

Image over Ideology

People running for office are often embarrassed about their résumés and eager to beef them up to present a more credible image as a community leader. But what may feel like a painful biographical note to the candidate can actually be an asset. For example, if a candidate is embarrassed because she dropped out of high school, she is overlooking the possibility that having earned her GED followed by working her way through college carries more weight because of her early struggles.

Candidates and campaign committees who are tempted to embellish personal history should think long and hard before doing so. It's a crime to place any false statement into a voters' pamphlet and takes only an accusation by the opposition to activate an investigation.

Manners Matter

As important as dress and appearance are, there is more to looking the part of a serious public servant. The candidate must adopt the kind of manners a mother would be proud of. Do not chew with your mouth open, pick your nose, clean your ears, or floss in public. Cover your mouth when you yawn.

When appearing as a dinner speaker, eat only moderately at the event or, better yet, have a light meal beforehand and skip the public dinner. When people are nervous, digestion slows down. You cannot afford to have a stomach upset from nervous energy and burp through a speech. In general, eating and greeting don't mix well for candidates, which is ironic, given that food and drink are often the bait used to pull potential supporters to a political event.

Avoid drinking alcohol while running for public office. Besides the fact that alcohol adds empty calories and affects one's ability to deal with stress, people have tons of issues around alcohol, and it's not worth the grief or uncertainty of how drinking, even as little as one glass of wine, will play. Similarly, if you're a smoker, keep it closeted.

Bring along a sweater or light jacket to cover nervous perspiration. Wear deodorant and clean shirts. Previously worn clothes can carry body odor that might be activated with nervous perspiration. Avoid perfume and after-shave. Do not chew gum. Place a few breath mints in your pocket for easy and unnoticed retrieval. In fact, avoid all public grooming: hair combing, lipstick, and the like. Also, you can avoid problems if you think ahead. For instance, when I get nervous, my mouth gets dry, so I always go to the po-dium with a glass of water. Marco Rubio's impromptu water break during his GOP State of the Union response in 2012 would have gone unnoticed if he had a glass of water with him from where he was speaking. Similarly, if you have a tendency to sweat when nervous, bring a folded handkerchief to wipe your brow.

From experience, a woman candidate should leave young children at home. Not only does that enable her to be more focused, but it also meets the voters' need to see her in a professional role. It is difficult for many people to accept a woman as a leader if the only image they have of her includes children clinging to her, asking for attention. This is absolutely not true for men. In fact, men are given bonus points for being seen with their children. Society assumes that men are professional, and seeing a man with his children gives the voters the idea that they are getting a glimpse into his private life. He seems warmer (figure 10.1).

While Jeff Golden chats with supporters, daughter Sarah Beth gets an eyeful of photographer.

Golden celebrates wir

New commisioner's daughter accompanies him

Candidates each bring their own style and special approach to politics, sometimes they carry a lot of political baggage.

But only Jeff Golden carries a baby on his back.

For much of Tuesday evening – ev live TV interview – the Ashland D wore a baby backpack that held hi daughter, Sarah Beth, born a year giving.

FIGURE 10.1 A Candidate with a Baby

When it comes to children, there is a double standard in society, and the standard carries over into campaigning. Where women are penalized for campaigning with their children, men are rewarded.

Judicial and Law Enforcement Races

Candidate races that fall under law enforcement or judicial posts have specific areas of caution:

- Candidates must be above reproach when it comes to ethics. Even one ethics violation filed against a campaign can be the end for a candidate.
- Do not use or take pictures of a judge behind the bench.
- Omit pictures of a candidate clad in robes. Typically, a judge wears robes only when behind the bench. If the individual is pictured outside that venue in robes, it looks contrived. This is especially true for pro tem judges, as it implies incumbency, which is an ethics violation.
- Whether in robes or out of them, comport yourself as though you were in the courtroom. Be judicial at all times, and exemplify all the best virtues of the vocation.
- Distribute no political literature in buildings owned by the taxpayer (this is true for all candidates). Not only is it illegal, but it suggests laziness.
- Do not campaign in buildings owned by the taxpayer. If a supportive staff member wants to help your candidacy and asks how at the office, explain why you cannot discuss it at the office.
- Use nothing that was bought by the taxpayers such as copy machines, telephones, and paper—this is true for all candidates.

- If you have cut corners as a law enforcement officer or judge, it will be revealed by the opposition during the campaign; count on it.
- If you have not withheld taxes for laborers in your home, from babysitter to gardener to housekeeper, it will be revealed during a campaign.
- Do not blame others for your mistakes; own them and move on.
- Whether running for judge or sheriff, have others fundraise for you.

Groomers

Given the importance of image, it's a good idea to have a "groomer" for the campaign. As a candidate, recruit a friend whose only campaign job is to let you know how you look and to make suggestions on what to wear and how to better project your image. In all three of my campaigns for mayor, I had a groomer who proved to be invaluable.

When I work for other candidates, I usually assign a groomer and look for a man or woman with an eye for fashion and detail. If my candidate needs a haircut, I encourage him or her to get the best one available. Have the campaign pick up the cost of a studio photo shoot. The groomer and I will often discuss the kind of look we want out of the shoot and share those ideas with the candidate and the photographer. For example, if I have a candidate who smiles very little and is somewhat hesitant, I look for a photo where he or she leans into the lens. Whatever may be a weakness of your candidate in personality or appearance, your photo shoot is an opportunity to make it look otherwise. In one campaign, the candidate was strikingly unattractive. To address this, his strategist used a series of three head shots of him on his walking piece, one after the other. I don't know why, but it worked, making him look more attractive. Many believe that a photo starting low, looking up at the candidate, projects power and one from above angled down the opposite. Personally, I think nostril shots are unflattering and don't use them. I like the photographer to work with the camera coming straight on.

A groomer must be willing to attend early debates and public gatherings to observe the candidate's behavior. Talk with the groomer after an event and discuss how delivery can be improved, and then share that with the candidate. All such suggestions, however, should be cushioned with a lot of praise. Candidates' egos can be fragile, and you don't want them to be self-conscious at the next event.

A few years back, I was running a campaign for a very capable, well-educated, professionally successful candidate. However, after a debate, I was called by the groomer, whom I had asked to attend to observe the candidate in action. She did not have much to say about his dress but told me that his answers were rambling, that he continually said he agreed with his opponent, and that his opening and closing statements were weak.

I immediately called him and asked if he could come over. Although the candidate and I had previously gone over all issues and discussed possible answers, he had not yet made debate cards as instructed. So for two hours we revisited the issues and made debate cards together. (Note: This is not something you can do for the candidate; the candidate needs to be in on this task.) In addition to issue cards, we discussed how no candidate should ever say he agrees with his opponent and why. Finally, we prepared opening and closing statements. No matter how great your candidate, this kind of coaching is invaluable to his or her success. For the campaign manager, getting the candidate's speaking and debating skills in order is every bit as important as printed materials, ads, lawn signs, and letters to the editor. As the candidate left my home, he said it was the best two hours he had spent since the beginning of the campaign. After that he became focused and had a level of comfort we had not seen before. All of that came from having a groomer.

Stay on Message

Although message development is handled in depth in Chapter 4, as a reminder, a message is an organizational tool for the candidate to stay focused on an issue that's important to the voting population. The answers to all questions lead back to your message. As exampled in Chapter 4, Bill Clinton's message "It's the economy, stupid" provided a focus for all issues. The environment, education, health care, or whatever—all came back to his message: the economy.

Once you've developed your message, don't let your opponent pull you off of it. Ever. Develop a message that builds relationships between the candidate and the voters. A benchmark poll can really help here.

If you have no money for a benchmark poll, then with the team list all of the candidate's positives and why the team feels voters will support this individual. The list might include programs in which the candidate was involved, stands on controversial issues, votes in previous offices, his vision, her character, and experience. It might be nothing more than a clear list of issues and beliefs that the candidate embraces.

You must also develop a list of issues and concerns that might hurt the candidate's support. It is this list that you will use in preparing the candidate for negative questions and in formulating strategies to defuse negative perceptions. For example, if the candidate has an image of being slick, the team sends him to neighborhood meetings, where he can be seen as one of the people. This requires a candidate who is open to observation and criticism and a close campaign team to develop the campaign message.

Once you have developed your campaign message and strategy, stick to it. When your opponent hits you, respond and move the discussion right back to your message. Keep in mind that the public is observing everything during the campaign: your stand on issues, your presence and composure, your appearance, how you handle stress, and your ability to answer questions. In particular, the public is looking for how well you react under pressure and how hard you work to get into office. That will tell them something about whether they can expect you to keep your head and work hard once you are in office.

Staying on message can be particularly hard for candidates under attack. It's important to respond to attacks, but how you do translates into whether you're on your message or have moved over to that of your opponent.

In a recent local campaign for district attorney, the incumbent's opponent was accusing him of running an inefficient office in a newspaper article. Truth be told, the incumbent had an increasing caseload with a stagnant tax base. The challenger had left the DA's office a few years before to go into private practice and now wanted back in as boss.

The incumbent, being the first to speak at the debate, stood and said, "I would take issue with anyone who says I'm not running my office efficiently." Just like that, he was on his opponent's message. The following day, the debate was covered in the local paper. The headline: "DA Denies Allegations of Mismanagement." Instead, he should have promoted his achievements while preempting any criticism that his opponent might be tempted to wage, and he could have done it all without sounding defensive. He would be safe under the umbrella of disclosure.

Equally problematic was that the incumbent DA who had been attacked by his opponent in the press responded to that attack in a completely different medium: a live forum. As stated earlier in this manual, attacks should be answered using the same medium on which they were first asserted. So if an attack is made in letters to the editor, that's where the counter is made and so on. The DA should have waited for the opposition to go after him at the event and then countered the attack.

While looking professional, minding your manners, working hard, and being on message, you must find some way to minimize stress. As noted above, stress can be reduced by eating well, exercising (hopefully canvassing), getting your personal attire together, eliminating alcohol, and developing issue cards for public debates and appearances. Another is to do nothing that, once done, will lead you to tell a lie.

One dramatic example of a lie gone bad occurred a few years back, when a county commissioner was undergoing a recall. The recall looked dead, even though its proponents were able to gather the signatures and actually get it to a vote. It was a vote-by-mail election, and as is often the case in vote by mail, the computer spit out a few ballots whose signatures did not quite line up. One of these was the wife of the county commissioner targeted in the recall. The local elections office, in conjunction with the secretary of state's office, asked the county commissioner if the ballot had, in fact, been signed by his wife or someone else. The commissioner said his wife did indeed sign it. They checked again, and it still came out as a no-match. They asked the commissioner and his wife again. Both said she signed it. The secretary of state's office continued to press. Finally, the commissioner confessed to signing his wife's ballot because she was in the hospital and had directed him to do so. While the commissioner had easily beaten the recall, he now had to resign and was charged with and convicted of a Class C felony for forging his wife's signature. Obviously, he shouldn't have signed the ballot to begin with, but had he said from the get-go, "My wife asked me to take care of it for her while she was in the hospital; isn't that okay?" the secretary of state told me he very likely would have said, "No, don't do it again," and dropped the matter. It is rarely the act that gets candidates in trouble but rather the lie that follows the act.

If a candidate is caught in a lie while on the campaign trail, it can be sudden death. As one of the ten commandments of campaigning and one of the cardinal sins, being caught in a provable lie is about the worst thing that can happen to a candidate.

Outsider Campaign Versus Incumbent Campaign

If you are in government already, you are an insider; if not, you're an outsider. Insiders and outsiders typically run very different campaigns because the voters expect the insider to defend what government is doing and the outsider to challenge it with a fresh outlook. In reality, however, skillful politicians who have been in office for years have, when the need arises, waged outsider campaigns against first-time candidates. Insider or outsider status is as much a state of mind as a fact. Whatever the actual status of the candidate, insider and outsider campaigns require distinctly different strategies.

Whether you are the incumbent or the challenger, you should list all personality characteristics of both the officeholder and the challenger, both strengths and weaknesses. Your objective is to contrast your strengths with your opponent's weaknesses.

Outsiders

To run an outsider's campaign, you must first legitimize yourself through establishment endorsement (no matter how tangential the endorsement might be). The public record the incumbent has amassed while in office actually defines that person—but in terms of image, not specifics. If you're an outsider, it's important for your team to define the test the voters will apply. Obviously, you want to stay away from experience, since an incumbent would easily pass that test. Your best hope is to define the test the voters will apply as that of "time for a change." Ultimately, as an outsider, you will find that it is more important to present sound reasons for why an incumbent should be cast out of office than to explain why you should be elected.

Attacks on the system are effective if they plant seeds of doubt about how things are being done or where attention and public money are being focused. You cannot just throw complaints against a wall to see what sticks. You have to know what you're talking about. Research how things have worked or not worked, and explain them to the voters. Remember, you must sound like a potential officeholder rather than a malcontent. That requires offering solutions, not just criticizing. This is where your homework really pays off.

Before my first run for mayor, I went to the local college library, checked out ten years of city council minutes, and read them all. I also checked out every current report on every system for which the city had hired a consultant. I read the city's comprehensive plan and the downtown plan. This put me at a decided advantage: Because it was so fresh in my mind, I could recall the information more quickly than my opponent, who had been a sitting city councilor for ten years. Incumbents who live through the events compiled in such reports while in office will find it difficult to recall the details, and they make matters worse by believing they can. Typically, an incumbent will underprepare for an election; outsiders should not make that mistake and indeed take advantage of it.

Incumbents

If you are an incumbent, you must show that the average citizen still supports you and show how, working cooperatively with other elected officials, you have made a positive contribution. In other words, your campaign should make the test applied by the voters that of experience and accomplishment. This is a strong theme when voters have a grasp of the complexities of government. Again, your public record defines who you are, but avoid looking at each vote individually; this definition is more about image than specifics. Although you may not actually use the word, stick close to a theme of "proven" leadership. Make your record the focal point of the campaign by using examples that the average person will understand and that apply to the day-to-day lives of those being served. Avoid speaking in governmentalese—that is, using acronyms and jargon that only those in government would know.

An Opponent

You may breathe a sigh of relief when you discover that you are unopposed in your election or groan when you find that at the last minute, someone has filed to run against you. However, an opponent in any campaign is a blessing. Without an opponent, your race will be ignored by the press, and the programs and issues you want to get before the voters will be that much more difficult and expensive to get there. If you are involved in a hotly contested race, the press will more likely provide front-page coverage, which greatly reduces the amount of advertising you will have to buy. Just compare the Republican presidential primary of 2008 with the Democratic presidential primary. Barack Obama and Hillary Clinton were lead stories every day, whereas John McCain could not get the press's attention. This inattention contributed to McCain's loss, just as Obama's primary momentum contributed to his win.

If you have a primary race in which you are unopposed, you may never build the momentum and party support that are necessary to win the general election. Do not lament if someone declares against you. Thank your lucky stars, and organize a great campaign. Bring forward programs you want to begin or to maintain, changes you feel are needed, and use the election as a mandate to muscle these into place. Use the campaign as a reminder of who you are and what you stand for and as a rallying point to get people behind your efforts.

Debates

Don't use debates to attack your opponent; rather, use them to share what you know and would do once elected. Keep on the sunny side. Debates can be turning points for a campaign or amount to nothing. I've seen amazing mistakes made during debates that had little or no effect on the campaign and seen other items that should have gone unnoticed blow up.

There are a number of ways you and your campaign committee can minimize the risk factor and make a debate work in your favor. Small precautions include familiarizing yourself with the room before the event and making sure that some friendly faces are in the audience. However, preparation is your best tool for positioning yourself. When you are well prepared, political debates are surprisingly easy and great fun. As a political candidate, you should welcome the showiness of debates, the pressure, and the opportunity to get your opinions in front of voters. When you have successfully positioned yourself as a candidate, people recognize who you are and what you do will make sense to them.

The central rule of debating is that the voters should know more after the debate than they did before. Come armed with a lot of information.

Preparation

To get ready for a political debate, choose eight to ten subjects that are important to you or the community; include among them issues that are part of your campaign platform. For each of the subjects you have chosen, list on one side of a five-by-eight-inch index card the information and points that you feel are relevant. Use only one card per subject and only one side of the card.

For example, development in the forest interface is of great concern in my community. As an incumbent, I would list on the left side of a card all that government (with my help) has done to limit development in these fire-prone areas as well as fire mitigation implemented on existing structures. On the right side, I would list remaining concerns of fire danger and what government still needs to do to make the forest and the community safer. If I were running an outsider's campaign, for the same subject I would list all that is being done, how this is not enough, what has gone wrong (being specific), and exactly what I would do to correct the course. This information is just listed on the card, not written out. The idea is to be very familiar with the information before the debate and to use the cards to focus on specific points you want to make, not exactly what you will say.

Once you have the subject cards filled out, color-code each card with a single stripe along the top. For example, your card for budget issues might be red; for forest interface, brown; for park issues, green; for recycling, yellow; for air quality, blue; for transportation, black; and so on. Once the cards are color-coded, they can be placed in a tier in front of you during the debate. With just the color bar showing, the appropriate card can be found in a glance. By color-coding in advance, you can avoid disorienting yourself looking through all the cards to find the one you want. And once you have the card you need for a particular subject on top of the stack, you can glance at it while looking around the audience. When looking at the cards, you should appear to be collecting your thoughts rather than reading or reminding your-self with notes.

Do not kid yourself that you can guess all the subjects or questions that will be asked in a debate—unless, of course, you received them ahead of time. You will undoubtedly prepare for areas that are never addressed and have nothing for areas that are covered. Even so, with the preparation done ahead of time, you will be much more relaxed and "on" during the debate because some of the answers will be in front of you. Be sure to bring extra blank cards to jot down thoughts during the debate. This will help you remember on rebuttal what you want to say.

Familiarize yourself with any ballot measures or propositions coming be-fore the voters or any initiative petitions being circulated. The press, your opponent, or an audience member may ask you about your position, so have a clear idea of where you stand and why.

The importance of your image and how you present yourself cannot be overstated. Smiling and speaking clearly and slowly enough so those in the audience can hear and understand are very important. A certain amount of tension surrounds a campaign in general and a debate in particular, and peo-ple will notice how you deal with that tension. Be aware that your image gets projected in a hundred ways.

Mock Debates

Mock debates are fun and very helpful for a candidate. For a successful one, you must have a moderator, an opponent, and an audience. High school government teachers, newspaper reporters (though not those who will be covering the campaign), and people who are politically active and involved make the best audience. Your objective is to have seven or eight people who are well versed in public speaking and politics, are smart, and can communi-cate suggestions without offending the candidate.

Rearrange the furniture in the living room so that it looks more like a classroom. Use bar stools for the real and the pretend opponent to perch on. The moderator should be armed with questions that most certainly will come up in a campaign. This is the time to focus on your questions. Let all involved know that everyone will be in character throughout the mock debate. The moderator should be dressed up, and whoever is playing the op-position candidate should study how the opponent dresses, moves, answers questions, and attacks in real life. This does not take long: Read the literature, and watch him or her on a commercial, interview, or public appearance, and you're there.

Have everything in place when the real candidate and the pretend opponent arrive. Establish guidelines and time the answers, just as would be done in a real debate.

After the debate, questions are taken from the audience and answered by both the real candidate and the pretend opponent. If the campaign is concerned about how the candidate will respond to a question, this would be the time to have someone in the audience persist in asking it.

This is followed by a frank discussion of the candidate's performance, which questions posed problems, and what made the candidate defensive. Cover body language, the brevity and clarity of answers, hairstyle, and clothes.

Most public speakers are best when they have a command of the material and can talk off the top of their head. However, if you are working with a candidate you have told time and again not to read speeches because he or she is horrible at it, be sure to send the debate questions ahead of time. In general, candidates read because they feel uncertain of their ability or the material. If you provide the questions ahead of time and a clear directive that reading is not a choice, the candidate will prepare content and fret only about delivery. Helping a candidate gain confidence works best if specific aspects of a debate or speech are isolated and worked on one at a time. You don't teach someone to swim by throwing the person in the deep end of the pool.

If possible, have someone videotape the mock debate. This way, the candidate and team can review it later.

Recently, we set up a mock debate for a novice candidate. The candidate was given questions ahead of time, and the audience was also prepped. The reporter who attended was smart and direct with questions, as were a US history teacher from the high school, a teacher from the middle school, and an assortment of people from the campaign committee.

The whole debate took over two hours, including the question-and-answer period that followed. It was very successful except for one thing: The candidate was furious with the individual playing the role of her opponent, who was in character right down to the cheap suit and flag pin and who vaguely answered questions all while subtly going after our candidate, just as we had seen the opponent do in real debates. The candidate was so upset, she never watched the video of the mock debate.

However, at her next debate, when the real opponent seemingly reenacted what had occurred at the mock debate, our candidate was brilliant. Her response to a demeaning comment made by her opponent brought the conservative crowd to a round of boisterous applause. She was so good and her opponent so bad that we cut a TV ad by simply juxtaposing the two candidates answering a question at the debate.

Fielding Negative Questions

You will very likely get nasty questions and innuendos during a debate. Look at such questions as an opportunity to demonstrate how well you respond under fire. People know that being subjected to negativity is part of serving in public office, and they will want to see how you handle it. Never be defensive. If possible, be humble and self-effacing; if you can come up with a little joke that turns the attack to your advantage, so much the better. Find anything that uses the ammunition of the opposition and redirects it at them. If you redirect attacks, it is important to do so with class, without sounding defensive or mean-spirited. This is your opportunity to sound smart. Being quick on your feet is a function not of IQ but of preparedness, confidence, and poise.

Responding to Attacks

In general, there are four options for responding to an attack:

1. I did not do it.
2. I did it, but it's not how you think.
3. I did it, I'm sorry, and I won't do it again.
4. Attack the source.

If you are attacked and do not respond, you are presumed guilty, especially if the attack is considered fair. When you do respond, you should do so on the same level as the attack. For example, if you were attacked in direct mail, respond with direct mail.

One way to prepare yourself for attacks is to sit with your campaign team and brainstorm on every possible negative question that might come your way. Practice responding to questions concerning your weaknesses. This allows your support group to deliberate on the best possible responses. These responses may be placed according to topic on your five-by-eight-inch cards for handy reference during the debate. Even if the attack is not exactly what your team predicted, this level of preparation lends comfort, poise, and organization to the candidate, resulting in better responses in high-pressure situations.

At one debate, my opponent brought up a program I had initiated to use volunteers to clear ladder fuels (dead and dying brush) from the forest interface. He cited how the program had been a miserable failure and had placed the city at risk of potential litigation because of possible worker (volunteer) injury. I picked up my forest card and took the microphone. I said that while the outcome of the program had been different from what was first envisioned, it raised community awareness of the need to mitigate fire danger. Moreover, the voters needed to make a decision for the future: Did they want leadership that never tried anything out of fear of failure or leadership that solved problems creatively at the risk of an occasional partial success? By using this attack as a gift, I was able to direct attention to the limited success of the program and then shift back to my message, which was strong, creative leadership: leadership willing to take risks. And for those who knew nothing of my efforts to get volunteers into the forest interface to prevent wildfires near homes, it planted a seed that there may be other things I was doing quietly on behalf of citizens.

Another approach to leading or negative questions is the "Yeah, so?" response. For example, the opposition might say, "Since you became mayor, the city has acquired more and more programs that should be run by the private sector." Your "Yeah, so?" response might be, "I'm sorry. How is this a problem? The proof is in the pudding. We are extraordinarily successful at providing a broad range of outstanding programs, programs that our community may never have enjoyed if left to the private sector. And we do so while saving the taxpayers money." While you may not use these exact words, this is the tone: "Yeah, so what's your point?"

In Debates, Attacks Can Backfire

Hitting your opponent with a negative during a debate is somewhat unpredictable and ill-advised. As noted above, more often than not, attacks waged in debates can backfire and strengthen the candidate under attack. For example, I worked for a candidate whose opponent, an incumbent, was receiving a lot of PAC money, and my candidate wanted to hit him for a disproportionate amount of PAC money over average citizens from the district. Because the campaign team had heard rumors that the incumbent had a story to die for whenever he was hit on PAC money, the campaign team felt uneasy about the strategy.

At the next debate, however, our candidate went after the credibility of the incumbent because of the type of money fueling his campaign and suggested the incumbent was bought and owned by the lobby. True to the rumors, the opponent stood up and said that when he was first elected, a supporter who had given a $3,000 campaign contribution visited his office at the capitol. According to the story, the contributor was looking for a particular vote on a bill and felt that the size of the campaign contribution warranted this vote. Our opponent went on to say that after hearing the demand, he went to the bank, took out a personal loan, and returned the money to the contributor. He concluded by saying that no one owned his vote.

In about thirty seconds, our opponent showed that he was of modest means like everyone else in the room—after all, he had to take out a personal loan to pay back the $3,000 contribution—and that he had integrity. In hindsight, with our candidate so insistent about using this issue, we would have served him better if research could have unequivocally established a correlation between votes and money; if there were none, he may have dropped the attack, and if there were many, it would have called his opponent's credibility into question.

In debates, you just never know how your opponent will turn an attack around. So, unless you are armed with concrete information, avoid rehearsed attacks. If, however, your opponent leaves himself or herself open, seize the opportunity. For example, a few years back, a Democrat and a Republican were facing off for a US Senate seat. The Democrat had been criticizing the Republican for using federal Superfund money to clean up industrial waste in his family-owned business. During a debate, the Republican, who was worth millions, was challenged by the Democrat to pay back the money to the taxpayers. The Republican stood and said, "I'll pay it back just as soon as you pay back the honoraria you said you would never take when you ran for Congress." In a very flustered voice, the Democrat said, "Why . . . why, you've insulted my integrity!"

This is an opportunity that doesn't come along very often. The Democrat should have seen this coming and been ready. He missed an opportunity to reach into his pocket to pull out a checkbook and say, "Deal. I'll pay back all the money I received for giving speeches. You get out your checkbook and do the same for the federal cleanups, which amounts to $XYZ. And while you're at it, make it out to the federal deficit because the only way we're going to get our arms around it is if those who have stop taking from those who don't." While the Democrat had received thousands in honoraria, the Republican had received millions in Superfund money—an easy exchange.

Public Speaking

Before my very first debate as a candidate, I was genuinely excited about what was ahead of me. I was charged up and armed with enough information to handle any question thrown at me. Afterward, I thought I'd done a great job. So when someone from the audience handed me a slip of paper, I was certain it would be the name and phone number of a potential campaign volunteer. The note said, "You said 'um' 48 times during your speech and the question and answer period that followed. Why don't you join us at Toastmasters?"

Unless you're a top-notch public speaker—either a natural or an actor—you need to get some skills, quickly. Even after three campaigns and twelve years in public office, I still got nervous before a speech; it didn't matter how perfunctory it was or how young the audience. But remember, it isn't what you say that's important but rather how you say it. Given how quickly people form opinions of candidates, the candidate who gets some early help in giving speeches will have a longer shelf life than the candidate who receives none. Training in public speaking does not need to take a whole lot of time and can ultimately make the journey much more enjoyable.

The following are ten simple things the candidate and team can do to improve speech giving, debates, and public appearances.

1. *Prepare your introduction.* Few will remember anything you said, but most notice how you are introduced. Prepare a strong introduction that gets read at each venue you attend; include your experience and specific qualities you will bring to the office.

2. *Keep speeches short and end on a positive note.* Tell the audience what you will say, say it, and then tell them what you just said. Always keep on point.

3. *Practice topics on-camera.* Have a friend or campaign worker ask the candidate questions that might come up in the campaign while videotaping. After the interview, the candidate and someone with experience in public speaking should go over the video. Look at everything: Does the candidate have verbal tics ("you know," "quite frankly," "like," "um"); does he scratch his chest, toe the ground, stroke his chin, fluff the hair, or jut the chin? Does she hold her hand to her cheek when seated? Does she do a nervous yawn? Tap her foot? Click a pen?

4. *Be aware of your surroundings.* Before giving a speech, familiarize yourself with the room ahead of time. For TV interviews, think about where you will position yourself and know what will be behind you. If seated, choose the chair carefully; avoid overstuffed chairs, which can affect delivery and make a candidate look slouchy.

5. *Look the part.* Clothes, mannerisms, eyes, hair—everything.

6. *Don't overload the audience with too many facts.* Use facts to make a point, no more.

7. *Be authentic.* The candidate's job is to appear likable, so smile and visually engage with the entire room. Show passion.

8. *Practice your stump speech again and again so the delivery is both fluid and authentic.* Never read a speech. If you cannot remember everything, use the back of a number 9 (business) envelope to jot each point you want to make.

9. *Start small.* One way to help candidates find their feet is to start with coffees before they head out on the speech or debate trail. A coffee

may draw unknown faces, but they're usually a forgiving crowd. Send committee people or those with public speaking skills to give feedback following the event.

10. *Share an experience that happened to you on the campaign trail.* "The other day, while I was canvassing . . . " can be an effective way to make known that you canvass and care what voters think; plus, it provides an opportunity to communicate an important idea that is part of your platform. Remember, campaigns are not about the candidate; they're about the voters.

Write-In, Third-Party, and Nonpartisan Candidates

In some circumstances, you may be running at a distinct disadvantage as a write-in or third-party candidate. In other situations, depending on the laws of the area, the first election the candidates face might be the deciding election. All these situations require specific approaches.

The Write-In Candidate

After the sudden death of a city councilor just weeks before a general election, a few of us got together to help a write-in candidate. This turned out to be a great campaign. There were a lot of volunteers, plenty of money, great ads, well-placed lawn signs, an excellent brochure, and a solid candidate—one who was both hardworking and willing to do anything her campaign committee asked, from walking neighborhoods to modifying her "look." She had been actively involved in city politics and had served on volunteer boards and commissions, she was smart and well spoken, and she did her homework. She got strong endorsements from both local newspapers. Although the race was nonpartisan, she was also a very progressive Democrat running for office against a conservative Republican in a community with an overwhelming Democratic registration advantage. The opposition really ran no campaign other than two or three ads and about as many lawn signs. We made no mistakes during the campaign, and still we lost.

Write-in campaigns, under the best of circumstances, are tough to win. Can it be done? Absolutely. There are examples everywhere of people pulling it off. Washington State elected a congresswoman on a write-in ticket. Write-ins are really no more work than a regular election. However, depending on the ballot type, voting for a write-in can be more complicated for the voter. In the case of our write-in candidate, our county was using a punch-card ballot, requiring voters to do more than just write a name next to a position. Our voters had to write "city council," the actual position number of the council seat, and the candidate's name in an area completely separate from where the actual punch position was on the ballot. They also had to remember not to punch the corresponding number of the opponent on the ballot itself. The name had to be the same on all write-ins. For example, my name is Cathy, but if someone wrote in Kathy, Cathie, or even Catherine, our clerk would not accept it.

To visually reinforce what was required of the voter, we re-created a ballot to use as our campaign logo and put it on everything: lawn signs, the brochure, and direct mail. Still, according to the county clerk, the voters made so many mistakes—such as failing to put the proper council position or any position on the ballot, writing only the position number without specifying "city council," and so on—that hundreds of write-in votes did not count.

The following is a list of things to consider before jumping in on a write-in candidate:

1. You must know the ballot type used by your county and what it looks like.
2. Find out precisely how a write-in vote must be cast at the ballot box. Does the voter have to write in the full name and the position of the office?
3. Know the law: Laws for financial disclosure are the same for a write-in as for a candidate on the ballot.
4. Know when the absentee ballots are mailed. To win you must both identify support and turn out your absentees on or before Election Day.
5. Know what percentage the absentees are of those who vote—not the registered voters, but of those who actually vote. For example, although 25 percent of all registered voters may request and vote absentee, on Election Day they may represent 50 percent or more of the voter turnout.
6. Run two campaigns: one for absentees and one for poll voters.
7. In your campaign literature and advertising, even on the lawn signs, illustrate and reinforce what voters will see on their ballot; make the ballot your logo.
8. Get your candidate on the speaking circuit with the opponent(s).
9. Conduct all other business as you would for any other campaign, keeping in mind item 7 above.
10. If your state has one, get in the voters' pamphlet.

You might think this sounds convoluted, but write-in campaigns are actually more fun than running a regular campaign. No one really expects a write-in to win, so everyone is rooting for you. Also, because write-in campaigns are so rare, the media gives the campaign more attention with feel-good stories during the news, especially if the candidate is working his or her tail off in an obviously well-organized effort. This kind of campaign creates a sense of urgency that brings out the best in volunteers, so they really go the extra distance for the campaign.

It is usually difficult to raise money for a candidate who appears to be losing. With a write-in, however, people perceive being behind not as the fault of the candidate but rather due to circumstances beyond the candidate's control. As a result, if you have a strong write-in candidate, it is surprisingly easy to raise money.

Finally, because people know the odds are long on a write-in winning, when you lose, your efforts get far more attention than they would in a more traditional race. Depending on the kind of campaign you run, the candidate ends the race with more stature, power, and respect in the community than before the campaign and, ironically, is not portrayed as the loser. If you don't win your write-in effort, next election cycle get on the ballot and you will win.

Third-Party Candidates

As in all campaign activities, a third-party candidate can be a blessing or a curse. If you're a third-party candidate, you will benefit most by presenting the Republican and the Democrat as one and the same. You and you alone provide an alternative. To win as a third-party candidate, you must be able to pull votes from both major parties, all age groups, and all income levels, which is pretty rare.

Most often, third-party candidates act as spoilers by splitting the vote of one party and thereby increasing the likelihood of a win by the other. Voters registered as nonaffiliated will track the party of greatest registration within their precinct, so the candidate running as an independent has little claim to any voter and will pull votes from either the Democrats or the Republicans, depending on how he or she stands on the issues. In 1990 a very conservative independent went on the gubernatorial ticket in Oregon. He ran on an anti-choice, anti-sales-tax, anti-land-use-planning platform and successfully pulled conservative votes from a very popular and moderate Republican and, as a consequence, effectively gave the Democrat the win.

In New Mexico, Republican Bill Redmond won a congressional seat in a district registered heavily Democratic by using a third-party candidate to pull support from his Democratic opponent. Redmond's win was due primarily to three strategies: target the Democrat with negative ads, boost the Green Party candidate to split the Democratic vote, and turn out the Republican base. Redmond's campaign even sent literature to registered Democrats *for* the Green Party candidate.

Nonpartisan Races

There are typically two kinds of nonpartisan races: The first matches all candidates in a primary and requires a runoff of the top two only if no one receives 50 percent or more of the votes cast. The other is when all the candidates face each other in a single election, usually the general, and whoever receives the majority of votes cast wins.

If your election is the first animal, that is, you must get 50 percent or have a runoff, your mission is to accurately predict voter turnout for each of the parties in the primary and employ strategy accordingly. Not all primaries are the same. Depending on what is on the ballot, there could be more Democrats or Republicans weighing in the election. In other words, predicted voter turnout is a function of other ballot noise. The goal is to lock in the party that will perform the best in the primary, and then come back and get the other in the general. Even if the campaign does not garner the requisite 50 percent to win the primary outright, the general will be more winnable with this strategy.

Let me give you an example: By the time the 2008 Oregon primary rolled around in May, John McCain already had a lock on the Republican nomination, but Hillary Clinton and Barack Obama were still in full tilt. That presented an unusual opportunity for nonpartisan primary races in our county, where the Republicans, who held a three-point registration advantage (3,400), underreported for their civic duty with a 53 percent primary turnout. Meanwhile, a whopping 75 percent of the Democrats turned out to vote. The net result was 7,400 more Democrats who voted in the primary than Republicans. That translates into nearly an 11,000-vote advantage the Democrats would not have in the general. With 7,400 more Democrats casting a ballot in the primary than Republicans, any Democrat looking to garner the 50 percent vote in a nonpartisan race should have been able to pull off a win—as long as the voters "sort of" knew which candidate was which. However, running for a nonpartisan seat means that in this scenario, if the "Republican" works the Democrats in the primary—and holds on until the general—he only needs to come back in and get the Republicans to win outright in November.

Negative Campaigning

Negative campaigning is inherent in the process. After all, you are running because you embrace issues or values that differ from those of your opponent. You are working on a campaign—whether for a candidate or an issue—for a reason, and as you define that reason, you define both your campaign and that of your opposition. The inverse is true as well.

Although the thought of being attacked in public can cause panic for a candidate or campaign team, remember that it is yet another opportunity to get your message out and to show how you comport yourself under pressure. As I said before, do it well, and an attack can actually help.

If your campaign goes negative, keep in mind that numerous studies conducted on the impacts of negative campaigning indicate that only four areas consistently fall in fair territory when it comes to attacks: actual voting records, current ethical problems, business practices, and money received from special-interest groups. Finally, do not think you can win in a direct-mail war; your campaign must be smarter and have scores of volunteers assisting your efforts.

So what do you do if you are attacked? The University of Maryland conducted a study, the Campaign Assessment and Candidate Outreach Project, that looked at the effects of negative campaigning on voters. Charges that voters considered unfair placed the attacking candidate in serious trouble, whether the opposition responded or not and regardless of whether the voters considered the counterattack fair. Charges that were deemed fair (such as a voting record) caused problems for the candidate being attacked, especially if he or she did not respond or did so in an unfair manner. The best outcome for the candidate under attack is to counter with a "fair charge" in return.[2]

Dos and Don'ts of Attacks

1. Don't start a campaign with an attack.
2. Define yourself before going on the attack, especially if you're running against an incumbent or community leader the voters respect.
3. Be forthcoming to your inner circle on anything in your past that can be used against you. This allows the campaign manager and committee to develop a response to counter potential attacks.
4. Don't mix together a lot of unnecessary arguments.
5. Don't mix positive and negative issues within the same ad or directional piece.
6. Avoid inconsistent, misleading, or unconvincing arguments.

7. Be sure that any attacks are believable and fair: Anything questionable will lead the voter to doubt everything.

8. Do your homework so that you can back up any charges you make, and be prepared for a counterattack.

9. Do not attack using revelations uncovered from divorce proceedings. Voters assume things are said (and done) during a divorce that may not be true or representative of the individual in normal circumstances—whether it is child or spousal abuse, being arrested for back child support, or restraining orders.

10. And, in a related topic, avoid themes that may be related to a potential attack. For example, if the candidate *was* arrested for failure to pay child support, even for a good reason, do not run him on a "greatest dad" platform; leave his current wife and children out of the campaign literature and run him on his experience, record, or leadership abilities. If a candidate has declared bankruptcy, do not present her as a financial wizard. Too often it's not the failing itself that sinks a candidate but rather the perceived hypocrisy.

11. Understand that not all candidate indiscretions are treated equally. For example, there's a difference between Mark Sanford's affair and Anthony Weiner's tweeted crotch shots. Voters understand an affair; they do not understand aberrant behavior.

12. If you're caught, fess up. For example, Weiner's initial lies (compared to Sanford's immediate confession) also reflected poorly on him and further brought into play integrity and judgment, both of which were underscored in subsequent behavior. Voters forgive mistakes long before exaggerated self-opinion or lies.

13. Look for patterns. Behaviors don't change. If a candidate is accused of unnecessary roughness in intramural sports in the distant past, chances are it happened in areas other than on the playing field. Corruption doesn't usually happen just once. If a candidate embellishes in one arena, he or she probably has done so in others as well. Follow the behavior for more examples to establish a pattern to the voters.

14. Time your attack carefully. An attack launched too early in a campaign may not have the intended impact, and one launched too late may not have enough time to sink in with the voters.

15. As Robert A. Heinlein once said, "Never insult anyone by accident."

Recall

As with the initiative and referendum process, recalls require a number of signatures of registered voters equal to a specific percentage of those who voted in a specific election. For example, the number of signatures for a recall for a state office might be equal to 8 percent of the number who voted in the last election for governor, whereas a recall of a city official might be 10 percent of those who voted in the last mayor's election. Once a petition is pulled, it must be filed within a specific time (depending on the state or local statutes), and a special election must be held within a specific number of days after verification of the signatures. In Oregon the whole process can last no more than 140 days: 90 to gather the signatures, 10 to have them verified, and 40 to organize the special election. You cannot begin a recall until someone has been in office for 6 months after his or her *last* election. This goes for those who are in their second or third term of office as well.

From my experience, recall attempts are often prompted by one specific action that, coupled with the personality of the officeholder, means trouble. The recall attempts often focus on strong, smart, outspoken women and strong, smart, soft-spoken men with an overriding theme that the officeholder doesn't know who butters his or her bread. If you find that you are the subject of a recall, remember, you only need to survive; they need to conquer. A failed recall attempt generally leaves the officeholder in a politically stronger position than before (think of Scott Walker). Whether you believe enough signatures will be gathered is really not the point. Once the attempt has begun, do not hang your head: Fight back. There are a lot of people who do not believe in recalls—76 percent of black voters in California, for example, according to data from the 2003 recall of Governor Gray Davis. From my experience having conducted a postmortem analysis after a county commission recall, seniors don't like them either.

Fighting a recall is no different from running a regular campaign. As soon as you hear of an attempt being waged against you, organize a campaign committee. If the organizers of the effort against you claim that you are supported by only one segment of the population, or one community in the county, then be sure that you have representatives from every city and people from all walks of life. If you're being thrown out because of your connection with special-interest groups, then be sure they are nowhere to be seen in the campaign; show broad-based support.

Begin by fundraising. You want to amass a war chest that will scare the opponents before they file the papers. Depending on the circumstances, fundraising events for officeholders subjected to a recall are often surprisingly easy and raise tons of money. A bonus is that because you're undergoing a recall while serving in office, no one expects you to do more on the campaign than just show up. So enjoy: Raise money and support, and marginalize your opposition. If you cannot find a way to do this yourself, have it said by others in blogs, social media, and letters to the editor, and do it again and again and again.

The campaign defending an officeholder is actually made easier because the recall communication is all negative. Obviously, little is positive about a recall—all communication, TV, direct mail, and radio will be on the attack. After all, the recall proponents must make the case of why someone should be thrown out of office in the middle of a term. Negative campaigning tends both to disengage voter participation and to create sympathy for the person subjected to the public execution. Further, if voters feel the attack is unfair, you're gold. Unfair recall attempts can generate a lot of money for the subject of the recall. Use the opportunity to raise money for your reelection.

If you're thinking about recalling an elected official, stop and reconsider. Recalls are almost never warranted. They generally take on the atmosphere of a public flogging. Recalls also scare off other qualified, honest, hardworking people, the kind of people we need, from serving in public office. If you're mad enough to want to recall an officeholder, get over it and run a campaign against the target in the next election.

A Petition Is Pulled!

Whether you are fighting a recall, an initiative, or a referendum, once a petition has been pulled, there are many things you can do to prepare for the inevitability that the petitioners will get the required signatures. Do not make the mistake of waiting to see whether it actually happens. If you do, the momentum will be with the petitioners, and you will not have enough time to mount a viable campaign. Remember, the best way to prevent signatures from getting collected is to organize, fundraise, and line everything up for a full-on frontal assault. You want petitioners to believe that you're really enthused, delighted, and looking forward to the possibility of going toe to toe with them. Here's what you do:

1. Organize a campaign committee.
2. Send at least one mailing and email blast to your house list, explaining what is going on, and alert your Facebook followers. Ask for money.
3. Begin voter identification of support immediately of low-performing nonaffiliated voters in areas of fifty-fifty registration.
4. Know who is opposed to the recall or referendum; getting them out on Election Day will be critical to survival. Start with older voters, who typically do not support recalls, who vote, and who will actually answer their phones.

5. While you're on the phone, secure lawn sign locations and names for an endorsement ad or list of supporters on your webpage. It will be important to show broad community support for your side. Secure field sign locations as well.

6. Whether the movement is local or statewide, when it comes to referrals and recalls, voters are hugely influenced by their neighbors and community. The best way to fight a recall or referendum is to focus in close. The battle is waged neighborhood by neighborhood. Show individual support if you're facing a recall, and show individual opposition (rebellion) if your tax measure is being targeted.

7. Establish a speakers' bureau, and put the speakers on the circuit immediately.

8. Do not let petitioners define you. If your efforts are backed by unions, they should stay in the closet. If your efforts are backed by big business, keep it at a distance.

9. You must go on the offensive; define the opposition, and communicate that those referring the tax measure are self-serving or supported by special interests. Have proof.

10. As soon as a petition is pulled, start fundraising, especially if the opposition's campaign is being bankrolled by special-interest groups. If the law does not allow fundraising until petitions are verified, then ask for pledges you can call in the moment the opposition qualifies for the ballot. But remember, if you have kept your campaign bank account open, you do not need to wait until your opposition gets the signatures. Supporters can give to your existing committee. If you closed your campaign account, simply reopen it under your same committee name. Since committees are often called "Committee to Support Whoever or Whatever," you can continue to use that committee name to fight the recall.

11. Line up letters to the editor and supporters to monitor and respond to newspaper blogs. Remember, while your opponents are gathering signatures, you are, too—signatures for letters, contributions, endorsements, and the get-out-the-vote effort. As a campaign, review these letters and decide when they go to the paper(s). Letters need a mix of emotion, pragmatism, and ridicule of the petitioners. Keep 'em short and post them on your website after they're published.

12. Consider TV ads even if you chose not to do them to get into office. Why? Typically, recall elections are special elections, and special elections have lower voter turnout. When you're dealing with a low-turnout election, the first (and sometimes only) people to vote are seniors, and seniors watch local news and television.

13. If you're fighting a recall, sing long and hard on accomplishments and service, but make the messenger the average person. If you're fighting a referendum, do not fight the actual referral, but rather promote and protect what is being referred. Remember, you are selling hope, opportunity, independence, and investment in the future. Don't get on the opposition's message by defending how little money the program costs.

14. Know your audience, and ask sales reps in both television and radio to set up schedules for airtime. You don't actually have to buy, but you want to know the cost, penetration, reach, and frequency that will get you what you need. The nice thing about recalls is that they happen at a time when other campaigns are not competing for airtime, so you can purchase time up to the last minute.

15. If you don't already have them from the previous election, design your lawn signs and brochures, and have the camera-ready art at the respective printers with a directive to wait for your phone call.

16. The moment the petitions are filed and certified, you want to be able to make five calls and quickly move the whole process into high gear.

As a candidate, think beyond just selling political views. Voters are looking for leaders who are committed and exude honesty, ones who both look and act the part. Voters want individuals who will represent their city, county, state, or nation with class and integrity. The only real qualifications a candidate needs to run and win elected office is a willingness to work hard, communicate honestly, and present an image that meets the voters' expectations of leadership.

11

The Issue-Based Campaign

It doesn't make sense to talk about successful corporations in a
society whose schools, hospitals, churches, symphonies, or libraries
are deteriorating or closing.
—CLIFTON C. GARVIN JR.

We shape our buildings; thereafter our buildings shape us.
—WINSTON CHURCHILL

IN THIS CHAPTER:

- Initiative and Referendum
- Competing Measures
- Local Preemption
- Polling and the Issue-Based Campaign
- Saving Our Public Buildings
- Special Districts
- Flies in the Ointment: The Double Majority, Independents,
  and the Supermajority
- The State Initiative and Referendum Process

AN ISSUE-BASED CAMPAIGN IS ANYTHING THAT GOES BEFORE THE
voters other than a candidate. Issue-based campaigns can cover money
measures for publicly owned buildings, infrastructure—like water systems
or wastewater—parkland acquisition, air-quality regulations, and various
taxes, like a gas tax to fix roads. Issue-based campaigns can also limit government, such as term limits, and can also limit or direct social issues, like
abortion and sexuality laws. Issue-based campaigns can come to the ballot

either through a government body placing it on the ballot or through an initiative process.

Initiative and Referendum

The initiative and referendum process arose out of the fundamental controversy about whether government should come directly from the people or through representatives to the various levels of government. Primarily a western-state phenomenon, the state initiative process enables citizens to bypass the legislature and directly place proposed statutes and constitutional amendments on the ballot by gathering signatures. Each of the twenty-four states with citizens' initiative authority has different criteria to activate the process. Before you begin an initiative campaign, contact your local elections office or secretary of state's office to learn all the necessary details.

The referendum process, by contrast, serves as a check on the governing body by forcing adopted legislation to a vote of the people, allowing them to accept or reject it. The signature requirement for referring legislation out to a vote is usually less than the initiative process.

Increasingly, the initiative process is being used to amend state constitutions in an effort to keep legislative bodies from tinkering with voter-approved initiatives. The result is that state constitutions and city and county charters are needlessly cluttered. However, in defense of this practice, in the 2003 legislative session alone, the Oregon Legislature tried to undo a number of voter mandates. One mandate, a measure to increase the minimum wage in the state, had received voter approval just three months before the Republican house majority advocated undoing the law at the behest of the business interests that funded their campaigns. Another mandate attempted to undo a ban on the use of bait and traps for cougars and bears; voters had previously affirmed the mandate on two occasions. Also, during each session, legislators revisit voter directives related to reproductive rights.

Initiative and referendum processes are also available in many local jurisdictions, and their requirements and scope usually mirror state requirements. Local initiatives can be very useful tools for school districts, libraries, and municipal and county government.

In a local initiative, although most of the guidelines are established by state statutes, the percentage of signatures that need to be gathered varies by locale. Voters may also refer (through referendum) any legislation passed by the local governing body to the voters. As with the state, the number of signatures required is some percentage of the number of people who voted in a specific election—for example, 10 percent of those who voted in the last mayoral election.

The local referendum process differs from the initiative process only in the number of signatures required for qualification and in a time limit; that is, the referendum must be referred within a certain number of days after adoption by the governing body. However, if enough people are opposed to a law, it can, in essence, be repealed through the initiative process at any time. Because both the initiative and the referendum processes circumvent the legislative body, they have some inherent problems. If you're not working in conjunction with the local elected officials, be prepared: They have more tricks in their bag.

Who drafts the ballot title may have a decided advantage. Some titles are prepared in such a way that you cannot tell whether a yes vote is actually a yes or a no (for example, "yes: repeal it" versus "yes: don't repeal it").

Also, some states have limitations, such as allowing only a single subject to be covered in a measure. Meeting this limitation can be a little more difficult than it sounds. Often citizens are eager to throw in a couple of ideas, each of which may strengthen the other and are quite related, and then, after collecting the signatures or running the winning campaign, the participants find that their wording covered more than one subject and it all gets undone. It really isn't for the local governing body to determine whether you have more than one question.

There are many restrictions on initiatives and referenda. In Oregon, for example, local government cannot put land-use matters to a vote, only legislative matters. So before spending a lot of time and money, learn what your parameters are and hire an attorney with experience in government law.

Another caution: Those signing the petition must be registered within the jurisdiction of the area that will be affected by the proposed legislation. For example, if your school measure is to be voted on by those within your school district, then only those registered within the school district will qualify as signers on the petition. Similarly, if your proposed legislation affects your city, then only those registered within the city limits would qualify. In this way, only those affected get to weigh in on the decision.

Also, in a statewide initiative or referral, the people whose signatures are on the petition must be registered in the county in which they signed the petition. This requirement stems from the fact that signatures are verified at the county level where voters are registered.

If it is your intention to gather signatures at tables in front of the local grocery store, be sure to get at least 10 percent more signatures than is required for qualification. An alternative approach would be to use the neighborhood-captain organization covered in Chapter 12, on getting out the vote (GOTV). In this approach, your campaign would actually canvass for signatures using canvassing maps listing the registered voter in a given neighborhood. By methodically canvassing registered voters, talking with them at their door, and securing their signature, the campaign would know that all the signatures are good, thereby avoiding the need to gather more than the required number. The added bonus is informing the voters while gathering signatures.

Of the states with no statewide initiative process, many have provisions for initiatives and referenda at the local level.

Competing Measures

Competing measures are two initiatives, referrals, or propositions appearing on the same ballot that compete with each other for the same vote; they have two forms. The first, which results from a legislative body's responding to a qualifying initiative, is designed to give voters an alternative to the citizen-drafted law. In this case, the governing body places before the voters legislation that is linked in some way to an initiative or a referral generated by the public. A competing measure is a powerful tool that can be used effectively to squelch another ballot proposal. For example, Ashland voters approved a prepared-food and beverage tax to fund an open-space land-acquisition program and state-mandated upgrades on its wastewater treatment plant. It was a divisive campaign that had local restaurants, real estate agents, and the state food and beverage industry on one side and the parks commission, environmentalists, and citizens buckling under potentially astronomical utility bills (should it fail) on the other. Although the proponents were outspent five to one, the voters approved the tax by a narrow margin. Opponents immediately referred it back to the voters.

In the meantime, the state legislature decided to place a statewide sales tax before the voters. The timing was such that the referral of the meals tax would appear on the same ballot as the sales tax proposal. One would assume the proponents of the food and beverage tax repeal would use the scare tactic that the food and beverage tax would be added on top of a statewide sales tax. Although a statewide sales tax was unlikely to pass, given that it had been previously defeated eight times, Ashland had always been supportive of such a tax. However, while the voters might approve a 5 percent local food and beverage tax, few would stand still for a 10 percent tax that would result from the two combined. To head off this predicament, the city placed a competing measure on the ballot along with the food and beverage tax referral. The competing measure said that if the state sales tax passed, Ashland's food and beverage tax would be repealed, and if people voted in larger numbers for the competing measure than to repeal the tax, it would override the initiative on the food and beverage tax. Citizens chose the competing measure over an outright repeal of the tax.

Just a note: Measures approved by voters, no matter how narrow the margin, are rarely overturned when rereferred. Voters historically come back on the referral and reaffirm previous intentions by even larger margins. The same is true with recalls: Officials typically hold on to their office in the face of a recall by a larger margin than they were voted into office.

The other type of competing measure occurs when two or more unrelated money measures appear on the same ballot. They can come from the same governing body, such as two county measures requesting funding through the property tax, let's say one for juvenile services and another for an adult detention center, or from different governing bodies placing money measures on the same ballot, such as a county, city, school, or special district.

These days, counties and cities often place competing measures on ballots because so many needs are falling by the wayside. However, doing this increases the likelihood that all will fail. For example, in one election, our county placed three bond measures before the voters, and all went down. The reason is fairly simple. Among voters, some will vote no on any new taxes, and others will vote yes. Of the yes voters, some will vote for more than one money measure, and some will choose between the measures, effectively splitting the yes vote. They compete with each other.

The survival rate of competing measures is further complicated when statewide initiative-driven legislation is placed on the ballot and inflames one group over another, such as legislation dealing with gun control, reproductive rights, or sexual orientation. Issues of this sort will bring out a voter who might otherwise stay home, and as long as they're at the voting booth, they'll weigh in on your issue-based campaign.

Despite these problems, there are times when a competing measure can actually help. If one of the money issues on the ballot is poorly constructed, the campaign is poorly conducted, or fatal flaws have been committed right out of the gate, voters may choose to overwhelmingly dump it. When they do, there is a fairness doctrine that kicks in, and other measures get a little more of the swing vote than they might normally receive.

Local Preemption

State legislatures love to preempt local government; as moneyed interests have discovered, fighting targeted taxation and legislation is much easier in a state capital than in a hundred municipalities. For example, in 2002, two statewide grassroots initiatives on the Oregon ballot went down in flames. One, a proposal for universal health care, was outspent thirty-two to one, and the other, which would have required labels on genetically modified foods, was outspent sixty-one to one. The latter prompted the agricultural industry, which dumped $5 million into defeating the food-labeling measure, to get legislators to introduce a bill prohibiting local government from implementing any food-labeling laws.

Years ago the city of Ashland, which owns the electric utility, brought in high-speed data services and cable television as part of the electric utility system upgrade. It was also a boon for our emerging software industry and graphic design businesses. Although the private sector had no intention of providing high-speed data services before the city stepped up, cable companies urged the Oregon Legislature to introduce legislation prohibiting other cities from doing what Ashland had done—and tried to make the law retroactive in an effort to undo Ashland's system. Government participation in creating this kind of infrastructure is no different from when it participated in state highway systems or rural electric development in days gone by, and it may be one of the best tools for strengthening local economic development.

More recently, in 2014, county residents where I live garnered enough signatures to place a GMO (genetically modified organism) ban on the ballot, as did another county directly to the west. This time the agricultural interests again knocked on the door of the state legislature, saying that the legislature should take control and disallow GMO bans to roll out county by county. The statewide ban was attached to a completely unrelated bill, and if not for our legislators holding up state budget bills in both chambers until our county was allowed to vote on the GMO ban, the industry would have been victorious in blocking the county vote. The GMO ban overwhelmingly passed.

Polling and the Issue-Based Campaign

Political consultants and pollsters generally agree that to make it through the campaign process, an issue-based campaign must begin with polled support of at least 60 percent. While this is certainly the case for any issue in which something is requested of the citizens, such as a tax increase, issues that restrict government, such as term-limit legislation, track a different polling pattern; for limiting the powers of government, the polling data need only to show a voter preference in initial polls to successfully pass on Election Day.

Further, there are other considerations in reading polls than a simple majority in favor of or opposed to the polled issue. For example, a statewide poll looking at proposed legislation to reintroduce term limits in Oregon showed voter support at 56 percent and opposition at 30 percent. At first glance, it looks as if this proposal does not meet the 60–70 percent threshold for passage following a heated campaign. But comparing the support and opposition numbers shows almost a two-to-one voter preference for term limits. The other thing to consider is the "hard" support and "hard" opposition of the proposed issue-based campaign. In this term-limit example, the hard numbers in favor (definitely for) came in at 35 percent, and the hard numbers in opposition (definitely against) came in at only 20 percent.

Here are some things to consider before embarking on an issue-based campaign:

1. It must be simple and straightforward.
2. It must have voter appeal and speak to emotion. You are selling an idea, not a person, so there are some inherent challenges. Issue-based campaigns that sell hope and opportunity tend to do best.
3. It must be self-serving. The voter must feel that he or she will personally get something upon passage: a park, better schools, a library, reduced taxes, or a shifted tax burden (e.g., to tourists, business, or the wealthy).
4. For fundraising purposes, it must have populist appeal. Remember, money is thy savior.
5. Timing is everything. The best cycle to place an issue-based money measure on the ballot is a midterm primary where a well-organized and comprehensive GOTV can urge lazy supporters to vote. Typically, a low-turnout cycle coupled with a fantastic GOTV equals a win.
6. Is there enough time to make your case to the voters, and do you have people willing to head up the campaign?
7. Who will be drafting the ballot title and summary—a friend or a foe?
8. What are the polling numbers? If you're working on a losing campaign from the beginning, you will finish the race exhausted and will actually set your cause back.
9. Who will carry the measure? Who will carry the opposition? The chair, speakers' bureau, endorsers, and opponents of an issue-based campaign are often the biggest clues the voters have for supporting or rejecting an idea.
10. Have mistakes been made that could sink your efforts even before the decision to place the issue on the ballot?
11. Finally, an issue-based campaign designed to raise taxes must answer four questions: How high will (can) the tax go? Where will it be spent? (Dedicate the funds.) When will it go away? (It has a sunset clause.) And is there a nexus between what is being taxed and where the revenue will be spent? An example would be a cigarette tax to fund health care or a gas tax to fund road improvements. If there is not a logical connection, your campaign must make one. For example, in the prepared-food and beverage tax, we pointed out that tourists and residents alike use city parks and flush toilets, so both locals *and* visitors should help improve these systems that will benefit from the tax stream.

FIGURE 11.1A Historical Photograph of Ashland's Carnegie Library

This photo was used on the front of the "Campaign for the Carnegie" brochure.
(Photo courtesy of Terry Skibby, Ashland historian)

FIGURE 11.1B Inside the "Campaign for the Carnegie" Brochure

We used this image to show voters what they were buying. In issue-based campaigns, use a mix of the old with the new. Civic buildings reflect who we were as well as who we are.

Saving Our Public Buildings

In the age of technology, voters often look at libraries as a throwback and consider funding them a frill. Schools have also suffered, as the classroom remains out of sight and therefore out of mind to the voter. Unlike new wastewater treatment plants or water pipelines, both of which can be funded through revenue bonds, libraries and schools have suffered under taxpayer revolts. Still, if your mission is to get money to build a new school or library or to remodel and expand an existing one, there's plenty of hope.

There are basically three steps involved in setting up a facility bond campaign for capital improvements and a number of choices within each of those steps.

1. Establish a committee to examine needs, opportunities, and direction. Your first step is to gather a select group of community members to usher your project through to the elected body. Although some may end up working on the campaign, that is not the purpose of this committee. Its members' job is to serve as the community voice regarding the project. Assemble people who represent the many sides of your community and are well respected in their circle. You may select a businessperson, representatives of influential city boards or commissions (such as planning and historic), a builder, librarian, teacher, architect, lawyer, baker, and thief. If the facility is city or county owned, it is also important to have the appropriate representative there for guidance and administrative support. It doesn't matter if all the committee members are not 100 percent on board for the project at the beginning; it's actually better if opinions are spread. Don't worry—people will come around or the project won't fly anyway.

2. Once you have the committee in place, working with the local government, hopefully municipal, you will need to select an architectural team. The architectural team should be committed to the community process and inclusivity. You want architects who are interested in what the community wants, not what they think is best for the community. Through a community visioning workshop, a clear idea of what people want will emerge. From this the architects can draft architectural renderings and come up with a money figure to place before the voters (figures 11.1A and 11.1B).

3. Using the money figure generated by the architectural team and backed by your committee, the governing body should place the matter before the voters.

Note: If the cost estimate of your project comes in on the high side and sticker shock among voters is a concern, reduce the size of the expansion but maintain quality. Don't panic and agree to a portable building stuck to the side of the existing structure: Nothing is more permanent than a temporary building.

Keep the Vote Within City Limits

Those living in the unincorporated areas can be the most conservative of American voters and often want little or nothing to do with what government has to offer. They have wells and septic drain fields, and many heat exclusively with wood or some other fuel shipped directly to their homes, and when it comes to being taxed, they're a no vote. People living in cities, however, tend to want what government offers and are willing to tax themselves to get it. If you have an opportunity to run an election without the unincorporated vote, do it.

The no vote of the unincorporated voter can keep city residents from getting what they want. If you want programs for your school district or library system and can keep the vote within the city limits, your chances of passage increase significantly. Here are five reasons to keep the vote within city limits for programs benefiting both those in and out of town:

1. The assessed valuation (per acre) is often greatest within the city, so even if you include county residents in the overall funding scheme, it won't have a huge impact on the cost per $1,000 of the property tax.
2. People within city limits have a higher voter turnout in general than those living rurally.
3. It's easier to run an election and bring in votes within city limits because of the population density.
4. The percentage of people favoring taxes for anything is higher within city limits than in the unincorporated areas.
5. By holding your voting district to the city limits, you eliminate a greater proportion of nonsupporters because of the voting tendencies of those living in unincorporated areas.

Think Creatively

For years, our community leaders had been advocating for upgrades to the county library system. Each library had unique challenges for meeting long-overdue improvements to the point that a system-wide upgrade would easily run tens of millions of dollars. The county commissioners were reluctant to put it to a vote prior to other county improvements they felt were more important. The county Library Committee also seemed hesitant, as a countywide vote could ultimately be turned down by the voters, leaving them with dilapidated buildings and less hope for passage of future taxing measures.

Back then the Ashland Friends of the Library was unsuccessfully dogging the county to move forward to fix libraries in the system. Finally, they came to me (as the mayor) and asked whether the city could help. Given the Ashland branch building was actually owned by the city, we were in a unique position to step up.

I proposed that the Ashland renovation move ahead of the countywide upgrades, but the county officials wanted no part of this proposal. They believed that Ashland voters would not support county upgrades on top of the Ashland branch renovation and expansion. The county also felt that without a strong Ashland vote, the countywide tax measure would have more difficulty surviving an election. Those in the Ashland contingent were concerned about a countywide measure passing, period, with or without Ashland, and were further concerned about meeting a countywide double-majority requirement, which would be very difficult. Meanwhile, county officials were not moving.

To get all the parties what they wanted, we moved Ashland's city library upgrades to be voted on ahead of the county vote with a promise that we would hold off on issuing bonds to pay for the project until the county had an opportunity at the polls. This approach had many benefits. First, it got us off our knees begging the county to do something, as a citywide initiative required only the Ashland City Council to vote to place the tax measure before the voters—an easy prospect. Second, it would guarantee Ashland voters that a specific amount would be spent on our branch and that the renovation outcome would reflect what citizens had agreed upon in the community visioning process. Finally, for those who did not want to pay twice, holding off on issuance of bonds for the project negated those concerns. To underscore this, we agreed to communicate with the voters that a vote for the county system upgrades would result in lowering the debt load for the Ashland improvements with our taxpayers. The latter is important because the first vote held in the city would mean that only city residents would pay for upgrades, while folding our improvements into the county bond would mean that those surrounding the city would also share in the tax burden. In this way, we locked in how much money would be spent in Ashland and exactly what the upgrades would look like. The countywide vote simply reaffirmed what Ashland wanted but for less money because of an economy of scale.

In the spring, the city bond measure passed easily and with an ample double-majority turnout. In the fall, when the county put the whole system before the voters, it was approved, and the double-majority requirements were also met. Eighty-five percent of those casting a ballot in Ashland voted for the countywide upgrades. Given that the second vote actually lowered Ashland's tax on the library upgrade, one would have to wonder what the 15 percent who voted no were thinking.

The worst thing we could have done would be to place an Ashland library upgrade before the voters at the same time as a countywide library upgrade, where the two would become competing measures. Although these two sides had plenty of history and suspicion of each other, we were ultimately able to craft an agreement that met all concerns. And given that the city would hold off on floating the voter-approved bonds only until the next election, it pushed the county commissioners into action.

Know What You're Working On

There are two kinds of issue-based campaigns when it comes to libraries, schools, or government efforts: operating and maintenance (O&M) and facility upgrades (capital improvements or CI).

If your campaign is for operation and maintenance, it will typically be supported by a property tax levy, which goes out for voter approval. When it comes to "selling" operations and maintenance to the community, the test placed before the voters is one of hope and opportunity such as extended operating hours, smaller class sizes, and cocurricular programs. When asking voters to fund facility upgrades, the test is one of need: roof repair to protect the books inside, crumbling infrastructure, dangerous heating systems—that sort of thing. You are basically making the case that improving the facility protects the public asset, which will actually save money in the long run.

There are two ways that facility upgrades can be funded: One is through revenue bonds; the other is general-obligation bonds (GO bonds). With revenue bonds, the government entity guarantees payment of the bond through a reliable revenue stream. For example, you want to upgrade your water treatment facility, so you sell bonds on the bond market, and the repayment is guaranteed through the revenue stream of water rates. The government may raise water rates to pay back these loans. Revenue bonds do not need voter approval.

If you intend to fund your project through GO bonds, then the repayment of those bonds typically comes from the property tax. Depending on your state and local guidelines, GO bonds usually require voter approval. Also of note is that GO bonds get a better interest rate because property tax is seen as more stable than a revenue bond's income stream. Obviously, some publicly held interests—like schools and libraries—make no revenue, so they must go to the voters for approval as a GO bond.

Special Districts

One option for funding, operating, and maintaining libraries, public transportation, historic preservation, water, sewer, agricultural extension services, and such is through a special district. Note that some states have requirements as to when a special district may be placed before the voters, such as even-year cycles only.

If you're sick of begging the county elected officials to keep libraries open, consider a special district. To understand how they work, you only need to think of school districts where an elected board, an administrative arm, and citizen budget committee oversee revenues and expenditures, and you have the model for any special district.

With increased demands on county revenues from law enforcement, elected officials are gutting library, historic preservation, public transportation, and agricultural extension service funding. In other areas where water is scarce, money is being moved from libraries or law enforcement to find more water. The only way to ensure ongoing and permanent funding for programs your elected officials choose to defund is through a special district. Special districts cannot be touched by a governing body outside of the district board.

Typically, any city within a proposed district must decide at the municipal level whether it wants its citizens to even vote on a special district; similarly, your county elected officials must be willing to allow voters in unincorporated areas to participate in the election. If neither the city nor the county government is willing to cooperate, then the interest group must take the issue through an initiative process in states where that is allowed. Keep in mind, when it comes to gathering signatures to place special districts on the ballot, the bar is set very high; in fact, I would argue it is too high for success in this regard.

However, proposing a district to keep an established department open is in the best interest of all concerned and should be presented as such to elected bodies in both city and county government. After all, their expenditure requirements are increasing in the face of stagnant revenue streams, and you're offering a solution that will free up funds for other uses. It's a win-win. And with the help of county government, a special district is easily within the reach of a motivated group of citizens. One small caution: Pushback may come from county officials who would rather not lose control of the new revenues and, therefore, will urge or demand that special-district proponents support a *service district* instead.

A service district often funds more than one type of program (such as historic preservation, libraries, and water combined) into one service district. Under a service district, the existing elected board, the administrator, and the citizen budget committee determine how the revenues will be dispersed. And if they decide the money is better spent on water than libraries or law enforcement, then the money can be siphoned for one of the other items included in the service district. It's a bad exchange. A service-district model denies you of your most persuasive campaign arguments: dedicated funding. Selling a special (versus service) district is much easier because voters know that the new revenues will be used for one and only one voter-approved entity.

Passing a Special District or a Taxing Measure

If your goal is to pass a special-district or tax measure, here's what you need to do:

1. Break the geographic area into zones of similar voting blocs.
2. Look at the election returns of the last (likely failed) tax proposal for the same kind of money measure: library, school, parks, roads, fire, or the like. Look for tax measures that cover a similar focus: operating and maintenance or facility bonding. Nothing? Find something similar in order to assess the percentage by precinct of yes and no votes.
3. Next, determine predicted voter turnout. As noted in Chapter 2, "Precinct Analysis," predicted voter turnout can be calculated by using the percentage turnout of similar election cycles (midterm primary, presidential general, special election, and so on) and multiplying that by the current registration numbers, precinct by precinct. Multiply the predicted voter turnout by the yes and no vote percentage from the last similar tax proposal. This will give you predicted yes and no numbers for all the precincts in all the zones in the taxing area if a measure were placed before the voters today.
4. Finally, play with the predicted turnout numbers. For example, if you have two zones that consistently vote no on similar money measures to yours by 70 percent, rerun those numbers with a 10 percent shift— that is, just 60 percent voting no. What does that do for your bottom line? If zones that typically vote no by 60–40 could be moved to a 50–50 split on your measure, what does that do to your bottom line?

Still need more? What if you can pump up the turnout in zones that typically vote yes? Let's say you have a zone that usually votes in favor of libraries by 80 percent, always have, always will, but they turn out only by 34 percent in the election cycle you're in—such as a typical midterm primary. Can you pump those numbers up so that 65 percent turn out to vote? Look at your bottom line again. Are you there?

This final step will tell you where you must focus attention and where you must lay low to get the outcome you desire. It is a simple and strategic approach to organize your campaign. Once you know which zones need attention and which must be ignored, you will know where to send mail, in which local papers to advertise, where canvassing is detrimental or unnecessary or where it is imperative. This approach will also inform the campaign where lawn signs should be concentrated—in other words, where to activate voters. It will also inform your budget.

In the 2014 midterm primary, I managed a library district campaign for Jackson County, Oregon. The county covers nearly 3,000 square miles—bigger than either Delaware or Rhode Island—and profiles like much of the nation: People have moved to their respective corners and vote like their neighbors. I broke the county into seven zones of similar voting populations:

- Two had a history of overwhelmingly voting "no" on *any* library measure (70 percent no).
- Three had a history of narrowly defeating prior library tax measures (55 percent no).
- Two zones consistently voted to support library funding. Of those two, one did so by 75 percent and the other by 62 percent.

With the exception of the zone that historically voted 75 percent in favor, voters were identified for four months prior to the May election, that is, from January to April. I ran each zone as its own independent campaign with weekly meetings and employed strategy specific to the types of voters within a specific zone. In areas of little support, dedicated volunteers identified library support among Democrats and "Republican women of a certain age." In areas of marginal support, only underperforming nonaffiliated voters were identified, and in areas of overwhelming support no voter ID was necessary. One of the most effective parts of the campaign was my weekly pilgrimages to the far corners of the county, bringing the campaign to them rather than requiring the desperate zones to come to me in a more central location.

For the zone that voted overwhelmingly for library measures in the past, we used that team to do all clerical work for the campaign—stuffing parties, phoning, raising money, assembling lawn signs, and all of those miscellaneous odds and ends that constantly need doing in a campaign. This was also the zone that got most of the lawn signs.

Zones that historically showed little interest in library funding, or any tax measure, were denied lawn signs, canvassers, advertising in local poop sheets, or any untargeted activity. You will recall that lawn signs do not persuade but rather activate, and a campaign should never place them in an area that will activate 70 percent "no" votes to 30 percent "yes." That's just stupid.

Let me caution you: This type of campaign is not for the faint of heart. It is counterintuitive, and many will say, "I see no campaign, no lawn signs, and no mailings. You will lose." And if you do lose, people will say, "Not surprised—they ran no campaign." Controlling those who support your efforts and who want to do "something" because they see nothing is crazy making. Let me repeat: Nowhere do people confuse motion with progress more than in political campaigns.

Well-meaning supporters of the library district campaign printed their own flyers, heralding the services of the local library with the idea of changing minds. I would remind them that libraries are not a new idea that needs explaining. Some would storm out of meetings, never to return, because the idea of quietly running a targeted campaign made no sense; after all, political campaigns are big, noisy, expensive things.

Fortunately, most of the volunteers drank the Kool-Aid. It was a disciplined, well-oiled machine, and the outcome followed the strategic model: Voters of the two zones who typically voted "no" 70–30 moved to "no" 60–40, the zones that previously voted "no" 55–45 went to 50–50, and then we swamped the boat with the two zones that historically supported library measures on the ballot. In the 75–25 "yes" zone, which typically turned out 34 percent in a midterm primary, we pushed 70 percent of the voters out, and they delivered a 75 percent "yes" vote. The way we were able to increase the turnout in favorable areas is covered in the next chapter: getting out the vote.

The most interesting takeaway was that we flipped a previous twenty-point loss to a four-point win without substantially changing the yes vote. Indeed, out of the 63,396 votes cast in 2014, the yes vote improved by only 2,690, while the no vote decreased by a whopping 14,460 votes. By ignoring the areas of little support and registrants that typically would never vote yes, the no voter disengaged, giving us the win.

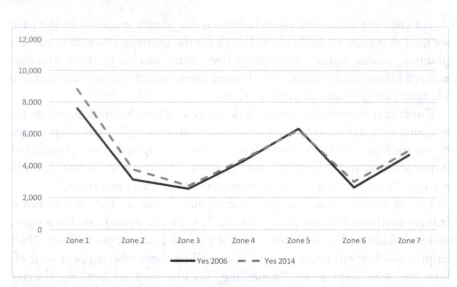

FIGURE 11.2A 2006 Versus 2014: "Yes" Vote by Number

A twenty-point loss in 2006 was converted into a four-point win in 2014 by identifying support and then running a robust GOTV to be sure the vote got in. Above, the yes vote increased 2,690 votes from 2006 to 2014.

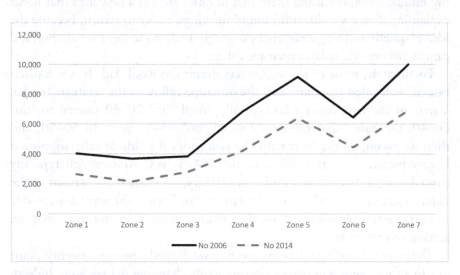

FIGURE 11.2B 2006 Versus 2014: "No" Vote by Number

The other side of converting a previous twenty-point loss into a win is keeping a low profile so "no" voters are not activated. Between the two campaigns, the "no" vote fell by 14,460, which, coupled with the increased "yes" vote, equaled a net gain of 17,150—a twenty-four-point flip between 2006 and 2014. And we ran it for less than half the price.

Flies in the Ointment:
The Double Majority, Independents, and the Supermajority

The Double Majority

Under a *double majority*, there must be at least a 50 percent voter turnout before ballots are counted to determine if a majority of those casting a ballot actually support the proposal. This means that the challenge becomes one of turning out at least 50 percent of the vote, not just a majority of support. Those opposing taxes or annexations under a double majority understand that not voting and urging their friends to stay home as well can defeat tax measures quicker than if they actually participate in an election and vote no on a proposal. In counties and states that do not routinely update voter rolls, those who have died or moved get a de facto vote, making it more difficult to reach the 50 percent turnout threshold.

Nonaffiliated Voters (Independents) and the Double Majority

In primary elections where nonaffiliated voters are not allowed to participate in the partisan races, turnout of these voters can be too low to achieve an overall turnout of 50 percent. In these cycles, there is little you can do to meet the required 50 percent turnout unless the campaign covers a small area (city or school district) with an active electorate. Although you may win the vote, you'll lose the election because of turnout. Ironically, these same campaigns, coming back for a second shot in the non-double-majority general election, often lose because of support. It is almost as though everyone who stays home in the primary votes no in the general. A postmortem analysis on a primary will not give you solid predictors for a general because the primary support numbers simply do not carry over. To predict these elections, you must take another general midterm election for an issue-based campaign that lost in a primary.

The upside of double-majority requirement is that it creates a sense of urgency on the part of the protax voter as well as the volunteers needed to prod them, and it has the added benefit of scaring away competing measures on the ballot.

Some states, like Hawaii, require that the double-majority turnout carry over to all those casting a ballot. In this way, even though 50 percent may turn out to vote, if voters undervote a double-majority tax measure, then the ballot issue fails.

The Supermajority

The supermajority rule applied to tax measures requires that either two-thirds or 60 percent of those voting approve the measure before it may take effect. Here your objective is dramatically different from a double majority. The best defense is to place your money measure on an election with the lowest voter turnout possible and no competing measures. Then you must identify your supporters and have a top-notch GOTV effort to get them to the polls or to mail their absentee ballots.

A few years back, in Marin County, California, supporters of a school facility plan used an interesting tactic to pass their bond measure under the supermajority rule. The supporters of the measure determined that those sixty-five and older were both a no vote and likely voters. To move this age group over to the yes column, the bond measure excluded them from having to pay, but did not exclude them from the vote. The campaign then worked hard to turn out the sixty-five-and-over age group, who had nothing to lose by voting yes. The facility plan passed.

The State Initiative and the Referendum Process

Three Types of Initiatives

1. *Direct initiative:* The completed petition places a proposed law or amendment directly on the ballot, bypassing the legislative process.
2. *Indirect initiative:* The completed petition is submitted to the legislature, which then may enact the proposed measure or one substantially similar to it. If the legislature fails to act within a specified time, the proposal is placed on the ballot.
3. *Advisory initiative:* The outcome provides the legislature with a nonbinding indication of public opinion.

Four Kinds of Referenda

1. *Mandatory referendum:* Requires the legislature to refer all proposed amendments to the constitution as well as measures regarding tax levies, bond issues, and movement of state capitals or county seats to the voters.
2. *Optional referendum:* The legislature may refer to the citizens any measure that it has passed. This is often called a referral.
3. *Petition referendum:* Measures passed by the legislature go into effect after a specified time unless an emergency clause is attached. During that interval, citizens may circulate a petition requiring that the stat-

ute be referred to the people either at a special election or at the next general election. If enough signatures are collected, the law is not implemented, pending the outcome of the election. The signature requirement is usually lower and the time allowed to gather signatures less than for a straight initiative.

4. *Advisory referendum:* The legislature may refer a proposed statute to the voters for a nonbinding reflection of public opinion.

Initiative and Referendum Procedures

1. *Preparing the petition:* Preparing the initiative petition and organizing the collection of signatures are the responsibility of the chief petitioner(s). The text of the proposed measure is drafted by the chief petitioner(s), with legal assistance if desired, and filed with the secretary of state for state initiatives and the local election office for local initiatives.

2. *Filing the petition:* Any prospective petition must include the names, addresses, and signatures of the chief petitioner(s); a statement of sponsorship signed by a certain number of registered voters and verified by county election officials; a form stating whether the circulators of the petition will receive payment; and the complete text of the proposed measure.

3. *Obtaining the ballot title:* State statutes usually provide strict timelines for moving a filed petition through the process to obtain a ballot title. For statewide initiatives, all petitions are filed with the secretary of state, and two additional copies are sent to the attorney general, who prepares a draft of the ballot title.

4. *Preparing the cover and signature sheets:* The chief petitioner(s) must submit a printed copy of the cover and signature sheets for approval prior to circulation. The cover sheet must include names and addresses of the chief petitioner(s), the proposal itself, the ballot title, and instructions to circulators and signers. The cover sheet must be printed on the reverse of the signature sheet and contain instructions to signature gatherers. Notice of paid circulators must be included. Signature sheets must never be separated from the cover sheet and the measure's text.

5. *Circulating the petition:* As soon as approval is obtained from the election officer, the ballot is certified and may be circulated for signatures. Usually you can withdraw the petition at any time. Any registered voter may sign an initiative or a referendum petition for any measure being circulated in a district where the registered voter resides. All signers on a single sheet must be registered voters residing in the same county.

6. *Filing the petition for signature verification:* There's a deadline for signature verification statewide (usually four months) and locally (usually less time).

7. *Filing campaign and expenditure information:* Within a specified period after filing petition signatures for verification, the chief petitioner(s) must file a statement of contributions received and expended by the petitioner(s) or on their behalf.

Before a political committee receives or expends any funds on a measure or proposition that has reached the ballot, the committee treasurer must file a statement of organization with the secretary of state, and subsequent contributions and expenditures must be reported. Sometimes this must be done even if a petition is withdrawn.

There are few things you can do, including serving in office, that would impact your community more than running and passing an issue-based campaign. Seeking and receiving voter approval for such things as public buildings, parks, education, municipal water systems, and the like is very rewarding. And, conversely, stopping elected officials from heading in the wrong direction through referral is empowering. If you live in a state where initiatives and referrals are not allowed, then run for office, win, and once sworn in seek voter approval for programs that will last long after you're gone.

Getting Out the Vote (GOTV)

By Catherine Shaw and Daniel Golden

Word of mouth appeals have become the only kind of persuasion that
most of us respond to anymore.

—MALCOLM GLADWELL

IN THIS CHAPTER:

- The Shifting Landscape
- The NC-GOTV System
- The Absentee Ballot and Early Vote
- Poll Watching

THE SUCCESSFUL GOTV EFFORT FOCUSES ON SURGICALLY PRECISE
activation of lazy supporters. People get busy: Kids get sick, cars break down,
an old friend calls—in short, life gets in the way, and somehow, despite the
best intentions of your base to do their civic duty, it falls down their list
of priorities. Now, your one and only job is to help remove obstacles. This
chapter will walk you through it with a system developed over thirty years of
research and campaign/field refinement. It really works.

The Shifting Landscape

Before the days of ubiquitous caller ID and wireless phones, GOTV was
primarily an exercise in phone banking. The campaign team would find volunteers to spend a few hours at a call center, and over several days they'd prod
every supporter in their database to get to the polls. In the 2006 midterm

general, I worked on a facility campaign for the largest school district in southern Oregon: Three hundred volunteers—teachers, school board members, principals, classified workers, parents, and students—called on twenty phone lines in fourteen two-hour shifts. The volunteers often knew the voters on their lists, and the familiarity was central to the passage of the $184 million bond that won by just 313 votes out of 30,000 ballots cast.

Four years later, phone bankers were reaching fewer than 10 voters per two-hour shift, and it was clear that something had to change. In 2014 we rolled out a totally reengineered approach for a countywide library district measure, a GMO agricultural ban in the midterm primary, followed by a partisan race in the midterm general. The results were unprecedented in our region. The county had voted down an earlier iteration of the library measure in the same election cycle by twenty points. This time we passed it by four points, an incredible twenty-four-point swing. One targeted zone, with an 75 percent rate of support for public libraries historically, typically had a midterm primary voter turnout of 34 percent—this approach increased it to 70 percent. Putting the same system to work in 2017, we successfully passed a funding measure for a fire department in one the most anti-tax cities in the county.

The NC-GOTV System

Your GOTV effort can only be as successful as your voter identification (ID) effort, and your voter identification can only be as strong as your precinct analysis (see Chapter 2). About four months before Election Day, you will break your district into *zones*, or congruous precincts demonstrating similar voting patterns—strongly supportive of your political party or issue (*saint zones*), mixed support for your political party or issue (*mixed zones*), or strongly unsupportive of your political party or issue (*sinner zones*).

Next you'll break each zone into *turfs*, or congruous neighborhoods of fifty to sixty voters apiece, and assign each of them to one or two *neighborhood captains* (NCs), sometimes called *neighborhood coordinators*. Always pick reliable volunteers for your NCs, and whenever possible, make sure they live within the turf you've assigned them. Some volunteers prefer not to make phone calls, and others prefer not to canvass—in this case, try to pair them with each other as co-NCs for a single turf. Each NC will be issued the list of voters living within his or her turf (voter list) and is responsible for identifying support within their lists in the months leading up to Election Day: Are they supportive (*friendly*) or unsupportive (*unfriendly*) of your candidate or issue?

The NCs assigned to turfs within mixed zones will ID the nonaffiliated voters on their voter list. Those assigned to turfs within saint or sinner zones, however, should only ID voters if you are managing a long-shot campaign, and they will *not* be contacting NAVs. Further details are provided in the next section, but if your resources are too tight to expand your ID effort to saint zones and sinner zones, it will not be necessary to break them into turfs so early. The turf and NC assignments for saint zones will be required only a few weeks before Election Day. Sinner zones, on the other hand, will not be broken into turf or assigned NCs at all—unless you ID voters in these zones, you will assume that all of them are unfriendly. Your best bet is to keep your campaign totally invisible to unfriendly voters.

In the weeks leading up to the election, each NC will canvass or call the voters on his or her list to make sure they vote—on average, activating twenty lazy voters per week. That might sound like a big lift, but feedback questionnaires after the election indicated an overwhelming preference for the NC-approach GOTV over traditional phone bank and canvassing efforts. Some NCs even wrote thank-you letters to the campaign. Whatever persuasion or voter identification you might have done is over now. The GOTV phase is all about activation of lazy friendlies, so NCs won't have to confront hostile neighbors.

The NC system affords your volunteers a lot of flexibility. No more meeting at a parking lot on Saturday morning to knock on the doors of voters who usually don't answer—NCs can contact voters on their list at their own convenience, canvassing a few homes in their neighborhoods each night while walking the dog. They can even bring their kids along. And for NCs unwilling or unable to reach voters by calling or knocking, we distribute "Please Vote" door hangers (figure 12.1) to NCs during the training session.

FIGURE 12.1 Generic Door Hanger for the Neighborhood-Captain GOTV System

Not listing candidates or issue-based campaigns on the door hanger expands the volunteer base as supporters of noncompeting campaigns join forces. "Please Vote" was printed in bright orange on white background and visually linked voters to the library district campaign lawn signs that were also orange and white. (Crystal Castle Graphics)

Turf assignments make expectations unambiguous. It's frustrating for a volunteer when a campaign asks for more time than he or she signed up for (*job creep*), and frustrated volunteers are less likely to return for your next campaign. This GOTV system will empower your volunteers with a feeling of ownership for their own neighborhood and contains their responsibilities within literal borders.

Finally, the NC system is just plain more effective. Voters are more inclined to answer a screened phone call or open the door to a familiar face, and the NCs that had previously identified voters in their turf will have the benefit of a preexisting relationship.

Eight Steps to a Winning GOTV

Let's review the NC-GOTV system thoroughly.

1. *Consult your precinct analysis, and assign each of your precincts to one of three zone types.* The three zone types are saint zones, mixed zones, and sinner zones (details on precinct analysis and zone selection are in Chapter 2). A typical *zone bracket* might be 75 percent—25 percent votes owed—that is, saint zones are composed of precincts owing more than 75 percent of votes to your candidate or issue, sinner zones are composed of precincts owing less than 25 percent of votes to your candidate or issue, and the remaining zones are mixed. However, the zone brackets you choose should be informed by the outcome of your precinct analysis.

Your GOTV approach will be party specific—you will need to know who to count in *your party* before you begin. Of course, if you are managing a partisan race, *your party* is simply the political party of your candidate. However, if your campaign is nonpartisan or issue based, you will need to map voter preferences to party registration. In general, your party will be Democratic for perceived liberal issues or relatively liberal candidates in nonpartisan races, and your party will be Republican for perceived conservative issues or relatively conservative candidates in nonpartisan races. More detail on party mapping is provided in Chapter 2, but the bottom line is to go with your own judgment—it's usually pretty obvious which party is yours. We'll call the other party the *opposition party*. Your zone-specific strategies will be as follows:

- *Saint zones:* Include all voters in your party and all NAVs on the voter lists—the NCs will try to activate them all. If you are managing a long-shot campaign, your NCs will ID voters registered with the opposition party in the months leading up to your GOTV push, adding the friendly voters to be contacted during the GOTV push. Otherwise, voters registered with the opposing political party should be ignored entirely.

- *Mixed zones:* All voters in your party will be targeted for GOTV. Your NCs will ID NAVs in the months leading up to your GOTV push and keep friendly voters on their list; unfriendly voters are scrubbed and never contacted again. Voters registered with the opposition party should be ignored entirely.

- *Sinner zones:* Assume all voters are unfriendly and remain invisible to voters in these zones—no turf assignments or NCs are necessary. The exception would be if you are managing a long-shot campaign. In this case, ignore all NAVs and voters registered with the opposing political party, but assign NCs to ID voters in your party. The turfs will cover a considerably greater area, since voters registered in your party are sparser in sinner zones by definition, so you may choose to give shorter voter lists to the NCs managing turfs in these zones. All voters that NCs identify as friendly will be targeted to GOTV. Never place lawn signs within these zones.

2. *Request the voter file with history from your county clerk's office or secretary of state elections office.* This will tell you each voter's name, address, party registration, voter identification number (the unique tag assigned to track voters), and a record of the elections for which they turned in ballots (whether you turn in a ballot is public information—how you voted is not). You will need to grade each voter according to the number of ballots they cast over the past four *similar* elections—for example, if your election is a midterm primary, each voter's grade is determined by the number of midterm primaries in which he or she voted:

- A (always vote): voted in four out of the past four similar elections
- B (usually vote): voted in three out of the past four similar elections
- C (sometimes vote): voted in two out of the past four similar elections
- D (rarely vote): voted in one out of the past four similar elections
- F (never vote): haven't voted in any of the past four similar elections
- N: no voting history available

Election offices typically save election data for only five years, which isn't enough to properly score your voters: It would be ideal to have a *sixteen-year* voter history because the election cycle is four years. If you're making a career out of campaign management, be sure to save the data you collect from your county clerk so you'll have a longer voting history in the next election. If you cannot acquire extended voting histories, or if you are trying to grade a voter too young to have participated in four similar elections, you might have to take a shortcut: Use the past two similar elections and double the score, or use the past four semisimilar elections (e.g., the previous four general elections, even though two would be presidential and two would be midterms). You can also get data from other political operatives in your region or your state political party (more on that in the next step). If data are too hard to find but you have the last four years and a voter has voted in every single one of them plus special elections, I'd call that an "A" voter.

3. *Build a voter database.* It should have column headers for voter identification number, first name, last name, special pronunciation of names or nicknames, address, turf ID, zone ID, political party, voting score (A–F), gender, others in household, contact information, age, and special notes. State political parties typically offer detailed voter data online by subscription—for example, the Democrats offer a service called the Voter Activation Network (the "VAN"). These databases can help you complete your voters' histories for grading as well as fill out the relevant fields in your voter database.

4. *Cut your turf.* Break each zone into contiguous areas of about fifty to sixty households or voters each. Turfs in urban areas and turfs assigned to multiple NCs can have more, but make sure to keep turfs in rural precincts small—they're more difficult for NCs to canvass.

We use BatchGeo to cut turf, but other mapping platforms are available. BatchGeo supports imports of spreadsheet data and generates dots on a city map from the address column, and then each row of individual voter data can be accessed by clicking a dot. However, the following voters should be excluded from your GOTV effort and therefore not be imported into your mapping platform:

- "A" or "F" graded voters: Don't expend GOTV resources on people who always vote or never vote
- Opposition party voters in mixed zones and sinner zones
- NAV voters in sinner zones
- Party voters in sinner zones and opposition-party voters in saint zones unless you are managing a long-shot or issue-based campaign

As mentioned in the previous section, you will need to cut all turf for which voter ID is necessary about four months before Election Day—all the turf within mixed zones and, if you're managing a long-shot campaign, the turf inside saint and sinner zones as well.

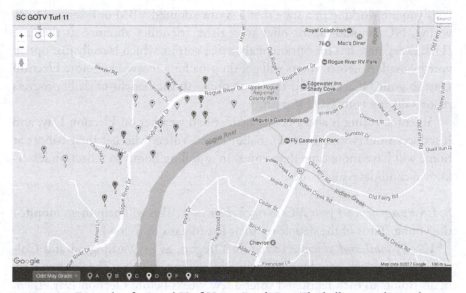

FIGURE 12.2 Example of a Rural Turf Using BatchGeo. The balloons indicate the voting grade by color.

5. *Assign each turf to one or two neighborhood captains.* Ideally, they should live inside their own turf, and you should provide them with the voter lists (figure 12.2).

6. *Assign district coordinators (DCs) to oversee the work of the neighborhood captains.* Each DC can supervise about fifty neighborhood captains.

7. *Identify voters according to their zone-specific strategy in step 1 by canvassing or phone.* NCs responsible for turf with voter ID activity should have about three months to reach the neighbors on their voting list beginning four months before Election Day.

The ID process can be lengthy, and it gets more difficult to identify intent as Election Day approaches. It's critical that you get the process started with time to spare; you don't want to find yourself in the GOTV push without knowing where to find your supporters. Furthermore, planning for a healthy buffer between the ID push and the GOTV push will prevent unnecessary activation of unfriendly voters, whom your NCs will find and strike from their lists. (Be sure they report each removal back to the campaign, however—you will exclude these voters from your GOTV effort, but you'll want to keep track of them for future campaigns.) Remember that winning on the undervote requires that you keep the unfriendlies in the dark: The less they see of your campaign, the less likely they are to vote against you.

If you are working in a state that has not adopted VBM or extended early voting, NCs should *always* offer to register friendlies absentee as they are ID'd. Every state has the option of absentee voting, which is really just opt-in vote by mail. Absentee voters will get their ballot a few weeks before Election Day, so your NCs can prod them to vote with the benefit of daily progress reports during your GOTV push.

Absentee voting is also a hedge against bad weather on Election Day, and it reduces undervoting in down-ballot races. Voters who get their ballots at home will have more time than voters in a polling booth to reflect on lesser-known candidates and issues.

8. *Create a system for your NCs to track their turfs.* This will help them monitor the voting status of the people on their list (details to follow).

Vote-by-mail and absentee voting. In Oregon, as in Washington and Colorado, we have all vote by mail in lieu of polling stations. The county clerk mails ballots to each registered voter a few weeks before Election Day. Then, as the completed ballots are mailed back, the campaign can order an activity list for a nominal fee that is then emailed to the campaign. During the GOTV push, ballots received are automatically updated by our team using the activity list sent by the county. Through the webpage created for the GOTV, our NCs see in real time when a ballot is received by the county because a "1" is dropped into their voter lists (see figure 12.7). This allows the NC to focus only on the lagging friendlies. Obviously, the task becomes much more difficult wherever voters go to the polls to cast their ballot on Election Day. The best an NC can do is really emphasize the importance of the election to lower-graded friendlies, hoping it all sticks on the big day. Poll watching in areas of saints will mitigate some uncertainty. More on poll watching later.

Identifying Voter Intent

Your precinct analysis is the key to an efficient GOTV. Precinct-level votes-owed calculations will help you wisely allocate resources by rapidly grouping neighborhoods of overwhelming support and opposition, freeing your volunteers to focus their ID effort in mixed precincts. In these precincts, the campaign must identify who is with you among the lazy NAVs, who is a question, and who is not willing to support your candidate or cause.

You will especially be interested in parsing friendlies from unfriendlies among NAVs—on average, they fail to cast a ballot 20 percent more often than partisan voters. Most tight down-ballot races are lost by the undervote, so the winning campaign is usually the one that activates more base voters and friendly NAVs to actually vote and fill in the bubbles for their candidate or issue. Once you give your NCs their voter ID assignments, they are free to contact voters throughout the campaign season, by canvassing or by phone. Drive-by canvasses work in some towns and basically involve nothing more than scanning a home for identifiers. In my area, for example, statues of Buddha in the garden or at the front door and Tibetan prayer flags reveal Democrats. On the other hand, bumper stickers that celebrate the Second Amendment ("If it's hootin' I'm shootin'" or "Support gun control: Use both hands") are reliable indicators of Republican voters. Canvassers should always keep an eye out for demographic clues because canvasses typically yield few actual contacts. A volunteer once reported to me that he ID'd a voter as Democrat when he found an old VW bus in the driveway with a Grateful Dead bumper sticker. In my area Democrats tend to like older homes and porches, and Republicans tend to have no-trespassing signs and garages that greet the street. You may find different giveaways in your neck of the woods, but they will be there if you look.

When it comes to taxes for publicly held entities, areas of very little tax support may require more nuanced assumptions. For example, conservative neighborhoods are usually unfriendly to property tax increases, but I've found loyalty and support for firefighters among the most ardent no-tax voter. Libraries are popular among Democrats, but also Republican women of a certain age. If you're looking for unlikely pockets of support for an issue campaign, you might find friendly demographics with the help of micro-targeting data (see Chapter 2). For example, you would ordinarily exclude opposition-party voters living in mixed zones from the voter ID effort, even if you're running a long-shot campaign. But suppose you contract a polling firm, and it reports that young voters in that party reacted well to your specific issue. You might then choose to have NCs managing turf in mixed zones to ID opposition-party voters in that age bracket (but do ID them—*never* add opposition-party voters to your GOTV list automatically, no matter what the demographic data show).

So how many voters do you need to identify? Looking at your precinct analysis, determine the typical percentage of voter turnout based on the election cycle. If you're running a campaign during an off-year election, typical turnout may be as low as 20 percent. In that case, you would multiply total registration by 0.20 and divide the product in half—the result will give you one fewer voter than you need to win. Do not pay attention to volunteers and supporters of an issue-based campaign that say something will pass, no sweat. As the saying goes: Trust in Allah, but tie your camel.

When your NCs ID the voters in their turf, the ideal friendly is one who says, "Keep your literature; I'm a supporter." Money measures for schools, libraries, building upgrades, and O&M (operating and maintenance) aren't exotic to anyone: Most voters will be familiar with the idea, and if they show any hesitation with their support at all, they will almost certainly vote "no." The voter who asks how much your issue-based item costs is a no voter. NCs may disclose technical details if they like, but make sure the ID is "no"—you will not be activating these voters during the GOTV. A money measure isn't about the fifty-cents-per-thousand increase on property taxes, it's about expanded hours, a new facility, or smaller class sizes. It's not like voters keep an itemized budgetary limit for each public service in their back pocket—if fifty cents per thousand is too high, ten cents per thousand will be, too. And while we're here: You cannot sell a money measure with clever comparisons like "For the cost of a cup of coffee . . . " I don't even advise campaigns to include cost information in their literature; if the voter wants to know, it'll be on the ballot title.

Grading Voter Performance

Grading voters saves campaign effort. We know that NAVs are closet partisans who track the voting behavior of their neighbors (see Chapter 2). You should never expend resources identifying NAVs in saint zones or sinner zones—include them in your GOTV effort and ignore them, respectively. Only identify NAVs in mixed zones (also, if you are managing a long-shot campaign, possibly your party voters in sinner zones and opposition-party voters in saint zones).

When you cut the turf in step 4, I advised you to omit the "A" and "F" voters from your mapping-software drop. It would be a waste of resources to ID anyone who always votes or never votes, and therefore you don't need to expend GOTV resources on them. Instead, your NCs should focus their efforts on "D," "C," and possibly "B" voters (in my experience, those who vote in three-quarters of elections are nearly always "A" voters who missed a year for some extenuating circumstance—you should really only ID them if you're flush with volunteer hours). A campaign can expand its base only by activating friendly lazy voters, which are usually found among NAVs living in mixed zones and saint zones. The lazy unfriendly voters your NCs find in mixed zones are likely either to not vote or undervote your down-ballot race if you leave them alone. You will use voter apathy to your advantage inasmuch as you succeed in surgically activating lazy voters.

Mapping Neighborhoods (Turfs)

Consider the following when you cut your turf:

1. In urban areas, avoid creating turf that spans both sides of man-made or natural barriers like large parks, wide streets, rivers, streams, gullies, and highways.
2. NCs assigned to rural areas will have to travel longer distances to reach the voters on their list, so don't give them as many as NCs assigned to urban areas. You won't necessarily group voters into the same turf just because they live on the same street—it might be easier on your NCs to divide very long roads into more than one turf.
3. If you are managing a long-shot campaign, you might have chosen to ID voters in your party within sinner neighborhoods. In this case friendly voters will be sparse by definition, even in urban areas. Assign shorter voting lists to NCs in charge of sinner districts as their canvassing job will cover more distance.

You can't effectively cut turf from a spreadsheet—you need to map the voters in your district geographically, and that will require a mapping platform. As mentioned above, we use BatchGeo to convert our voter list into a graphical map interface, which color-codes voters according to their grade and helps NCs to visually review who on their list has voted notated with a "1" (see figure 12.7).

In states with vote by mail and extended early voting, elections offices update individualized turnout data frequently during the voting period. If you don't live in such a state, it's important that your NCs try to register their ID'd friendlies as absentee voters in the months leading up to the election. Absentee voters usually get their ballots in the mail weeks before the election, and elections offices will include them in their updates of turnout data.

Your campaign must use these reports to provide real-time progress reports to your NCs, or they will not know which voters are dragging their feet. It would be impractical and annoying to hassle every single voter in your database every day; you need your NCs to stay on top of only the lazy voters. Activation is also a lot more powerful with data in hand—imagine a neighbor knocking on your door to tell you that everyone else on the block has voted except for you.

Ideally, your NCs will have access to an online graphical interface that automatically updates their turf data as your election office revises turnout data. If you can't find a volunteer savvy enough to build such a website, have your county clerk email turn out reports to you on a nightly basis as a spreadsheet. They will provide the same voter identification numbers that you included in your database, which you can use to update the status of each voter's ballot. Then re-import the revised spreadsheet into BatchGeo or your mapping platform so your NCs can review their progress the following morning.

Although it's a safe bet to exclude "A" voters from your GOTV effort, you may prefer to keep them in your database when you cut turf in your mapping platform. Like I said, these voters will most always cast a ballot, so you won't ever ID them, and at the very most your NCs will leave a "Please Vote" door hanger at their residence during the GOTV push. It also won't be necessary to register "A" voters absentee. But if you have streamlined an easy system for your NCs to review their progress, and yours is a state with extended early voting or vote by mail, including "A" voters in your voter list can be motivating for NCs. All they'll really have to do is watch them as they turn in their ballots, and it's exciting to see the to-do list rapidly shrink. If you do include "A" voters in your turf, you'll need to include 100–125 in each voter list instead of 50–60.

Finding and Assigning Neighborhood Captains

The power of using neighborhood captains is the social pressure they exert on neighbors; it puts the voter on notice that someone is watching—indeed, someone they know or someone their friends may know. This is extraordinarily important for activation. Nothing works quite as well as social pressure to impress upon a voter to vote.[1]

Anyone who signs up to help a campaign to canvass or phone bank is a candidate to serve as an NC, but you may have difficulty finding volunteers living in all the turf you cut. If you must assign turf to an NC living outside of it, do your best to make sure he or she works there, lives nearby, or doesn't mind a little travel. Still, you likely will not find willing captains for some of your turf. On the webpage we created for this system and for which I've included screen shots, turfs with no NC are labeled as "orphans," and volunteers are urged to adopt—and sometimes you'll find a volunteer willing to NC for more than one turf. Even if you opted not to expand your voter ID targets for a long-shot strategy, you may still find yourself scrambling to find NCs for orphaned turf as you're getting ready to launch the GOTV phase of your campaign. In this case, start cold-calling "A" voters within the orphaned turf until somebody volunteers to adopt it. The gravy is that you might expand your volunteer base for future campaigns.

It's good practice to solicit feedback from your NCs, and volunteers in general, after an election. A common request from our NCs was a method to make notes on the turf pages to keep track of conversations with voters or the number of contact attempts, and we accommodated the feedback by the next election cycle. (In figure 12.7 you can see notes taken by the NC.) If you can,

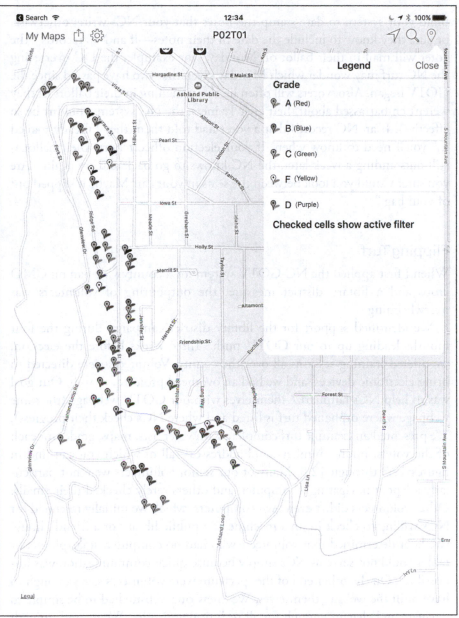

FIGURE 12.3 Example of a Turf Map Created for a Neighborhood Captain Using BatchGeo

This is an urban area, so it covers more voters over a smaller area than a rural area map, as shown in figure 12.2. Each of the letter grades is color-coded so the neighborhood captain can isolate voters by clicking on the balloons he or she wishes to feature on the map. When your cursor is held over a balloon, the voter's name appears, along with address, grade, and any other information you have included in your spreadsheet, like a phone number. Voters represented by the balloons are listed below the map in BatchGeo.

build your system to date stamp the notes that your NCs write; otherwise, be sure they know to include the date in their notes—if an NC records "The voter will mail in their ballot on Monday," for example, the DC overseeing the NC turf may wonder which Monday given that two have passed since the GOTV began. Also, voters will often lie about mailing in their ballots (if they weren't embarrassed about their civic laziness, the NC system wouldn't be so effective). If an NC records that a voter had told them they "already mailed it," you'll need to know when. If your election office reports their ballot is still outstanding a week later, the NC knows to go back and try again. "Are you sure? Could you look between the seats in your car? Maybe it slipped out of your bag."

Flipping Turf

When I first applied the NC-GOTV system for a countywide ban on GMO crops and a library district measure, the outpouring of volunteers was overwhelming.

We identified support for the library district campaign during the four months leading up to our GOTV push. Three weeks before the election, we offered training sessions all over the county. Volunteers were directed to bring electronic devices, and we had an overhead projector as well. Our goal was to help NCs familiarize themselves with our GOTV webpage (the same webpage where orphaned turf is listed and where NCs check their progress). We presented an example turf complete with voter lists, maps, grades for each of the voters, phone numbers, and addresses—all of which you can find in figures 12.3 through 12.8. Many of our senior volunteers were not particularly adept at navigating a computer, and others rarely checked their emails. Other volunteers didn't even own computers, which we initially tolerated for NCs willing to check in on a machine at a public library or a friend's house (we later determined that volunteers who had no computer, smartphone, or tablet could not serve as NCs simply because quick communication was impossible). On the other end of the spectrum were volunteers savvy enough to have built the website themselves. We knew our website had to be simple to navigate and elegant enough for all technical aptitudes. We wound up with four hundred neighborhood captains, but far more had volunteered initially and were placed on a backup list.

What we had not anticipated was the number of NCs who backed out of their commitments, complaining of computer confusion, falling ill, or remembering some other priority in their lives. Within two days of our website going live—just ten days until the election—about one hundred of our four hundred NCs had dropped out. Three of us on the core campaign team spent days flipping turf from one volunteer to another. We became turf day traders, working tirelessly to assign newly orphaned turfs. Notwithstanding the uncommon deluge of willing volunteers, it was stressful on our team, and you should be prepared for last-minute orphans to be stressful on yours as well. On the other hand, we suffered only one turf turnover during our 2017 issue-based campaign for additional firefighters, but then we had only ten turfs in the entire district.

Finally, you should require that all NCs check their email regularly—ideally, through a notification-enabled app on their phone. If you have to flip turf, the quick communication with your volunteers will be a lifesaver. And with a single email, you can respond quickly to emergencies—such as a nasty hit piece—with a targeted canvass in a matter of hours.

District Coordinators

DCs were integrated into the NC-GOTV framework following feedback from campaign leadership that additional resources were needed to oversee the progress of our hundreds of NCs and to help manage last-minute turf flips. DCs oversee about fifty NCs apiece to ensure their progress stays on schedule.

We ask all our NCs to check in with their DC on a daily basis, unless they show progress in their notes (see figure 12.7) or complete a daily Survey Monkey (see figure 12.8). If an NC is falling behind schedule or failing to keep their DC informed of their progress, the DC must reach out by phone or email to ask if assistance is needed from the campaign. I've had DCs call stalled NCs repeatedly and even drop by their homes to check in. If no contact can be made with a stalled NC, the campaign must orphan his or her turf and look for an adopter immediately.

Operation GOTV Website

As I've covered above, this system was designed for states with vote by mail, extended early voting, and campaigns that succeed in registering friendly voters absentee during the ID phase. If your state polls voters only on Election Day, this system will still be helpful in your volunteer organization by breaking voters into units small enough that a neighborhood captain can personally remind his or her neighbors to vote on Election Day.

If you have trouble finding a volunteer capable of building a platform from scratch modeled after our screen shots, it may be worth the effort to raise the money and subscribe to a tool called Fulcrum that can handle basically all of this: BatchGeo, check-ins, notes, and automated time stamps, pretty much everything except the automated updates from the election office. It has apps

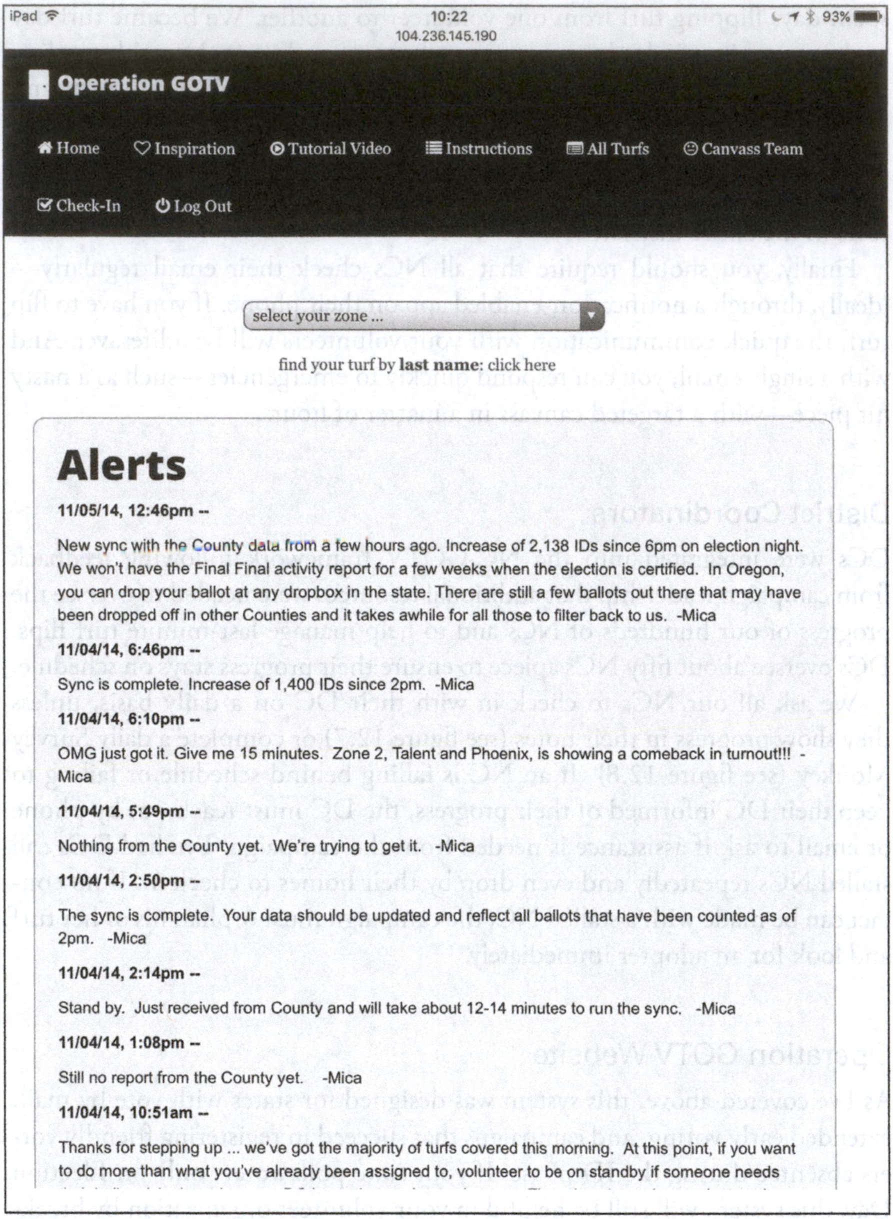

iPad 📶   10:22   🔋 93%
104.236.145.190

▌ Operation GOTV

🏠 Home   ♡ Inspiration   ◉ Tutorial Video   ☰ Instructions   ▦ All Turfs   ☺ Canvass Team

☑ Check-In   ⏻ Log Out

select your zone ...

find your turf by **last name**: click here

Alerts

11/05/14, 12:46pm --

New sync with the County data from a few hours ago. Increase of 2,138 IDs since 6pm on election night. We won't have the Final Final activity report for a few weeks when the election is certified. In Oregon, you can drop your ballot at any dropbox in the state. There are still a few ballots out there that may have been dropped off in other Counties and it takes awhile for all those to filter back to us. -Mica

11/04/14, 6:46pm --

Sync is complete. Increase of 1,400 IDs since 2pm. -Mica

11/04/14, 6:10pm --

OMG just got it. Give me 15 minutes. Zone 2, Talent and Phoenix, is showing a comeback in turnout!!! -Mica

11/04/14, 5:49pm --

Nothing from the County yet. We're trying to get it. -Mica

11/04/14, 2:50pm --

The sync is complete. Your data should be updated and reflect all ballots that have been counted as of 2pm. -Mica

11/04/14, 2:14pm --

Stand by. Just received from County and will take about 12-14 minutes to run the sync. -Mica

11/04/14, 1:08pm --

Still no report from the County yet. -Mica

11/04/14, 10:51am --

Thanks for stepping up ... we've got the majority of turfs covered this morning. At this point, if you want to do more than what you've already been assigned to, volunteer to be on standby if someone needs

FIGURE 12.4 Operation GOTV Home Page

The campaign can communicate with the NCs regarding turf updates or other news about the effort under "Alerts."

for every tablet and smartphone model, as well as permission settings (e.g., NCs can look at and modify only their turf, DCs can look at and modify all the turfs they oversee, and outsiders cannot access anything).

Figure 12.4 is a screen shot of the Operation GOTV home page. Neighborhood captains are instructed to visit the page each day leading up to the election. As noted above, we update turfs daily as ballots are received and alert NCs when that will happen. I am constantly surprised by the delight NCs take when they find progress in their turf every day, as reward for their effort—this is why we always include "A" voters in our voter lists. As you can see, in figure 12.4, an NC may either go to his or her name directly or navigate the site by zone and then name. On the dashboard are various links for the NC, including (from left to right) "Inspiration," which, in this case, was a moving testimonial for the candidate from a coworker produced for the candidate's Facebook page; a "Tutorial Video" designed to walk NCs through the webpage; "Instructions" (figure 12.5); "All Turfs," which is exactly what it says—a sample of the turfs in Zone 1 (figure 12.6); "Canvass Team" (created for a special-interest group who was paying NCs for their work on a partisan state legislative election and needed a shortcut to supervise their workers apart from the rest of the effort); "Check-In" (figure 12.8); and "Log Out."

By way of background: Figure 12.6 is a partial list of NCs located in Zone 1, Precinct 2. The first, Turf 201, has John and Jane Stromberg as the NCs. When they click on "Get Turf Data" on the same line as their names, figure 12.7 is what they see. When they click on their map URL, figure 12.3 is what they see.

As an aside, we update all of the ballots received after the election so NCs can see how they did overall.

Clearly, the system outlined in Operation GOTV is simply a way to organize volunteers so that their work is presented in manageable and predictable units. The webpage allows seamless access to voter performance and provides a mechanism for the campaign to communicate with hundreds of volunteers quickly.

Further, an organized effort, as laid out above, actually builds community. Neighbors meet neighbors, friendships are formed, and campaigning falls into a pleasurable, indeed fun, activity.

Activate Voters by Making Them Care

If your campaign is struggling to make your message resonate with base voters, it won't get any easier during the GOTV. With that said, there's plenty you could do to make your situation worse in the home stretch. Resist the temptation to attack your opponent in the final hours of a campaign.

◀ Safari 🛜   10:23   google.com ▶

← GOTV instructions all zones   👤+ 💬 ⋮

Operation GOTV Instructions

Tutorial Video: click here

Find your neighborhood turf(s) either by zone or by last name. Your turf will have names of ID'd voters, phone number (if available), address, grade, and more. Your mission is to begin contacting those individuals on October 24 and reminding them to vote before 8 PM on November 4. The earlier, the better. Begin contacting voters whose grades are either C, D, or F. This gives early voters a chance to get their ballots in without being bothered. Lower-performing voters will need to be reminded repeatedly to get their ballots in (A and B voters will probably remember on their own).

We can provide a limited number of door hangers that say "PLEASE VOTE" on them. Click here for pickup locations.

Although door-to-door reminders from neighbors are the most effective way of activating lower-probability voters, you may opt for a combination of door knocks and phone calls, or in some cases just phone calls. You know your neighborhood and your limits better than we do. If you find that you are unable to complete either of those functions, please let us know by email: BatesCampaign2014@gmail.com and we'll do our best to find someone to help you out.

Suggestions for what to include in your script:

On October 27th:"Hi, I'm _____ and I'm calling to let you know that the county ballot boxes are now open 24/7." (Let ID's know where the closest ballot drop box is according to your zone. Don't know? Check Jackson County Dropsite Locations: click here

On Thursday October 30th: "Hi, this is _____ I wanted to let you know that tomorrow is really the last day to mail your ballot and be assured it will safely make it to the clerk's office by Tuesday."

On Friday October 31st: "Hi, I'm _____ working to get the vote out. I wanted to remind you that it's now really too late to mail your ballot and be assured it will be received by County Elections in time. So you'll want to drop it in a County Ballot Box; they're now open 24/7."

"You say you've already voted? I'll make a note and keep a lookout to be sure it gets in. I'll give you a call back once I know they've received it so you don't worry."

"You're having trouble finding your ballot or some other election issue? Here is the number for the county elections office, 541 774-6148."

FIGURE 12.5 The Instructions Page for Operation GOTV

It includes sample scripts for the neighborhood captains. Note that scripts provide information, as the NC must appear to be helpful rather than nagging.

iPad 🔋   12:25   📶 ✴ 100% ▰

<   >   📖   104.236.145.190   ⟳   ⬆   +   ▭

Ar   7-Day Fo| Letters to…   Controls   Login   Operation…   ⊗ Operati…   TV IDs f…   Vide…

■ **Operation GOTV**

🏠 Home   ♡ Inspiration   ◉ Tutorial Video   ☰ Instructions   📖 All Turfs   ☺ Canvass Team

☑ Check-In   ⏻ Log Out

Turfs in Zone #1

Turf ID	First Name	Last Name	Location Description	Notes	GetTurfData	Map URL	Check-In
201	Jane & John	Stromberg	Ridge Rd./Terrace		click here	click here	click here
202	Doug	Shipley	Ashland St.to Morton		click here	click here	click here
203	Morgan	Cottle	Long Way to Merrill Street		click here	click here	click here
204	Paul	Fisher	Holly, Kearney, Taylor		click here	click here	click here
205	Adrienne	Fansler	Pracht, Harrison, Holly		click here	click here	click here
206	Ann	Sierka	Idaho to Terrace; Iowa to Holly		click here	click here	click here
207	Jennifer	Bacon	Morton to Union, Iowa to Siskiyo		click here	click here	click here
208	Nancy	Blum	Terrace, Meade, Gresham		click here	click here	click here
209	Sara	Brown	Union to Enders Alley along Sisk		click here	click here	click here
210	Paul	Rostykus	Pioneer to Vista		click here	click here	click here
211	Robert	Sorrell	Granite	Shared	click here	click here	click here
211	Barbara	Casey	Granite	Shared	click here	click here	click here
212	Ruby	Whalley	Church, Bush, High		click here	click	click

FIGURE 12.6 Example of a Portion of Turfs in Zone 1

The Turf ID is a combination of the precinct number followed by the turf. For example, 201 is Precinct 2, Turf 1. The NC's first and last names are provided. "Location Description" must be done after the maps are made and takes a bit of time, as it must all be done by hand, but is very important for NCs to know where they are working or to assist volunteers in the adoption of an orphan within a precinct. "Notes" are details from the campaign, like when a turf is shared (e.g., 211). When "GetTurfData" is clicked, the list of voters (as illustrated in figure 12.7) appears. Click the "Map URL," and the canvass map pops up for the turf (the map for 201 is featured in figure 12.3). Finally, the Survey Monkey appears when "Check-In" is clicked, as illustrated in figure 12.8.

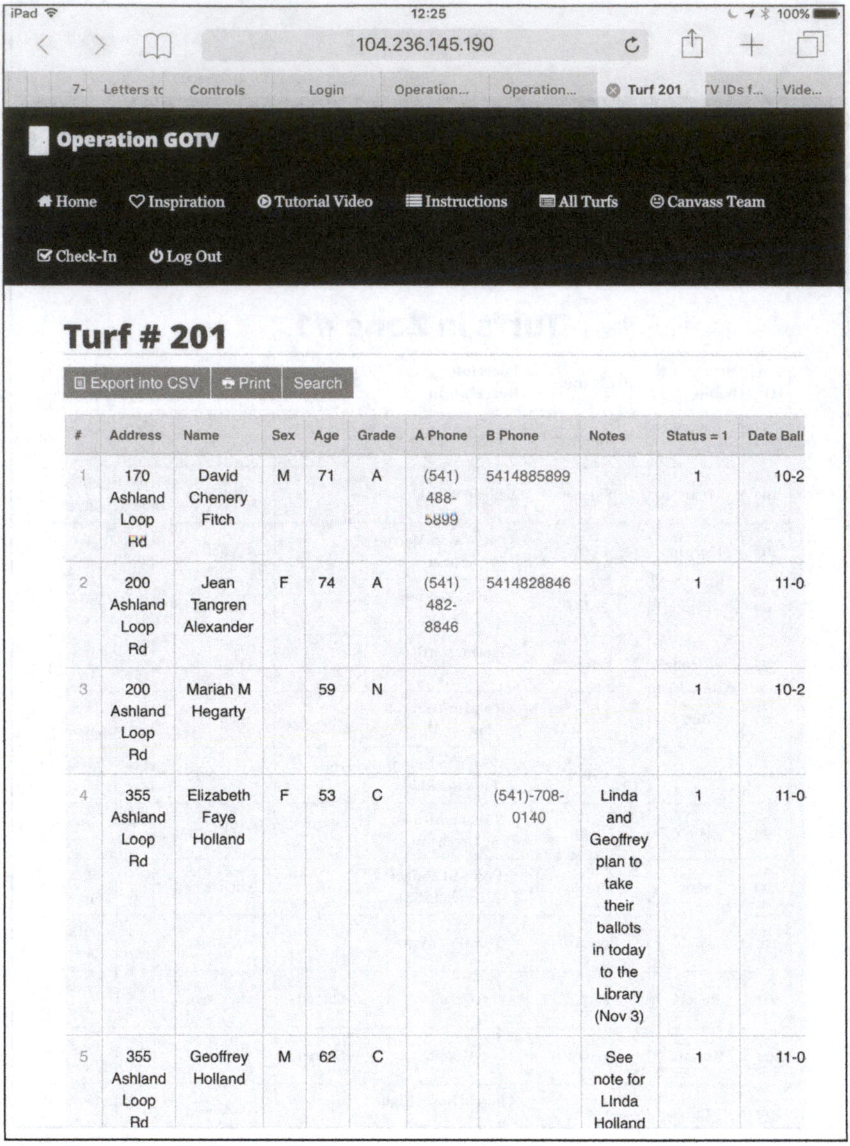

#	Address	Name	Sex	Age	Grade	A Phone	B Phone	Notes	Status = 1	Date Ball
1	170 Ashland Loop Rd	David Chenery Fitch	M	71	A	(541) 488-5899	5414885899		1	10-2
2	200 Ashland Loop Rd	Jean Tangren Alexander	F	74	A	(541) 482-8846	5414828846		1	11-0
3	200 Ashland Loop Rd	Mariah M Hegarty		59	N				1	10-2
4	355 Ashland Loop Rd	Elizabeth Faye Holland	F	53	C		(541)-708-0140	Linda and Geoffrey plan to take their ballots in today to the Library (Nov 3)	1	11-0
5	355 Ashland Loop Rd	Geoffrey Holland	M	62	C			See note for LInda Holland	1	11-0

FIGURE 12.7 Example of What Neighborhood Captains See When They Click on Their Turf Data

In this example John and Jane Stromberg, who were the NCs of Turf 201, click on their names (at the top of figure 12.6), and their turf pops up. The campaign automatically updates the "status" of the ballot with a number 1, which indicates a ballot was received by the elections department, followed by the date it was received. A blank in the status column indicates the voter's ballot is still outstanding. NCs are able to include notes, as shown under voters 4 and 5. This NC had 100 percent participation in his turf.

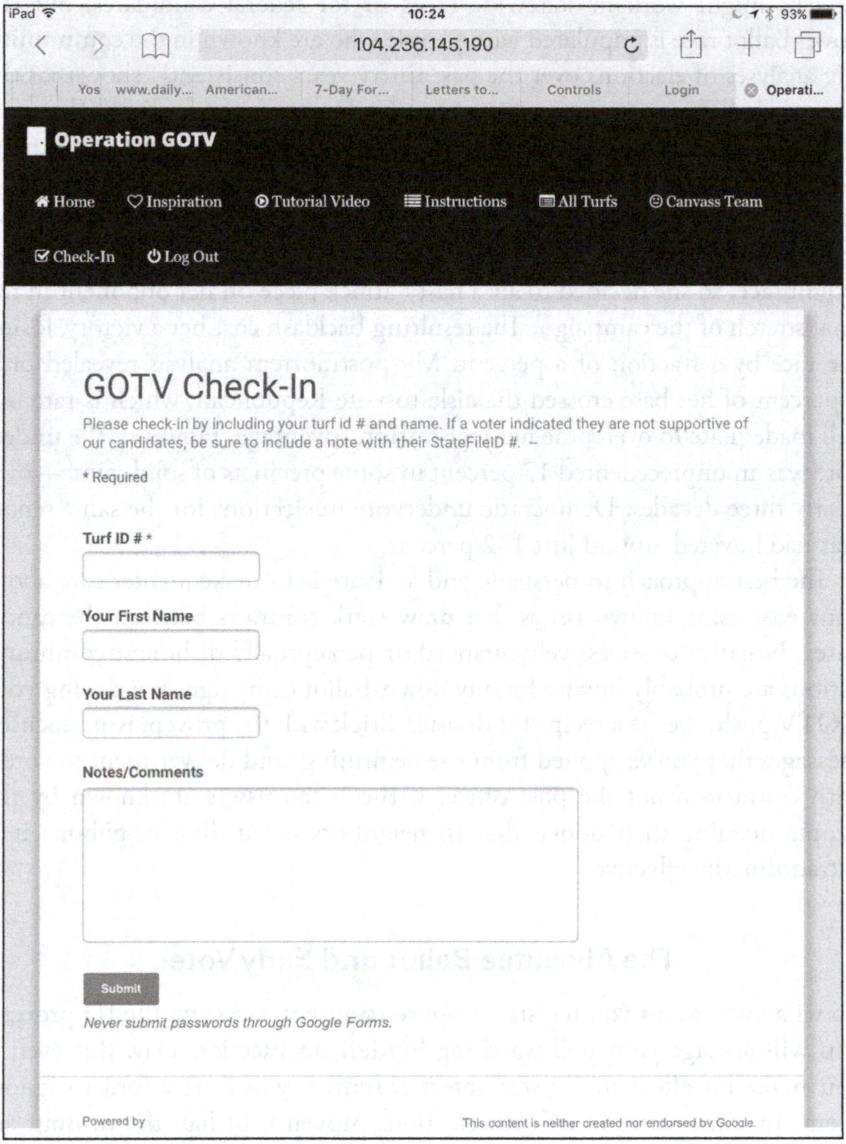

FIGURE 12.8 Sample of the Survey Monkey for Neighborhood Captains

This Survey Monkey allows NCs to alert the district coordinator or the campaign that they're active.

Attacks might work in statewide races or for federal candidates, but the down-ballot race is populated with people who are known in the community. My analyses of elections over the past thirty years consistently show that the biggest challenge a campaign faces is an undervote from the base. The most common explanation for undervoting is apathy, but it can also be an expression of protest against candidates who ran unsavory campaigns. For example, one Democratic candidate for state senate enjoyed an eight-point registration advantage in my district when she ran in 2016. But her polling data predicted a tight race, so she decided to air a nasty attack piece on her opponent in the final stretch of the campaign. The resulting backlash cost her a victory, losing the race by a fraction of a percent. My postmortem analysis revealed only 3 percent of her base crossed the aisle to vote Republican, which is rare but still inadequate to overcome her registration advantage. However, the undervote was an unprecedented 17 percent in some precincts of solid saints—over nearly three decades, Democratic undervote in elections for the same senate seat had hovered around just 1–2 percent.

The best approach to persuade and activate is to make a voter care about your race using known issues that draw stark contrasts between the candidates. Negative or excessively nuanced or perceptually dishonest communications are probably unwise for any down-ballot campaign, but during your GOTV push, they're a recipe for disaster. Stick with the proven, issue-focused messages that you've applied from the beginning, and deliver them to voters with canvassers, not the post office. If those canvassers are known by the people opening their doors, that is, neighbors persuading neighbors, it is extraordinarily effective.

The Absentee Ballot and Early Vote

To whatever extent you register supporters absentee during the ID process, you will assuage your poll-watching burden on Election Day. But even if you make no effort to register voters absentee, you can't afford to ignore them. In some states in off-year elections, upwards of half the turnout are voters registered absentee; it's a lot easier to monitor them in your GOTV effort than Election Day poll voters. In Oregon, when the state still had poll voting but allowed voters to permanently register absentee, campaigns could access the entire list of permanent absentee voters for a nominal fee from county elections. Back then, absentee voters made up 60 percent of the turnout.

In many states, the option to register absentee is open to anyone for the asking, up to the day before the election, and those who request absentee ballots within the three weeks before an election are the most likely to actually

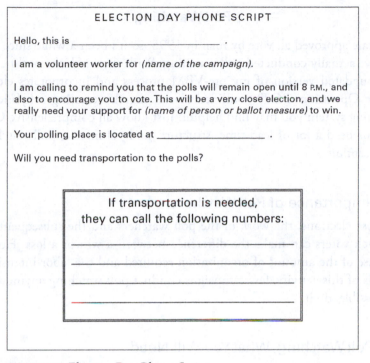

FIGURE 12.9 Election Day Phone Script

vote. Some states have a cutoff date for an absentee ballot request; however, for those that allow requests up to Election Day, your county elections office may be able to provide updated lists as requests come in. If your election office cannot provide a list of those who request an absentee ballot, someone must visit their office on a regular basis to get (and update) your GOTV targeted lists with the voters' names making the request. The campaign should immediately contact and ID these voters to include and watch in the GOTV effort in order to minimize a down-ballot undervote among support.

As with absentee voting, early voting gives a campaign an opportunity to lock in votes before the election. However, it does require that a campaign peak twice: once for the early voting and absentees and once for Election Day. Make sure you know when your elections office drops absentee ballots in the mail so your GOTV apparatus will be ready.

If it is your intention to use phone banks to activate voters for the GOTV, see the section "Phone Banks," in Chapter 3, "The Campaign Team and Volunteer Organization."

Poll Watching

My state approved all vote by mail in 1998, so it's been a while since any of us have actually conducted poll watching. With that said, the outline below is an updated version of my pre-VBM process and incorporates elements of the Operation GOTV outlined above, thereby creating a hybrid poll-watching system you may find helpful. Just know all comprehensive GOTV systems need a lot of lead time, structure, and volunteers; poll watching is no exception.

The Importance of Poll Watchers

In close elections, the work of the poll watchers and the subsequent effort to reach voters can make the difference between a win or a loss. However, because of the amount of organization required and the labor-intensive demands of this activity, few campaigns conduct poll watching anymore. If at all possible, do it.

For Poll Watching, What You Will Need

1. An army of ready volunteers with a manager to coordinate them
2. Someone on registration-list management
3. Knowledge of local laws and regulations surrounding the activity

Your target areas will look a lot like the target areas for the above GOTV effort, but given the typical resources of a down-ballot campaign, they may need to be consolidated some. The following reflects the strategic approach a campaign must undertake for this effort.

As above, poll watchers must be focused only in areas of high or moderate support; forget low-support areas. And poll watchers will need to pay special attention to lazy voters that are harder to get to the polls; don't worry too much about "A" and "B" voters.

To that end, your voters should be graded according to voting performance. Each poll watcher must have a tablet or smartphone that includes only the registered voters of his or her specific precinct being watched—providing all registered voters to each of the poll watchers would simply be overwhelming. So, for example, if you have a rotating team overseeing Precinct 2, which has 3,000 registered voters but only 500 known lazy friendlies, then you may just be watching for and knocking on the doors of just those lazy voters.

The poll watcher will update his or her lists as voters announce their arrival at the polling station; that informs canvassers, phone banks, and transportation teams to be aware of who may still need help to get to the polls. How the poll watcher determines if a specific voter has voted depends on the rules and regulations of the election office. If you are unable to view the voting log at your polling places, your poll watchers will have to write voter names down as they are called to check against their list.

Precinct Captains

Each polling place must have a precinct captain to manage the precinct team. The precinct captain will be responsible for two duties:

1. The captain is responsible for recruiting four to eight poll watchers and standbys (depending on the size of the precincts or how many precincts report to a polling station). These people need to be certified by the clerk, trained, and supervised by the campaign. Poll watchers should meet with their team captain the weekend before the election. Signed certificates, obtained from the election office, for each poll watcher are provided to the precinct captains at that time. Your county clerk or county elections office will supply you with all the information and forms you need for certification.
2. The captain must be present at his or her precinct when it opens and supervise the precinct on and off throughout the day.

Poll-Watcher Responsibilities

1. Arrive a few minutes early at the polling place.
2. Give your signed certificate to the election judge, who is a member of the polling board.
3. Do not engage in conversation with the election board. You may, of course, answer questions, but do not discuss other topics with the board.
4. As voters arrive and give their names to the board, listen for the name so it can be noted within your assigned area on your tablet or smartphone.

Regulation of Persons at the Polls

You should be literate in election laws for all of your campaign activities, but that's especially true of poll watching. The polling place has special regulations that cover everything from how close individuals may stand to the polls if they are not voting and are not certified poll watchers to what topics those present may discuss. The campaign should contact the county clerk well beforehand and get the regulatory information to the precinct captains in written form.

Authorized poll watchers are allowed in the polling place and must sign a specific section of the front cover of the poll book. Only as many poll watchers are allowed as will not interfere with the work of the election board.

Poll watchers must have written authorization from one of the following:

1. For the purpose of challenging electors at the polling place, from either the county clerk or a political party
2. For the purpose of observing the receiving and counting of votes, from a candidate

Poll watchers *may*
- Take notes
- Have access to poll books, so long as it does not interfere with the work of the board
- Challenge persons offering to vote at the poll
- Challenge entries in the poll book
- Wear campaign buttons
- Distribute sample ballots as long as there is no campaigning involved (we did this in Ohio in 2008—as people stood in long lines, they were given sample ballots to familiarize themselves for what lay ahead)

Poll watchers *may not*
- Campaign in any way
- Circulate any cards, handbills, questionnaires, or petitions
- Fail to follow the instructions of the election board
- Take poll books off tables

Remember, everything you've done to get here was all preparation for the GOTV push. You can't win if your supporters don't make a showing on Election Day. If you've come this far, you are no doubt exhausted, but don't allow yourself to run out of steam just yet. Reach deep for that second wind and get your team across the finish line.

13

The Campaign Plan

Simply reacting to the present demand or scrambling because of tensions is the opposite of thoughtful planning. Planning emphasizes conscious, disciplined choice.

—VAUGHN KELLER

IN THIS CHAPTER:

- Begin with a Flowchart
- The Campaign Calendar
- The Campaign Plan

IF YOU'RE RUNNING FOR ANY OFFICE WHERE YOU HOPE TO ATTRACT outside money from special-interest groups or the lobby, they will first ask to see your campaign plan before investing in your candidacy. Campaign plans demonstrate organization and forethought; both are necessary to pull off a win, especially in a close election, and offer comfort for big-money investors, the campaign team, and the candidate.

Basically, a campaign plan lays out exactly what your team intends to accomplish daily from the first day of the race through the days immediately following the election. For a partisan race with both a primary and a general election or one that requires a candidate to receive 50 percent of the votes cast in one election or face a runoff in the general, the campaign will need a plan for both the primary and the general.

Although the process may seem daunting, below you will find a very easy process to complete a campaign plan within a few hours.

Begin with a Flowchart

Although you will be guided through making a flowchart and should familiarize yourself with the process, there are easy how-to programs for both

295

Word and Excel available online. Just Google "Creating a flowchart." Meanwhile, know that this process is the first step in creating a campaign plan.

To make a campaign flowchart, start by listing the tasks you need to complete before the election. These might include canvassing, development and printing of a walking piece, media, phone banks, fundraising, and lawn signs. Your choices, of course, are dictated by your resources and the type of campaign you are running. Obviously, you will not place anything in the flowchart that you have no intention of doing. For instance, you may not be able to afford direct mail, or you may have decided you do not want to do lawn signs or paid media.

Once you have the list of campaign tasks, all you need to do is transfer them onto your campaign flowchart in the proper sequence. A mock-up of a campaign flowchart is included in this chapter (see figure 13.1).

To construct your flowchart, you will need a long, unbroken wall and the following items:

- Five or more Post-it pads in assorted colors
- A long roll of paper; butcher paper works best
- At least six different-colored marking pens
- A yardstick
- Masking tape
- One or two key campaign people (no more) to help you think

If possible, pull in someone who has worked on other campaigns to help you. Although an experienced campaigner is an invaluable aid in building the flowchart, you can also use the table of contents of this book. That's what I do, and I've done dozens of flowcharts.

To begin your chart, unroll about ten feet of the butcher paper and tape it to a wall. On the bottom right hand of the chart, place the date of the day after the election. On the bottom left-hand corner, place the date of the beginning of your campaign. It may be the date that you start your flowchart or the date of your first "formal" campaign activity, such as your announcement. Draw a single line along the bottom between the two dates (this is your X axis). Divide the line into fairly equal monthly or weekly parts by drawing in all the dates between the day your campaign begins and the day it will end. On the Y axis, there will be a list of all the things you intend to do in your campaign: lawn signs, walking piece, canvassing, media, fundraising, and so on.

Using different-colored marking pens, draw a horizontal line straight across for each campaign activity the campaign intends to execute. So, for example, clerical may be blue; media, red; lawn signs, green; and so on. You now have on your butcher paper a line across the bottom with dates on it,

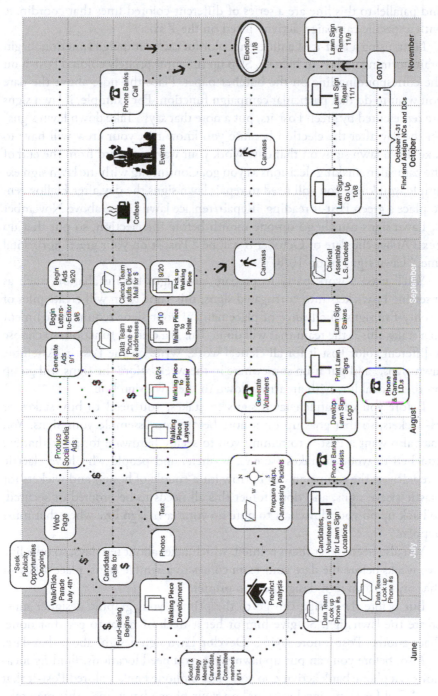

FIGURE 13.1 Example of a Campaign Flowchart

and parallel to this line are a series of different-colored lines that coordinate with a specific campaign activity listed on the Y axis.

Next, using a Post-it of a different color for each campaign function, begin brainstorming with your helpers. Slap up the appropriately colored Post-it on the corresponding line on the butcher paper. Place the note above the date you want to do that particular campaign function. For example, if lawn signs are represented by green Post-its, put a note that says "Take down lawn signs" on the day after the election because you know that your crew will have to take down lawn signs on that day. Work your way backward from the end of the campaign, making decisions as you go. Continuing with the lawn sign example, you know you will need to repair lawn signs the day after Halloween, so place a green Post-it reading "Repair/replace lawn signs" above November 1. Lawn signs usually go up one month before the election, so put that up next: Above the date of October 8 will be a Post-it on your green horizontal line, "Lawn signs go up 10/8."

You'll need a work party to prepare lawn signs for installation, such as inserting H-wickets into corrugated signs; this same team will create piles of twenty-five signs in advance of placement; if your signs require attachment to a stake, this is the team that will do it. This is a clerical function, so choose a different color Post-it for all clerical work. Write on the Post-it "Assemble lawn signs," and put it up somewhere in the week before the signs will go up on the clerical line with an arrow down to the lawn sign line.

Before you can attach lawn signs to stakes, you need to buy stakes or H-wickets, so that goes up on a note before you assemble your signs. You may also want a Post-it to remind you to secure hardware for signs that are attached to wooden stakes (screws, washers, and people who have electric screwdrivers the campaign can borrow for a couple of hours) and wickets for plastic-sleeve signs, and don't forget this all needs to be ordered or secured, so back up on your flowchart to note on your lawn sign line when that must happen.

You also need to get them printed, which takes about ten days, so on a line two weeks before the date your team comes to assemble signs, place a Post-it that says, "Lawn sign design goes to printer."

But before the design can go to the printer, your graphic designer must create the lawn sign. So give him or her a week or more to get that done. Place another Post-it note saying "Develop lawn sign design" above that date.

Also, before you can put up lawn signs, you need locations. Finding locations is a phone bank activity, so you place a phone bank–colored Post-it that says "Call for lawn sign locations" on your phone bank line. This may take two weeks, so you are showing this activity on your phone bank line with an arrow to your lawn sign line.

But before your volunteers can call, you need lists of people they can call. So you make a Post-it that says "Secure lists for calling for lawn signs." Also, before you can call, you need to secure a location for the phone banks. That goes on a Post-it that is placed on a line representing the week before the phone bank team begins to call.

Keep working your way back (back mapping), thinking through each of the campaign activities you have on your list. Review the chapters and headings in this manual. Think in terms of the progression of an activity and all the subactivities needed to support it. Begin at the end.

Spread Out the Activities

With this method, time periods with too much campaign activity become immediately apparent. For example, if you find by the concentration of multicolored Post-its that walking-piece development, two direct-mail pieces, and a phone bank for an event are all happening at the same time, you may consider moving something to another time slot. Developing a walking piece could move up and be done sooner, and the direct-mail pieces may be handled (just this once) by a mail house, or they may be prepared earlier and kept in a box at the door for a drop at the post office at the desired date of delivery. Your Post-its are mobile for a reason, and you want to take advantage of that during this campaign planning activity. Spread out the activities so that you and the volunteers do not get overworked or overwhelmed. If nothing can move, you will know to line up extra help to organize the work.

By using colored Post-its for every function on the chart, you build a visual representation of the campaign. The process is simple: Just take whatever it is you want to do, give it a color, and work your way back from the date you want to see that function completed to the point where that task must start to be completed on time. Some of the functions will end when others begin. For example, your walking piece must be ready in time for canvassing. If canvassing will take you two months, working each day after work plus weekends, then the walking piece must be back from the printer by this time. Therefore, the Post-its for "Walking-piece development" and "Printing" will end on the flowchart before canvassing activities start. Although not all activities are listed in figure 13.1, add or subtract what you intend to do. Here is a partial list of activities that should be represented on your flowchart:

- Precinct analysis
- Ads—print, radio, and television
- Lawn signs, field signs
- Webpage design and social media upkeep

- Coffees, fundraisers, special events
- Letters to the editor
- Direct mail
- Walking piece
- Canvassing
- Phone banks
- GOTV

Convert the Flowchart to a Campaign Plan

If you're working on a small down-ballot campaign, you may prefer to keep your campaign organized using a permanent flowchart. Since Post-its tend to fall off after a couple of days, tape them in place or create a hard copy of your working flowchart. Another option is to convert it to a campaign calendar (figure 13.2) or campaign plan.

The Campaign Calendar

I now exclusively use campaign calendars that we create using Excel. At the bottom of the file, each tab is marked with the month (see figure 13.2). It's a good idea to include on the campaign calendar the outside schedule of the candidate, especially if he or she is involved in volunteer activities or already holds office with daytime meetings. Keeping the committee informed of the candidate's schedule helps avoid mishaps. Another way is to assign one person to do all scheduling; this is the same person who maintains and emails the calendar to committee members.

The Campaign Plan

To create your plan, simply transfer everything from your flowchart to a Word or Google document or calendar with a date at the top of each page and the number of days left till the election. List each activity or job that must be completed on that day.

A campaign plan will organize a team so that each of the necessary tasks may be implemented in an orderly and stress-free manner. Done well and rigorously followed, a campaign plan will reduce stress and lighten the load for all involved.

Sunday	Monday	Tuesday	Wednesday	Thursday	Friday	Saturday
15	16 Committee working on Brochure wording Lawn Sign to Graphic Designer	17	18	19	20 Lawn Sign to Printer	21
22 8PM Campaign Team Meets	23 Brochure copy to Graphic Designer Call for Volunteers to put up Lawn Signs	24	25 Review Brochure with Committee	26	27 Pick-up Brochure from Graphic Designer	28
29 8PM Campaign Team	30 Brochure to Printer	1 11AM Ground breaking for Senior Center 4PM Opponent on Ken Linbloom Show KCMX Call for $	2 10AM Temple Emek Shalom Ribbon Cutting Golden Class: Meet the Candidates Candidate call for $	3 Pick-up Lawn Signs from Printer Organize Lawn Sign Cards	4 Clerical Party to Staple Lawn Signs - Bundle Stakes	5 8-10AM Lawn Signs Go up 12 - firefighters 2 - Carole, Ken 2 - Bill Street Canvass?
6 Canvass 8PM Campaign Team Meets	7 Candidate Calls for $	8 5:30-7PM Chamber of Commerce - Meet the Candidates, AHI	9 12 noon LWV Lunch at the Mark 5-6 Canvass $ Calls	10 Canvass Ashland Mine 6:30-10PM Kathleen Brown Dinner SOWAK, Red Lion	11 12 Noon Welcome Leadership Conference 4-6 Canvass	12 10AM Canvass 3-6PM Make informercial SOU for Cable Access $ Calls
13 Canvass 12-3 3-5 Canvass 8PM Campaign	14 5-6 Canvass $ Calls	15 7AM Lithia Springs Rotary Debate 5 min. + Q&A $ Calls	16 4 PM Office Hours 5-6 Canvass $ Calls	17 10AM Meet the Candidates 1023 Morton St. DEBATE - AAUW/LWV	18 Letter-to-Voters Ad to Graphic Designer 4-6 Canvass Kennedy Roosevelt Dinner	19 10-1 Canvass 4-6 Ribbon Cutting of Environmental Center Design and Write Experience Ad
20 10AM Crop Walk 12-3 Canvass 3-5 Canvass 8PM Campaign	21 Experience Ad to Grahic Designer Camera-ready Letter-to-Voters Ad to paper 4PM Ken Linbloom Radio Show	22 7PM Cable Access Debate	23 5-6 Canvass	24 Camera-ready Experience Ad to paper Run Letter-to-Voters Ad Noon Rotary Debate	25 Run Letter-to-Voters Ad again 4-6 Canvass	26 Bob Miller 2-1001 Welcome Lions Club AHI 10-1 Canvass 3-5:30 Canvass Letter-to-Voters Ad again Call for EndorsementAd
27 12-3 Canvass 3-5 Canvass 8PM Campaign Meeting	28 Run Experience Ad Layout Endorsement Ad Canvass	29 Run Experience Ad Camera-ready Endorsement Ad to paper Canvass	30	31 Run Experience Ad	1 Run Endorsement Ad Lawn Sign Team Clean-up 4-6 Canvass	2 Run Endorsement Ad Canvass 10-1 3-5:30 Canvass
3 12-3 Canvass 3-5 Canvass 8PM Campaign Meeting	4 Run Endorsement Ad	5 - ELECTION DAY -	6 Lawn Signs come down			

FIGURE 13.2 Example of a Campaign Calendar for a Nonpartisan General Election

After the Ball

When the fall is all there is, it matters.
—PRINCE RICHARD, *LION IN WINTER*

Once the game is over, the king and the pawn go back into the same box.
—ITALIAN SAYING

IN THIS CHAPTER:

- Election Night
- Retiring a Campaign Debt

WIN OR LOSE, THERE ARE MANY THINGS YOU MUST DO TO PUT YOUR campaign to bed. However, before taking down your lawn signs, bundling your stakes or H-wickets, paying your bills, finishing reports for the state, closing out bank accounts, and reassembling your house, you must first face Election Night.

Election Night

On Election Night, if you are not in a well-known location with other candidates and their volunteer teams, you should let the press know where they can find you. Establish a meet-up location with your team, and then email your volunteers to let them know where you will be, urging them to join you. Spend Election Day or even the weekend before the election calling and personally thanking volunteers; this is also a good time to remind them of the

Election Night gathering. Don't wait to thank them until after the election. If you lose, volunteers are anxious to console, and you are anxious to sit alone in a dark closet with the door closed.

There is no preparing for a loss, and I'm not sure people *ever* get over it. It will change your life, just as winning will. But win or lose, you must be prepared to face the media and do it with class.

In one election on which I worked, I sat with the candidate as the first big returns came in. The shock that went through us as we realized we were losing is indescribable. I remember cameras pointing at our faces. There is something predatory and morose about our society when it comes to watching a leader fall. We had expected a win and were not prepared for what was before us.

The next day, our pictures were in the paper. I looked for shock, disbelief, upset, disappointment. None of it was there. We just sat, stunned, looking at the huge TV screen in the restaurant. In the story that followed, the candidate thanked his volunteers, his campaign team, and his supporters. He thanked everyone for a chance to serve. The end.

Win or lose, that is the speech.

I recently had a candidate who believed he would win, 100 percent—frankly, we all did. He had everything going for him and was running against a complete idiot. When he lost, he went into hiding, and his campaign manager evaporated. The campaign did nothing to retire their debt. In fact, they did the opposite; for example, campaign phones were not disconnected, and bills continued to roll in. While it is completely understandable, when a candidate and manager do not follow through on the day-to-day business necessary to exit the stage, it creates validation for those who undervoted or jumped ship and voted for the opposing team. Always take care of your business, always exit with class, and be graceful.

If you lost, say you put together a great effort but that your opponent put together a better one. Give your opponent a little of the limelight if you won and a lot of it if you lost. Don't blame your loss on an insufficient campaign effort. That translates to "My volunteers are responsible for my loss." The most common feeling among volunteers of a losing campaign is "What a waste of time that was." Say that you had a great campaign team that put in countless hours and that the whole thing was a ball—challenging, instructive, and fun from beginning to end. Take heart in the fact that you have come to know yourself and the democratic process better. Should you ever run for office again, you will be glad you acted magnanimously.

Retiring a Campaign Debt

I counsel all candidates to spend within their means. Lending money to your own campaign sends the wrong message to the voting public. A campaign that is chronically short of funds is a sure sign of one that is in trouble. Nevertheless, it happens, and when it does, it is up to you, the candidate, with the help of the campaign team and manager, to retire the debt.

Never walk away from debt: Graphic designers, print shops, photographers, and even your strategist and campaign manager are trying to make a living and generally are well connected with the community in which you live and hope to serve. In politics, nothing is more important than your reputation. But short of taking a second mortgage out on your home, there are a few things you can do to ease your debt. Win or lose, it is tough to retire a campaign debt. However, if you win, you tend to have more options.

If you ran and won for the state assembly, go through the contributions of your opponent and find any who gave to him or her but not to your campaign. Contact those representing "moderate" interests, and ask them to match the contribution given to your opponent. It should be obvious which among them will double give, and it should be obvious which ones you do not want listed on your finance form.

Win or lose, go to your most faithful donors for help. The simplest and most cost-effective way is to review all individuals who contributed previously and email those you know personally, whether you're the candidate, the campaign manager, or part of the team. Explain that the campaign has a small debt to retire and ask the previous donors whether they are willing to help. Do not send to the contributors as a group but rather email individually—it must be a personal ask. Besides being efficient, emailing contributors for an additional contribution adds no further drain to the finances.

As you exit or enter the stage, be graceful and appreciative; thank your family, volunteers, supporters, and the community. If you win, you must be humble, acknowledge the efforts of your opponent, and immediately begin mending fences that might have been broken during the process. If you lose, there is one call you must make: to your opponent. Congratulate that person and say you are on board to help make his or her time in office as successful as possible.

Afterword

YOU ARE NOW PREPARED TO BEGIN ON THAT TIME-HONORED PATH OF A political campaign. Campaigns are enormously fun and exhilarating. If you do everything right, you greatly improve your chances of winning. Just a few reminders before you begin:

1. Know the law.
2. Stay on your campaign theme and message, and you will be in control.
3. Deliver that message to your targeted voters.
4. Redirect negative campaigning at your opponents, and use it as an opportunity to restate your message.
5. Work hard, and others will work hard for you.
6. Be humble, and listen more than you speak.
7. Know who you are and why you are running.
8. Smile. Always look as though you're having a great time.

Win or lose, you will emerge from the process a different person, a leader within your community.

Notes

Chapter 2: Precinct Analysis: The Sinners, the Saints, and the Savables

1. See "Urban and Rural America Are Becoming Increasingly Polarized," *Washington Post*, November 17, 2016, https://www.washingtonpost.com/graphics/politics/2016-election/urban-rural-vote-swing/; Josh Kron, "Red State, Blue City: How the Urban-Rural Divide Is Splitting America," *Atlantic*, November 30, 2012; Ronald Brownstein, "How the Election Revealed the Divide Between City and Country," *Atlantic*, November 17, 2016, https://www.theatlantic.com/politics/archive/2016/11/clinton-trump-city-country-divide/507902/; and Emily Badger, "What's Your Ideal Community? The Answer Is Political," *New York Times*, November 3, 2016, https://www.nytimes.com/2016/11/04/upshot/whats-your-ideal-community-the-answer-is-political.html.

2. Wendy K. Tam Cho, James G. Gimpel, and Iris S. Hui, "Voter Migration and the Geographic Sorting of the American Electorate," *Annals of the Association of American Geographers* (October 15, 2012), doi:10.1080/00045608.2012.720229.

3. Bill Bishop, "You Can't Compete with Voters' Feet," *Washington Post*, May 15, 2005, B2.

4. Pew Research Center, "Party Affiliation Among Voters, 1992–2016," September 13, 2016, http://www.people-press.org/2016/09/13/2-party-affiliation-among-voters-1992-2016/.

5. Alex Lundry, "Microtargeting: Knowing the Voter Intimately," *Winning Campaigns* 4, no. 1 (2004).

6. Rhodes Cook, "Moving On: More Voters Are Steering Away from Party Labels," *Washington Post*, June 27, 2004, B1.

7. For additional reading regarding swing voters, see Pew Research Center, "Political Polarization in Action: Insights into the 2014 Election from the American Trends Panel," October 17, 2014, http://www.people-press.org/2014/10/17/political-polarization-in-action-insights-into-the-2014-election-from-the-american-trends-panel/.

8. Joshua Kalla, David E. Broockman, "The Minimal Persuasive Effects of Campaign Contact in General Elections: Evidence from 49 Field Experiments," Standford University Graduate School of Business Research Paper No. 17-65, September 25, 2017. https://papers.ssrn.com/sol3/papers.cfm?abstract_id=3042867.

Chapter 3: The Campaign Team and Volunteer Organization

1. Jim Gimpel, "Computer Technology and Getting Out the Vote: New Targeting Tools," *Campaigns & Elections* (August 2003): 40.

Chapter 4: Campaign Messaging

1. Karl G. Feld, "What Are Push Polls, Anyway?," *Campaigns & Elections* (May 2000): 63.

2. Sam Stein, "Nasty Anti-Obama Push Poll Launched in Ohio," *Huffington Post*, September 11, 2008, http://www.huffingtonpost.com/2008/09/11/nasty-anti-obama -push-pol_n_125607.html.

3. For a general description of the Bradley effect, see *Wikipedia*, s.v. "Bradley effect," http://en.wikipedia.org/wiki/Bradley_effect. For the Confederate-flag issue, see Sean Wilentz, "How the Confederate Flag Flap Helped the GOP," *Salon*, November 12, 2002, http://dir.salon.com/story/politics/feature/2002/11/12/confederate_flag/index .html.

4. John Ritter, "City Council Pays for Lessons in Civility," *USA Today*, October 4, 2007, http://www.usatoday.com/news/nation/2007-10-04-citycouncil-help_N.htm.

Chapter 5: Fundraising

1. "Case Study: MyBarackObama.com," Blue State Digital, http://www.bluestate digital.com/casestudies/client/obama_for_america_2008.

2. Center for Responsive Politics website, http://www.opensecrets.org.

3. David Erickson, "Barack Obama's Online Fundraising Machine," January 1, 2009, http://e-strategyblog.com/2009/01/barack-obamas-online-fundraising-machine.

Chapter 6: Digital and Social Media

1. Colin Delany, *How to Use the Internet to Win in 2016: A Comprehensive Guide to Online Politics for Campaigns & Advocates* (Epolitics.com, Kindle ed., 2013), Kindle locations 477–478.

2. Jakob Nielsen, "Why You Only Need to Test with 5 Users," Nielsen Norman Group, https://www.nngroup.com/articles/why-you-only-need-to-test-with-5-users/.

3. Delany, *How to Use the Internet to Win in 2016*, Kindle locations 273–277.

4. Pew Research Center, "Social Media Update, 2016," November 11, 2016, http:// www.pewinternet.org/2016/11/11/social-media-update-2016/.

5. Pew Research Center, "Social Media Fact Sheet," January 12, 2017, http://www .pewinternet.org/fact-sheet/social-media/.

6. Monica Anderson, "More Americans Are Using Social Media to Connect with Politicians," Pew Research Center, May 19, 2015, http://www.pewresearch.org/fact-tank /2015/05/19/more-americans-are-using-social-media-to-connect-with-politicians/.

7. "Global Trust in Advertising: Winning Strategies for an Evolving Media Landscape," Nielsen, September 2015, https://www.nielsen.com/content/dam/nielsenglobal /apac/docs/reports/2015/nielsen-global-trust-in-advertising-report-september-2015 .pdf.

8. A. J. Agrawal, "Why Influencer Marketing Will Explode in 2017," *Forbes*, December 27, 2016, https://www.forbes.com/sites/ajagrawal/2016/12/27/why-influencer -marketing-will-explode-in-2017/#3232bab320a9.

9. "Rethinking Your Digital Spend," *Campaigns & Elections* (July–August 2012): 46.

10. http://www.brainrules.net/vision.

11. Jakob Nielsen, "Photos as Web Content," Nielsen Norman Group, November 1, 2010, https://www.nngroup.com/articles/photos-as-web-content/.

12. Matt Mansfield, "27 Video Marketing Strategies That Will Have You Hitting the Record Button," *Small Business Trends*, https://smallbiztrends.com/2016/10/video -marketing-statistics.html.

13. Belle Beth Cooper, "How Twitter's Expanded Images Increase Clicks, Retweets and Favorites," Buffer Social, April 27, 2016, https://blog.bufferapp.com /the-power-of-twitters-new-expanded-images-and-how-to-make-the-most-of-it.

14. Andiranes Pinantoan, "How to Massively Boost Your Blog Traffic with These 5 Awesome Image Stats," Buzzsumo, May 20, 2015, http://buzzsumo.com/blog/how -to-massively-boost-your-blog-traffic-with-these-5-awesome-image-stats/.

15. Marko Saric, "Facebook Analysis for March—Videos and Photos Rule Engagement Totally!," Locowise blog, April 21, 2015, https://locowise.com/blog/facebook -analysis-march-videos-and-photos-rule-engagement-totally.

16. Megan O'Neill, "The 2015 Video Marketing Cheat Sheet," Animoto blog, May 7, 2015, https://animoto.com/blog/business/video-marketing-cheat-sheet-infographic/.

17. "The Ultimate List of Marketing Strategies," Hubspot, https://www.hubspot .com/marketing-statistics?_ga=1.22602811.1887974499.1460390947.

18. Pew Research Center, "Presidential Candidates' Changing Relationship with the Web."

19. Pew Research Center, "Social Media Update 2016," November 11, 2016, http:// www.pewinternet.org/2016/11/11/social-media-update-2016/.

20. Kathleen Chaykowski, "Number of Facebook Business Pages Climbs to 50 Million with New Messaging Tools," *Forbes*, December 8, 2015, https://www.forbes.com /sites/kathleenchaykowski/2015/12/08/facebook-business-pages-climb-to-50-million -with-new-messaging-tools/#6268adaf6991.

21. Rob Peterson, "6 Studies Show Why Facebook Organic Reach Is Declining So Quickly," Business2Community, June 6, 2016, http://www.business2community.com /facebook/6-studies-show-facebook-organic-reach-declining-quickly-01564179 #StcKxyDWwivjjwGW.97.

22. Michael Barthel, "Running for President, and Announcing It with a Tweet," Pew Research Center, April 17, 2015, http://www.pewresearch.org/fact-tank/2015/04/17/running-for-president-and-announcing-it-with-a-tweet/.

23. Sahil Patel, "85 Percent of Facebook Video Is Watched Without Sound," *Digiday*, May 17, 2016, https://digiday.com/media/silent-world-facebook-video/.

24. Pew Research Center, "Social Media Fact Sheet," January 12, 2017, http://www.pewinternet.org/fact-sheet/social-media/.

25. Delany, *How to Use the Internet to Win in 2016*, Kindle location 333.

26. James Doubek, "Political Campaigns Go Social, but Email Is Still King," National Public Radio, July 28, 2015, http://www.npr.org/sections/itsallpolitics/2015/07/28/426022093/as-political-campaigns-go-digital-and-social-email-is-still-king.

27. Delany, *How to Use the Internet to Win in 2016*, Kindle location 333.

28. Peter Kafka, "2016: The Year Election Ads Finally Come to the Internet," *Recode*, April 7, 2016, https://www.recode.net/2016/4/7/11585922/facebook-google-political-campaign-ads.

29. Russell Brandom, "Facebook Is Helping Campaigns Target Politically Active Users," Verge, November 4, 2015, https://www.theverge.com/2015/11/4/9671826/facebook-campaign-political-user-targeting.

30. Adam Broder, "Do TV Political Ads Still Matter in the Age of Social Media?," *Broadcasting & Cable* (May 3, 2017), http://www.broadcastingcable.com/blog/bc-guest-blogs/do-tv-political-ads-still-matter-age-social-media/165517.

31. Donald P. Green and Alan S. Gerber, *Get Out The Vote: How to Increase Voter Turnout* (Washington, DC: Brookings Institution Press, 2008), 83–84.

Chapter 7: Traditional Media: Print, Radio, and TV

1. Pew Center for the People and the Press, "Key News Audiences Now Blend Online and Traditional Sources," August 17, 2008, http://people-press.org/report/444/news-media.

2. Pew Center for the People and the Press, "Political Polarization & Media Habits, Section 1: Media Sources: Distinct Favorites Emerge on the Left and Right," October 21, 2014, http://www.journalism.org/2014/10/21/political-polarization-media-habits/.

3. L. Marvin Overby and Jay Barth, "Radio Advertising in American Political Campaigns: The Persistence, Importance, and Effects of Narrowcasting," *American Politics Research* 34, no. 4 (2006): 451–478.

4. Ibid.

5. Ibid.

6. http://www.ad-mkt-review.com/public_html/docs/fs075.html.

7. Josh Katz, "'Duck Dynasty' vs. 'Modern Family': 50 Maps of the US Cultural Divide," *New York Times*, December 27, 2016, https://www.nytimes.com/interactive/2016/12/26/upshot/duck-dynasty-vs-modern-family-television-maps.html?_r=0.

8. Jennifer L. Elgin, "Copyrights and Campaigns: Five Tips for the Unwary," *Campaigns & Elections* (May–June 2012): 58–61.

Chapter 8: Targeting Voters

1. Alan Gerber, Donald Green, and Ron Shachar, "Voting May Be Habit-Forming," *American Journal of Political Science* 47 (2003): 540–550.

2. Wendy K. Tam Cho, James G. Gimpel, and Joshua J. Dyck, "Residential Concentration, Political Socialization and Voter Turnout," *Journal of Politics* 68 (2006): 156–167.

3. http://www.fairvote.org/what_affects_voter_turnout_rates.

4. http://www.demos.org/data-byte/voter-turnout-income-2008-us-presidential-election.

5. Oregon Secretary of State, http://www.sos.state.or.us.

6. http://www.sos.ca.gov/elections.

7. http://www.census.gov/compendia/statab/cats/elections/voting-age_population _and_voter_participation.html.

8. Scott Keeter, Juliana Horowitz, and Alec Tyson, "Young Voters in the 2008 Election," Pew Research Center Publications, November 12, 2008, http://pewresearch.org /pubs/1031/young-voters-in-the-2008-election.

9. Joe Green, "Software Will Revolutionize Local Politics," *Campaigns & Elections* (September–October 2012): 51.

10. Alan S. Gerber and Donald P. Green, "The Effects of Canvassing, Telephone Calls, and Direct Mail on Voter Turnout: A Field Experiment," *American Political Science Review* 94, no. 3 (2000): 653–663.

11. George Washington University Graduate School of Political Management, *Young Voter Mobilization Tactics* (Washington, DC: George Washington University, 2006), http://www.civicyouth.org/PopUps/Young_Voters_Guide.pdf; Center for Information and Research on Civic Learning and Engagement (CIRCLE), Tufts University, http:// www.civicyouth.org.

12. Donald P. Green and Alan S. Gerber, "Getting Out the Youth Vote: Results from Randomized Field Experiments," unpublished report, Yale University, December 29, 2001, http://www.yale.edu/isps/publications/Youthvote.pdf.

13. Green and Gerber, "Getting Out the Youth Vote," 19.

14. Gerber and Green, "Effects of Canvassing, Telephone Calls, and Direct Mail."

15. Kathleen Hall Jamieson, *Everything You Think You Know About Politics, and Why You're Wrong* (New York: Basic Books, 2000), 107–110.

16. Dan Romer, Kathleen Hall Jamieson, and Joseph Cappella, "Does Political Advertising Affect Turnout?," ibid., 111–120.

17. Pew Research Center, "Political Polarization in Action: Insights into the 2014 Election from the American Trends Panel," October 17, 2014, http://www.people-press .org/2014/10/17/political-polarization-in-action-insights-into-the-2014-election -from-the-american-trends-panel/.

18. https://www.usps.com/business/every-door-direct-mail.htm.

Chapter 10: The Candidate Campaign

1. Michael Lewis, "Obama's Way," *Vanity Fair*, October 2012.

2. Owen Abbe et al., "Going Negative Does Not Always Mean Getting Ahead in Elections," *Campaigns & Elections* (February 2000).

Chapter 12: Getting Out the Vote (GOTV)

1. See Alan S. Gerber, Donald P. Green, and Christopher W. Larimer, "Social Pressure and Voter Turnout: Evidence from a Large-Scale Experiment," *American Political Science Review* 102, no. 1 (2008); and Donald P. Green and Alan S. Gerber, "Introduction to Social Pressure and Voting: New Experimental Evidence," in "Social Pressure and Voting," special issue, *Political Behavior* 32, no. 3 (2010): 331–336.

Appendix A: Glossary of Campaign Jargon

Absentee voting: Voting by mail in a state that holds poll voting.

Advocacy mailers: Mailers that sing the praises of a candidate.

Attack mailers: Mailers that go after a candidate on a personal or public level.

Backmap: Mapping a campaign activity starting with the end and moving to the present, a.k.a. a flowchart.

Ballot roll-off: The practice of voting the top of a ballot and then leaving down-ballot categories blank. May also occur from voter fatigue on long, confusing ballots.

Base party vote: Voters who only vote their party of registration.

B-roll: Supplemental footage that can be inserted into an ad to enrich the story being told.

CI: Civic improvements.

Comparison mailers: Mailers that highlight distinctions between candidates.

CRM: Constituent relationship management.

DCs: District coordinators. Individuals who oversee the work of a portion of neighborhood captains.

District: General term referencing a campaign's area of focus. It could be a county, a legislative district, state senate seat, and so on. It is unrelated to a district coordinator. *Your district* means *the region in which registered voters will vote on a ballot that includes your race.*

Down-ballot: Candidates and issues that appear on a ballot below statewide races.

Earned media: Refers to publicity gained through efforts other than paid advertising.

EDDM: Everyday direct mail.

Field op: Field operative; responsible for finding and getting volunteers to campaign activities.

Flats: Unfolded direct mail usually printed on eight-and-a-half-by-eleven-inch, or larger, card-stock paper.

Flipping turf: The process of assigning orphan turf to new neighborhood captains.

Friendly voters: Individuals of your political party or supporters of your issue-based campaign.

GO bonds: General-obligation bonds typically paid with a voter-approved property tax.

GOTV lists: List of voters who have been identified to turn out in the get-out-the-vote effort.

Homogeneous populations: Areas of voters overwhelmingly registered in the same party and overwhelmingly supportive of or opposed to specific issue-based campaigns.

Hybrid voting: Voting areas (state and local) where people can vote by mail or poll vote.

ID: Voter identification.

Independents: Misnomer for nonaffiliated registrants.

IP: Internet protocol. An IP address is the unique number that identifies your computer.

Job creep: Assigning an individual one job and then expanding the job beyond that.

Long shot: Underdog campaigns.

LTEs: Letters to the editor.

Microtargeting: A marketing activity that utilizes demographic, social, and commercial data to predict voting tendencies.

Mobilizing voters: Getting registered voters to actually vote.

NAVs: Nonaffiliated voters: those registered in no party.

NC-GOTV: Neighborhood-captain system for a GOTV effort.

NCs: Neighborhood captains. Individuals who oversee a portion of a precinct or neighborhood.

O&M: Operating and maintenance.

Opposition party: Registrant in a political party other than yours or individuals who do not support an issue-based campaign effort.

Orphans: A turf of voters without a neighborhood captain to activate.

Overvote: Voters who vote for more than one person in one ballot category or vote both yes and no for a particular issue-based ballot item.

PAC: Political action committee.

Poll book: The official book of registered voters located at a polling station.

Poll voting: Voting in person, not by mail.

Postmortem analysis: Study of previous elections, typically the immediately past election, to help figure out what went wrong or right.

Revenue bonds: Civic bonds typically repaid with a revenue stream.

Social context: Typically refers to a voter's immediate neighborhood or precinct but can also extend to all those in a small city that profile similarly.

Swing precincts: Precincts in which voters vote outside their party.

Swing voters: Those who will vote for candidates registered in another party.

Ticket splitting: Voting for candidates in different parties on the same ballot.

Undervote: Can happen anywhere on a ballot and is created by voters who do not vote for every item on the ballot, skipping (undervoting) some. As opposed to roll-off, it does not happen on all down-ballot categories but randomly.

Unearned media: Refers to paid advertising.

Unfriendly voters: Voters who will not support your efforts (a.k.a. sinners).

VBM: Vote by mail.

Vendors: People or organizations producing and selling mail, television, radio, and other communication services to campaigns.

VNW: Votes needed to win. Calculated by averaging turnout of similar election cycles, dividing that total by two and then adding one to your side of the ledger.

VO: Voice-over used in television ads.

Voter activation: Any activity that engages a voter to cast a ballot.

Voter classification according to voting history:
- **A (always vote):** voted in four out of the past four similar elections
- **B (usually vote):** voted in three out of the past four similar elections
- **C (sometimes vote):** voted in two out of the past four similar elections
- **D (rarely vote):** voted in one out of the past four similar elections
- **F (never vote):** haven't voted in any of the past four similar elections
- **N:** no voting history available

Voter file with history: Lists of registered voters that includes a history of elections in which voters have participated.

Voter ID: Any activity that is designed to identify voter intent.

Voter identification number: A unique number assigned to each registered voter.

Voter lists: Registration lists obtained (usually) from government offices.

Votes owed: A prediction of votes that a Republican or Democratic candidate can expect to receive in each precinct. It is calculated by adding only Democratic and Republican registration together and then dividing that total by the registration of each of the parties. This process will yield a percentage that can then be multiplied by total registration for both the Republican and the Democrat. Doing so allows a campaign to predictably assign NAVs and third-party registrants to each of the parties.

Zones: Areas of like-minded voters, through either party registration or issue-based support.

Appendix B: Campaigning on a Shoestring

Everything should be made as simple as possible, but not simpler.
—ALBERT EINSTEIN

IN THIS APPENDIX:

- Getting Started
- The Walking Piece
- Voters' Pamphlet or Voters' Guide
- Graphics
- Name Recognition
- Lawn Signs
- Show Me the Money
- Webpage and Social Media
- And We're Out

IN THE FOLLOWING PAGES, YOU WILL FIND THE BARE MINIMUM YOU need to know to execute a successful campaign in three months while spending less than $3,000.

Getting Started

This section is not for all campaigns; it is designed specifically for city or down-ballot county races and will work only if you live in a homogeneous city or are running in a nonpartisan race. For specific strategy in partisan, legislative, or countywide races, consult the pages of the entire book.

A campaign is a lot of work: Take it seriously and run to win. In general, you will need the following:

- A walking piece/brochure
- Lawn signs and a strategy for placement, maintenance, and removal
- House parties
- A webpage
- A Facebook page
- Three grand and two to three months

A Committee

Should you decide to get a volunteer committee together (and I advise you do), you want one person to oversee and take responsibility for each of the above activities. Although everyone will help execute the duties of any given category, one individual dogging a job is very helpful.

Campaign Manager

A campaign manager is generally a pretty good friend who will stick with you from beginning to end. But let me caution you here that campaigns eat friendships and marriages alive, so unless you're positive your "pretty good friend" will follow through and truly help, get someone else and consider paying that person a small stipend.

Graphic Designer

I do not pretend to know how to lay out campaign literature or design logos. This is a really inexpensive cost to the campaign, so find someone to do it for you who knows what he or she is doing. This is important: You do not want any campaign materials to look amateurish. It costs very little to class up a campaign, so do it. Similarly, you need some professional photos for your print and online materials.

In Oregon you can spend $3,000 on a campaign and never have to file a contributions and expenditures (C&E) form with the secretary of state. Each state is different, so check with your local election department. Not having to file all that paperwork is liberating. Nevertheless, keep track of all your expenses and contributions. Make copies of checks or maintain a paper trail, and be sure to have a completely separate bank account from your personal account. Never commingle campaign funds with personal funds: Treat a campaign like a business. If you're ever called upon to prove anything, you'll be glad you did.

The Walking Piece

Your walking piece should be no more than 325 words and should include the following:

- *Occupation.* Include years—not "27" but rather 1983–2010, that sort of thing.
- *Occupational background.* Include names of companies or jobs held and actual years worked at each. If you have a laundry list, then forgo the years to save on your word count.
- *Prior government experience.* This is where you list the planning commission and such—not Little League coach or pink lady at the hospital.
- *Educational background.* Include degrees starting from the lowest, and then work your way up; give the universities or schools and years you attended. If you did not get a degree, just list the school with no actual dates, and hopefully voters will think you finished. There's no need to list your high school, as voters will assume you went in order to get into a college; the exception might be if you want to demonstrate longevity in a community.
- *Military service.* If you served in the military, this is important; indicate years and rank. If you never served, omit this category.
- *Community service.* This is where the Little League, pink-lady, and Chamber of Commerce stuff goes; if you received special awards or recognition, list those as bullet points here as well.
- *Proven leadership.* Next you will list things you accomplished that somehow relate to the office you seek. If you're running for reelection, you will list what you and the body on which you served accomplished while you were in office. Bullet-point this stuff. People are going to look at your walking piece for exactly ten seconds, so be brief and articulate.
- *Together we can do more.* This section will offer bullet points regarding issues your town or community could do to make the world a better place. For example, dealing with the homeless, upgrading the wastewater treatment plant, placing electric lines underground to prevent future outages, safeguarding the water system by removing dead and dying timber from the watershed, getting sidewalks installed near schools—that sort of thing.
- *Values we respect.* Depending on word count, this final section will feature two to four quotes from prominent community leaders. They, not you, will say just how great you are. They, not the committee,

will describe the crumbling school or closed library or dilapidated park system that increased taxes will fix. This is also where you provide some reassurance to the voter. For example, if you're a businessperson, you will balance that strength with a quote from a credible person who may be outside the business community. If you're on the Left, get a quote from someone on the Right. One caution: Do not choose people who are extreme; you want to balance a weakness with someone just slightly over the line in the other camp. Think about your strengths versus the strengths of your opposition, and enhance yours at the opposition's expense.

When asking people for a quote, also ask permission to edit it for space if necessary. No one says no to that. Most will ask that the campaign generate the quote and run it by the endorser. Make the individual sound smart and believable. Also important to note here is that your endorsements can actually say what you highlighted under "proven leadership" above. So if you want to say you worked the floor of a cannery and everyone came to you for advice, have a former coworker say, "He was always there for us with great advice, and he set an example by working hard. He's a born leader" (Sally Smith, Borden Foods supervisor).

- *And now a word from our sponsor.* Once you have completed all the above sections and find you still have a few words, this is where you, the candidate, make a special appeal: "It would be an honor to serve our city. I hope I can count on your vote." Then sign it and have your printed signature appear on the walking piece under your appeal.

Off to the Photographer

Every walking piece needs at least one picture of the candidate. If you're working on an issue-based campaign, you may need two or three pictures to evoke emotion to create urgency and appeal for the voters.

Candidates with families should consider a picture of the entire family as well as a solo of the candidate. Your family will be affected by your campaign, so involving them in this small way completely works. But never use a photo that makes any member of your family look bad—especially if a child is a teenager. Be considerate.

Family photos can be of your last vacation together or in your backyard. Indeed, if you already have a great photo that looks spontaneous, it will work better than a studio shot and save you money.

If your family is your dog or cat, then include your pet in the photo; it makes you look genuine and accessible. But if you have dozens of pets and include them all, you will look like a nut, so use some common sense.

Voters' Pamphlet or Voters' Guide

If your state or locality has a government-produced voter guide, now is the time to review the requirements and fill out the required information. If a fee goes with it, pay it; getting into a government-sponsored voter guide that goes to each and every home or one that is available online is completely worth the effort and expense. I have won campaigns using a voters' pamphlet entry as the entire campaign.

Graphics

Next you will take the 325-word copy from your completed form above plus a few carefully selected photos to a graphic design professional.

Create a Logo

Your graphic designer should first create a logo; this will go on your walking piece and also becomes your lawn sign. A logo is your name and the office you seek presented in a memorable way. If you already hold office, be sure to get that "reelect" label in there somewhere. If you do not already hold the office you seek, you cannot place the office name before yours, only after. If you want to include a slogan, you and the committee should mull that over and give it to the designer along with the 325-word copy and the photos. A slogan is unnecessary, but a lot of people like them. Generally, they're along the lines of "Building a Better Community" or "It's About Community" or something that involves leadership, like "Leadership Matters."

If you're working on an issue-based campaign, there's always the inclination to guilt voters into supporting a tax measure, but in general I think it's best to go with optimism. "A Great Community Deserves a Great Library" works better than "Save Our Library." Same goes for schools: "Create Possibilities" works better than "Our Children Deserve Better." Keep it on the "hope and opportunity" side.

The Layout

Your walking piece should be printed on both sides and no bigger than a half sheet of eight-and-a-half-by-eleven-inch paper. The first section (occupation, occupational background, education, and so forth) should be boxed and to one side; it becomes an easy reference for those who want to know whether you're actually qualified to serve. The second section includes what you've done or will do or both, and then the quotes and the pictures get placed where they look best; your designer will get it right. You basically want your piece to breathe. Too much copy, and no one will read any of it; too little, and you will insult the voter. Keep the copy to 325 words, and all will be right with the world.

An alternative is to see what other candidates have done in terms of layout and design and then steal ideas.

To the Printer!

After you're satisfied with the layout and design of the walking piece, it goes to the printer, usually electronically. Next you will consult with the print shop about the best and most affordable paper to use. Generally speaking, you do not want to use colored paper, anything that's too absorbent, or paper that's high gloss. Use something with just enough finish to allow the copy and photos to pop off the page and enough weight to easily get shoved into doorjambs or screen doors. I really like eighty-pound Xerox Digital Color Elite.

Also, know that printing costs have really come down. Full color at big print houses costs no more than black and white with spot color at a local print shop. We send our full-color walking pieces to get printed in Los Angeles, where 6,000 runs around three hundred dollars. I then save small print jobs for my local printer—such as the remit envelopes.

Quantities

Your walking piece will go wherever you go: canvassing, house parties, farmers' markets, everywhere. Knowing this, you may be inclined to print "enough," which can easily be too many. Considering how small the difference in cost per piece between 500 and 2,000 is, I suggest you begin with a shorter run. You can always print more, and a short run provides an opportunity to swap out quotes, depending on where you're canvassing.

If you're running for office in a really small city of a few hundred to a few thousand, consider printing your walking piece on your home printer, especially if that printer is of good quality. Otherwise, begin with a few hundred and be prepared to order more. One caution: Short runs of full color at small print shops will bleed your campaign dry.

Paying for Your Walking Piece Without Money

You have now generated two expenses: one with the graphic designer (one to two hundred dollars) and another with the printer (two to five hundred dollars). To get around paying these bills before you have any money, open accounts with the vendors and request that you get billed for their service. You just bought yourself thirty days.

When it comes to paying vendors, do so with online bill pay, and your bank will issue the check, post an online copy for your records, and pay the postage to get the check to the vendor. The packet of starter checks the bank provides when an account is opened is plenty for a short campaign season.

Name Recognition

If you have never run for or served in office, you need to let the voters know who you are, and there are a number of ways to do that:

- Television, radio, and newspaper advertising
- Direct mail
- Letters to the editor
- Lawn signs, field signs, and billboards
- Canvassing—that is, walking door to door and introducing yourself (or the issue-based proposal) to the voter
- Social media or online advertising

TV, Radio, and Newspaper Advertising

If you're running a campaign in a small market, television may be very affordable to you, but given how fractured the audience is and the number of spots you will need to run to get noticed, your three grand would be gone in less than a week.

Like TV, radio and print media are all outside the budget of a small down-ballot race. Although social media is cheap, including online advertising, where you pay only if the viewer clicks, for it to be truly effective you need someone who can execute and monitor your presence and knows something about targeting.

Direct Mail

Direct mail is expensive, and all but those making money sending it believe it is of little value.

Still, I would be remiss if I did not tell you there are a couple of things you can do to bring the cost of sending direct mail to within your reach—especially for a small city election.

A saturated-mail piece—a piece of mail that goes to every single house within a given postal route—brings down the postage considerably, and you don't even need a bulk-mail permit. Clearly, you will spend more money to print and mail to homes of residents who are not registered and have no intention of voting, but the cost difference of targeted mail versus saturated mail makes the decision simple. A saturated-mail piece will work best for nonpartisan or homogeneous voting districts—which means you're in luck because most small towns in America are predominantly "like living with like."

If you want to keep this option on the table, here are a few figures for you to use in calculating the cost: Postage for a 5.5-by-8.5-inch postcard sent by bulk mail runs about 14 cents per piece, and the printing will run you another 4 to 5 cents each for full color. So if you live in a city of 10,000 households, you can send one piece of mail for just over $2,000—that's $165 for layout, $460 for printing, and $1,440 for postage. But if you live in a city of just 3,000 households, you could send a piece of mail for around $800. Remember: Flip-flip-throw; make it memorable.

Letters to the Editor

While many people will tell you they'll write a letter and send it to the local paper, few will actually execute the mission. Indeed, so few follow through that your campaign should assign a person to oversee this task; make sure this individual has no other campaign activities to execute. That's how hard this job is.

Once an individual is identified as willing to write a letter to the editor, someone in the campaign must follow up. Early letters get read and have more impact than letters submitted closer to Election Day. Also, shorter letters get read over long letters. Make sure your supporter keeps his or her letter to just eighty words: one thought, three sentences, two paragraphs, and it's done.

Field Signs and Billboards

Printed field signs run hundreds of dollars each and billboards even more. Neither of these offer as good a return for the investment as lawn signs. In a $3,000 campaign, I'd put field signs at the bottom of my list, especially given that many cities will not allow them within city limits.

Lawn Signs and Canvassing

Lawn signs are a great way to get your name before the voters—problem is, you actually need yards in which to place them, and that requires getting permission. One way to get the green light is to simply call people: your friends, business associates, Little League coaches, anyone you know. You can also "cold call" strangers if you want signs on a particular high-traffic street.

Another way to secure lawn sign locations is to canvass. It's time-consuming, but if done right it works and serves more than one purpose—always a plus in a cash-strapped, time-limited campaign.

Lawn Signs

The logo designed for your walking piece will now be used for your lawn signs. To save money, use only one color on your lawn signs. Given that the stock is white, you can create the look of two colors by leaving only the lettering white while printing the rest of the lawn sign with your color. Although it costs about the same to print your logo on stock that's eighteen by twenty-four inches as eleven by twenty-four inches, nine by twenty-four inches is considerably cheaper. I've been moving to the smaller sign for a couple reasons. For starters, it will force your design into a bold look—typically just your name and the office you seek—so it has a clean and memorable look. Second, the smaller size, on H-wickets, is more stable in wind and weather. If you intend to use wooden stakes with screws and washers, I'd go with the eighteen-by-twenty-four-inch sign. With that said, I've seen signs that are printed nine inches wide by twenty-four in height. It's a different look that could make your campaign stand out. I came up with this layout for a pool campaign with a woman diving straight down the long vertical sign into the slogan: Take the Plunge. Heads-up: If you do this long, narrow look, you must use wooden lawn sign stakes. Other ideas, plus sample signs, can be found in Chapter 9, "Lawn Signs."

As a rule of thumb, one-color lawn signs printed on both sides run about two dollars each; add another color and you can add thirty cents per sign. Full-color signs run around five dollars each, and that's without the H-wickets or lawn sign stakes to hold them in the ground. (H-wickets add about one dollar per sign.) The fewer signs you print in any given run, the more they cost per sign, so print the right amount or too many. Do not print too few.

Since lawn signs are generally placed five to six weeks before an election, you have enough time to call local printers to compare costs to those on the Web. Many shops print lawn signs, and some are pretty competitive, so get on this task immediately. Don't forget if you're doing business with a Web printer, you will have shipping on top of the printing costs. And be sure to check the final color before going to print. Indeed, have your graphic designer send the actual color number to the printer to make sure that what you get is what you pay for.

Personally, I save H-wickets and lawn sign stakes plus hardware (screws and washers) for reuse. If you have neither in your barn, garage, or basement, call around to other candidates who previously ran for office or to party headquarters to see if they have any you can borrow. If not, you'll have to buy them and can often get the best deal if they're ordered from the place that prints your signs. But check online for deals on metal brackets.

If you intend to use wooden stakes with washers and screws, the lawn sign must be printed so there's room for the stake without blocking the logo, and the interior tubing of the material must run horizontally; otherwise, it will fold in the wind and look bad—really bad. For H-wickets, the interior tubing of the material runs vertically. If you have no idea what I'm talking about, go to a shop that prints lawn signs and take a look at them.

Another alternative is to use plastic bags that fit on top of huge croquet wickets. Companies lure you in with very affordable printing quotes on the plastic bag, and then you're hit with the cost of the wickets and shipping charges (they weigh a ton). If you have access to the wickets, this can be a pretty cheap way to go, but beware: Wickets, like the plastic sleeves, come in all sizes, so get the correct-size sleeve printed for the wicket you're borrowing. If you have to buy both the sleeve and the wickets, this is no cheaper than the H-wicket sign and looks cheesier.

Canvassing for Lawn Sign Locations

So let's say you have every intention of knocking on each and every door in your voting district. Easy to do if you live in a small city, and it's effective. But let me suggest that no matter the size of your town or voting district, you begin by canvassing homes on arterial and collector streets. Collectors are the sort of large streets that "collect" the traffic of smaller streets, and arterials are the busiest streets running through your town.

A sign placed on an arterial is worth two on a collector and ten on a side street. Plus, when you canvass arterials and collectors, people see you, and voters who see you canvassing others consider themselves canvassed as well. Once you hit all of the arterials and collectors, you can knock on the doors of everyone else.

Anyone who seems even remotely supportive gets asked to host a lawn sign and is told when it will go up and when it will come down. If you're not working with a handheld GPS system to note voter support, then write everything down, including a name, address, email, and phone number in case those placing the lawn signs cannot find the address during installation. Some cities and counties have regulations that limit size and how political signs can be placed. Be sure to verify dates. You do not want to start your run for public office by breaking the law or appearing to be above it.

Installation of Lawn Signs

If you're running in a small town, chances are you have only fifty to two hundred signs for placement. If that is the case, just get them up as soon as the law allows. Also of note is that when candidates actually install their own signs, people notice and like this humble touch. Normally, I would say that a candidate's time would be better spent dialing for dollars, but in a small-town race, you have more options as to how you can make a positive impression.

Show Me the Money

There are a lot of ways to raise money; unfortunately, most of them require money to do so. For example, you can mail a solicitation letter to your family and friends, but each one requires you print the letter as well as the envelope and remittance envelope (remit) that gets stuffed inside. Add to this a first-class stamp, and each piece will cost the campaign close to a dollar. So let's say you mail two hundred pieces for a buck each; given that mail solicitation generally has a rate of return of 6 percent, you will get back about twelve envelopes with checks. Just to break even, every one of those must contain a seventeen-dollar check. Not a tall order. So let's assume all twelve send twenty-five dollars; that means your mailing will generate one hundred dollars after expenses. That's a lot of work for a hundred bucks.

If you hold events, such as an auction or a yard sale, the bookkeeping alone will drive you to drink. Think about it: Someone donates a book and you sell it; the campaign claims as a donation the money received but must list as an "in-kind" the difference between the value of the book and the actual cash received. Likewise, the donor can claim as a political contribution only the difference between the worth of the book and the amount you actually sold it for. Multiply that effort by hundreds of items, and add to this the simple reality that these kinds of events raise very little money while eating up tons of committee and volunteer time, and I say no way, not in a three-month campaign.

Still, there will be many who tell you that events are "friend raisers," and even in a three-month effort, with the right person overseeing the project, they can be successful with relatively little demand on the committee. (For ideas, see "Fundraising Ideas That Take Less Than One Month of Preparation" in Chapter 5, "Fundraising.")

Online Contributions

The era of texting ten dollars to a campaign in a room full of people appears to be limited now to nonprofits or huge races, such as for president. Still, money can be raised online with virtually no expense, and let's face it, most of us have no idea where our checkbook is anymore. Stay tuned—I will cover this next.

Meanwhile, you need to raise money, and given that everything must do double duty in a three-month campaign, so should your fundraising efforts. To that end, house parties or coffees offer a modest financial return for the effort while getting your message out in a personal and believable way. Further, attendees typically give more than money; they will often take a lawn sign, offer to do a coffee for *their* friends, and volunteer time for the campaign.

House Parties

A successful house party begins with the hosts. Your committee volunteer in charge of house parties will call potential or known supporters and ask him or her to sponsor an evening get-together. The host can decide whether to invite neighbors, friends, or both. Generally, tea, coffee, and some sort of dessert, such as cookies or brownies, are served to those attending, but I've had people put on house parties that draw hundreds and raise thousands with simple finger food, donated wine, and nonalcoholic beverages. If you can get a big name to a house party, such as the governor or a local celebrity, that will up the attendance as well as the returns.

The committee member overseeing house parties must give some attention to the effort; for example, if not enough people have responded to the invitation, then calls must go out to all the invitees. If too few are willing to attend, put off the event to another date to bring up attendance. Be flexible: Poorly attended coffees or house parties are assumed to be the candidate's fault.

Because the hosts send the invitations and provide the refreshments, the campaign incurs no cost. The best parties are when two or more friends get together to cosponsor one. They then draw from a broader friends list. Some quick facts:

- Typically, a house party will last ninety minutes.
- Someone from the campaign must arrive early to help the host set up the event, to lay out materials, and greet people at the door.
- The candidate must arrive early as well, and it is lovely if he or she brings a small gift for the host—such as flowers or a bottle of nice wine.

- Enough time must be allowed for late attendees to arrive and get settled before beginning the evening introductions—usually about thirty to forty-five minutes into the event.
- Once people have gathered, the host welcomes attendees and introduces the candidate (the campaign should provide the copy for the introduction that underscores the candidate's experience and qualifications for the job).
- The candidate thanks the host, then briefly speaks; this is followed by Q&A.
- When the candidate is done and all the questions have been asked and answered, someone with some talent must stand before the group and make the "ask" for money. This individual could be from the committee or another elected official you invite for this purpose alone.
- Walking pieces, a basket for contributions, and remit envelopes are available at a table near the door along with any other materials the campaign may have generated, such as buttons and bumper stickers.
- Be sure to have a sign-up sheet for potential volunteers and lawn sign locations.

Since it is remarkably hard to get people to attend house parties during the summer, when the whole world is numb to politics, they can be delayed until September for a general election or two months before any primary.

Meanwhile, what to do about money?

Candidates can bridge their campaigns to the house parties by spending a couple of hours a day calling friends, family, and business associates to contribute. These are well-spent hours because no one wants to turn down the candidate. If you're running for a judicial position and the law does not allow you to solicit directly for money, you will need to have friends and committee members do this task for you.

Webpage and Social Media

Every campaign must have a webpage, if for no other reason than to have a donate button that allows people to contribute to the campaign. Campaigns can spend thousands on a webpage, but simply having one is actually enough. Get a professional to put your page together so that everything works, but do not pay a lot of money for it.

The information included in your 325-word walking piece is actually enough for your webpage, but it will be broken up a bit according to buttons on your home page. People love to tell you that you need to generate all kinds of "white papers" on issues of the day, but this is not necessary. Only your opponent will read long narratives you post regarding your position on controversial issues. I'm not saying your webpage should be vacuous, just rather brief on all pages.

Everything you place online should be well written. Typos, grammatical errors, and misspellings will cost you votes. Don't be stupid: If you do not know how to write, get help. Even if you do know how to write, always put more eyes on your words: Run all copy by at least one committee member who is capable of writing and editing. Do not group-edit the copy.

You should have more photos than appear in your walking piece, so dig around for some nice ones. This is where a professional photo shoot can come in handy. Typically, this will run you about five hundred dollars, but believe me, when you are digging daily to find pictures in boxes in the back of your closet, you'll wish you'd just done it.

Have your graphic designer alter your lawn sign logo to fit comfortably across the top of your webpage.

To be effective, you will need to generate at least a little information for those who visit. Typically, buttons across the top of a webpage for a political candidate include the following:

- Home
- Bio
- Experience
- Donate
- Volunteer
- Facebook

When it comes to listing those who support or endorse you or your cause, I strongly suggest you have a method of scrolling the names. If your Web master cannot do this function, you may need to find and pay someone else to set it up. It's worth it and allows names to be added as people jump on board. This is far more effective than a page listing columns of names. Scrolling names are mesmerizing to the visitor. As an aside, this feature should move with the visitor no matter what page she or he visits on your site.

Your campaign should have a Facebook page; it's free and easy to set up. However, if you're not the sort of person who lives on social media sites and your Facebook page has no activity, it's a problem. To remedy this, have a volunteer or committee member monitor your site and post your activities as well as pictures of your daily travels as you move through the campaign. If you are willing to update your travels yourself, then set aside some time each night before retiring. It needs to be done on a regular basis.

And We're Out

I've omitted some things from these pages because I consider them common sense; for example:

- Send thank-you notes for contributions, house parties, and volunteerism.
- Maintain your lawn signs so they do not look like litter, and quickly remove them after the election.
- Call and knock at reasonable hours.
- Never waste people's time: Keep meetings brief and organized and have materials ready for volunteers, no matter the task they're doing.
- Always dress and act the part of the candidate.

Have fun and remember that additional information on any of the above topics can be found within the pages of this manual.

Index

Pages shown in bold refer to information within tables; pages shown in italics refer to information within figures.

About the Authors

Catherine Shaw served three terms (twelve years) as mayor of Ashland, Oregon. First elected in 1988, she was the youngest person and the first woman elected to her city's highest post. She also served as a member chief of staff in the Oregon Legislature.

For three decades, she has managed and consulted for scores of political campaigns, successfully passing innovative taxing measures for funding public education, recreation, parks, open-space programs, libraries, and civic buildings.

Outspent in every election, sometimes as much as five to one, Shaw developed and perfected techniques to combat big money and to engineer seemingly impossible wins. She has been a frequent guest speaker and instructor for political science classes and campaign schools.

Shaw currently works as a political consultant. For questions regarding any portion of this book, please contact her by email: cathyshaw@mind.net.

Sarah Golden is a strategic communications expert with more than a decade of experience developing creative communication campaigns for political, environmental, and social impact issues. Sarah holds a BA in politics and environmental studies from Whitman College and was an Annenberg Dean Scholar at the University of Southern California, where she earned an MA in journalism and communication.

Daniel Booker Golden holds a BA in economics from Pomona College and a BS in chemical engineering from Oregon State University. He is a graduate of the Oregon Bus Project Poli Corp program and cofounder of Oregon Climate (now Our Climate). He has worked as a chemical engineer in the biodiesel, petrochemical, electronics, and energy-efficiency industries. He is currently writing a book on ketogenic nutrition for cancer patients.